D1400317

FileMaker Pro 5
Companion

Maria Langer

QA
76
.9
.D3
L3644
2000

Morgan Kaufmann

AN IMPRINT OF ACADEMIC PRESS
A Harcourt Science and Technology Company

San Diego   San Francisco   New York   Boston
London   Sydney   Tokyo

CARROLL COLLEGE LIBRARY
WAUKESHA, WISCONSIN 53186

This book is printed on acid-free paper.

Copyright © 2000, 1998 by Academic Press
All rights reserved.

No part of this publication may be reproduced or transmitted in any form or by any means, electronic or mechanical, including photocopy, recording, or any information storage and retrieval system, without permission in writing from the publisher.

All brand names and product names mentioned in this book are trademarks or registered trademarks of their respective companies.

Requests for permission to make copies of any part of the work should be mailed to the following address: Permissions Department, Harcourt, Inc., 6277 Sea Harbor Drive, Orlando, Florida 32887-6777

Academic Press
A Harcourt Science and Technology Company
525 B Street, Suite 1900, San Diego, CA 92101-4495 USA
http:// www.academicpress.com

Academic Press
Harcourt Place, 32 Jamestown Road, London, NW1 7BY, UK

Morgan Kaufmann
A Harcourt Science and Technology Company
340 Pine Street, Sixth Floor, San Francisco, CA 94104-3205 USA
http://www.mkp.com

Library of Congress Catalog Card Number: 00-102246
International Standard Book Number: 0-12-436151-X

PRINTED IN THE UNITED STATES OF AMERICA
00 01 02 03 04 IP 9 8 7 6 5 4 3 2 1

CARROLL COLLEGE LIBRARY
WAUKESHA, WI 53186

FileMaker Pro 5
Companion

To Kevin Mallon, Steve Ruddock,
and the rest of the folks at FileMaker, Inc.
for your support and for developing a great product.

Contents

Part I: FileMaker Pro Basics

Part III: Exploring Advanced Features

Chapter 9: Using Field Entry Options 341

Chapter 15: Sharing Information. 561

Chapter 16: Publishing Data on the Web. . . . 581

Appendices

Introduction

So you've purchased FileMaker Pro 5, the latest version of File-Maker, Inc.'s popular database application. Or maybe someone else—like your boss or the guy or gal responsible for your computer—has purchased it for you. Either way, it's a good decision, and one you can be happy about.

Not only is FileMaker Pro the top-selling database program among Mac OS users, but it's quickly gaining favor with Windows users. And why shouldn't it? It has an easy-to-use interface to disguise its power, making it the perfect database management tool for beginners and power users alike. With the ability to create documents that can be accessed via network *simultaneously* by both Mac OS and Windows users, it's a dream come true in cross-platform, networked environments.

But good purchase decisions don't stop with FileMaker Pro. You also have this book, which will help you learn all about FileMaker Pro without a lot of time-consuming experimentation and guessing. Whether you're brand new to databases or FileMaker Pro, or you've been using FileMaker Pro for a while, you'll find plenty of information between this book's covers.

This introduction provides some important background information for folks who are exploring the world of databases for the first time. It explains what databases are and how they differ from the other documents that you might create on your computer. It also tells you about this book, what it contains, and how you can use it to learn about FileMaker Pro.

Database Basics

If you've never worked with a database program before, you might be wondering exactly what a database is and what it can do for you. If so, read on. I'll explain it all in this section.

What Is a Database?

A *database* is a collection of related information that is organized into fields and records. A *field* is a category of information. A *record* is a collection of fields relating to one item.

Think about a phone book—that's a database (see Figure 1). Each listing is a record. The listing's name, address, and phone number are fields.

JONES Arlen Ray 100 W Main St	685-0435
JONES Brian & Wendy 8457 W Jones Rd	685-9019
JONES Chester L 11254 W Rabbit Rd	685-2161
JONES FORD-MERCURY 4550 W Main St	685-1000
JONES Robert & Helen 15 Palo Verde Dr	685-4978
JONES T 630 S Mariposa Dr	685-8423
JOSEPH K B 181 S Front St	685-9432
JOSTEN Thomas 458 W Caballeros Dr	685-4158

FIGURE 1. Your local white pages are a good example of a database you might use every day.

Now think about a mail order catalog, like the one you threw away last week or the one that's still sitting on your desk. That's a database, too. Each item is record. The item name, description, number, available colors or sizes, price, and photograph are fields.

Think of some other examples. A teacher's grade book. A company's employee files. A doctor's billing records. A library's card catalog file. A dictionary. We're surrounded by databases!

So even if you think you're a raw beginner when it comes to using a database, you have more experience than you think.

How Does Database Software Work?

Database software like FileMaker Pro enables you to build database document files, which are often referred to simply as *databases*. You build a database by creating individual fields for each category of information that you want to manage. Then you enter information into the fields for each item's record.

For example, if you were going to recreate the white pages of your local phone book on your computer, you'd create fields for each last name, first name or initial, address, and phone number. You'd create a record for Tom Jones at 1616 Elm Street by entering his last name, first name, address, and phone number in the appropriate fields. You'd create a new record for Betty Smith at 123 Main Street and another new record for Eric Johnson at 111 Pine Tree Way. You'd continue until all the information had been entered in appropriate records and fields.

What Can Database Software Do for You?

There are several benefits to using database software like FileMaker Pro to organize and maintain information:

- Databases can be searched quickly to find records that match the criteria you specify.

- Database records can be sorted quickly by any combination of fields to display information in the order you desire.

- Database fields can be displayed in any combination on screen or on paper.

- Databases are easy to update and, if properly designed, can be shared by many individuals who need access to the information they contain.

These are only a few of the benefits of using database software. As you work with FileMaker Pro and see some of the examples in this book, you'll think of many more.

It's Alive!

One thing most people don't realize is that databases differ from the other document files that they create on computers. Unlike those other documents, databases are *alive*.

Let me explain.

Think about the last note or letter that you wrote on your computer using your favorite word processing software. When you were finished perfecting your prose, you probably printed it and sent it to the addressee. Have you opened and used that document since? Probably not. How many other documents like that one reside in a folder on your hard disk, feeling neglected? I don't know about you, but I've got hundreds of them—they're in a folder on my hard disk called "File Cabinet," and some of them date back to 1991.

A database document file is different in that, once created, it is often reopened and used. You may open an existing database to search for information. Or print a report. Or add, remove, or edit records.

Here's a real-life example. One of my clients uses a FileMaker Pro template I created for them to build a database of jobs processed within the department. The database file is opened and used by department personnel on a daily basis. Throughout the year it grows in size from the first record entered on January 2 to the 6487th or 7153rd record entered on December 31. Staff people use the database to see what jobs are open and to log out completed jobs. Supervisors use the database to calculate how long it takes to complete each job and how many jobs are completed by each staff person. Management uses the database to obtain statistics that prove how valuable the department is to the company as a whole.

If you agree that databases are alive (and I hope you do), then you must also agree that they require a bit more attention than the one-shot deal documents saved for prosperity in your electronic file cabinet. In effect, they require what I call "care and feeding"—almost like a pet or the plants in your garden. Here are a few things you need to keep in mind.

Database Design and Construction

Before you begin creating a database, you should have a good idea of what you want the database to accomplish for you. Here are some questions to ask:

WHAT INFORMATION WILL BE RECORDED IN THE DATABASE? This will determine what fields you need to include. It may also determine the importance of the database file, which will, in turn, help you decide how often to back it up.

HOW WILL RECORDS BE ORGANIZED? This will determine whether certain types of information—like a name or address—need to be broken out into multiple fields. For example, it's a lot easier to sort by last name when last names and first names are in separate fields.

HOW WILL DATABASE INFORMATION BE USED? This will determine how information is presented on screen or on paper.

WILL OTHERS HAVE ACCESS TO THE DATABASE FILE? This will determine whether the file requires special instructions, special field options to validate input, buttons and scripts, and/or security. It may also determine whether the server version of FileMaker Pro should be used and how network-related options should be set within the FileMaker Pro application on each user's computer.

WILL THE DATABASE BE PUBLISHED ON THE WEB? This will impact the database's design—its fields and layouts—and determine its security features and network location.

Database Management

A database also needs to be managed. Here are some examples of the kinds of things you may need to do:

CHECK FOR CONSISTENT DATA ENTRY You enter information in a State field using standard post office abbreviations like FL, OK, and AZ. Mary Jane likes to spell things out, so she enters them as Florida, Oklahoma, and Arizona. The temp your boss hired while Joe was away abbreviates the old fashioned way, so she entered Fla., Okla., and Ariz. This might not seem like a big deal, but it will be a very big deal when you try to sort, summarize, or search for information based on the inconsistent field.

T_{IP} *FileMaker Pro's validation features can help prevent inconsistent data entry. I tell you all about that in the section titled "Validation Options" on page 350.*

CHECK FOR (AND DELETE) DUPLICATES Every time someone orders a product from your catalog, his name and address are added to your Customers database. What about the folks who order every other week? Duplicates make your database larger than it needs to be and can be misleading on reports. It can also be costly if you use a database with duplicates for a bulk mailing. I explain how to search for duplicates in the section titled "Creating a Find Request" on page 136.

CHECK FOR (AND REVISE OR DELETE) OUT-OF-DATE INFORMATION Information, like bread, tends to get stale with age. (Unless you live in a damp climate; then it gets moldy.) Out-of-date information isn't much use to you or anyone else so revise, archive, or delete it.

Database Protection and Maintenance

It's November. My client's Job database—the one I told you about a few pages ago—has 4,956 records. But when Nauri tries to open it one Monday morning, the database refuses to open. Or it opens and half the records are gone. Either way, my client is not going to be happy. And neither am I when I have to fly to New Jersey (where it's cold in November) to explain what happened.

The importance of protecting and maintaining a database cannot be understated. Here are some of the things you should be thinking about:

BACK UP YOUR DATABASE FILES Heck, back up *all* your important files on a regular basis. You shouldn't have to hear this from me. You'll miss those files when they're gone if no up-to-date backup exists. Believe me—I've been there and it ain't fun. You can learn more about backup strategies in Chapter 18.

SECURE YOUR SENSITIVE FILES Got some secret information in a file? Keep it secret by password-protecting the database and restricting access to the sensitive fields. I tell you how in Chapter 17.

PREVENT FILE CORRUPTION Yes, an ounce of prevention is worth at least a pound of cure. FileMaker Pro has its own built-in tricks for preventing files from being corrupted—and recovering them if you waited too long to use them. I tell you how to fight back against the corruption gremlin in Chapter 18.

About This Book

In this book, I tell you everything you need to know to build, use, and maintain database files with FileMaker Pro. I start with the basics (important concepts and definitions, an interface overview, and instructions for creating and entering data into simple database files) and finish with advanced techniques (importing and exporting data, scripting, and Web publishing) covering everything in between along the way. I provide important background information, step-by-step instructions, illustrations, and tutorials to:

- Build a foundation of vital information and ideas on which you can build effective database files.

- Explain why things work the way they do, so you understand the underlying logic of databases and FileMaker Pro.

- Teach you how to complete specific tasks, so you can use FileMaker Pro without a lot of time-consuming trial-and-error experimentation.

- Show you what your Mac or Windows screen looks like as you work, so you know you're on track.

- Give you a chance to review concepts and tasks and see how they can be applied to real-life situations.

I've written this book in a friendly, conversational tone, with plenty of humor, brief anecdotes, tips, and real-life examples. I'm a firm believer that learning should be fun. Who's going to read a book that puts you to sleep? (Other than insomniacs, of course.) Although you might not like all my jokes, I promise you won't be bored. And I think you'll learn a heck of a lot about databases and FileMaker Pro along the way.

Three Learning Tools in One

This book combines elements from all three major types of computer books:

HOW-TO BOOK/USER GUIDE This book provides instructions for completing specific tasks with FileMaker Pro. How-to information is provided in a narrative style that begins with an introduction and then presents illustrated instructions with examples for using commands, buttons, dialog boxes, or whatever.

REFERENCE BOOK This book covers all features and interface elements of FileMaker Pro and provides three appendices of useful reference material. Its thorough index and table of contents make it a complete reference guide.

TUTORIAL Each chapter of this book includes step-by-step instructions for creating and modifying database files that meet real-life needs: contact management, product inventory, and invoicing. Use these exercises to review and reinforce the chapter's concepts.

This Book Is for You If...

This book is for just about anyone who wants to use FileMaker Pro to store, manage, and use data.

DATABASE BEGINNERS If you've never used a database program—even if you're not quite sure what a database is—this book is for you. It provides all the information you need to understand how databases work and how you can use them to organize and store information.

FILEMAKER PRO BEGINNERS If you've worked with databases before, but have never used FileMaker Pro, this book is for you. It provides all the basic how-to information you need to get started quickly. You'll find the tutorials both educational and fun.

EXPERIENCED FILEMAKER PRO USERS If you've used FileMaker Pro before—either this version or a previous version—this book is for you. It provides tips, tricks, and in-depth discussions of features, making it a valuable resource for taking FileMaker Pro to its limits.

SMALL AND HOME OFFICE BUSINESS OWNERS If you want to take control of the information that's a part of your business, but don't want to pay an expensive consultant to create a custom solution for you, this book is for you. It provides information that gives you the power to be your own database designer, builder, and manager. You'll find the real-life examples and tutorial exercises especially inspiring, since they'll give you plenty of creative ideas.

The Inside Scoop

This book is fat for a reason: it's jam-packed with information. Its logical organization makes it easy to find, understand, and use the information you need.

The book has five parts, each of which has two or more chapters. Here's a summary of the parts and their chapters.

Part I: FileMaker Pro Basics

This part of the book introduces you to FileMaker Pro and provides information and instructions for creating, entering data into, and working with simple database files. Its four chapters are:

Chapter 1: Getting to Know FileMaker Pro

Chapter 2: Creating a Database and Defining Fields

Chapter 3: Entering and Editing Data

Chapter 4: Finding and Sorting Records

Part II: Developing Layouts and Reports

This part of the book provides detailed information about using one of FileMaker Pro's most powerful features: layouts. Its four chapters are:

Chapter 5: Understanding Layouts

Chapter 6: Creating New Layouts

Chapter 7: Arranging Layout Objects

Chapter 8: Polishing Layout Appearance and Functionality

Part III: Exploring Advanced Features

This part of the book begins to go beyond the basics of FileMaker Pro by covering more advanced topics. Its four chapters are:

Chapter 9: Using Field Entry Options

Chapter 10: Tapping into the Power of Calculations

Chapter 11: Developing Relationships between Files

Chapter 12: Working with Scripts and Buttons

Part IV: Sharing Database Information

This part of the book offers information for sharing database contents with others via import/export, printing, networking, and Web publishing. Its four chapters are:

Chapter 13: Importing and Exporting Data

Chapter 14: Previewing and Printing Reports

Chapter 15: Sharing Information

Chapter 16: Publishing Data on the Web

Part V: Protecting and Maintaining Database Files

This part of the book provides information to help you protect your database files from unauthorized access and data loss. Its two chapters are:

Chapter 17: Securing Database Files

Chapter 18: Backing Up and Maintaining Database Files

Appendicitis

If you're a fan of reference stuff at the end of a book, I've got you covered. There are three appendices:

Appendix A: Menu and Keyboard Shortcut Reference

This appendix illustrates all of FileMaker Pro's menus and lists all of its keyboard shortcuts.

Appendix B: Function Reference

This appendix lists and describes all of FileMaker Pro's calculation functions, providing a great reference tool when specifying calculations for fields or scripts.

Appendix C: ScriptMaker Reference

This appendix lists and describes all of the ScriptMaker's commands, providing a useful reference tool when taking advantage of FileMaker Pro's scripting feature.

Batteries Not Included

I'll admit it: This book doesn't tell you *everything* you need to know to use FileMaker Pro. It doesn't tell you how to turn on your computer, use a mouse, or launch a program. It doesn't tell you how to select a command from a menu or resize a window.

In writing this book, I've assumed that you know all of that. If you don't, it's time to learn. Take out the manuals that came with your computer and spend some quality time with them. When you know how to point, click, drag, launch a program, enter and edit text, and quit or exit a program, you'll be ready to start working with FileMaker Pro and this book.

This book also omits in-depth discussions of advanced FileMaker Pro features such as custom database application development and custom Web publishing. Although I provide enough information to get you started with these features, you'll have to let other authors help you become an expert. After all, if I covered every aspect of FileMaker Pro in detail, this book would weigh a ton!

How to Use This Book

You can use this book in a number of ways:

- Turn off the phone, pick up the book, and read it cover to cover. It's not the latest Tom Clancy novel, but as I mentioned earlier, I'll try to keep you entertained while you learn.

- Read through the chapters that interest you most. If you're just getting started with FileMaker Pro, this may be the best way to quickly learn just what you need to know.

- Skip to the tutorials at the end of each chapter and read them first. They'll give you a feel for how FileMaker Pro can be used in real life, while giving you a chance to complete specific tasks for yourself. This is especially useful if you already have some FileMaker Pro experience.

- Keep it on your shelf and reach for it when you need information about a specific topic or task. You'll find the index and table of contents particularly helpful for looking things up.

- Use it to keep papers from blowing off your desk when the window is open. On second thought, don't use it for that. That's what old modems are for.

Yes, There Are Icons

Like most computer books, this one includes icons. I've used them in the margins to draw your attention to three things: notes, tips, and warnings.

NOTE   *A note is a bit of information you don't need to know but that you might find useful or interesting.*

TIP   *A tip is a tidbit that can make it easier or quicker to get something done. Look for tips when you understand the basics and are ready to become a power user.*

WARNING   *A warning is a piece of information that can save you a lot of grief. Read all the warnings—they're there for a reason!*

The Database Files

At the end of each chapter are exercises with step-by-step instructions for building three database files for Spot Ink, Inc.: Contacts.fp5, Products.fp5, and Invoices.fp5. (Spot Ink, which is a fictional company named after my dog, sells pens, ink, and related products.) By following the instructions, you can review many of the chapter's concepts and procedures while learning how they can apply to real-life situations.

You may have noticed that this book didn't come with a disk or CD. Why? Well, have you ever gotten a disk or CD with a book that was really worth the extra $10 to $20 tacked onto the price of the book? I never have. And do you think it would be worth that extra $10 to $20 to get the FileMaker Pro database files that you could build from scratch by simply following my instructions? I don't!

Don't worry, I won't *force* you to build the files from scratch. If you want to review the files I created for each chapter, you can get them (for free, of course) two ways:

- Download them from this book's companion Web site, where you'll also find additional files and information that you might find helpful as you work with FileMaker Pro. The URL is *http://www.gilesrd.com/fmprocomp/*.

- Send an e-mail message to *info@gilesrd.com* with the words *FMP5 Companion* and your computer platform (*Mac* or *Win*) in the message subject. (For example, putting *FMP5 Companion Win* in the subject of the message would request the Windows version of the files.) The files will be sent to you in a return e-mail message within a day or so.

About Your FileMaker "Pro"

If you're wondering who I am and why the nice folks at Morgan Kaufmann let me write (and then revise!) this book, let me tell you.

I've been a freelance computer consultant since 1990, when I quit my day job as a Financial Analyst in a Fortune 100 corporation. In the beginning of this second career, I spent quite a bit of time doing computer applications training in a classroom setting. This taught me a very valuable skill—how to explain procedures in a way that people can understand. It also taught me how to anticipate questions and head them off with explanations before they're asked.

I co-authored my first computer book way back in 1992 and have written 25 Mac OS and Windows books since then—including *FileMaker Pro 2.0 for the Mac in a Nutshell* for Sybex (way back in 1993) and *FileMaker Pro 4 Companion* for FileMaker Press (in 1998). FileMaker Pro is one of my all-time favorite software applications, so I'm thrilled to be writing about it again.

In addition to writing books, I write columns for *FileMaker Pro Advisor* and *Mac Today* magazines, speak at Macworld Expo, and develop Web sites for budget-conscious small businesses. When I'm not working (which isn't often these days), I enjoy horseback riding, motorcycling, photography, reading, and travelling. Last year I started learning to fly a helicopter; I'm hoping to finish that up sometime soon.

I don't consider myself a "computer geek" and hope you don't either. After all, there's a lot more to life than punching keyboard keys and mousing around in front of a computer screen. I urge you to do what you can while you can. Life's too short to waste a moment of time.

Tell Me What You Think

I like to hear from people who read my work (especially if they have nice things to say). If you want to drop me a line, do it via e-mail. My address is *maria@gilesrd.com*. Although I can't promise to answer your message—I get an awful lot of e-mail—I do eventually read every message I get.

You can also visit my Web site: *http://www.marialanger.com/*. That's where you'll find a list of all my books; links to sites I've created to support my books and answer frequently asked questions; pictures of my Ducati, dog, and horses; and links to some of my favorite Web sites.

Acknowledgments

I'd like to take this opportunity to send my thanks to the following people.

To Ken Morton for giving me the opportunity to write and revise this book for Morgan Kaufmann.

To the production folks at Morgan Kaufmann for seeing my book safely through the production process, especially Angela Dooley, Production Editor; Victor Curran, Production Manager; Adrienne Rebello, Copy Editor; and Shawn Girsberger, Cover Designer. And to the other folks at MK who worked on this project without me ever knowing who they were.

To Andy Knasinski, for another excellent technical editing job.

To Kevin Mallon, Steve Ruddock, and Bill Shissler at FileMaker, Inc., for helping me get the software and support I needed to write this book.

To Mike, for the usual set of reasons.

– Maria Langer

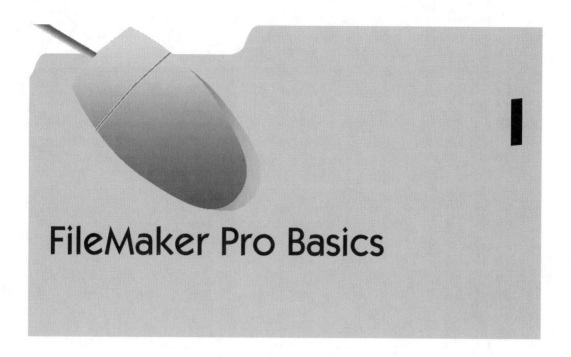

FileMaker Pro Basics

This part of the book offers basic information about using File-Maker Pro. Written especially for brand-new FileMaker Pro users, its four chapters are:

Chapter 1: Getting to Know FileMaker Pro

Chapter 2: Creating a Database and Defining Fields

Chapter 3: Entering and Editing Data

Chapter 4: Finding and Sorting Records

Getting to Know FileMaker Pro

In this chapter, I introduce you to the FileMaker Pro interface—its terminology, window elements, standard menu commands, and preference settings. The things I cover in this chapter form the basis of all work with FileMaker Pro.

NOTE   *If you've never used any version of FileMaker Pro before, this chapter is required reading. In it, you'll find important terms and concepts that you'll encounter again and again when working with FileMaker Pro databases.*

Important Terms and Concepts

There are a number of important terms and concepts that you need to know to work with FileMaker Pro. I discussed two of them—*fields* and *records*—in the Introduction. In this section, I review those standard database terms and define others that are unique to FileMaker Pro.

Field

A *field* is a category of information. An address book database, for example, may include the following fields: First Name, Last Name, Street Address, City, State, Zip Code, Home Phone, and Work Phone (see Figure 1-1).

```
                        Fields
                          |
      First Name    Tom
       Last Name    Jones
  Street Address    1616 Elm Street
            City    Cresskill
           State    NJ
        Zip Code    07626
      Home Phone    (201) 568-5555
      Work Phone    (212) 555-1212
```

FIGURE 1-1. Fields you might find in an address book database.

WARNING *Don't confuse fields with field labels. A* field *is a box in which you can enter information. A* field label *is text that appears on a layout to identify a field. I define the term* layout *a little later in this section.*

There are two important things to remember about fields:

- The same kind of information must be entered in a field for each record. (More on records in a moment.) For example, the First Name field should include first names only—not addresses or phone numbers.

- A database should contain a separate field for each category of information by which you want to sort or summarize records. That's why a good address book database will have separate fields for first and last name and will break the address into its separate components: street address, city, state, and zip code.

FileMaker Pro offers eight different types of fields. You can learn more about them in the section appropriately titled "Types of Fields" on page 55.

Record

A *record* is a collection of fields for one item. In our address book example, a record would consist of *all* the information—and *only* the information—for one particular person (see Figure 1-2).

First Name	Tom
Last Name	Jones
Street Address	1616 Elm Street
City	Cresskill
State	NJ
Zip Code	07626
Home Phone	(201) 568-5555
Work Phone	(212) 555-1212

Record

First Name	Betty
Last Name	Smith
Street Address	123 Main Street
City	Harrington Park
State	NJ
Zip Code	07640
Home Phone	(201) 768-5555
Work Phone	(914) 555-1212

Record

First Name	Eric
Last Name	Johnson
Street Address	111 Pine Tree Way
City	Wickenburg
State	AZ
Zip Code	85390
Home Phone	(520) 685-5555
Work Phone	(602) 555-1212

Record

FIGURE 1-2. Database records.

Here are some mildly interesting facts about records:

- The contents of a FileMaker Pro field may differ from one record to another. This makes sense—would you enter the same phone number for every person in an address book database? Yet more than one person may live in a particular city or state.

- A FileMaker Pro record can have any number of fields.

- The number of records in a FileMaker Pro database file is limited by the size of the file—a FileMaker Pro database cannot exceed 2 GB in size. That's a heck of a lot of records!

Layout

A *layout* is an arrangement of fields and other elements such as text and graphics that determines how database contents are displayed on screen or paper. An example of a layout for an address book database might be the entry form that you use to enter information into the database. Another example might be mailing labels that you print for each record.

TIP *Layouts are often referred to as* reports. *Technically, a report is something you print—usually for your boss—that is based on a layout. A FileMaker Pro layout, however, can be used for on-screen display or printed documents.*

Here are some important things to remember about layouts:

- A FileMaker Pro layout can contain any number or combination of fields. As you can see in the examples shown in Figure 1-3, an address book layout might include all fields; a telephone list layout might include only the First Name, Last Name, and Home Phone fields; and a mailing label layout might include only the First Name, Last Name, Street Address, City, State, and Zip Code fields.

Addresses			
Name Tom		Jones	
Address 1616 Elm Street			
Cresskill		NJ	07626
Home Phone (201) 568-5555			
Work Phone (212) 555-1212			

Phone List		
First Name	**Last Name**	**Home Phone**
Tom	Jones	(201) 568-5555
Betty	Smith	(201) 768-5555
Eric	Johnson	(520) 685-5555

Name Betty   Smith
Address 123 Main Street
   Harrington Park   NJ   07640
Home Phone (201) 768-5555
Work Phone (914) 555-1212

Tom Jones
1616 Elm Street
Cresskill, NJ 07626

Betty Smith
123 Main Street
Harrington Park, NJ 07640

Name Eric   Johnson
Address 111 Pine Tree Way
   Wickenburg   AZ   85390
Home Phone (520) 685-5555
Work Phone (602) 555-1212

Eric Johnson
111 Pine Tree Way
Wickenburg, AZ 85390

FIGURE 1-3. Layout examples: an address book (left), a phone list (top right), and mailing labels (bottom right).

- The contents of a FileMaker Pro field do not differ from one layout to another. That means the First Name field for the first record will be the same no matter what layout it appears on.

- A FileMaker Pro database can contain any number of layouts.

FileMaker Pro layouts are flexible and easy to use. They're also one of FileMaker Pro's most powerful features. That's why I devoted four whole chapters (Chapters 5–8) to them.

Database

A *database file* or just plain *database* is a collection of records, with information entered into the same group of fields, along with the layouts defined for on-screen or printed display. A FileMaker Pro database file can be easily identified by its icon (see Figure 1-4).

FIGURE 1-4. A FileMaker Pro document icon.

Related Files

FileMaker Pro is a *relational* database. That means you can have several databases that are related—they share information in specific fields.

Here are two examples that you'll explore in detail in Chapter 11, where I tell you all about developing relationships between files.

INVOICE/CUSTOMER DATABASE SOLUTION An invoicing database usually includes fields for customer information. That information is entered over and over for repeat customers. You could create a separate customer database and fill it with all kinds of information about the customer, then use a relationship to include necessary fields from the customer database in the invoicing database. The customer information would be entered only once and used over and over by the invoicing database. As an added benefit, updating the customer information in one place would update it everywhere.

INVOICE/PRODUCT INFO DATABASE SOLUTION An invoicing database also includes fields for product information. That information is entered over and over each time a product is sold. You can create a product database that stores information about all the products and, then use a relationship to include necessary fields from the product database in the invoicing file. This would speed data entry for invoicing and could update inventory automatically, each time an invoice is prepared.

TIP *FileMaker Pro can still be used to create* flat-file *databases—database files that are not related to other files.*

Saving Files

FileMaker Pro will never ask if you want to save changes to a document when you close it. Why? Because it automatically saves as you work and when you close the file.

NOTE *Although FileMaker Pro has no Save command, it does have a Save a Copy As command. This command is discussed in Chapter 18.*

Modes

FileMaker Pro has four different modes for working with database files. Each mode lets you work with different program features. You can switch from one mode to another by choosing the mode that you want from the View menu (see Figure 1-5), or by using the appropriate keyboard shortcut.

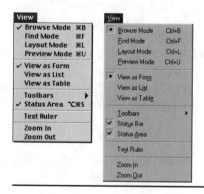

FIGURE 1-5. The View menu on Mac OS (left) and Windows (right).

TIP *There are two ways to identify the current FileMaker Pro mode: look at the Mode menu to see which of the top four commands are checked or marked (see Figure 1-5) or look at the mode pop-up menu at the bottom-left of the window (see Figure 1-27).*

Browse Mode

Browse mode (see Figure 1-6) is the mode you use to view, create, edit, and delete records. Each field appears as an edit box where you can enter and change information.

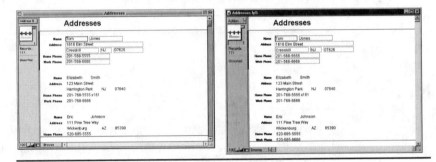

FIGURE 1-6. Browse mode on Mac OS (left) and Windows (right).

NOTE *Although you can also view records in Preview mode, you can only change them in Browse mode. I tell you about Preview mode in the section titled "Preview Mode" on page 14.*

The phrase *records being browsed* is used often in FileMaker Pro. It refers to the records that appear in Browse mode. This can be either:

• All records in the database.

• The records in the *found set*—those records displayed after using the Find or Omit commands.

TIP *It's a good idea to keep track of what records are being browsed since many File-Maker Pro commands work only on the found set. You can consult the book in the status area to learn more about how many records are being browsed. I tell you about that in the section titled "Book Icon" on page 18.*

When in Browse mode, the Records menu (see Figure 1-7) offers commands for working with records. The Format menu's options are limited to those you can use with selected field contents (see Figure 1-8).

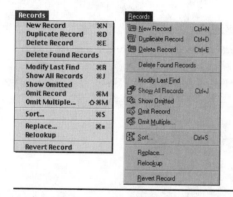

FIGURE 1-7. The Records menu in Browse mode on Mac OS (left) and Windows (right).

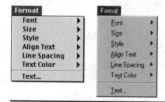

FIGURE 1-8. The Format menu in Browse mode on Mac OS (left) and Windows (right).

Find Mode

Find mode (see Figure 1-9) is the mode you use to specify search criteria and perform a search. When you switch to Find mode, each field on the current layout appears as a box in which you can enter criteria.

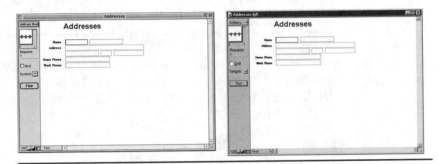

FIGURE 1-9. Find mode on Mac OS (left) and Windows (right).

When in Find mode, commands on the Requests menu (see Figure 1-10) let you work with find requests.

FIGURE 1-10. The Requests menu on Mac OS (left) and Windows (right).

After entering criteria in Find mode, you can click the Find button to begin the search. FileMaker Pro displays the records that it found in Browse mode so you can work with them.

Layout Mode

Layout mode (see Figure 1-11) is the mode you use to view, create, modify, and delete layouts. You can create, modify, or move layout *objects*—fields, field labels, and graphic elements.

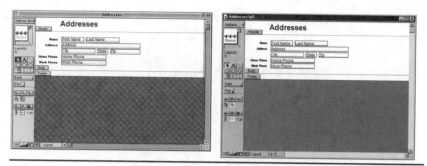

FIGURE 1-11. Layout mode on Mac OS (left) and Windows (right).

When in Layout mode, commands on the Layouts menu (see Figure 1-12) let you work with layouts. The Arrange menu (see Figure 1-13) offers additional options and commands for working with selected layout objects. The Format menu expands to add commands for working with layout objects (see Figure 1-14).

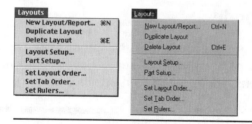

FIGURE 1-12. The Layouts menu on Mac OS (left) and Windows (right).

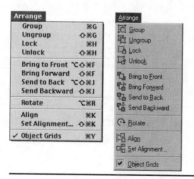

FIGURE 1-13. The Arrange menu on Mac OS (left) and Windows (right).

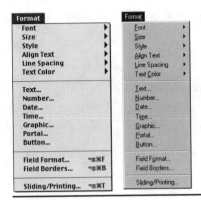

FIGURE 1-14. The Format menu in Layout mode on Mac OS (left) and Windows (right).

After making changes to a layout, you can see how your changes affect the appearance of data in Browse or Preview mode.

Preview Mode

Preview mode (see Figure 1-15) is the mode you use to view documents before printing them. Preview mode shows exactly how your document will appear when printed.

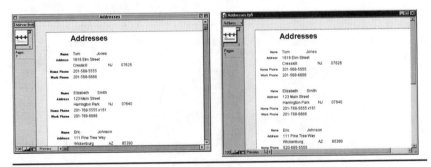

FIGURE 1-15. Preview mode on Mac OS (left) and Windows (right).

NOTE *Although Browse mode also lets you see the records of a database, it does not show each individual page of a printed report. In addition, some layout features such as header, footer, and summary parts are not accurately represented in Browse mode. I describe Browse mode in the section titled "Browse Mode" on page 10.*

When in Preview mode, the Records menu looks a lot like the Records menu in Browse mode, but most of the commands are gray (see Figure 1-16).

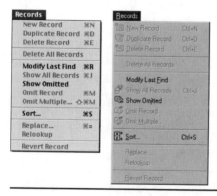

FIGURE 1-16. The Records menu in Preview mode on Mac OS (left) and Windows (right).

Views

There are three ways to view data in Browse mode or find requests in Find mode: as a form, list, or table. Although one view may be more appropriate than the other for some layouts or purposes, you can select any view for any layout.

To select a view, choose one of the View commands from the View menu (see Figure 1-5).

TIP *The option you choose is applied to the current layout. This means you can set different views for different layouts.*

Form View

Form view displays one record at a time in the window. You can use the book in the status area, which I tell you about in the section titled "Status Area" on page 17, to switch from one record to another. As the name implies, this option is most appropriate for form layouts. Figure 1-9 shows an example of Form view in Find mode.

List View

List view displays all records in the found set in a scrolling list in the window. You can use the vertical scroll bar to scroll through the records. This view is most appropriate for columnar reports, mailing labels, and other layouts in which you want to view more than one record at a time. Figure 1-6 shows an example of List view in Browse mode.

Table View

Table view displays all records in the found set, organized in rows and columns. Each row displays a specific record; each column displays a specific field. You can use the vertical scroll bar to scroll through the records. You may also need to use the horizontal scroll bar to scroll through the fields, depending on how many fields the layout displays. You can resize columns and sort data by a specific column by dragging or clicking within the window. Figure 1-17 shows an example of Table view in Browse mode.

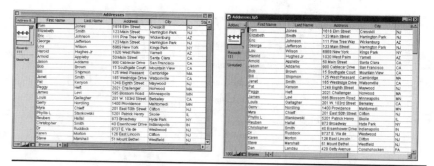

FIGURE 1-17. Table view in Browse mode on Mac OS (left) and Windows (right).

Components of the Document Window

FileMaker Pro's document window contains a mixture of familiar Mac OS or Windows elements and FileMaker Pro tools and controls. The Mac OS or Windows elements—title bar, scroll bars, close box or button, etc.—remain the same from window to window and work just like they do in all of your other programs. In this section, I tell you all about the tools and controls inside the FileMaker Pro document window.

NOTE *As I mention in the Introduction of this book, I assume you already know Mac OS or Windows basic operations, so I don't cover them in this book. If you don't know the basics, consult the manuals that came with your computer or operating system.*

Status Area

The status area appears on the left side of the document window (see Figure 1-18). It provides information and controls that you can use while working with FileMaker Pro database files.

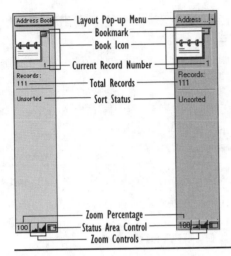

FIGURE 1-18. The status area in Browse mode on Mac OS (left) and Windows (right).

Although the appearance and functionality of the status area changes depending on the current mode, the following items always appear:

LAYOUT POP-UP MENU   The *Layout pop-up menu* always shows the name of the current layout. You can use it to switch from one layout to another (see Figure 1-19).

FIGURE 1-19. The Layout pop-up menu on Mac OS (left) and Windows (right).

BOOK ICON   The *book icon* is a tool for navigating within the current mode:

- In Browse mode, use the book icon to switch from one record to another.

- In Find mode, use the book icon to switch from one Find request to another.

- In Layout mode, use the book icon to switch from one layout to another.

- In Preview mode, use the book icon to switch from one page to another.

You can use the book icon in a number of ways:

- Click the top or bottom "page" of the book icon to switch to the previous or next item. If a book page has lines on it, you can click it to switch to another item. If the book page is blank, it means you're looking at the first (top page) or last (bottom page) item. Figure 1-20 shows some examples of how the book can appear.

FIGURE 1-20. The book icon when the first item (left), a middle item (center), and last item (right) is displayed.

- Drag the bookmark to move to another item quickly.

- Click the current item number at the bottom of the book icon to select it (see Figure 1-21, left), type a new item number (see Figure 1-21, center), and press Return or Enter to move quickly to that item (see Figure 1-21, right).

FIGURE 1-21. The book icon after selecting the current item number (left), typing in a new item number (center), and pressing Enter to go to that item number (right).

ZOOM CONTROLS The two zoom control buttons let you increase or decrease the magnification within the window. The button with the short mountains (the "New Jersey mountains," as I call them) is the zoom out button; it decreases the magnification. The button with the tall mountains (the "Colorado mountains") is the zoom in button; it increases the magnification. Each time you click one of these buttons, the magnification changes. The current magnification is indicated on the zoom percentage button. You can zoom from 25 to 400 percent.

TIP   *To return quickly to 100 percent magnification, click the zoom percentage button.*

STATUS AREA CONTROL   The status area control button toggles the display of the status area. Click it once to hide the status area. Click it again to display the status area.

The Status Area in Browse Mode

In Browse mode, the status area can provide several other pieces of information (refer to Figure 1-18).

TOTAL RECORDS   The total records is the total number of records in the database.

FOUND RECORDS   After successfully performing a find, the status area displays the number of records in the found set (see Figure 1-22).

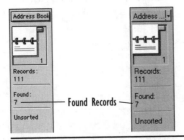

FIGURE 1-22. Found records indicated on Mac OS (left) and Windows (right).

SORT STATUS   The sort status indicates whether the records are sorted.

The Status Area in Find Mode

In Find mode, the status area offers options that can be used when specifying search criteria and performing a find (see Figure 1-23).

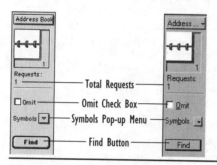

FIGURE 1-23. The status area in Find mode on Mac OS (left) and Windows (right).

TOTAL REQUESTS Total requests indicates the total number of find requests. You use multiple find requests to find records with different values in the same field, such as all contacts in NY or NJ.

OMIT CHECK BOX The Omit check box enables you to omit (rather than find) records matching specified search criteria, such as all contacts except those in NJ.

SYMBOLS POP-UP MENU The Symbols pop-up menu (see Figure 1-24) displays a list of symbols or operators that can be used as part of search criteria.

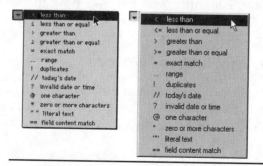

FIGURE 1-24. The Symbols menu on Mac OS (left) and Windows (right).

FIND BUTTON   The Find button is what you click when you've entered search criteria and are ready to perform the Find.

The Status Area in Layout Mode

In Layout mode, the status area fills with a variety of tools for adding or modifying layout objects (see Figure 1-25).

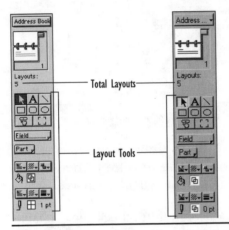

FIGURE 1-25. The status area in Layout mode on Mac OS (left) and Windows (right).

TOTAL LAYOUTS   Total layouts indicates the total number of layouts within the database.

LAYOUT TOOLS   The status area is jam-packed with layout tools in Layout mode. I identify and tell you how to use these tools in Chapters 5, 7, and 8.

The Status Area in Preview Mode

In Preview mode, the status area is nearly empty (see Figure 1-26).

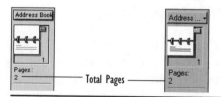

FIGURE 1-26. The status area in Preview mode on Mac OS (left) and Windows (right).

TOTAL PAGES Total pages indicates the total number of pages that would emerge from your printer if you printed the records being browsed (or found set).

NOTE *A question mark appears in the total pages area if FileMaker Pro has not yet calculated the total number of pages.*

Mode Pop-up Menu

The Mode pop-up menu appears at the bottom of the FileMaker Pro window in every mode. It performs two functions:

- The Mode pop-up menu displays the name of the current mode.

- The Mode pop-up menu can also be used to switch from one mode to another (see Figure 1-27).

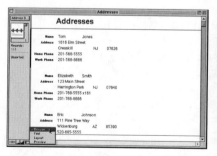

FIGURE 1-27. The Mode pop-up menu on Mac OS (left) and Windows (right).

Status Bar (Windows Only)

The status bar is a narrow area commonly found at the very bottom of the screen when a Windows program is running (see Figure 1-28). On the left side of the status bar, you can find instructions for opening onscreen help or details about a currently highlighted menu command. On the right side of the status bar, you can find indicators to tell you whether the Caps Lock, Num Lock, or Scroll Lock keys on your keyboard are enabled.

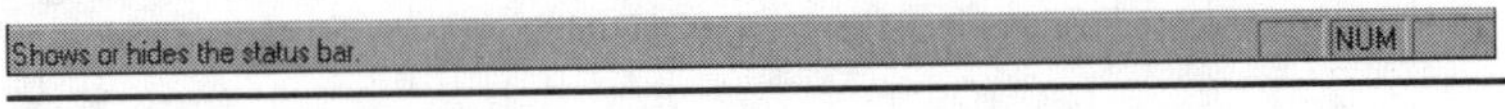

Shows or hides the status bar.   NUM

FIGURE 1-28. The status bar with a menu command highlighted.

You can show or hide the status bar by choosing the Status Bar command from the View menu (see Figure 1-5, right). If a check mark appears beside the command, the status bar is already displayed.

Standard Menu Commands

Like most Mac OS and Windows programs, FileMaker Pro includes a number of standard commands. These commands work just they way you expect them to, so I don't spend too much time explaining them here.

File Menu Commands

The File menu (see Figure 1-29) offers the usual collection of file-related commands.

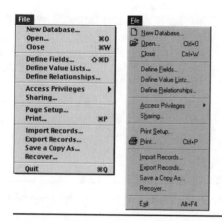

FIGURE 1-29. The File menu on Mac OS (left) and Windows (right).

NEW DATABASE   Use the New Database command to create a new FileMaker Pro database. I tell you more about that in the section titled "Creating a New Database File" on page 47.

*T**IP*** *There is no keyboard shortcut for the New Database command in FileMaker Pro. The normal shortcut, Command-N (Mac OS) or Control-N (Windows) will create a new record, find request, or layout, depending on the current FileMaker Pro mode.*

OPEN   Use the Open command to open an existing database file or to create a database based on information in a file created with a program other than FileMaker Pro. When you choose this command, a standard Open File dialog box appears (see Figure 1-30). Use it to locate and open the file with which you want to work.

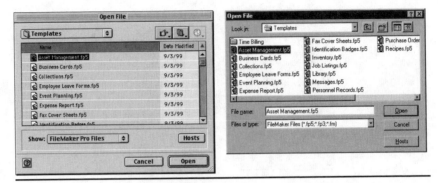

FIGURE 1-30. The Open File dialog box on Mac OS (left) and Windows (right).

TIP   *On Windows, to open a FileMaker Pro database file that was named without the .fp5 extension, choose All Available (*.*) from the Files of Type menu in the Open dialog box. I tell you about file name extensions in the section titled "Naming and Saving Files" on page 52.*

CLOSE Use the Close command to close the active document window.

WARNING   *Closing a document window is not the same as quitting or exiting the FileMaker Pro application. You must use the Quit or Exit command under the File menu to close the FileMaker Pro application.*

NOTE   *FileMaker Pro will never ask if you want to save changes to a document when you close it because it automatically saves changes as you work.*

PAGE SETUP (MAC OS), PRINT SETUP (WINDOWS), AND PRINT Use these commands to prepare a document for printing and print it. I tell you all about printing database files in Chapter 14.

QUIT (MAC OS) OR EXIT (WINDOWS) Use the appropriate command to close the FileMaker Pro application when you are finished working with it. This clears FileMaker Pro out of RAM, freeing up memory for other applications you may want to use.

Edit Menu Commands

The Edit menu (see Figure 1-31) offers the usual collection of editing commands.

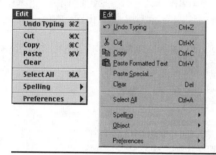

FIGURE 1-31. The Edit menu on Mac OS (left) and Windows (right).

UNDO The first command on the Edit menu is the Undo command. Its wording varies depending on the last thing you did. If it's gray when you want to undo something, you're out of luck.

REDO The Redo command takes the place of the Undo command right after you use the Undo command. It basically undoes the Undo command. Try it sometime and see for yourself.

CUT, COPY, AND PASTE Use the Cut, Copy, and Paste commands to cut, copy, and paste selected text or objects. These commands work the same way they do in other Mac OS and Windows programs.

 On Windows, the exact wording of the Paste command varies depending on what was last copied or cut.

CLEAR Use the Clear command to delete whatever is selected.

SELECT ALL Use the Select All command to select all the text in any box or field with a blinking insertion point or all the objects on the current layout in Layout mode.

Window Menu Commands

The Window menu (see Figure 1-32) offers commands you can use to hide windows (Mac OS only), arrange windows (Windows only), and switch from one active window to another.

FIGURE 1-32. The Window menu with two database files open on Mac OS (left) and Windows (right).

HIDE WINDOW (MAC OS ONLY) This command removes the active window from view without actually closing it. Once hidden, a window's name appears in the Window menu with parentheses around it (see Figure 1-33). Simply select the window name to display it again.

FIGURE 1-33. The Window menu on Mac OS with a hidden window listed.

TIP *Windows users can "hide" a window by minimizing it. Just click the Minimize button on the window's title bar.*

TILE HORIZONTALLY AND TILE VERTICALLY (WINDOWS ONLY) These commands arrange the open document windows by resizing them and placing them edge to edge in the application window (see Figure 1-34).

CASCADE (WINDOWS ONLY) This command arranges the open document windows by resizing them and placing them one atop another so all their title bars show (see Figure 1-34).

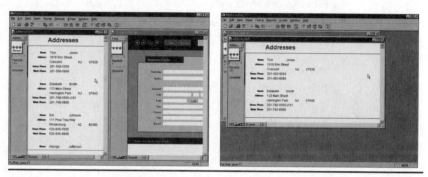

FIGURE 1-34. Two document windows arranged with the Tile Vertically (left) and Cascade (right) command on Windows.

ARRANGE ICONS (WINDOWS ONLY) This command arranges the title bars for minimized windows along the bottom of the application window.

Help Menu Commands

The Help menu (see Figure 1-35) offers a number of commands you can use to access FileMaker Pro's online help system and, on Mac OS, Balloon Help.

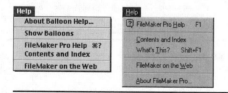

FIGURE 1-35. The Help menu on Mac OS (left) and Windows (right).

SHOW BALLOONS (MAC OS ONLY)   Use the Show Balloons command to display balloon help for FileMaker Pro. Those little cartoon balloons may be annoying, but you might find them useful for identifying the things you see onscreen. When you're sick of them, choose Hide Balloons from the Help menu.

FILEMAKER PRO HELP AND CONTENTS AND INDEX   These two commands display FileMaker Pro's onscreen help feature. Use this feature to get additional information about using FileMaker Pro.

WHAT'S THIS? (WINDOWS ONLY)   Use this command to display context-sensitive help. Choose the command, then click on anything in the FileMaker Pro application or document window. FileMaker Pro's onscreen help feature displays a window with information about the item on which you clicked.

Context Menus

Like most other Mac OS and Windows programs, FileMaker Pro supports Context menus. These menus appear at the mouse pointer and offer commands that can apply to the currently selected item.

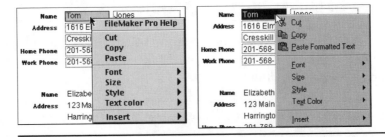

FIGURE 1-36. The Context menu that appears on Mac OS (left) and Windows (right) for selected text in a field.

Using a Context Menu

To use a Context menu, begin by pointing to the item for which you want the Context menu to appear. Then:

- On Mac OS, hold down the Control key and press the mouse button.

- On Windows, press the right mouse button.

The Context menu appears (see Figure 1-36). Choose the command that you want to use.

Dismissing a Context Menu

To dismiss a Context menu without choosing a command, click anywhere in the document window other than on the Context menu. The menu disappears.

NOTE   *I'm not a big fan of context menus. I'm used to doing things the old fashioned way—with regular menu commands or keyboard shortcuts. (Besides, I usually use a Mac and like single-handed mousing.) Don't be upset if I don't point out every instance where you can perform a task with a Context menu command. There are enough other things to tell you and this book is already fatter than it was supposed to be. If you like Context menus, explore them on your own.*

Toolbars

FileMaker Pro also includes toolbars that you can use to access commands. Simply click a toolbar button or choose a command from a toolbar menu to access the command.

NOTE *The toolbar feature was added to FileMaker Pro in version 5 to help make it more familiar to Microsoft Office users. Many of the buttons on the Standard and Formatting toolbars are identical to buttons on the Standard and Formatting toolbars in Microsoft Office products.*

FileMaker Pro's Toolbars

FileMaker Pro offers two different toolbars: Standard and Text Formatting.

STANDARD TOOLBAR By default, the Standard toolbar (see Figure 1-37) appears beneath the menu bar. This toolbar offers access to many commonly used commands on the File, Edit, and Records menus.

FIGURE 1-37. The Standard toolbar on Mac OS (top) and Windows (bottom).

TEXT FORMATTING TOOLBAR The Text Formatting toolbar (see Figure 1-38) offers access to commands found under the Formatting menu. In most cases, you'll have to select a field's contents in Browse mode or a field or label object in Layout mode before you can use Text Formatting toolbar options.

FIGURE 1-38. The Text Formatting toolbar on Mac OS (top) and Windows (bottom).

Displaying and Hiding Toolbars

You can display or hide a toolbar using commands on the Toolbars submenu under the View menu (see Figure 1-39). Simply choose the toolbar name to display or hide it. If a check mark appears beside the toolbar name, it's already displayed.

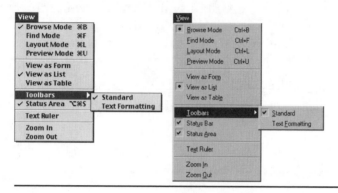

FIGURE 1-39. The Toolbars submenu under the View menu on Mac OS (left) and Windows (right).

Moving Toolbars

If, for some reason, you don't like seeing the toolbars right beneath the menu bar, you can move them. Position your mouse pointer on the drag handle on the far right end of the toolbar. Then press your mouse button down and drag the toolbar into the document window. When you release the mouse button, the toolbar turns into a floating toolbar (see Figure 1-40). You can then drag the toolbar by its title bar to position it anywhere on screen—even back where it originally was.

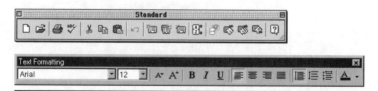

FIGURE 1-40. The Standard toolbar displayed as a floating toolbar on Mac OS (top) and the Text Formatting toolbar displayed as a floating toolbar on Windows (bottom).

Preferences

Every time I fire up a brand new software program for the first time, the first area I explore is the program's preferences. I've found that reviewing a program's preferences gives me insight to many of its features and enables me to customize it for my own use, right from the start.

FileMaker Pro has two different kinds of preferences: application and document.

Application Preferences

Application preferences govern the way the FileMaker Pro application works. These preference settings are in effect no matter which document file is open.

To view or change application preferences, choose Application from the Preferences submenu under the Edit menu (see Figure 1-41).

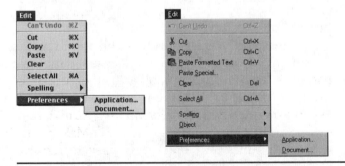

FIGURE 1-41. The Preferences submenu under the Edit menu on Mac OS (left) and Windows (right).

The Application Preferences dialog box appears (see Figure 1-42). To switch from one category of application preferences to another, click its tab at the top of the dialog box.

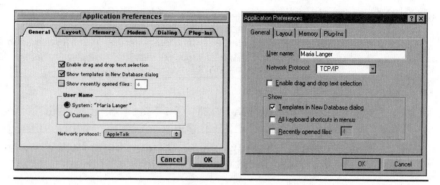

FIGURE 1-42. The default settings for General preferences in the Application Preferences dialog box on Mac OS (left) and Windows (right).

General

General application preferences (see Figure 1-42) are a hodge-podge of preferences that can't be categorized logically elsewhere.

ENABLE DRAG AND DROP TEXT SELECTION When turned on, this check box makes it possible to drag selected text from one field to another, thus copying it to the destination location.

SHOW TEMPLATES IN NEW DATABASE DIALOG This check box includes an option in the New Database dialog box to create a file based on templates that come with FileMaker Pro.

SHOW RECENTLY OPENED FILES When turned on, this check box displays a list of recently opened FileMaker Pro files on the File menu. This makes it quick and easy to reopen files that were recently open. You can enter the number of files that you want to display on the File menu in the option's box.

SHOW ALL KEYBOARD SHORTCUTS IN MENUS (WINDOWS ONLY) When turned on, this option displays all keyboard shortcuts beside their corresponding commands on menus.

NOTE *Although this option is turned off by default, I recommend turning it on. It will help you learn shortcuts for the commands you use most often. This option is turned on in all menu illustrations from this point forward throughout this book and in Appendix A. (All keyboard shortcuts are displayed by default on Mac OS.)*

USER NAME (MAC OS) On Mac OS, the User Name area enables you to select either the System Name recorded in your computer's network settings or a Custom Name that you can enter into an edit box. Select the radio button for the option that you want.

USER NAME (WINDOWS) On Windows, the User Name box displays the user name entered for your copy of FileMaker Pro. This is either the name you entered when you installed FileMaker Pro or the name set up in the network settings for the computer. You can change this name by entering a new one.

NETWORK PROTOCOL Use this menu (see Figure 1-43) to select a protocol for sharing FileMaker Pro files on a network. On Mac OS, your options are AppleTalk, TCP/IP, or <none>. On Windows, your options are IPX/SPX, TCP/IP, or <none>.

FIGURE 1-43. The Network Protocol menu on Mac OS (left) and Windows (right).

Layout

Layout application preferences (see Figure 1-44) govern the way tools work in Layout mode, as well as whether newly defined fields are added automatically to the current layout.

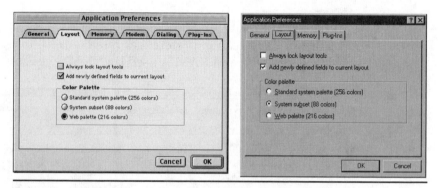

FIGURE 1-44. The default settings for Layout preferences in the Application Preferences dialog box on Mac OS (left) and Windows (right).

ALWAYS LOCK LAYOUT TOOLS   When turned on, this option keeps the layout tool you select active until you select another tool or press Return or Enter.

ADD NEWLY DEFINED FIELDS TO CURRENT LAYOUT   When turned on, this option automatically adds each newly defined field to the current layout.

COLOR PALETTE   These three options let you set the number of colors offered for formatting options throughout FileMaker Pro:

- **Standard system palette** is the 256-color palette commonly available in your computer system. Select this option to access the most colors within FileMaker Pro.

- **System subset** is the 88-color palette traditionally offered within FileMaker Pro. You might find this option useful if you're accustomed to working with previous versions of FileMaker Pro.

- **Web palette** is the 216-color palette that corresponds to "Web-safe" colors. This palette is particularly handy if you plan to publish your database files to the Web using File-Maker's Instant Web publishing feature.

Memory

Memory application preferences (see Figure 1-45) govern the way files are saved and RAM is used by FileMaker Pro.

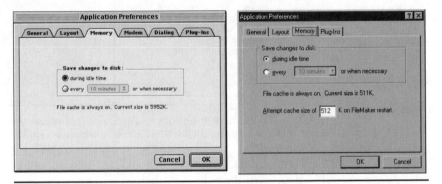

FIGURE 1-45. The default settings for Memory preferences in the Application Preferences dialog box on Mac OS (left) and Windows (right).

SAVE CHANGES TO DISK OPTIONS Select an option to determine when you want FileMaker Pro to save changes to the open database files.

- **During idle time** saves when you're not performing tasks with the database.

- **Every 10 minutes or when necessary** saves periodically or when database information changes. If you select this option, you can use the menu (see Figure 1-46) to set the save frequency.

FIGURE 1-46. The save frequency menu on Mac OS (left) and Windows (right).

TIP *If you're using FileMaker Pro on a laptop computer that is running from battery power, set the save frequency to 30 minutes or higher to help save battery power.*

FILE CACHE   The file cache is a place in your computer's RAM that is used by FileMaker Pro to store changes to the database between saves. On Windows, you can change the cache size requested by FileMaker Pro by entering a new value in the Attempt cache size box.

TIP *On Mac OS, you can change the cache size by changing the amount of RAM allocated to FileMaker Pro. In the Finder, select the FileMaker Pro application icon. Choose Get Info from the File menu or press Command-I to display the FileMaker Pro Info window. On some versions of Mac OS, you may have to choose Memory from the Show pop-up menu to display Memory options like those shown in Figure 1-47. Then change the value in the Preferred Size edit box. Close the window to save your changes. Increasing the RAM allocation is the best way to fix or prevent "out of memory" messages that may appear when you work with large files or import large images.*

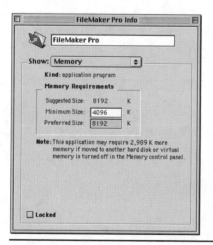

FIGURE 1-47. The FileMaker Pro Info window on Mac OS.

Modem (Mac OS Only)

On Mac OS, you can also set Modem preferences (see Figure 1-48) that help FileMaker Pro control your modem.

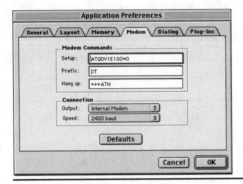

FIGURE 1-48. The default settings for Modem preferences in the Application Preferences dialog box on Mac OS.

MODEM COMMANDS Use these boxes to change default modem setup (initialization), prefix, and hang up strings for your modem.

WARNING *If you are not sure what the Modem Commands settings should be, leave them alone. Chances are, the default values will work just fine for your modem. If not, consult the manual that came with your modem.*

CONNECTION Use these two menus (see Figure 1-49) to choose the output method (speaker, port, or internal modem) and maximum speed of your modem.

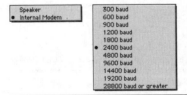

FIGURE 1-49. The Output (left) and Speed (right) menus. Output menu options vary depending on your computer model; these options are on an iMac.

DEFAULTS Clicking this button returns all settings to the default values. (You'll find this especially helpful if you didn't heed the previous warning and messed up the Modem Commands settings.)

Dialing (Mac OS Only)

On Mac OS, you can set Dialing preferences (see Figure 1-50) that FileMaker Pro uses to dial phone numbers from different locations.

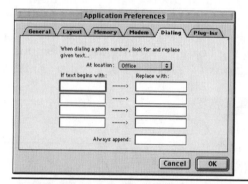

FIGURE 1-50. The default settings for Dialing preferences in the Application Preferences dialog box on Mac OS.

The idea behind these settings is that you may or may not want to dial certain telephone number digits based on your location. The settings in this dialog box are used by the Dial Phone script step.

To set these preferences, start by choosing a location from the At location pop-up menu (see Figure 1-51). Enter the digits that File-Maker Pro should search for in the edit box(es) on the left side of the dialog box. Then enter the digits that FileMaker Pro should replace the found digits with in the edit box(es) on the right side of the dialog box. If you always want FileMaker Pro to dial certain digits at the end of the phone number, enter those in the Always append edit box.

FIGURE 1-51. The At location pop-up menu.

The best way to understand this feature is with an example. Say you work in an office building where the phone numbers all begin with area code 520 followed by the exchange 684. When dialing a co-worker in the building, you don't have to dial all these numbers—just the last four digits of the phone number. When dialing from FileMaker Pro, you can automatically omit the first six digits of the phone number by entering them in an edit box on the left side of the dialog box and leaving the corresponding edit box on the right side blank (see Figure 1-52).

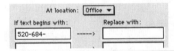

FIGURE 1-52. Dialing preferences example.

NOTE *If you're having trouble understanding Dialing preferences or imagining how you would set them up for your use, don't panic. This preferences setting is for advanced users who take advantage of the Dial Phone script step only—and it isn't even required to use that step.*

Plug-Ins

Plug-Ins application preferences (see Figure 1-53) let you set up FileMaker Pro plug-ins, such as Local Data Access Companion, Remote Data Access Companion, and Web Companion. Plug-ins add functionality to the core FileMaker Pro application. In addition to the plug-ins that come with FileMaker Pro, you can obtain and install plug-ins from third-party vendors. Check the File-Maker, Inc. Web site (http://www.filemaker.com/) for more information.

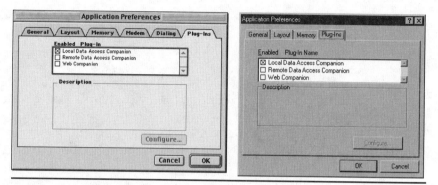

FIGURE 1-53. The default settings for Plug-In preferences in the Application Preferences dialog box on Mac OS (left) and Windows (right).

You can learn more about a plug-in by selecting it and reading the contents of the description area within the dialog box. You can enable or disable a plug-in by toggling its check box on or off. Finally, you can configure a plug-in by selecting it and clicking the Configure button.

Document Preferences

Document preferences govern the way FileMaker Pro works with specific documents. These preference settings affect only the documents for which they are set.

General Preferences

General document preferences (see Figure 1-54) control a variety of document operations.

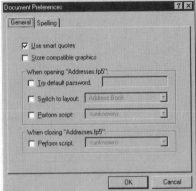

FIGURE 1-54. The default settings for General preferences in the Document Preferences dialog box on Mac OS (left) and Windows (right).

USE SMART QUOTES (' ', " ") When turned on, FileMaker Pro automatically enters curly or smart quote characters when you type single or double quote characters.

WARNING   *If you plan to publish your database on the Web using FileMaker Web Companion or any other Web publishing tool, make sure the Use smart quotes option is turned off! Smart quote characters are not properly interpreted by Web browser software so they may not appear correctly on Web pages.*

STORE COMPATIBLE GRAPHICS When turned on, this option stores all graphics in a format that can be read and understood by both Mac OS and Windows computers.

TIP   *If your database file includes graphics and will be used on both Mac OS and Windows computers, turn this option on. Otherwise, leave it turned off to conserve disk space.*

WHEN OPENING FILE OPTIONS These options apply when opening the database file.

- **Try default password** instructs FileMaker Pro to try opening the file automatically with a specific password. This option is useful only if the file is password protected. To set it, turn on the check box and enter the password in the edit box.

WARNING

If you enter the master password in the Try default password edit box, you grant full access to anyone who opens the file! I tell you all about password protecting files in Chapter 17.

- **Switch to layout** instructs FileMaker Pro to switch to a specific layout automatically when opening the database file. To set this option, turn on the check box and choose a layout from the pop-up menu.

- **Perform script** instructs FileMaker Pro to perform a specific script automatically when opening the database file. To set this option, turn on the check box and choose a script from the pop-up menu.

WHEN CLOSING FILE OPTION This option applies when closing the database file.

- **Perform script** instructs FileMaker Pro to perform a specific script automatically when closing the database file. To set this option, turn on the check box and choose a script from the pop-up menu.

Spelling Preferences

Spelling document preferences (see Figure 1-55) control the way the spelling checker works for the database file.

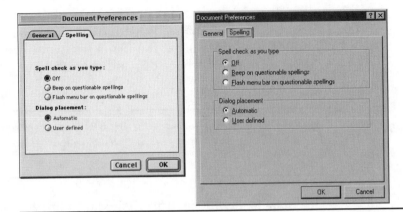

FIGURE 1-55. The default settings for Spelling preferences in the Document Preferences dialog box on Mac OS (left) and Windows (right).

SPELL CHECK AS YOU TYPE These radio buttons enable you to set up automatic spell checking. Select one of three options:

- **Off** disables the automatic spell checking feature.

- **Beep on questionable spellings** tells FileMaker Pro to sound an alert each time you type a word it doesn't recognize.

- **Flash menu bar on questionable spellings** tells FileMaker Pro to blink the menu bar each time you type a word it doesn't recognize.

DIALOG PLACEMENT These radio buttons enable you to specify where the Spelling dialog box will appear. There are two options:

- **Automatic** puts the Spelling dialog box where FileMaker Pro wants to put it.

- **User defined** puts the Spelling dialog box where you position it.

Creating a Database and Defining Fields

Ready to get started working with FileMaker Pro? Then let's hop to it. In this chapter, I tell you how to create a new database file, define fields, and view the default layout.

Creating a New Database File

FileMaker Pro offers two ways to create a new database file: with a template or from scratch. No matter which method you use, you choose the same command to get started: the New Database command under the File menu (see Figure 2-1). This displays the New Database dialog box (see Figure 2-2).

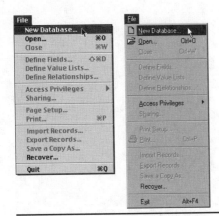

FIGURE 2-1. Choosing New from the File menu on Mac OS (left) and Windows (right).

FIGURE 2-2. The New Database dialog box that appears when you use the New command on Mac OS (left) and Windows (right).

NOTE *When you launch FileMaker Pro by double-clicking its application icon (Mac OS) or choosing it from the Start menu (Windows), FileMaker Pro also displays the New Database dialog box. But as shown in Figure 2-3, that version of the dialog box also enables you to open an existing file. You can prevent the dialog box in Figure 2-3 from appearing by turning on the No longer show this dialog check box.*

FIGURE 2-3. The New Database dialog that appears when you open the FileMaker Pro application icon on Mac OS (left) and Windows (right).

Using Templates

FileMaker Pro comes with a number of templates on which you can base new database files. This enables you to create a FileMaker Pro-based solution with the least amount of effort.

About the Templates

The templates can be found in the FileMaker Templates (Mac OS) or Template (Windows) folder inside the FileMaker Pro 5 folder. They are organized into two categories:

- **Templates** includes databases of use to business owners, as well as a few databases of interest to individuals.

- **Tips from Tech Support** includes templates with frequently asked questions about FileMaker Pro, as well as tips and tricks for learning more about the program.

TIP   *You can learn more about each of the templates by clicking the Template Info button in the New Database dialog box (see Figure 2-2 or Figure 2-3). This button displays a FileMaker Pro database full of template information.*

Pros and Cons of Using Templates

There's no denying it—the templates are nice. They were developed by FileMaker Pro experts who made them not only functional but also attractive. You'd need a lot of FileMaker Pro experience and time to build similar databases from scratch. The templates make it possible to start getting work done with File-Maker Pro virtually minutes after taking it out of the box.

But before you make your decision, consider these points:

- Basing a database on a template is not a custom solution. You still must have FileMaker Pro knowledge and time to customize the template for your own use.

- Some of the templates utilize advanced FileMaker Pro features, making them difficult for new FileMaker Pro users to understand and use.

- You must fully understand how a template-based solution works before modifying its structure. For example, deleting a match field that is used to relate two databases will break a relationship, thus "breaking" the solution.

- Creating a database from a template does not teach you the basics of building FileMaker Pro databases.

Are FileMaker Pro's templates for you? In some instances, they might be just what you need. Browse them and see for yourself.

Creating a New Database from a Template

To create a new database from a template, select the Create a new file using a template option in the New Database dialog box (see Figure 2-2 or Figure 2-3). Then choose a template category from the menu in the dialog box. Click once on the name of the template that you want to use and click OK.

The Create Copy dialog box, which looks and works like a standard Save As dialog box, appears (see Figure 2-4). Continue following instructions in the section titled "Naming and Saving Files" on page 52 to save the new file.

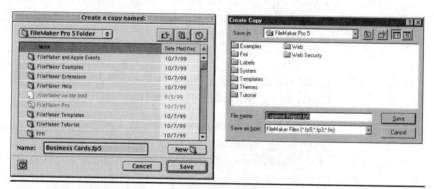

FIGURE 2-4. The dialog box that appears when you create a new database from a template on Mac OS (left) or Windows (right).

Starting from Scratch

The other way to create a new database file is the roll-up-your-sleeves-and-get-down-to-it way: from scratch. You start with an empty file and add fields and layouts as needed.

Pros and Cons of Starting from Scratch

The main benefit of building a database from scratch is that you can make it exactly the way you want it to be—fields, layouts, and options are to your precise specifications. Since you're in charge, you'll use only the FileMaker Pro features and options that you understand. This means you'll have no trouble using the database file when it's ready. And if you've never used FileMaker Pro or created a database before, starting from scratch is the best way to learn.

Of course, you do miss out on all the fancy graphics that the professionals included in the templates. And if your needs are close to those satisfied by a template, why reinvent the wheel?

Creating a New Database from Scratch

To create a new database from scratch, select the Create a new empty file option in the New Database dialog box (see Figure 2-2 or Figure 2-3). Click OK.

The Create New File dialog box, which looks and works like a standard Save As dialog box, appears (see Figure 2-5). Continue following instructions in the next section.

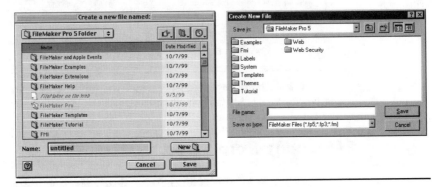

FIGURE 2-5. The Create New File dialog box that appears when you create a new database from scratch on Mac OS (left) or Windows (right).

Naming and Saving Files

Unlike most other computer programs you might use, one of the *first* steps in creating a FileMaker Pro database is naming and saving the file. Why? Because unlike those other programs, FileMaker Pro saves your database automatically as you work. That's why the Save command doesn't appear on any of FileMaker Pro's menus.

Whether you create a file from a template or from scratch, a Save As dialog box like the one in Figure 2-4 or Figure 2-5 appears. Your job is to give your new database a name, specify a location on disk, and save it.

What's in a Name?

You can name a FileMaker Pro file anything you like—as long as it follows the naming conventions of your computer platform:

MAC OS Mac OS users can use up to 31 characters, including spaces, numbers, symbols, and special characters to name their database files.

WINDOWS Windows users can use up to 256 characters, including spaces, numbers, and some symbols. Although you are not required to use the .fp5 extension that identifies a FileMaker Pro 5 file, doing so will ensure that the file automatically appears in Open dialog boxes.

WARNING *If your database file will be accessed by both Mac OS and Windows users, follow the old DOS 8-dot-3 file naming convention: an 8-character filename followed by the .fp5 file extension. This ensures that the filename will not be changed by the network software or a user's operating system—a situation that could damage relationships between files and external script steps.*

Entering the Name

To name the file, enter the desired name in the Create Copy (see Figure 2-4) or Create New File (see Figure 2-5) dialog box.

NOTE *If you are creating a file from a template, a default name appears in the Create Copy dialog box (see Figure 2-4). You don't have to use that name; edit it as desired.*

Choosing a Disk Location

Use the controls in the dialog box to select a location on disk for the file. This is standard Mac OS and Windows stuff, so I won't go into details. If you don't know how to use a Save As dialog box, consult the manual that came with your operating system.

WARNING
The location you select should be one that you always have access to—don't save the file on a server that can become unavailable without warning. Otherwise, FileMaker Pro may not be able to update the file when it needs to.

Saving the File

The last step is to click the Save button. This saves the file in the location and with the name you specified and dismisses the dialog box.

What Happens Next

What happens next depends on whether you created a database from a template or from scratch.

Creating a New Database from a Template

If you used the Create Copy dialog box (see Figure 2-4) to create a new database from a template, the new file appears (see Figure 2-6). This file is all ready for modification or data entry.

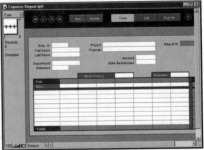

FIGURE 2-6. Two template examples—one on Mac OS (left) and the other on Windows (right). In both examples, the database's Form button was clicked to display the data entry form.

NOTE *When you create a database from a template, a new file with 0 records is created. If you want to start entering data, you must first create a new record. I tell you how to create records and enter data in Chapter 3.*

Creating a New Database from Scratch

If you used the Create New File dialog box (see Figure 2-5) to create a new database from scratch, an empty document window appears. Before you can say "FileMaker Pro," the Define Fields dialog box appears on top of it (see Figure 2-7). Your next step is to define the database's fields, which I discuss in the section titled "Using the Define Fields Dialog Box" on page 60.

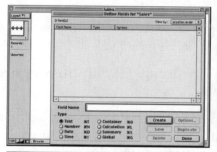

FIGURE 2-7. The Define Fields dialog box atop a blank document window on Mac OS (left) and Windows (right).

Types of Fields

Before you start defining fields for your database, take a moment to learn about the different types of fields FileMaker Pro offers. In this section I tell you what you need to know about each type so you can choose the correct one(s) for your database. I also provide some important tips on why the obvious choice isn't always the best choice.

WARNING *If you choose an inappropriate field type, you may have unexpected results when finding, sorting, and performing calculations based on field contents.*

Text

The first type of field—which is probably the one you'll use most often—is a *text* field. As the name implies, this field is designed to store text.

Here are some facts about text fields:

- A text field can store up to 64,000 letters, numbers, symbols, and special characters.

- Text fields can be used in calculations and for summarizing information.

- Text fields are sorted alphabetically from the first character in the field to the 20th.

- Text fields can be formatted as entry boxes with multiple lines of text (if necessary) or as scrolling windows. Other formatting options can also be applied.

TIP *Do yourself a big favor and create separate fields for components of names and addresses. This makes it a snap to sort and summarize by each component (i.e., last name, state, zip). And if you need the components put together, you can always use merge fields or create a calculation field to concatenate them.*

Number

The next type of field is a *number* field, which, as you probably guessed, is designed to store numbers, especially those on which you plan to perform calculations.

Here are some number field facts:

- A number field can store a number with up to 255 numeric and other characters. That's a big number.

- If characters other than numbers are included in a number field, those characters are not treated like part of the number.

- Number fields can be used in calculations and for summarizing information.

- Number fields are sorted numerically based on the numeric part of the field's contents.

- Number fields can only be a single line. Other formatting options can also be applied.

TIP *Which kind of field would you use to store a zip code? If you guessed number field, guess again. Zip codes and other numeric information (such as phone numbers, social security numbers, and item numbers) are best stored in text fields. This prevents leading zeros from mysteriously disappearing and allows you to include dashes and other punctuation in the field. Save the number fields for the numbers that you plan to use in calculations.*

Date

A *date* field is designed to store dates—and *only* dates. Here are some facts about date fields:

- The contents of a date field must be a valid date (no February 30!) in the range of years from 1 to 3000 (no Y2K problem!) entered in *month/day/year* format.

- Date fields can be used in calculations and for summarizing information.

- Date fields are sorted in chronological order.

- FileMaker Pro offers a variety of date formats, including custom formats, so you're not stuck with numbers and slashes.

Time

A *time* field is designed to store times—and *only* times. Here are some time field facts:

- The contents of a time field must be hours, hours and minutes, or hours, minutes, and seconds entered in *hour:minute:second* AM/PM format.

- Time fields can be used in calculations and for summarizing information.

- Time fields are sorted in chronological order.

- FileMaker Pro offers a variety of time formats, including 24-hour clock formats and custom formats, so you're not stuck with numbers and colons.

Container

A *container* field is designed to store graphics, sounds, or Quick-Time movies. On Windows, they can also be used to store OLE objects; more on that in the section titled "Inserting Data into Container Fields" on page 102. Here are a few container field facts:

- The method you use to enter data into a container field varies depending on the type of data that you want to enter.

- A container field can hold virtually any size graphic, sound, movie, or other object, since FileMaker Pro can store a reference to the object rather than the object itself.

- Container fields can be used in calculations and for summarizing information. (I admit, however, that I'm having a hard time coming up with examples of *how* you'd use them.)

- The formatting options available for container fields vary depending on their contents.

Calculation

A *calculation* field contains a formula. Rather than the formula appearing in the field, however, the results of the formula appear—just like in a spreadsheet.

Here are some calculation field facts:

- Calculation field formulas can reference database fields to end up with a different result for each record.

- Calculation field formulas can reference any type of field.

- A calculation field's formula result can be text or a number, date, time, or container.

- You cannot manually enter a value in a calculation field.

- The formatting options available for calculation fields vary depending on the type of result (text, number, date, time, or container).

 Calculations are one of FileMaker Pro's most powerful features. That's why I devoted a whole chapter to them: Chapter 10.

Summary

A *summary* field contains a summary of a field's values grouped by the contents of a field for multiple records in the database.

Here's an example. Say you've got a database of invoices. You can create a summary field that sums the invoice totals by date to obtain total sales amounts by date.

Want some summary field facts? Here are a few:

- A summary field can be a total, average, count, minimum, maximum, standard deviation, or fraction of a total.

- Summary fields are most often used in the summary parts of layouts to create reports that summarize data from all records or groups of records. I tell you more about summary parts in the section titled "Using Summary Parts and Fields" on page 265.

Global

A *global* field has the same value for every record in the database. For example, if you enter a value of 3 in a global field in one record, the same value appears in the field for all the other records in the database file.

Here are some global field facts:

- A global field can be text or a number, date, time, or container.

- Global fields are commonly used in calculations and scripts.

- You cannot perform a find based on the contents of a global field. (This makes sense if you think about it; all the records have the same value so all of them would be found!)

- In a database set up for multiple users, global fields are set on a per-user basis and are removed when the database is closed. I tell you more about sharing database files in Chapter 15.

Using the Define Fields Dialog Box

The Define Fields dialog box is your tool for creating fields with FileMaker Pro. In this section, I tell you how to use it to add, modify, duplicate, and delete fields.

But before I do that, let me explain how to open the Define Fields dialog box. Sure, it opens automatically when you create a new file from scratch (see Figure 2-7), but what if you want to open it manually to add, remove, or modify fields?

Choose Define Fields from the File menu (see Figure 2-8) or press Shift-Command-D (Mac OS) or Control-Shift-D (Windows). The Define Fields dialog box appears (see Figure 2-9).

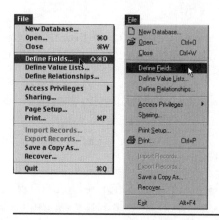

FIGURE 2-8. Choosing Define Fields from the File menu on Mac OS (left) and Windows (right).

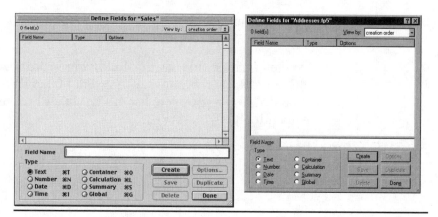

FIGURE 2-9. The Define Fields dialog box on Mac OS (left) and Windows (right).

Adding a Field

Adding a field is a three- or four-step process, depending on the type of field that you add:

1. Enter a name for the field in the Field Name box.

2. Select a field type option or press its keyboard shortcut.

3. Click the Create button.

4. Specify field options in the dialog box that appears when creating a calculation, summary, or global field and click OK.

Here's some additional information to help you complete these steps.

About Field Names

Field names must be unique and can be up to 60 characters long. If you plan to use a field in a calculation, you must observe the following field name restrictions:

- Do not begin the field name with a period or number.

- Do not include any of the following characters: , (comma), +, -, *, /, ^, &, =, ≠, >, <, (,), ", or ::

- Do not include any of the following words: AND, OR, NOT, XOR, or the name of any FileMaker Pro function. (You can find a complete list of FileMaker Pro functions in Appendix B.)

NOTE   *If you create a field that does not observe these field name restrictions, a warning dialog box like the one in Figure 2-10 appears, telling you about the problem. If you don't plan on using the field in a calculation, click OK to create the field anyway. If you do plan on using the field in a calculation, click Cancel to dismiss the dialog box and rename the field before creating it. You can also rename a field in the future if you decide that you want to use it in a calculation after all.*

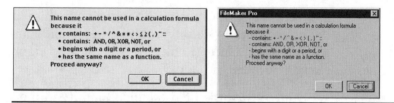

FIGURE 2-10. The dialog box that appears on Mac OS (left) and Windows (right) if you don't follow the field naming restrictions.

Completing the Definition for a Calculation Field

When you click Create to create a calculation field, the Specify Calculation dialog box appears (see Figure 2-11). You must use this dialog box to specify the calculation that you want FileMaker Pro to perform.

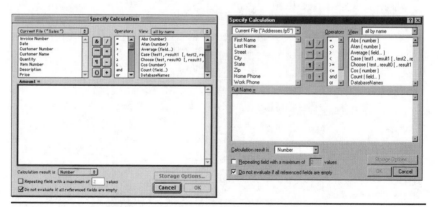

FIGURE 2-11. The Specify Calculation dialog box on Mac OS (left) and Windows (right).

You can enter a calculation two ways: by typing it in or by clicking or double-clicking the field names, operators, and functions that you want to include. The clicking method is usually better since there's less of a chance of entering typos that will prevent your calculation from working properly.

Here are two examples to get you started:

EXAMPLE I: MULTIPLYING TWO NUMBERS In this example, I want to define an Amount field by multiplying a field named Quantity by a field named Price. (Look at the left side of Figure 2-11 to follow along.) Here are the steps:

1. Double-click the field named Quantity in the scrolling list of fields on the left side of the Specify Calculation dialog box. That enters Quantity in the big box.

2. Click the * operator button once. That enters a multiplication symbol.

3. Double-click the field named Price in the scrolling list of fields. That enters Price.

The result (which you could type in if you prefer) is: Quantity * Price (see Figure 2-12).

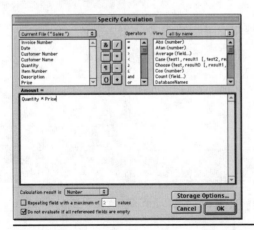

FIGURE 2-12. Calculation Example 1, completed on Mac OS.

EXAMPLE 2: CONCATENATING TEXT In this example, I want to define a Full Name field by concatenating a field named First Name, a space character, and a field named Last Name. (Look at the right side of Figure 2-11 to follow along.)

1. Double-click the field named First Name in the scrolling list of fields on the left side of the Specify Calculation dialog box. That enters First Name in the big box.

2. Click the & operator button once. That enters a concatenation symbol.

3. Click the "" operator button. That puts two double quotes in the big box with an insertion point between them.

4. Type a single space character between the two double quotes.

5. Click on the right side of the second double quote character to reposition the insertion point there.

6. Click the & operator button once. That enters another concatenation symbol.

7. Double-click the field named Last Name in the scrolling list of fields. That enters First Name.

The result (which you could type in if you prefer) is: First Name & " " & Last Name (see Figure 2-13).

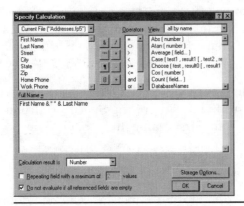

FIGURE 2-13. Calculation Example 2, completed on Windows.

TIP *Having trouble remembering what to double-click and what to single-click? Remember this rule: to select and enter an item in a scrolling list, double-click it; to select and enter an item represented by a button, click it just once.*

CHOOSING A RESULT TYPE When you're finished entering the calculation, choose an option from the Calculation result is menu (see Figure 2-14). Your options are Text, Number, Date, Time, and Container.

FIGURE 2-14. The Calculation result is menu on Mac OS (left) and Windows (right).

COMPLETING THE CALCULATION FIELD DEFINITION You're not done yet. You still have to cross your fingers and click OK to save your calculation and return to the Define Fields dialog box.

When you click OK, FileMaker Pro tries to evaluate your calculation for all the records in the database. If your calculation has an error in it, a dialog box like one of those in Figure 2-15 appears to tell you. (These are just examples; other messages like them can appear, depending on the problem.)

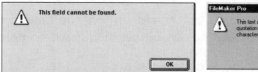

FIGURE 2-15. Two examples of messages that could appear on Mac OS (left) or Windows (right) if a calculation is invalid.

Click OK to dismiss the dialog box, then troubleshoot the calculation. You'll find that FileMaker Pro has kindly highlighted the problem area for you, making it a little easier to find and solve the problem. You won't be able to continue until you fix the problem or remove the calculation.

TIP   *For lots more information about working with calculations, be sure to check Chapter 10. I've only touched the tip of the iceberg here.*

Completing the Definition for a Summary Field

When you click Create to create a summary field, the Options for Summary Field dialog box appears (see Figure 2-16). You must use this dialog box to specify the type of summary and the field that you want to summarize.

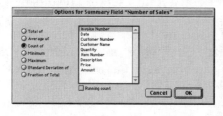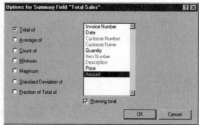

FIGURE 2-16. The Options for Summary Field dialog box on Mac OS (left) and Windows (right).

SELECTING A SUMMARY TYPE The first step to setting up the summary field is to select one of the options on the left side of the dialog box. Here's what each does:

- **Total of** adds up the contents of the field you specify. It can be used only on number or calculation fields.

- **Average of** calculates the average of the field you specify. It can be used only on number or calculation fields.

- **Count of** counts the number of entries in the field you specify. It can be used on text, number, date, time, container, and calculation fields.

- **Minimum** finds the minimum value or earliest date or time in the field you specify. It can be used only on number, date, time, or calculation fields.

- **Maximum** finds the maximum value or latest date in the field you specify. It can be used only on number, date, time, or calculation fields.

- **Standard Deviation of** calculates the standard deviation from the mean of the total of all values for the field you specify. It can be used only on number or calculation fields and is designed to work on a found set (the results of a find).

- **Fraction of Total of** calculates the ratio of the values in the field you specify to the total of all values in the field. It can be used only on number or calculation fields and is designed to work on a found set (the results of a find).

SELECTING A FIELD The next step is to select the field that you want to summarize. Click once on the name of the field in the scrolling list. You can only select a field that works with the summary type you selected earlier—the other fields will be gray.

ENABLING A SUMMARY OPTION Some of the summary field types also allow you to enable an additional option. This option appears as a check box beneath the scrolling window when available. Here's a quick list:

- **Running total** calculates the cumulative total for the current and all previous records. This option is available when you select the Total of option.

- **Weighted average** calculates the average in one field based on a value in another field that is used as a weight factor. This option is available when you select the Average of option. When you turn on the Weighted average check box, another scrolling list of fields appears in the dialog box (see Figure 2-17). Use it to select the field by which you want to weight the average.

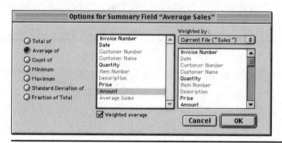

FIGURE 2-17. Setting up a weighted average summary field on Mac OS.

- **Running count** calculates the cumulative count for the current and all previous records. This option is available when you select the Count of option.

- **By population** calculates the population standard deviation where the formula is n-weighted. This option is available only when you select the Standard Deviation of option.

- **Subtotaled** enables you to define a subset of the group to sort and obtain a subtotal by. This option is available when you select the Fraction of Total of option. When you turn on the Subtotaled check box, another scrolling list of fields appears in the dialog box (see Figure 2-18). Use it to select the field by which you want to subtotal.

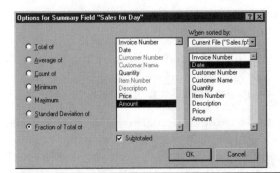

FIGURE 2-18. Setting up a Subtotal summary field on Windows.

TIP *You can calculate subtotals without using the Subtotaled option by creating a layout with a sub-summary part. I tell you more about that in the section titled "Using Summary Parts and Fields" on page 265.*

COMPLETING THE SUMMARY FIELD DEFINITION When the field's options are set just the way you want them, click OK to return to the Define Fields dialog box.

Completing the Definition for a Global Field

When you click Create to create a global field, the Options for Global Field dialog box appears (see Figure 2-19). You must use this dialog box to specify the type of data that will be stored in the field.

FIGURE 2-19. The Options for Global Field dialog box on Mac OS (left) and Windows (right).

SELECTING A DATA TYPE Choose the type of data you plan to put in the global field from the Data type menu in the dialog box. The menu looks just like the one in the Specify Calculation dialog box (see Figure 2-14).

COMPLETING THE GLOBAL FIELD DEFINITION Click OK to accept your settings and return to the Define Fields dialog box.

Setting Options for Text, Number, Date, Time, and Container Fields

You can also set options for text, number, date, time, and container fields. There are two ways to do this:

- To set options for a field while creating the field, click the Options button in the Define Fields dialog box before clicking Create.

- To set options for a field after the field has been created, click the name of the field once to select it, then click the Options button. Or just double-click the name of the field.

The appropriate Options dialog box appears for the type of field for which you want to set options. I tell you all about field options in Chapter 9.

Changing a Field Name or Type

Once you create a field, you can change it—even after you've entered information into it.

In the Define Fields dialog box's scrolling list of fields, click once on the name of the field that you want to change to select it. Then:

- To change the field's name, enter a new name in the Field Name box. Click the Save button.

- To change the field's type, select the option for the type that you want to assign and click the Save button. A warning dialog box like one of those in Figure 2-20 may appear, telling you about the consequences of the change. (These are just examples; other messages could appear depending on the change.) Click OK to make the change. Otherwise click Cancel to keep the field as is.

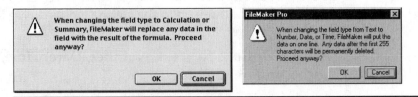

FIGURE 2-20. Two examples of messages that could appear on Mac OS (left) or Windows (right) when changing field types.

Duplicating a Field

Sometimes the easiest way to create a field is to duplicate an existing field. This is especially true if you need to create a field with a complex calculation similar to an existing calculation field or a field for which you have set many field options.

In the Define Fields dialog box's scrolling list of fields, click once on the name of the field that you want to duplicate to select it. Then click the Duplicate button. As shown in Figure 2-21, the duplicated field appears at the bottom of the list of fields. It has the same name as the field that you originally selected with the word "copy" appended to it.

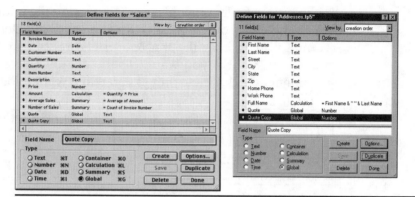

FIGURE 2-21. A duplicated field in the Define Fields dialog box on Mac OS (left) and Windows (right).

You can follow the instructions in the section titled "Changing a Field Name or Type" on page 71 to rename the duplicate field.

Deleting a Field

You can also delete a field. This removes the field—as well as any data that it contains—from the database and from any layout on which it appears.

WARNING   *When you delete a field, you permanently remove the field and any information that it contains from the database. Do not delete a field that contains data unless you are prepared to lose that data. You cannot undo this command!*

NOTE   *Deleting a field from a database is not the same as deleting a field from a layout. When you delete a field from a database, the field and its contents are permanently removed. When you delete a field from a layout, the field and its contents still reside in the database—they just don't appear on the layout from which they were deleted.*

In the Define Fields dialog box, click once on the name of the field that you want to delete to select it. Then click the Delete button. A warning dialog box like the one in Figure 2-22 appears, asking you to confirm that you want to permanently delete the field and its contents. Click Delete only if you really want to delete the field.

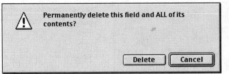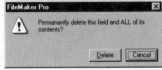

FIGURE 2-22. Warning dialog boxes that appear on Mac OS (left) and Windows (right) when you try to delete a field.

If you attempt to delete a field that is referenced by a calculation or summary field, a dialog box like one of those in Figure 2-23 will appear. Click OK to dismiss it, then either:

- Delete the calculation field that references the field that you want to delete.

- Change the calculation within the calculation field to remove the reference to the field that you want to delete.

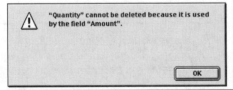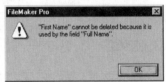

FIGURE 2-23. Warning dialog boxes that appear on Mac OS (left) and Windows (right) when you try to delete a field that is referenced by a calculation or summary field.

TIP *To see which fields are referenced by calculation fields, use the Print command to print all field definitions. Check the section titled "Printing Field Definitions" on page 557 for details.*

Changing the Field List Order

Once you have created a few fields, you can organize them as desired in the Define Fields dialog box. You can either use one of the built-in field orders or create a custom field order.

NOTE *The field order you specify in the Define Fields dialog box is the field order that will be used in other dialog boxes, such as the Sort Records dialog box.*

Choosing a Built-in Field View Order

To view the field names list in one of the built-in field view orders, choose an option from the View by menu (see Figure 2-24) at the top-right corner of the Define Fields dialog box (see Figure 2-9).

FIGURE 2-24. The View by menu in the Define Fields dialog box on Mac OS (left) and Windows (right).

- **Creation order** is the order in which the fields were created.

- **Field name** is alphabetical order by the name of the field.

- **Field type** is in order by the type of field. This is the same order in which field types are listed at the bottom of the dialog box—text, number, date, time, etc.

- **Custom order** is a custom order you specify.

TIP *You can quickly view fields by field name or type by clicking the Field Name or Type column heading within the Define Fields dialog box (see Figure 2-9).*

Creating a Custom Field View Order

You can also view the field names list in the Define Fields dialog box in a custom order by manually moving field names up or down in the list. Position your mouse pointer over the double-headed arrow to the left of the name of a field that you want to move. The mouse pointer turns into a pair of horizontal lines with arrows coming out of them (see Figure 2-25). Press the mouse button down and drag the field up or down in the list. Release the mouse button to complete the move. Repeat this process for every field that you need to move to get the list in the desired order.

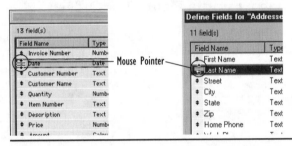

FIGURE 2-25. The mouse pointer when changing field order on Mac OS (left) and Windows (right).

Closing the Define Fields Dialog Box

When you are finished defining fields, click Done or press Esc to dismiss the Define Fields dialog box. FileMaker Pro will return to whatever layout and mode it was in when you opened the Define Fields dialog box. If you've just created a brand-new database file, FileMaker Pro will display the default layout in Browse mode.

The Default Layout

When you create a database file from scratch, FileMaker Pro kindly creates a layout that you can use to enter data. This default layout is named Layout #1 (see Figure 2-26). FileMaker Pro also creates an empty record so you can begin entering data immediately.

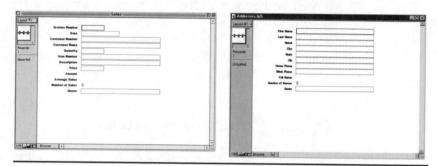

FIGURE 2-26. Layout #1 for example databases on Mac OS (left) and Windows (right).

NOTE   *In Figure 2-26, the first field is active and ready for data entry. If no fields are active, the entry boxes for each field will not appear. Press the Tab key to activate a field and enter data.*

Layout #1 includes all the fields that you defined when you first created the database. They're presented in the order in which they were created. To the left of each field is a field label that displays the field name.

An entry box appears for each field into which you can enter data. Boxes do not appear for calculation or summary fields since their contents are automatically calculated by FileMaker Pro for you.

The rest of the window's contents—the status area and mode indicator—are the same for all databases in Browse mode. I tell you about these window elements in the section titled "Components of the Document Window" on page 17.

Opening and Closing Existing Database Files

If you've been working with your computer for a while, you should know how to open and close existing documents. File-Maker Pro files can be opened and closed just like any other program's document files. But since there are a few special things to note, here's a quick review.

Opening an Existing Database

FileMaker Pro offers three ways to open an existing database file.

Opening a Database from the Mac OS Finder or Windows Explorer

No matter what operating system you use, you can open a File-Maker Pro database from your operating system's filing system: The Finder on Mac OS or Windows Explorer on Windows. This launches FileMaker Pro—if it is not already running—and opens the database.

OPENING THE DOCUMENT ICON Locate the icon for the document that you want to open. Then either double-click it or click it once to select it and choose Open from the File menu.

DRAGGING THE DOCUMENT ICON ONTO THE FILEMAKER PRO ICON Locate the icon for the document you want to open and drag it onto the icon for the FileMaker Pro program. When the FileMaker Pro icon becomes selected, release the document icon.

 TIP   *Using the drag and drop technique to open a file with FileMaker Pro is particularly useful for opening files that were not created with FileMaker Pro, such as tab-delimited text files or Excel worksheet files. I tell you more about opening non-FileMaker Pro files in the section titled "Opening a File Other Than a File-Maker Pro Database" on page 80.*

Opening a Database When You Start FileMaker Pro

When you first launch FileMaker Pro, the New Database dialog box that is shown in Figure 2-3 appears. Select the Open an existing file option and click OK.

An Open File dialog box appears (see Figure 2-27). Use it to locate and select the file that you want to open. Then click the Open button to open the file.

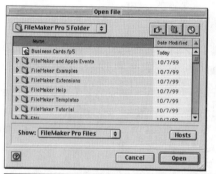 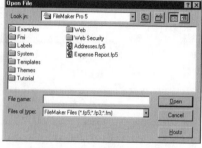

FIGURE 2-27. The Open File dialog box on Mac OS (left) and Windows (right).

NOTE *If you're using Windows and try to open a database file that has not been named with one of the filename extensions reserved for FileMaker Pro files—.fp5, .fp3, or .fm—the database may not appear in the Open File dialog box. If this happens, choose All Available (*.*) from the Files of Type menu at the bottom of the dialog box to display all files. Then select and open the one you want.*

Opening a Database from within FileMaker Pro

You can also open a database file from within FileMaker Pro while you are working with the program. Choose Open from the File menu (see Figure 2-28) or press Command-O (Mac OS) or Control-O (Windows).

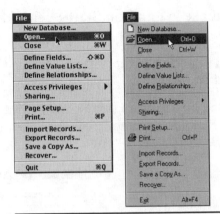

FIGURE 2-28. Choosing Open from the File menu on Mac OS (left) and Windows (right).

An Open File dialog box appears (see Figure 2-27). Use it to locate and select the file that you want to open. Then click the Open button to open the file.

 TIP *You can also open a recently used database by choosing its name from the File menu. To do this, however, you must turn on the Recently opened files option in the General tab of the Preferences dialog box. I tell you more about this option in the section titled "Show recently opened files" on page 35.*

Opening a File Other Than a FileMaker Pro Database

FileMaker Pro can also open files other than ones it created. It supports quite a few document formats, all of which are discussed in the section titled "File Formats" on page 502.

To open a document file saved in a supported format, choose Open from FileMaker Pro's File menu (see Figure 2-28). When the Open File dialog box appears (see Figure 2-27), choose the appropriate format from the Show (Mac OS) or Files of Type (Windows) menu (see Figure 2-29). Select the file that you want to open and click the Open button to open it.

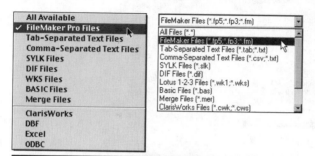

FIGURE 2-29. The Show menu on Mac OS (left) and the Files of Type menu on Windows (right). Both of these menus are in the Open File dialog box (see Figure 2-27).

If necessary, FileMaker Pro creates fields for the data in the file you opened. I tell you more about this feature of FileMaker Pro in the section titled "Importing Records into an Existing FileMaker Pro File" on page 505.

Closing a Database

You close a FileMaker Pro file the same way you close any other document file.

WARNING   *Closing a document window is not the same as quitting or exiting the FileMaker Pro application. You must use the Quit (Mac OS) or Exit (Windows) command under the File menu to close the FileMaker Pro program.*

Closing a Database with the Close Command

Make sure the database that you want to close is the active window; you can choose it from the Window menu if it is not. Then choose Close from the File menu (see Figure 2-30) or press Command-W (Mac OS) or Control-W (Windows).

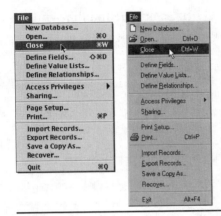

FIGURE 2-30. Choosing the Close command on Mac OS (left) and Windows (right).

Closing a Database with a Window Element

As you probably know, Mac OS and Windows document windows also include controls to close a window.

ON MAC OS Click the window's close box.

ON WINDOWS Click the document window's close button.

WARNING *Clicking the application window's close button on Windows will close the File-Maker Pro program. This closes all document windows and exits Filemaker Pro.*

Step-by-Step

In this section, I provide step-by-step instructions for creating the three database files that you'll work with throughout this book. I recommend that you follow all the instructions to build all three files. If you're feeling a bit lazy, however, you can find all three files at the companion Web site for this book, http://www.gilesrd.com/fmprocomp/.

Creating the Contacts Database

The first file is a contact management database called Contacts.fp5. It will store the names, addresses, and phone numbers for the customers and vendors of Spot Ink, Inc.

1. Choose New from the File menu to open the New Database dialog box.

2. Select the Create a new empty file option. Click OK.

3. The Create a New File dialog box appears. Use it to navigate to the folder in which you want to store the exercise files for this book. Then enter the name Contacts.fp5 and click Save to create the document.

4. The Define Fields dialog box appears. Use it to define the following fields:

Field Name	Type
Customer Number	Text
First Name	Text
Last Name	Text
Full Name	Text
Title	Text
Company	Text
Address	Text
City	Text
State	Text
Zip	Text
Voice Phone	Text
Fax Phone	Text
EMail	Text
Type	Text
Terms	Text
Limit	Number
Revision Date	Date

If you need help defining fields, check the section titled "Adding a Field" on page 62.

5. Select the field named Full Name. Then select the Calculation option and click Save.

6. In the Specify Calculation dialog box that appears, enter the following calculation:
First Name & " " & Last Name

7. Choose Text from the Calculation result is menu. Then click OK to save the calculation and return to the Define Fields dialog box.

8. Click Done to dismiss the Define Fields dialog box.

Creating the Product Inventory Database

Information about products purchased and sold by Spot Ink, Inc. will be stored in a product inventory database. Follow steps 1–4 and step 8 in the previous section to create a file named Products.fp5 in the same folder as Contacts.fp5. The database should include the following fields:

Field Name	Type
Item Number	Text
Item Name	Text
Item Description	Text
Purchase Price	Number
Selling Price	Number
Reorder Point	Number
Last Transaction Date	Date
Picture	Container

Creating the Invoicing Database

FileMaker Pro will also handle the invoicing for Spot Ink, Inc.

1. Follow steps 1–4 in the section titled "Creating the Contacts Database" on page 83 to create a file named Invoices.fp5 in the same folder as Contacts.fp5 and Products.fp5. The database should include the following fields:

Field Name	Type
Invoice Number	Text
Invoice Date	Date
Terms	Text
Due Date	Date
Customer Number	Text
Customer Name	Text
Company	Text
Address	Text
City	Text
State	Text
Zip	Text
Voice Phone	Text
Quantity	Number
Item Number	Text
Item Name	Text
Selling Price	Number

2. Create a calculation field named Extended price. The field's calculation should be: Quantity * Selling Price.

3. Create another calculation field named Invoice Total. Its calculation should be: Sum (Extended Price). (This calculation uses a function; I tell you more about functions in Chapter 10.)

4. Create a summary field named Total Sales. The options for this field should be: Total of Invoice Total.

5. Click the Done button in the Define Fields dialog box to dismiss it.

Viewing and Closing the Completed Files

Take a good look at each file in Browse mode. At the end of the next chapter, you'll enter information into each database file.

TIP *If you want to experiment with one of the files, use the Duplicate command (in the Mac OS Finder) or Copy and Paste commands (in Windows Explorer) to make a copy of it first. Then experiment with the copy. Remember, FileMaker Pro automatically saves your changes! If you experiment too much, your file may not look like the one you created when you're done.*

When you're finished checking out your work, choose Close from the File menu for each file to close it.

Entering and Editing Data

A database file isn't much good without data in it. In this chapter, I tell you how to enter and edit database information, as well as how to use FileMaker Pro's spelling checker to make sure everything is spelled just right.

More about Browse Mode

As I discuss in Chapter 1, Browse mode is the mode you use to enter and edit database information. When you create a database file, FileMaker Pro automatically displays the newly created database in Browse mode so you can begin to enter data. The quickest and easiest way to see if you're in Browse mode is to check the mode pop-up menu at the bottom of the document window. It should say Browse.

You can switch to Browse mode three ways:

- Choose Browse from the View menu (see Figure 3-1).

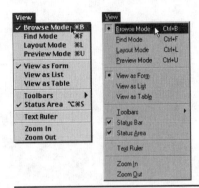

FIGURE 3-1. Choosing Browse from the View menu on Mac OS (left) and Windows (right).

- Press Command-B (Mac OS) or Control-B (Windows).

- Choose Browse from the mode pop-up menu at the bottom of the document window (see Figure 3-2).

FIGURE 3-2. Choosing Browse from the mode pop-up menu on Mac OS (left) and Windows (right).

*T**IP***   *Both the View menu and the mode pop-up menu display a check mark (Mac OS) or bullet (Windows) beside the current mode.*

Entering Data

In Browse mode, you can enter data into the following types of fields: text, number, date, time, container, and global. Entry boxes appear for each of these types of fields.

NOTE *You cannot enter data into calculation or summary fields because FileMaker Pro calculates the data for those fields for you—that's why no entry boxes appear for these fields, although data may appear.*

Entering data is usually a two-step process:

1. Create a new record.

2. Enter data into the new record's fields.

You repeat these steps over and over until you've entered all the data that you need to. In this section, I tell you how to complete both of these steps in a variety of ways.

The Importance of Consistent Data Entry

Before you begin entering data, it's important that you understand the importance of consistency. Although your FileMaker Pro databases won't self-destruct if you don't consistently enter data, you may wish that they did. Let me explain.

FileMaker Pro enables you to find, sort, and summarize records based on the contents of fields. If data is not consistently entered into fields, the results of a find request may not include all the records it should. Records may not sort the way you expect. And summaries will not be accurate.

NOTE *I tell you about finding and sorting records in Chapter 4 and about summarizing data in Chapters 6 and 7.*

Imagine the Consequences

Let's look at an example. Say your company uses an address book database that's available to you and two co-workers over the network. You enter data into the State field using standard post office abbreviations (NJ, OK, and AZ). Mary Jane spells out each state name (New Jersey, Oklahoma, and Arizona). Joe abbreviates the old fashioned way (N.J., Okla., and Ariz.).

Now say you want to search for all records that have New Jersey in the State field. If you search for NJ, you'll get only the records that you entered. If you search for New Jersey, you'll get only the records that Mary Jane entered. And you know whose records will appear if you search for N.J.

Although you can perform a more complex search that finds records with the State field entered as NJ, New Jersey, or N.J., this is more work than you should have to do to get the job done. In addition, what happens if Mary Jane made a typing error while entering a state and entered it as New Jorsey? It would never be found!

Now imagine how the records would sort by this inconsistently entered field. New York would appear between New Jersey and NJ. Does that make sense? And since summaries are based on field contents, you could end up with more summaries than states—one for each version of the entry. What a mess!

An Ounce of Prevention

The answer, of course, is to enter data consistently. If everyone stuck to the standard post office abbreviations, the potential problems with finding, sorting, and summarizing data by the State field would not occur. Keep this in mind when you set up and enter data into your databases.

---

*T*ıp   *The best way to ensure consistent data entry is to take advantage of validation field options. I tell you about them in the section titled "Validation Options" on page 350.*

Reading the Book

Before I explain how to create records and enter data, let me take a moment to tell you how to read the book. Not this book—you obviously already know how to do that. I'm talking about the book in the status area (see Figure 3-3 and Figure 3-4).

The Book for a New Database Created from Scratch

If you created a database from scratch (as discussed in the section titled "Creating a New Database from Scratch" on page 52) and are ready to enter data, you'll find that FileMaker Pro was thoughtful enough to create a new empty record for you. You can tell by consulting the book. It should look like the one in Figure 3-3, which shows a total of 1 record, of which record 1 is being browsed.

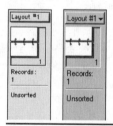

FIGURE 3-3. How the book appears when you create a database from scratch and view it in Browse mode on Mac OS (left) and Windows (right).

In this case, you can enter data for your first record right away, without first creating a new record. Then you create a new record for each additional record that you want to add.

The Book for a New Database Created from a Template

If you created a database based on a template (as discussed in the section titled "Creating a New Database from a Template" on page 50) and are ready to enter data, you'll see that the database might have some pretty spiffy layouts, but it has no records.

Again, you can see this by consulting the book in the status area. It should look like the one in Figure 3-4, which shows 0 records.

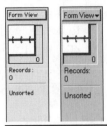

FIGURE 3-4. How the book appears when you create a database from a template and view it in Browse mode on Mac OS (left) and Windows (right).

In this case, you must create a new record before you enter any data in the database.

Creating a New Record

To create a new record, choose New Record from the Records menu (see Figure 3-5) or press Command-N (Mac OS) or Control-N (Windows).

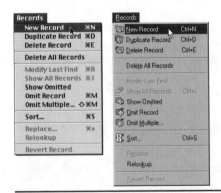

FIGURE 3-5. Choosing New Record from the Records menu on Mac OS (left) and Windows (right).

A new empty record appears. The first field is selected automatically and ready to receive your input.

Typing in Data

Although there are a number of ways to enter data into a database, most often, you'll use your keyboard to type in the data. This is a two-step process:

1. Select the field in which you want to enter data.

2. Type in the data.

Can't get any more basic than that, can you?

Selecting the Field

A field is selected when a solid border appears around it. If it is any type of field other than a container field, either a blinking insertion point appears inside it or some or all of its contents are selected. You can see this in Figure 3-6.

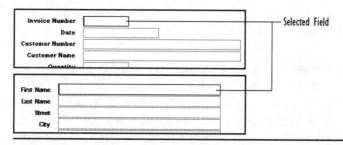

FIGURE 3-6. The first field selected on Mac OS (top) and Windows (bottom).

 Although you can select a container field, you can't type anything into it. Entering pictures, movies, or sounds into a container field requires other techniques, which I cover in the "Tip" on page 104.)

If you fail to select a field before you type, FileMaker Pro will let you know by displaying a dialog box like the one in Figure 3-7. Click OK to dismiss the dialog box, then select a field before you type.

FIGURE 3-7. The dialog box that appears on Mac OS (left) and Windows (right) when you try to type in data when no field is selected.

There are two ways to select a field:

- Click inside it.

- Press the Tab key until it becomes selected.

Typing in the Field's Contents

Once the field is selected, just type what you want to enter. When you press the Tab key or click to move to another field or you create or move to another record, the data is accepted into the field.

Here are a few important things to keep in mind for the various types of field.

ENTERING MULTIPLE LINES INTO A TEXT FIELD   A text field can contain up to 64,000 characters, including Return characters. This means you can enter more into a text field than you might think. The field expands as you type to accept what you enter, but when you advance to another field, the field's entry box closes up (see Figure 3-8). This doesn't mean data is lost; it just isn't showing.

FIGURE 3-8. A single-line text field entry box expands to accept text (left) but collapses back to a single line when you select another field (right).

NOTE *The same situation results when entering dates or times into fields that are not large enough to display them properly.*

ENTERING LENGTHY NUMBERS INTO NUMBER FIELDS A number field can contain up to 255 characters. If you enter more characters than can appear on a single line, the number may be displayed in scientific notation (remember that from high school?) when you advance to another field (see Figure 3-9). I tell you how to change the size of fields in the section titled "Resizing Objects" on page 248.

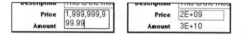

FIGURE 3-9. A lengthy number that appears to take up two lines (left) displays in scientific notation if it can't fit in the field when you select another field (right).

NOTE *The same situation results when FileMaker Pro displays the results of a calculation in a field that is not large enough to display the entire number.*

ENTERING FORMATTED NUMBERS INTO NUMBER FIELDS It is not necessary to include currency symbols, commas, or percent symbols when entering data into a number field. Instead, you can format the field's contents to display the number as desired for all records on a specific layout. This ensures consistency and flexibility for formatting numbers. I explain how to format numbers in the section titled "Number Formatting" on page 302.

ENTERING DATES INTO DATE FIELDS Dates must be entered in one of the following formats: *mm/dd*, *mm/dd/yy*, or *mm/dd/yyyy* where *mm* is the one- or two-digit month number, *dd* is the one- or two-digit day number, *yy* is the two-digit year number, and *yyyy* is the four-digit year number. If you leave out the year, FileMaker Pro assumes the current year (as recorded on your system clock). If you enter a two-digit year between 00 and 09, FileMaker Pro assumes you mean a year between 2000 and 2009. Otherwise, it assumes a year in the current century. If you enter the date incorrectly, a dialog box like the one in Figure 3-10 appears. Click OK to dismiss it and try again.

FIGURE 3-10. Dialog box that appears on Mac OS (left) and Windows (right) when you enter a date that FileMaker Pro does not understand.

NOTE *If you're reading this in the U.K. or somewhere else where dates are displayed in* dd/mm/yy *format, use* that *format, not the one we use here in the U.S. After all,* that *should be the format that your operating system and copy of FileMaker Pro recognize.*

ENTERING TIMES INTO TIME FIELDS   Times must be entered in one of the following formats: *hh, hh:mm,* or *hh:mm:ss* where *hh* is the one- or two-digit hour number, *mm* is the one- or two-digit minute number, and *ss* is the one- or two-digit second number. If you leave out the minutes or seconds, FileMaker Pro assumes 00. If you use a 12-hour clock, append AM or PM to the time; otherwise FileMaker Pro assumes AM. If you enter the time incorrectly, a dialog box like the one in Figure 3-11 appears. Click OK to dismiss it and try again.

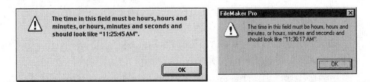

FIGURE 3-11. Dialog box that appears on Mac OS (left) and Windows (right) when you enter a time that FileMaker Pro does not understand.

"ENTERING" DATA INTO CALCULATION AND SUMMARY FIELDS

Although you cannot enter information directly into a calculation field, the field's entry is calculated automatically when you enter information into the fields that are referenced by the calculation. Figure 3-12 shows two examples. The same is true for summary fields, which display data when you are finished entering information into a record.

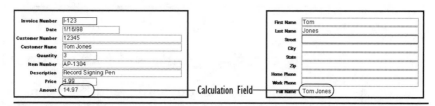

FIGURE 3-12. Entering data into fields referenced by calculations displays results in calculation fields.

Editing as You Type

You can edit the contents of a field as you enter data the same way you edit text in any other program as you type it. Here are some examples of what I mean:

- Press the Delete (Mac OS) or Backspace (Windows) key to delete the character to the left of the insertion point.

- Click anywhere in the field to reposition the insertion point and type to insert data.

- Select all or part of the field's contents and press the Delete (Mac OS) or Backspace (Windows) key to delete it.

- Select all or part of the field's contents and type to replace selected data.

Advancing from Field to Field

When you're finished entering information in a field, the quickest and easiest way to advance to the next field is to press the Tab key. If you prefer, however, you can click in the next field with your mouse pointer.

WARNING *Don't press Return (Mac OS) or Enter (Windows) when you are finished enter-ing data in a field. Doing so could enter a return character in the current field. If you do this by mistake, press the Delete (Mac OS) or Backspace (Windows) key to delete the extra character. Then press Tab to select the next field.*

Using the Copy, Cut, and Paste Commands

You can also use the Copy, Cut, and Paste commands under the Edit menu to enter data into fields. The information that you copy or cut can be in any document, including a document created with another application.

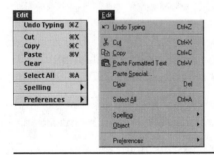

FIGURE 3-13. The Edit menu on Mac OS (left) and Windows (right).

The Copy and Paste commands are available in just about every Mac OS or Windows application you use. They work the same way in every program. If you've been using your computer for a while, you should already know how to use them. Here's a brief discussion to get you going.

Copying or Cutting Data

If the data you want to copy or cut resides in another document, open that document and scroll to the data so you can see it. Then select the information that you want to copy or cut. Normally, that means dragging over the information with your mouse pointer to highlight it, but other techniques may apply depending on the application that created the document in which the information resides.

Even though you can't enter information into a calculation field, you can still select and copy it.

Once the information is selected, choose Copy (Command-C on Mac OS or Control-C on Windows) or Cut (Command-X on Mac OS or Control-X on Windows) from the Edit menu (see Figure 3-13). No matter which command you choose, the information you selected is copied to the clipboard. If you choose Copy, the selected information remains in the source document. If you choose Cut, the information is removed from the source document.

NOTE *The clipboard is a place in RAM where copied or cut information is stored until one of two things happens: you use the Copy or Cut command again or you shut down your computer.*

Pasting Data

If necessary, switch to the FileMaker Pro document and record into which you want to paste the information you copied or cut.

Select the field into which you want to paste the information. Then choose Paste from the Edit menu (see Figure 3-13) or press Command-V (Mac OS) or Control-V (Windows). The information in the clipboard is pasted into the selected field.

NOTE *The exact wording of the Paste command may vary on Windows. For example, if text is in the clipboard, the command may be Paste Formatted Text (see Figure 3-13, right). Windows users can also take advantage of the Paste Special command (see Figure 3-13, right) to display the Paste Special dialog box (see Figure 3-14). This offers additional options for pasting the clipboard contents.*

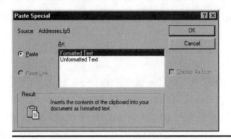

FIGURE 3-14. The Paste Special dialog box on Windows.

Using Drag and Drop

You can also use drag and drop text editing to drag selections into FileMaker Pro database fields.

Dragging Selections from Other Programs' Documents

If an application supports drag and drop editing, you can drag a selection from that document into a FileMaker Pro database field. Position the two document windows so that you can see the source document and destination field. In the source document, select the information that you want to use, point to it with your mouse pointer, press the mouse button down, and drag it to the destination field. When you release the mouse button, the selected data is copied to the field.

Dragging Selections from Other FileMaker Pro Fields

If the Enable drag and drop text selection option is turned on in the General Application Preferences dialog box, you can also drag selections from one FileMaker Pro field to another. This option is turned off by default so you'll have to turn it on; I tell you more about it in the section titled "Enable drag and drop text selection" on page 35.

To use this feature, in the source field, select the text that you want to drag, point to the selection with your mouse pointer, press the mouse button down, and drag to the destination field. When you release the mouse button, the selection is copied to the field.

 With the drag and drop text selection feature enabled, you can also drag the contents of FileMaker Pro database fields into documents created with other applications.

Using Insert Menu Commands

The Insert menu (see Figure 3-15) offers a number of commands that you can use to paste information into a selected field.

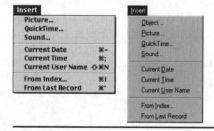

FIGURE 3-15. The Insert menu on Mac OS (left) and Windows (right).

To use one of these commands, select the field in which you want to paste an item. Then choose the appropriate command or use its keyboard shortcut.

Inserting Data into Container Fields

The first three (Mac OS) or four (Windows) commands under the Insert menu (see Figure 3-15) are for inserting data into container fields. Container fields, which I discuss in the section titled "Container" on page 58, are used for storing graphics, sounds, movie, and other multimedia data.

 TIP   *If your database file includes pictures that will be accessed by both Mac OS and Windows users, be sure to turn on the Store compatible graphics option in the General Document Preferences dialog box for the document. Check the section titled "Store Compatible Graphics" on page 44 for details.*

OBJECT (WINDOWS ONLY)   This option displays the Insert Object dialog box (see Figure 3-16), which you can use to insert an OLE object into a container field. To create a new OLE object, select the Create New option (see Figure 3-16, left), select an object type, and click OK. Windows launches the appropriate program to create the object, then inserts the object into the field. To insert an existing object, select the Create from File option (see Figure 3-16, right), then enter the pathname for the existing file and click OK. Windows inserts the object into the field.

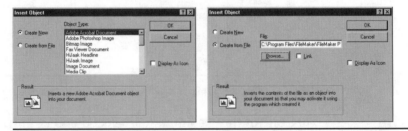

FIGURE 3-16. The Insert Object dialog box for creating a new object (left) and for inserting an existing object (right) on Windows.

TIP *If desired, you can display an OLE object in a container field as an icon. Simply turn on the Display as Icon check box in the Paste Special dialog box (see Figure 3-14) or Insert Object dialog box (see Figure 3-16) when pasting in or inserting the object.*

PICTURE This option displays the Insert Picture dialog box (see Figure 3-17), which you can use to select a picture file on disk. On Mac OS, FileMaker Pro recognizes pictures in GIF, JPEG, PICT, EPSF, MacPaint, and TIFF formats. On Windows, FileMaker Pro regcognizes files with .cgm, .bmp, .tif, .gif, .jpg, .pcx, .wmf, .drw, .pic, .sld, .pct, .mac, and .eps extensions. You can use the Show (Mac OS) or Files of type (Windows) menu (see Figure 3-18) to display only specific file types.

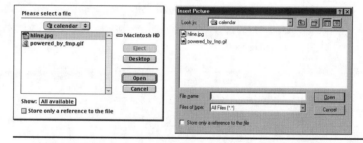

FIGURE 3-17. The Insert Picture dialog box on Mac OS (left) and Windows (right).

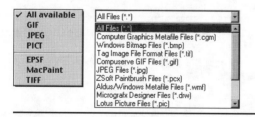

FIGURE 3-18. The Show (Mac OS, left) and Files of Type (Windows, right) menus. Both of these menus appear in the Insert Picture dialog box (see Figure 3-17).

TIP   *You can minimize file size by turning on the Store only a reference to the file check box in the Insert Picture dialog box (see Figure 3-17). There are two drawbacks to this: 1) If the picture on disk is deleted, FileMaker Pro cannot display it in the field and 2) the picture cannot be published on the Web using FileMaker Pro Web Companion.*

QUICKTIME   The QuickTime command displays the Insert QuickTime dialog box (see Figure 3-19), which you can use to locate, select, and open a QuickTime or other QuickTime-supported multimedia file. On Windows, you can use the Files of type menu (see Figure 3-20) within the dialog box to narrow down the list of files to show only those that are supported by FileMaker Pro—those with .avi, .mov, .qt, .aif, .au, .wav, .psd, or .qif extensions. Once the file has been inserted into the field, playback controls appear below the movie when you click to select the field (see Figure 3-21). Use the controls to play back the movie within the FileMaker Pro file.

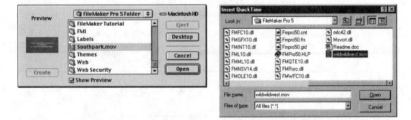

FIGURE 3-19. The Insert QuickTime dialog box on Mac OS (left) and Windows (right).

FIGURE 3-20. The Files of type menu in the Insert QuickTime dialog box in Windows.

FIGURE 3-21. The controls for playing back a QuickTime movie appear beneath the movie's first frame when you select its container field.

NOTE   *To insert and play a QuickTime movie in FileMaker Pro for Windows, QuickTime 3 or later must be installed on your computer. You can download QuickTime for free from Apple Computer's QuickTime Web site, http://www.apple.com/quicktime/.*

SOUND   This option displays the Sound Record dialog box (see Figure 3-22), which you can use to record a sound for the selected container field. Use the four buttons to record and playback a sound, using your computer's microphone. When the sound is just the way you want it, click the Save button. To play back a sound in a container field, double-click the sound icon in the field (see Figure 3-23).

FIGURE 3-22. The Sound Record dialog box on Mac OS (left) and Windows (right).

FIGURE 3-23. A sound icon in a container field.

NOTE   *Your computer must have a working microphone to record sounds and a work-ing speaker to play back sounds.*

TIP   *You can insert an existing sound file into a container field by using the QuickTime command, which is discussed in the section titled "QuickTime" on page 104.*

Inserting Data into Text, Number, Date, Time, and Global Fields

The remaining commands on the Insert menu (see Figure 3-15) enable you to insert data into text, number, date, time, or global fields.

CURRENT DATE   This option enters the current date as set on your system clock.

CURRENT TIME   This option enters the current time as set on your system clock.

CURRENT USER NAME   This option enters the user name as specified in the General Application Preferences dialog box. I tell you more about the User name preference in the sections titled "User Name (Mac OS)" on page 36 and "User Name (Windows)" on page 36.

FROM INDEX   This option displays the View Index dialog box (see Figure 3-24), which shows all entries in the current field for all existing records. You can display index items as complete field entries or, if you turn on the Show individual words check box, as separate words that appear in an entry. To enter one of the index items into the selected field, click it once to select it and then click the Paste button. I tell you more about FileMaker Pro's indexing feature in Chapter 9, where I discuss field options.

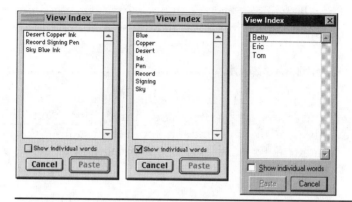

FIGURE 3-24. The View Index dialog box on Mac OS (left and center) and Windows (right). The center illustration shows the entries in the left illustration with the Show individual words check box turned on.

FROM LAST RECORD This option enters the value from the same field of the previous record.

 The From Last Record command is a great way to enter data quickly in a field when the last record you browsed has the same data in that field.

Working with Records

Once you create a few records, you have a database worth talking about. Congratulations!

In this section I provide instructions for navigating, editing, duplicating, and deleting database records.

Switching from One Record to Another

Sooner or later, as you work with your database in Browse mode, you'll probably find it necessary to move from one record to another. FileMaker Pro offers a variety of techniques for navigating among records.

Using the Book

In Browse mode, the book in the status area (see Figure 3-25), which I discuss in the section titled "Book Icon" on page 18, not only provides information about the total number of records and the current record, but also enables you to move from record to record.

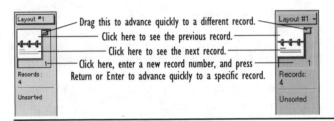

FIGURE 3-25. The book in Browse mode on Mac OS (left) and Windows (right).

- Click the top or bottom "page" of the book to switch to the previous or next item.

TIP *If a book page has lines on it, you can click it to switch to another item. If the book page is blank, it means you're looking at the first (top page) or last (bottom page) item.*

- Drag the bookmark to move to another item quickly.

- Click the current item number at the bottom of the book to select it, type in a new item number, and press Return or Enter to move quickly to that item.

Using Keyboard Shortcuts

You can also move from record to record by pressing keystrokes on your keyboard.

- To switch to the previous record, press Control-Up-Arrow.

- To switch to the next record, press Control-Down-Arrow.

Editing a Record

You can edit a record any time you like. First switch to the record that you want to edit, then make changes to fields as necessary.

Editing the Contents of a Field

How you edit the contents of a field depends on the type of field.

TO EDIT THE CONTENTS OF A TEXT, NUMBER, DATE, TIME, OR GLOBAL FIELD... Select the field that you want to edit. Then use standard editing techniques to change the field's contents. This includes inserting or deleting characters, using the Cut, Copy, and Paste commands to remove or replace selected characters, and using the Clear command under the Edit menu to delete selected characters.

NOTE   *Changing the contents of a Global field in one record changes its contents for all records.*

Here are some additional keystrokes and commands you might find useful for editing the contents of a selected field:

Task	Mac OS	Windows
Select next field	Tab	Tab
Select previous field	Shift-Tab	Shift-Tab
Move insertion point to end of text	Command-Down-Arrow	Control-End
Move insertion point to end of line	Command-Right-Arrow	End

Task	Mac OS	Windows
Move insertion point to next word	Option-Right-Arrow	Control-Right-Arrow
Move insertion point to previous word	Option-Left-Arrow	Control-Left-Arrow
Move insertion point to start of line	Command-Left-Arrow	Home
Move insertion point to start of text	Command-Up-Arrow	Control-Home
Select a word	double-click	double-click
Select a line	triple-click	triple-click
Select a paragraph	four clicks	four clicks
Select entire field	five clicks or Command-A or Choose Select All from the Edit menu	five clicks or Control-A or Choose Select All from the Edit menu
Delete selection or previous character	Delete	Backspace
Delete selection or next character	Del	Del

EDITING THE CONTENTS OF A CONTAINER FIELD   Select the field that you want to edit. Then press Delete (Mac OS) or Backspace (Windows), or choose Clear from the Edit menu (see Figure 3-13) to delete the field's contents. Follow instructions in the section titled "Using the Copy, Cut, and Paste Commands" on page 98 or "Inserting Data into Container Fields" on page 102 to reenter a different picture, movie, or sound.

EDITING THE CONTENTS OF A CALCULATION OR SUMMARY FIELD

You cannot directly edit the contents of a calculation or summary field. Instead, you must change the definition of the field using the Define Field dialog box. I tell you how to define fields in the section titled "Using the Define Fields Dialog Box" on page 60.

Undoing Edits

FileMaker Pro offers two ways to undo a change you make to a field or record:

UNDO The Undo command, which is the first command under the Edit menu (see Figure 3-13), lets you undo a change to a current field. To use it, you must select it *before* you advance to another field or record or use another FileMaker Pro command. I tell you more about the Undo command in the section titled "Undo" on page 27.

REVERT RECORD The Revert Record command under the Records menu (see Figure 3-26) undoes all changes to a record since you began editing it. To use it, you must select it *before* you advance to another record or use another FileMaker Pro command.

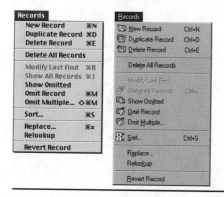

FIGURE 3-26. The Records menu on Mac OS (left) and Windows (right).

Replacing Field Contents

If you're interested in changing the contents of a field for all records, consider the Replace command. It works on the selected field for all records being browsed—not just the current record.

For example, say that you have a customers database with a field named Salesperson that contains the name of the salesperson assigned to each customer. Henrietta, one of the salespeople, leaves the company and Philip takes her place. You can use the Find command to find all records with *Henrietta* in the Salesperson field, then use the Replace command to replace the contents of the Salesperson field with *Philip* in all records of the found set.

WARNING   *The Replace command replaces the contents of a field for every record being browsed. You cannot undo a completed Replace command! Use this command carefully.*

To use the Replace command, select the field that you want to change and edit its contents to match the new desired value. With the field still selected, choose Replace from the Records menu (see Figure 3-26) or press Command-= (Mac OS) or Control-= (Windows). The Replace dialog box appears (see Figure 3-27).

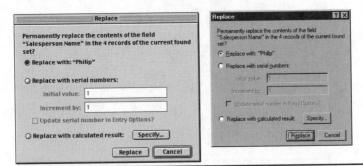

FIGURE 3-27. The Replace dialog box on Mac OS (left) and Windows (right).

Make sure the Replace with option is selected. Also, confirm that the data within the quotes matches the data that you want in the selected field of all records being browsed. Then click the Replace button. The contents of the field are replaced in all records being browsed.

TIP *This feature can also be used to serialize or reserialize numbers or replace the contents of a field with the result of a calculation. I tell you about these procedures in the sections titled "Reserializing Records" on page 346 and "Replacing Field Contents with Calculated Results" on page 378.*

Duplicating a Record

In some instances, you may have to enter information for a record that is very similar to an existing record. That's when the Duplicate Record command can help. It duplicates the current record and displays the duplicate. You can then edit the information in the duplicate record to create a new record with a lot less data entry.

To duplicate a record, begin by switching to the record that you want to duplicate. Then choose Duplicate Record from the Records menu (see Figure 3-26) or press Command-D (Mac OS) or Control-D (Windows). The record that appears is the duplicate, not the original.

TIP *You can confirm that a new record has been added by checking the book in the status area. It should display one more record than it displayed before you used the Duplicate command.*

Deleting a Record

FileMaker Pro enables you to delete the current record or all records in the found set.

WARNING *When you delete a record, all information in all of the record's fields is deleted. You cannot undo the Delete commands, so use them carefully!*

Deleting the Current Record

The Delete Record command lets you delete a single record from the database.

Begin by switching to the record that you want to delete. Then choose Delete Record from the Records menu (see Figure 3-26) or press Command-E (Mac OS) or Control-E (Windows). A dialog box like the one in Figure 3-28 appears. Click the Delete button only if you are sure that you want to delete the current record.

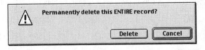 

FIGURE 3-28. The dialog box that appears on Mac OS (left) and Windows (right) when you choose Delete Record from the Mode menu.

Deleting All Records in the Found Set

The Delete All Records command lets you delete all records in the database or in the found set.

For example, say that Philip, the new salesperson I introduced several pages ago, leaves the company and takes all his customers with him. (That dirty &%$#@!) To delete all his customers from the customer database, find all records with *Philip* in the Salesperson field and then use the Delete All Records command to delete all records in the found set.

To delete all records, choose Delete All Records from the Records menu (see Figure 3-26). A dialog box like one of those in Figure 3-29 appears. Click the Delete button only if you are sure that you want to delete all the records being browsed.

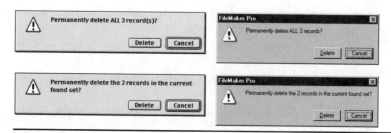

FIGURE 3-29. The dialog boxes that appear on Mac OS (left) and Windows (right) when you choose Delete All Records from the Records menu to delete all records in the database (top) or in the found set (bottom).

Using the Spelling Checker

FileMaker Pro's spelling checker uses two dictionary files to check spelling either all at once or as you type.

- Use commands under the Spelling submenu (see Figure 3-30) to select and edit dictionaries or check the spelling in a selection, record, or found set.

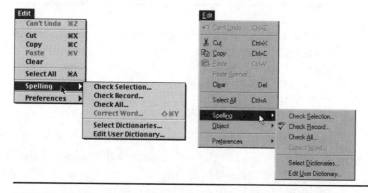

FIGURE 3-30. The Spelling submenu under the Edit menu on Mac OS (left) and Windows (right).

- Set up Spelling Document Preferences to enable automatic spell checking. Then work with the spelling checker to correct or learn potentially misspelled words as you type them.

In this section, I tell how to use FileMaker Pro's spelling checker to get your words right.

Setting Up the Dictionaries

The spelling checker uses two dictionary files:

- The *main dictionary* comes with FileMaker Pro and includes almost 100,000 words. FileMaker Pro checks your spelling against this dictionary first.

- The *user dictionary* is created and maintained by you. It includes words like proper names and company acronyms that you use but aren't included in the main dictionary. FileMaker Pro checks your spelling against this dictionary if it can't find a word in the main dictionary.

 TIP *You can have more than one user dictionary, each for a different purpose. If you have more than one user dictionary, be sure to select the one that you want to use before beginning a spelling check.*

FileMaker Pro allows you to select a main dictionary and user dictionary. It also lets you edit the user dictionary to add and remove words.

Selecting Dictionaries

Before you use the spelling checker feature for the first time, you might want to check (and change) the selected dictionaries—especially if you have the English version of FileMaker Pro, which includes two English dictionaries.

To see what dictionaries are selected, choose Select Dictionaries from the Spelling submenu under the Edit menu (see Figure 3-30). The Select Dictionaries dialog box appears (see Figure 3-31). It should automatically display the appropriate dictionaries in the folder in which dictionaries are stored:

- On Mac OS, dictionaries are stored in the FileMaker Extensions folder inside the FileMaker Pro 5 folder.

- On Windows, dictionaries are stored in the System folder inside the FileMaker Pro 5 folder.

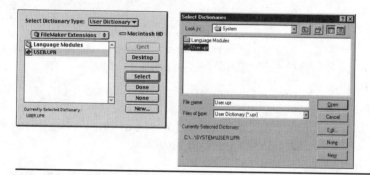

FIGURE 3-31. The Select Dictionaries dialog box for user dictionaries on Mac OS (left) and Windows (right).

By default, the Select Dictionaries dialog box displays installed user dictionaries. You can work with main dictionaries by choosing Main Dictionary from the Select Dictionary Type (Mac OS) or Files of Type (Windows) menu in the dialog box. The dialog box changes to list main dictionaries (see Figure 3-32). The name (Mac OS) or pathname (Windows) of the current dictionary is displayed at the bottom of the dialog box (see Figures 3-31 and 3-32).

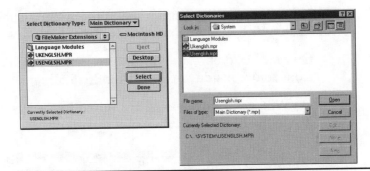

FIGURE 3-32. The Select Dictionaries dialog box for main dictionaries on Mac OS (left) and Windows (right).

SELECTING A DIFFERENT USER DICTIONARY Locate and click once on the user dictionary that you want to use. Then click the Select (Mac OS) or Open (Windows) button. To complete the process on Mac OS, click the Done button.

CREATING AND SELECTING A NEW USER DICTIONARY ON MAC OS Click the New button. In the Save As dialog box that appears (see Figure 3-33), enter a name for the dictionary file. You may want to include the .upr filename extension if you plan on sharing your user dictionary with a Windows user. Then click Save. The dictionary is created and becomes the selected user dictionary.

FIGURE 3-33. The dialog box that appears when you click the New button in the Select Dictionaries dialog box for user dictionaries on Mac OS.

CREATING AND SELECTING A NEW USER DICTIONARY ON WINDOWS Enter a name for the dictionary in the File name box. Be sure to include the .upr file name extension. Then click the New button.

The new dictionary appears in the list of dictionary files. Click it once to select it and then click the Open button.

IGNORING ALL USER DICTIONARIES   Click the None button. With no user dictionary selected, FileMaker Pro's spelling checker uses the main dictionary only when checking your spelling.

SELECTING A DIFFERENT MAIN DICTIONARY   Choose Main Dictionary from the Select Dictionary Type (Mac OS) or Files of Type (Windows) menu to change the list of dictionaries to main dictionaries. Locate and click once on the main dictionary that you want to use. Then click the Select (Mac OS) or Open (Windows) button. To complete the process on Mac OS, click the Done button.

TIP   *Main dictionaries for a variety of languages are available directly from File-Maker, Inc.*

Editing a User Dictionary

You can edit a user dictionary (but not a main dictionary) to add or remove words.

- Add words you use often that you know won't be in the main dictionary, like formal names, acronyms, and technical terms. This will prevent FileMaker Pro from stopping the spelling check when it encounters these words.

- Remove words that are misspelled. This will prevent FileMaker Pro from accepting an incorrectly spelled word.

NOTE   *You can also add words to the user dictionary while performing a spelling check. I tell you more about that in the section titled "Checking Spelling" on page 121.*

To edit the currently selected user dictionary, choose Edit Dictionary from the Spelling submenu under the Edit menu (see Figure

3-30). A dialog box like the one in Figure 3-34 appears. It lists all words in the user dictionary (if there are any).

FIGURE 3-34. The dialog box for editing a user dictionary on Mac OS (left) and Windows (right).

ADDING AN ENTRY Enter the word that you want to add to the user dictionary in the Entry box. Then click Add. The word is added to the list of user dictionary words.

NOTE *If the word you are trying to add is already included in the main or user dictionary, a dialog box like the one in Figure 3-35 appears to tell you. Click OK to dismiss the dialog box.*

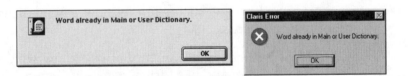

FIGURE 3-35. The dialog box that appears on Mac OS (left) and Windows (right) when you try to add a word that is already in the main or user dictionary.

REMOVING AN ENTRY Click once on the entry that you want to remove to select it. Then click the Remove button. The word is removed from the dictionary's word list.

CHANGING AN ENTRY Follow the instructions above to remove the word you no longer want and add the replacement word.

IMPORTING OR EXPORTING WORDS To add all the words in a text file to the user dictionary, click the triangle beside Text File (Mac OS) or the Text File button (Windows). This expands the dialog box to give you access to the Import and Export buttons (see Figure 3-36).

- Click the Import button to locate and open a text file containing words that you want to add to the user dictionary.

- Click the Export button to save the words in the user dictionary to a text file on disk.

FIGURE 3-36. The Import and Export buttons in the user dictionary editing dialog box on Mac OS (left) and Windows (right).

SAVING YOUR CHANGES When you are finished adding or removing words, click the OK button to save your changes and dismiss the dialog box.

Checking Spelling

FileMaker Pro offers two ways to check spelling:

- Manually check the spelling of a selection, record, or all records in the found set.

- Automatically check spelling as you type.

Here's how you can use both of these methods.

Manually Checking Spelling

To manually check the spelling of database entries (in Browse mode) or the contents of the current layout (in Layout mode), use the appropriate command on the Spelling submenu under the Edit menu (see Figure 3-30):

- **Check Selection** checks selected text. This command is available only if text is selected.

- **Check Record** checks all text in the current record. This command appears only in Browse mode.

- **Check Layout** checks all text in the current layout. This command appears only in Layout mode.

- **Check All** checks all text in the records being browsed.

When you select one of these commands, the spelling checker goes to work. When it finds a questionable word, it stops and displays the Spelling dialog box (see Figure 3-37).

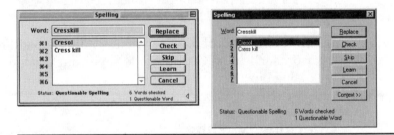

FIGURE 3-37. The Spelling dialog box on Mac OS (left) and Windows (right).

How you proceed depends on how you want to handle the questionable word:

REPLACING THE WORD WITH A CORRECT WORD Either select a correct word in the suggestions list or type the correct word in the Word box. Then click Replace.

CHECKING A WORD YOU TYPE IN THE WORD BOX If you think you know how to correctly spell a word that you want to use as a replacement for the questionable word, type it in the Word box. Then click the Check button to check the spelling of that word— the Status area at the bottom of the dialog box will tell you whether the spelling is correct. If it is correct, click the Replace button to replace the questionable word with the one you just typed and checked.

KEEPING THE WORD AS IS   Click the Skip button. This allows the word to remain in the document without adding it to the user dictionary.

ADDING THE WORD TO THE USER DICTIONARY   Click the Learn button. Once added to the User dictionary, the spelling checker will no longer bother you about it.

CANCELING THE SPELLING CHECK   Click the Cancel button. This dismisses the Spelling dialog box without completing the spelling check.

SEEING THE WORD IN CONTEXT   Click the Context button. This expands the dialog box to show the line in which the word appears. This option is only useful when the word appears in a phrase, sentence, or paragraph.

Automatically Checking Spelling

To automatically check spelling as you type, you must turn on the Spell check as you type option in the Spelling section of the Document Preferences dialog box. I tell you how to set up this option in the section titled "Spelling Preferences" on page 45. Once the Spell check as you type option is enabled for a document, all you need to do is type.

When you type a questionable word, FileMaker Pro alerts you with a sound or by flashing the menu bar. At that point—before you press the Tab key to move to another field—choose Correct Word from the Spelling submenu under the Edit menu (see Figure 3-30) or press Shift-Command-Y (Mac OS) or Control-Shift-Y (Windows). The Spelling dialog box appears (see Figure 3-37), listing the last word you typed as the questionable word. Follow the instructions in the previous section to handle the questionable word.

> ***NOTE*** *This feature is nice, but only if you're entering large blocks of text into fields. If you're entering only single words into fields (like name and address information), FileMaker Pro probably won't alert you about a problem until you've already pressed the Tab key—too late to use the keyboard shortcut for summoning the Spelling dialog box and fixing the problem.*

Step-by-Step

In this section, I provide step-by-step instructions for entering data into the three database files that you created at the end of Chapter 2. I recommend that you follow all the instructions to enter data into all three files. If you're not interested in entering lots of data, however, you can find the completed files at the companion Web site for this book, http://www.gilesrd.com/fmpro-comp/.

Entering Contact Information

Spot Ink, Inc. is a relatively new company, so it only has a few customers and vendors for its contact file.

1. Open the file named Contact.fp5 that you created at the end of Chapter 2.

2. If necessary, press the Tab key to select the Customer Number field.

3. Type in the following information for each field. Press the Tab key to move from field to field. If no data is provided for a field, leave it blank.

Field Name	Data
Customer Number	J101
First Name	Tom
Last Name	Jones
Title	

Company	ABC Songwriters
Address	1616 Elm Street
City	Cresskill
State	NJ
Zip	07626
Voice Phone	201-568-5555
Fax Phone	201-568-6666
EMail	tjones@anyisp.com
Type	Customer
Terms	Net 30
Limit	5000

4. With the insertion point blinking in the Revision Date field, choose Paste Current Date from the Paste Special submenu under the Edit menu or press Command-- (Mac OS) or Control-- (Windows) to enter the current date.

5. Choose New Record from the Mode menu or press Command-N (Mac OS) or Control-N (Windows).

6. Repeat steps 3–5 to enter the following two records:

Field Name	**Data**
Customer Number	S101
First Name	Elizabeth
Last Name	Smith
Title	Sales Associate
Company	Parkside Ink Company
Address	123 Main Street
City	Harrington Park
State	NJ
Zip	07640
Voice Phone	201-768-5555 x161
Fax Phone	201-768-6666
EMail	bettysmith@parksideink.com
Type	Vendor
Terms	Net 30
Limit	2000
Revision Date	*today's date* (see step 4)

Field Name	Data
Customer Number	J102
First Name	Eric
Last Name	Johnson
Title	Buyer
Company	Wickenburg Novelties Inc.
Address	111 Pine Tree Way
City	Wickenburg
State	AZ
Zip	85358
Voice Phone	520-685-5555
Fax Phone	520-685-6666
EMail	eric@wicknovinc.com
Type	Customer
Terms	Net 60
Limit	1000
Revision Date	*today's date* (see step 4)

7. Betty Smith has a co-worker in charge of selling pens. Click the top page of the book in the status area to switch back to record 2. Then choose Duplicate Record from the Mode menu or press Command-D (Mac OS) or Control-D (Windows) to duplicate Betty's record.

8. In record 4 (the duplicate record), edit the following fields to reflect the pen salesman's information:

Field Name	Data
Customer Number	J103
First Name	George
Last Name	Jefferson
Voice Phone	201-768-5555 x183
EMail	georgejeff@parksideink.com
Limit	3000

9. Switch to record 3 and change the Zip field to 85390.

10. Choose Check All from the Spelling submenu under the Edit menu to start a spelling check. Handle the words as

discussed in the section titled "Manually Checking Spelling" on page 121.

Entering Product Information

Right now, Spot Ink has only two products. It should be a snap to enter them.

1. Open the file named Products.fp5 that you created at the end of Chapter 2.

2. If necessary, press the Tab key to select the Item Number field.

3. Follow steps 3, 5, and 10 in the previous section to enter information and check spelling for the following two records:

Field Name	Data
Item Number	P100
Item Name	Signing Pen
Item Description	A high-quality writing instrument perfect for signing autographs.
Purchase Price	3.49
Selling Price	15.00
Reorder Point	20
Last Transaction Date	12/10/99

Field Name	Data
Item Number	I100-01
Item Name	Sky Blue Ink
Item Description	Style 100 ink cartridge filled with sky blue ink.
Purchase Price	.39
Selling Price	2.5
Reorder Point	30
Last Transaction Date	12/15/99

Entering Invoice Information

Spot Ink's invoicing system still needs some work, but you can enter the information for the single sale the company has had so far.

1. Open the file named Invoice.fp5 that you created at the end of Chapter 2.

2. If necessary, press the Tab key to select the Invoice Number field.

3. Follow steps 3, 5, and 10 in the section titled "Entering Contact Information" on page 124 to enter information and check spelling for the following record:

Field Name	Data
Invoice Number	98001
Invoice Date	1/2/00
Terms	Net 60
Due Date	3/2/00
Customer Number	J102
Customer Name	Eric Johnson
Company	Wickenburg Novelties Inc.
Address	111 Pine Tree Way
City	Wickenburg
State	AZ
Zip	85390
Voice Phone	520-685-5555
Quantity	10
Item Number	P100
Item Name	Signing Pen
Selling Price	15.00

4. Check the calculations performed in the last three fields. They all should equal 150. (The value will not appear in the Total Sales field until you deselect all fields.) If a calculation is incorrect, correct the formula stored for the field. Consult the section titled "Completing the Definition for a Calculation Field" on page 63 for more information.

Extra Credit

No, this isn't grade school and you really don't get any additional points for completing this part of the exercise. But you will get some more practice. To get the job done, however, you must have at least one graphic file on disk or be able to download two from the companion Web site for this book.

1. Open or switch to the file named Products.fp5.

2. If necessary, switch to record 1.

3. Click the Picture field to select it.

4. Use one of the techniques discussed in the section titled "Using the Copy, Cut, and Paste Commands" on page 98 or "Inserting Data into Container Fields" on page 102 to paste or insert images into the field. If you want to use the images I used, download them from the companion Web site for this book, http://www.gilesrd.com/fmprocomp/.

Finding and Sorting Records

No discussion of FileMaker Pro basics would be complete without coverage of two important features: finding and sorting. In this chapter, I tell you how to use the find feature to locate and browse the records that match criteria you specify and how to use the sort feature to put the records you browse in the order in which you want to see them.

About Finding and Sorting Records

If your FileMaker Pro database has a dozen records in it, you may never need to search it for a specific record or put records in a specific order. But if your database has dozens or hundreds or thousands of records, find and sort are two features you won't want to be without.

Here's an overview of each feature so you know what they do and how they work.

The Find Feature

The find feature searches the entire database file for records that match the criteria you specify and displays those records as the *found set*.

Here's how finding works. First, you switch to Find mode. You enter search criteria in the field(s) of a find request. If necessary, you can create multiple find requests to handle more complex search criteria. Then you click the Find button to submit the request. FileMaker Pro quickly searches the database for records that match the criteria you specified, then displays the found set in Browse mode.

The Sort Feature

The sort feature puts the records in the found set in the order that you specify.

Here's how sorting works. First, you use the Sort command to display the Sort Records dialog box. You specify the fields and order in which you want to sort. Then you click the Sort button. File-Maker Pro rearranges the records to put them in the order that you specified and displays them in the mode you were in when you chose the Sort command.

 NOTE   *Sort order is temporary. When unsorted, records always return to the order in which they were originally entered or imported into the database.*

Find and Sort—Together

Although the find and sort features do two completely different things, they are often used together. This is because the find feature displays the found set in the order in which records were entered into the database—*unsorted*. The sort feature works only on the records being browsed—that's either all the records in the database or the found set. As you can imagine, if you perform a find and end up with a hundred records, you'll probably want to put them in some kind of order before you work with them.

TIP *The most important thing to remember when using the find and sort features together is that you must use the find feature first, then use the sort feature to sort the records in the found set. If you sort and then find, the found set will be unsorted.*

Finding Records

FileMaker Pro's find feature is relatively easy to use and very powerful. In this section, I tell you what you need to know to enter search criteria to display the records that you want.

Before You Start

Before you use the find feature, it's a good idea to know the database and what you want to find. This will enable you to create effective find requests right from the start.

Know the Database

If you don't have a good idea of the design and contents of the database before you perform a find, it's unlikely that you'll be able to find what you're looking for without a lot of time-consuming trial and error.

Here are a few questions you should answer:

- What kind of information does the database contain?

- What fields does the database include?

- Is the data consistently entered? Consistency is vital, as I discuss in the section titled "The Importance of Consistent Data Entry" on page 89.

TIP *You can check the consistency of a field's data by viewing its index. Choose From Index from the Insert menu to display the View Index dialog box. When you are finished reviewing the entries for the field, click the Cancel button to dismiss the dialog box. I tell you more about the View Index dialog box in the section titled "From Index" on page 106.*

- What layouts are available for entering find requests? You can enter search criteria in a field only if that field appears on the layout when you switch to Find mode. I tell you more about layouts in Chapters 5 through 8.

If you created the database or work with it often, you should already know the answers to these questions. But if it is a database that was created by someone else or you seldom use it, browse it to answer these questions. The few minutes you spend now will save time later.

Know What You're Looking For

You should also have a clear idea of what you're looking for in the database. Jot it down on a piece of paper if you need to. This is especially helpful if your find request will be complex.

Here are some examples for the Contacts database:

- Find all records for contacts who are vendors.

- Find all contacts with last names beginning with the letter J.

- Find all contacts who are customers and have a credit limit of $2000 or more.

- Find all contacts who are located in the state of Arizona or who are vendors.

As you'll see later in this chapter, you can create very complex find requests. That's why it's important to have a clear idea of what you're looking for. If you make an error while entering a find request, you probably won't find the records you want.

Switching to Find Mode

Find mode is the FileMaker Pro mode that you use to enter find requests and initiate a find. Therefore, the first step to using the find feature is to switch to Find mode.

To switch to Find mode, choose Find from the View menu (see Figure 4-1) or press Command-F (Mac OS) or Control-F (Windows). The current layout appears in Find mode (see Figure 4-2).

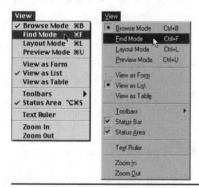

FIGURE 4-1. Choosing Find from the View menu on Mac OS (left) and Windows (right).

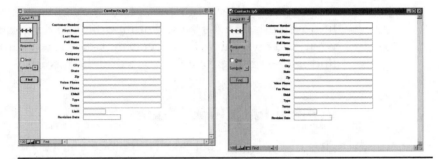

FIGURE 4-2. Find mode on Mac OS (left) and Windows (right).

Find mode looks a lot like Browse mode right after you create a new record. The fields that displayed data in Browse mode appear in Find mode as empty boxes. As you'll see in a moment, you create find requests by entering criteria into fields.

The status area also changes when you switch to Find mode. It displays controls and options that you can use to work with find requests. I introduce you to these controls and options in the section titled "The Status Area in Find Mode" on page 21; I tell you how to use them in this chapter.

Creating a Find Request

A *find request* is a collection of one or more field entries, entered in Find mode, that tells FileMaker Pro what you're looking for. A find request can include the following components:

- Text characters that appear in the same field for the records that you want to find. For example, a find request would include the characters *John* in a First Name field to find all records with John in that field.

- A number, date, or time that appears in the same field for the records that you want to find. For example, a find request would include *12/15/98* in a Date field to find all records with 12/15/98 in that field.

- Operators and other special symbols that modify a text, number, date, or time component. For example, a find request would include a greater than symbol (>) followed by a number in a Limit field to find all records with a value greater than the number in that field.

NOTE *For a find request to work, each criterion must be entered into the field in which the criterion's values will appear. For example, if you are searching for contacts who are located in a specific state, you must enter the state criterion in the State field. Entering it in a field in which it would not appear just won't do the job.*

What you include in a find request varies depending on what you want to find. In this section, I provide the steps for creating a simple find request, along with some examples to illustrate how find requests work.

NOTE *I tell you more about performing complex finds with multiple find requests later in this chapter, in the section titled "Performing Complex Searches" on page 147.*

Switching to an Appropriate Layout

To create a find request, you must be able to access the field in which you want to enter the criterion. That means the layout you view in Find mode must include that field.

If your database has more than one layout, you may want to use the layout menu at the top of status area (see Figure 4-3) to select a different layout—one that includes the fields by which you want to search for records.

FIGURE 4-3. The layout menu in the status area on Mac OS (left) and Windows (right).

TIP *If your database does not include an appropriate layout, create or modify one. I tell you how to create and modify layouts in Chapters 5 through 8.*

Entering Search Criteria

To enter search criteria, simply type it into the appropriate field(s). Use the Tab key or click with your mouse to move the blinking insertion point into the field in which you want to enter a criterion. Then type.

TIP *You can enter criteria into text, number, date, time, or calculation fields. You cannot enter criteria into—or search based on the contents of—container, summary, or global fields.*

Here are some tips for entering simple criteria:

FINDING RECORDS WITH ONE OR MORE WORDS THAT MATCH A CERTAIN WORD Enter the word in the appropriate field. For example, entering *Street* in the Address field would find all records containing the word Street in the Address field.

FINDING RECORDS WITH ONE OR MORE WORDS THAT BEGIN WITH A CERTAIN LETTER Enter the letter in the appropriate field. For example, entering *J* in the Last Name field would find all records that contain words that begin with J in the Last Name field.

FINDING RECORDS THAT MATCH A CERTAIN NUMBER, DATE, OR TIME Enter the number, date, or time in the appropriate field. For example, entering *1000* in the Limit field would find all records that have 1000 in the Limit field.

TIP *FileMaker Pro's find feature is not case sensitive. That means it would find the same records if you entered John, john, JOHN, or JoHn as a search criterion.*

Using Symbols

The Symbols menu in the status area offers a list of special symbols you can use in search criteria (see Figure 4-4). These symbols greatly increase the flexibility of criteria, making it possible to search for all kinds of things.

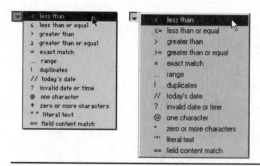

FIGURE 4-4. The Symbols menu in the status area on Mac OS (left) and Windows (right).

To use an item from the Symbols menu, position the blinking insertion point in the field where you want the symbol to appear. Then choose the symbol from the menu. Or, if you prefer, simply type the symbol with the keyboard.

Here's what each symbol is for, along with examples of how it can be used.

< LESS THAN   Finds records with values less than the text, number, date, or time that follows it. For example:

- *<L* finds records with any word that begins with a character before the letter L or any number (because numbers come before letters, alphabetically).

- *<1000* finds records with values less than 1000.

- *<1/1/98* finds records with dates before 1/1/98.

- *<12:15 PM* finds records with times before 12:15 PM.

≤ LESS THAN OR EQUAL (MAC OS) OR <= LESS THAN OR EQUAL (WINDOWS) Finds records with values less than or equal to the text, number, date, or time that follows it. For example:

- ≤*L* (Mac OS) or <=*L* (Windows) finds records with any word that begins with the letter L or a character before the letter L, or any number.

- ≤*1000* (Mac OS) or <=*1000* (Windows) finds records with values of 1000 or less.

- ≤*1/1/98* (Mac OS) or <=*1/1/98* (Windows) finds records with dates on or before 1/1/98.

- ≤*12:15 PM* (Mac OS) or <=*12:15 PM* (Windows) finds records with times on or before 12:15 PM.

TIP *To type the ≤ symbol on Mac OS, press Option-, (comma).*

> GREATER THAN Finds records with values greater than the text, number, date, or time that follows it. For example:

- >*L* finds records with any word that begins with a character after the letter L.

- >*1000* finds records with values greater than 1000.

- >*1/1/98* finds records with dates after 1/1/98.

- >*12:15 PM* finds records with times after 12:15 PM.

≥ GREATER THAN OR EQUAL (MAC OS) OR >= GREATER THAN OR EQUAL (WINDOWS) Finds records with values greater than or equal to the text, number, date, or time that follows it. For example:

- ≥*L* (Mac OS) or >=*L* (Windows) finds records with any word that begins with the letter L or a character after the letter L.

- *≥1000* (Mac OS) or *>=1000* (Windows) finds records with values of 1000 or more.

- *≥1/1/98* (Mac OS) or *>=1/1/98* (Windows) finds records with dates on or after 1/1/98.

- *≥12:15 PM* (Mac OS) or *>=12:15 PM* (Windows) finds records with times on or after 12:15 PM.

TIP   *To type the ≥ symbol on Mac OS, press Option-. (period).*

= EXACT MATCH   Finds records that contain an exact match of the text, number, date, or time that follows it. This symbol is not necessary when searching for numbers, dates, or times entered in number, date, or time fields. For example:

- *=John* finds records that contain the word John in the field. It won't, however, find records that contain the word Johnson. Other words or values may also appear in the field, so *=John* would also display records with John Smith, John Jones, or My Friend John in the field.

- = by itself in a field finds records with the field blank.

... RANGE   Finds records in the range beginning with the text, number, date, or time before the symbol and ending with the text, number, date, or time after the symbol. For example:

- *A...L* finds records with one or more words beginning with any letter between A and L.

- *0...1000* finds records with values between 0 and 1000.

- *1/1/97...6/30/97* finds records with dates between 1/1/97 and 6/30/97.

- *9:00 AM...5:00 PM* finds records with times between 9:00 AM and 5:00 PM.

TIP   *To type in the range symbol, simply type three periods in a row.*

! DUPLICATES   Finds records for which the field contains exactly the same data as the same field in another record. This symbol is normally used alone in a field to find duplicate records. For example:

- *!* in a Last Name field finds all records that contain the same last name in the field as another record.

- *!* in an Invoice Number field finds all records that contain the same number in the field as another record.

NOTE   *You cannot find duplicate values if the field has not been indexed. I tell you about indexing fields in the section titled "Indexing" on page 367.*

// TODAY'S DATE   Finds records with the current date. This can be used alone in a field or in combination with other operators:

- *<//* finds records with dates before the current date.

- *1/1/97...//* finds records with dates between 1/1/97 and the current date.

TIP   *The today's date symbol is especially useful for creating find requests that work with scripts. I tell you about scripting in Chapter 12.*

? INVALID DATE OR TIME   Finds records with invalid date or time data. This symbol normally is used alone in a date or time field.

@ ONE CHARACTER   A wildcard symbol that is used with text to specify criteria. The @ wildcard replaces a single character of text. Here are some examples:

- *jo@n* finds records with Joan, John, or join in the field.

- *S@@* finds records with a three-letter word beginning with the letter S in the field.

* ZERO OR MORE CHARACTERS Another wildcard symbol that is used with text to specify criteria. But rather than replace one character, the * wildcard replaces zero or any number of characters. Here are some examples:

- *jo** finds records with any word that begins with the characters JO in the field (like John, Johnson, or Joseph).

- *M* S** finds records with a word that begins with the letter M and a word that begins with a letter S in the field (like Main Street or M Smith).

"" LITERAL TEXT Finds records that exactly match the character string enclosed in the double-quote characters. For example:

- *", Inc."* finds record that contain the string ", Inc."

- *"Betty S"* finds records that contain the string "Betty S".

TIP *To find a double-quote character in a field, enter three double-quote characters. The two on the outside indicate literal text while the one between them tells File-Maker Pro what you want to find. If you want to find curly or smart quotes, make sure the Use smart quotes option is turned on in the General Document Preferences dialog box; see the section titled "Use Smart Quotes (' ', " ")" on page 44.*

== FIELD CONTENT MATCH Finds records that exactly match whatever follows the two equals signs. For example:

- *==Johnson* finds records with Johnson—and only Johnson—in the field.

- *==Betty S* finds records with Betty S—but not Betty Smith or anything else—in the field.

Omitting Records

If you want to show all records *except* those that match the criteria you specify, FileMaker Pro has you covered. Turn on the Omit check box in the status area before you initiate the find. This tells FileMaker Pro to find all records except those that match the criteria. It's like a "not equal to" check box for all the criteria you enter in the Find request.

 TIP *As you work with the find feature, you might often find it easier to omit the records that you don't want than to find the records that you do want.*

NOTE *I tell you more about using the Omit check box, including how to omit records when there are multiple find requests, in the sections titled "Omitting Records in a Complex Search" on page 150 and "More Omit Stuff" on page 152.*

Initiating a Find

Once you've entered search criteria, you're ready to tell FileMaker Pro to start looking for records. Click the Find button in the status area (see Figure 4-2), choose Perform Find from the Requests menu (see Figure 4-5), or press the Enter key on the keyboard.

FIGURE 4-5. Choosing Perform Find from the Requests menu on Mac OS (left) and Windows (right).

What happens next depends on whether FileMaker Pro found any records that match your search criteria.

The Found Set

If FileMaker Pro finds one or more records that match your search criteria, it displays the record(s) in Browse mode in the current layout (see Figure 4-6).

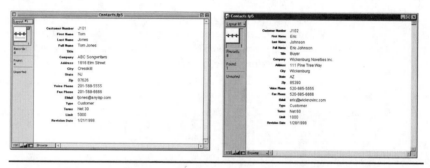

FIGURE 4-6. The found set: records with words beginning with the letter J in the Last Name field on Mac OS (left) and records with 1000 in the Limit field on Windows (right).

The most important thing to note after a successful find is the number of records in the found set, which is indicated in the status area beneath the word *Found*. This not only tells you how many records FileMaker Pro found, but it indicates that you are working with a found set—not all of the records in the database. These are the only records you will work with until you add records, remove records, or perform another find. I tell you how to work with all records again in the section titled "Finding All Records" on page 152.

What can you do with the records in the found set? Here are some suggestions:

- Browse the records for information that interests you.

- Switch to another layout to see the records in a different on-screen format.

- Use options under the View menu to view the records as a form, list, or table.

- Sort the records so they're in a desired order.

- Print the records to obtain printed reports.

 TIP *If the last find you performed didn't come up with the records you expected, you can edit the find request(s) and try again. Choose Modify Last Find from the Records menu (see Figure 4-7) or press Command-R (Mac OS) or Control-R (Windows) to display the find request(s) that resulted in the current found set. Then edit the find request(s) as desired and click the Find button to search for records matching the revised criteria.*

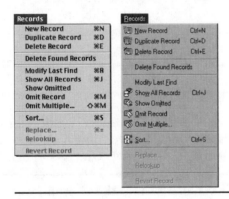

FIGURE 4-7. The Records menu in Browse mode immediately after performing a find on Mac OS (left) and Windows (right).

No Records Found

If FileMaker Pro is unable to find any records that match your search criteria, it displays a dialog box like the one in Figure 4-8.

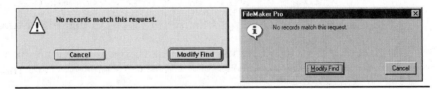

FIGURE 4-8. The dialog box that appears on Mac OS (left) and Windows (right) when no records match your search criteria.

You have two choices:

- Click the Cancel button to return to Browse mode. All records will be displayed.

- Click the Modify Find button to return to Find mode and modify your find request(s).

Performing Complex Searches

In a basic find, you enter a search criterion in a single field of a single find request and click the Find button. Although that might meet your needs most of the time, sooner or later you'll want to specify more complex search criteria. In this section, I tell you how.

Do yourself a favor—master the art of simple finds before you start getting fancy with complex search criteria. Then experiment, following the instructions here and carefully reviewing the found set to make sure it contains all the records—and only *the records—that it should.*

Finding Records that Match Two or More Criteria

At times, you may need to find records that match multiple search criteria. Here's an example. Say you want to search the Contacts database for customers with a credit limit of $2000 or more. In this case, there are two separate pieces of criteria:

- The contents of the Type field must be Customer **and**

- The contents of the Limit field must be greater than or equal to 2000.

The found set should include only those records that match *both* criteria.

To set up the search for these records, switch to Find mode and enter both criteria in the appropriate fields of the same find request (see Figure 4-9). Then click the Find button to find the records.

FIGURE 4-9. Two criteria entered into the same find request on Mac OS.

You can enter criteria into as many fields as you want, to fine-tune the search. Just remember that if the criteria is all in the same find request, FileMaker Pro will find only those records that match *all* of the criteria.

Finding Records that Match One Set of Criteria or Another

At other times, you may need to find records that match one set of criteria or another.

For example, say you want to search the Contacts database for all contacts who are located in the state of Arizona or who are vendors. This case also has two separate pieces of criteria:

- The contents of the State field must be AZ (or however Arizona is consistently entered in the database) **or**
- The contents of the Type field must be Vendor.

The found set should include the records that match *either or both* criteria.

To set up the search for these records, switch to Find mode and enter the first criterion in a find request (see Figure 4-11, left). Then choose New Request from the Mode menu (see Figure 4-10) or press Command-N (Mac OS) or Control-N (Windows) to create a new find request. Enter the second criterion into this request (see Figure 4-11, right). Then click the Find button to find the records.

FIGURE 4-10. The Mode menu in Find mode on Mac OS (left) and Windows (right).

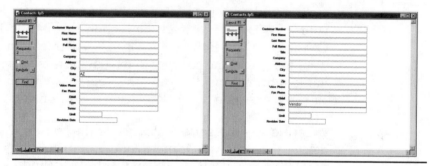

FIGURE 4-11. Two find requests on Windows. Note the request numbers on the book in the status area.

You can enter criteria into as many find requests as you want to expand the search. Just keep in mind that if the criteria is in separate find requests, FileMaker Pro will find those records that match *any* of the criteria.

Here are a few additional tips for working with multiple find requests:

SWITCHING FROM ONE FIND REQUEST TO ANOTHER Use the book in the status area (see Figure 4-11). I tell you all about using the book in the section titled "Book Icon" on page 18.

Viewing More than One Find Request at a Time in the Current Layout   Choose View as List from the View menu (see Figure 4-7). Remember, this will also display multiple records in the layout when you switch to Browse mode.

Creating a New Find Request that is Exactly the Same as the Current One   Choose Duplicate Request from the Requests menu (see Figure 4-10) or press Command-D (Mac OS) or Control-D (Windows). You can then modify the new request to specify the desired search criteria.

Searching for Records When Data is Not Consistently Entered in the Field   Create a separate find request for each version of the data entry. For example, if you're searching for Arizona in the State field, create a separate find request for AZ, Arizona, Ariz., and any other version of the entry in the State field. (Then do yourself a favor and read the section titled "The Importance of Consistent Data Entry" on page 89. After reading it, you may want to make some changes to the database to save yourself work in the future. Consider using the Replace command, which I discuss in the section titled "Replacing Field Contents" on page 112.)

Deleting a Find Request   Switch to the request that you want to delete, then choose Delete Request from the Requests menu or press Command-E (Mac OS) or Control-E (Windows). You cannot delete a find request if there is only one.

Omitting Records in a Complex Search

It is possible to find some records while omitting others. But there is a trick to setting it up so it works right: Make sure the last find request that you create omits the records that you don't want to find.

Here's an example. Say you want to search the Contacts database for all contacts who are located in the state of Arizona or who are vendors, but you don't want to see anyone with the last name Smith. (I don't know why; Betty Smith is a very pleasant person.)

In this case, there are two separate pieces of find criteria and one omit criterion:

- The contents of the State field must be AZ **or**
- The contents of the Type field must be Vendor **and**
- The contents of the Last Name field cannot be Smith.

To set up the search for these records, switch to Find mode and enter the first criterion in a find request (see Figure 4-11, left). Then choose New Request from the Requests menu (see Figure 4-10) or press Command-N (Mac OS) or Control-N (Windows) to create a new find request. Enter the second criterion into this request (see Figure 4-11, right). Now choose New Request from the Requests menu to create a third find request. Enter the third criterion in that request and turn the Omit check box on (see Figure 4-12). Then click the Find button to find the records.

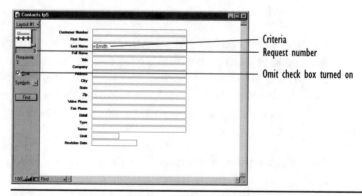

FIGURE 4-12. An omit request created as a third find request on Windows.

NOTE *Why create the omit request last? Because FileMaker Pro works through multiple find requests in the order in which they are created. If the omit requests aren't last, FileMaker Pro might find records you asked it to omit.*

Finding All Records

After successfully performing a find, the only records being browsed are those in the found set. If you want to work with all the records in the database again, you must find all records.

To find all records, choose Find All from the Records menu (see Figure 4-7) or press Command-J (Mac OS) or Control-J (Windows). All records return in Browse mode.

More Omit Stuff

Earlier in this chapter, in the sections titled "Omitting Records" on page 144 and "Omitting Records in a Complex Search" on page 150, I tell you how to use the Omit check box to omit records from the found set during a find. But that's not all the omitting you can do.

FINDING OMITTED RECORDS After successfully performing a find, the records being browsed are those in the found set. To see the records that weren't found rather than the records that were found, choose Show Omitted from the Records menu (see Figure 4-7). This command, in effect, turns the omitted set into the found set.

OMITTING A SINGLE RECORD While in Browse mode, you can omit a single record from those being browsed. Simply switch to the record to display it, then choose Omit Record from the Records menu (see Figure 4-7) or press Command-M (Mac OS) or Control-M (Windows). The record is removed from the found set.

OMITTING MULTIPLE RECORDS While in Browse mode, you can also omit multiple continuous records from those being browsed. Switch to the first record that you want to omit. Then choose Omit Multiple from the Records menu (see Figure 4-7) or press Shift-Command-M (Mac OS) or Control-Shift-M (Windows). The Omit Multiple dialog box appears (see Figure 4-13). Enter the number of records that you want to omit and click the Omit button. The records are removed from the found set.

FIGURE 4-13. The Omit Multiple dialog box on Mac OS (left) and Windows (right).

NOTE *Neither the Omit nor the Omit Multiple command delete records. Instead, they just remove the records temporarily from the found set. The records return if you find all records or perform a find that would include them in the found set.*

Sorting Records

FileMaker Pro's sort feature is very easy to use and quite powerful. In this section, I tell you how to sort—and unsort—the records in a database.

NOTE *I tell you about sorting portals for related fields in the section titled "Sorting Portal Contents" on page 441.*

Setting Sort Order

The first step to sorting records is to set a sort order—specify the fields by which you want to sort records and the order in which you want to sort them. You do this in the Sort Records dialog box.

Choose Sort from the Records menu (see Figure 4-14) or press Command-S (Mac OS) or Control-S (Windows). The Sort Records dialog box appears (see Figure 4-15). Use it to specify as many fields as you like for the sort order.

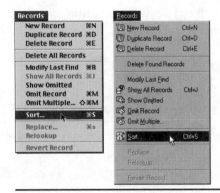

FIGURE 4-14. Choosing Sort from the Records menu on Mac OS (left) and Windows (right).

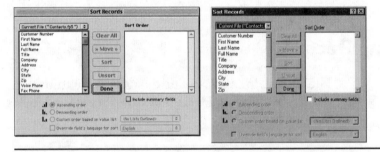

FIGURE 4-15. The Sort Records dialog box on Mac OS (left) and Windows (right).

 NOTE *You must be in either Browse or Preview mode to use the Sort command.*

Selecting a Sort Field

In the scrolling list on the left side of the Sort Records dialog box, click the name of the field that you want to use as a primary sort field. It becomes selected and the options at the bottom of the dialog box become available.

NOTE   *You cannot sort by a container field.*

Selecting the Field's Sort Order

Select one of the sort order options for the selected field. Your options are:

ASCENDING ORDER   This option sorts text from A to Z, sorts numbers from lowest to highest, and sorts dates and times from earliest to latest. This is the default option.

DESCENDING ORDER   This option sorts text from Z to A, sorts numbers from highest to lowest, and sorts dates and times from latest to earliest.

CUSTOM ORDER BASED ON VALUE LIST   This option sorts based on a sort order predefined in a value list. You must select this option and choose an appropriate value list from the menu beside it. You cannot use this option if no value lists exist. I tell you about value lists in the section titled "Value List" on page 353.

Overriding Field Language for Sort

If desired, you can turn on the Override field's language for sort check box. This enables you to choose a different sorting language from the menu beside it. Depending on the language you choose, this could change the order in which sorted records appear.

TIP   *Leave the Override field's language for sort check box turned off unless you are working with multiple languages.*

Adding the Sort Field to the Sort Order List

Click the Move button. The field name and sort order icon for the selected field appear in the Sort Order list on the right side of the Sort Records dialog box (see Figure 4-16).

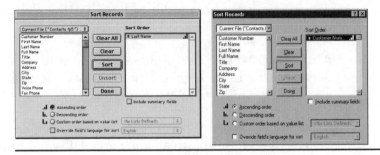

FIGURE 4-16. Examples of a field name in the Sort Order list on Mac OS (left) and Windows (right).

Sorting

When at least one field is in the Sort Order list, you can sort.

Click the Sort button or press Return (Mac OS) or Enter (Windows). FileMaker Pro returns to Browse mode and displays the records in the order you specified (see Figure 4-17).

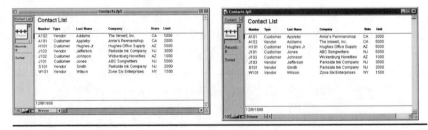

FIGURE 4-17. A columnar report showing records sorted as specified in Figure 4-16 on Mac OS (left) and Windows (right). Note the word *Sorted* in the status area.

Working with the Sort Order List

The Sort Order list remains the same until you change it. That means that when you open the Sort Records dialog box, the most recently set sort order appears. Although that might be handy if you always want records sorted in the same order, you're not stuck with it. Here are a few things you can do with the sort order list.

ADDING MORE FIELDS TO THE SORT ORDER LIST Follow the instructions in the section titled "Setting Sort Order" on page 153 to add as many fields as you like to the sort order list. FileMaker Pro sorts by the first field listed, then uses subsequent fields as tie-breakers. For example, if the first listed field is Limit and the second field is Customer Number, if there is more than one contact with the same limit, they are put in order of customer number. Figures 4-18 and 4-19 show two examples of multiple-level sorts.

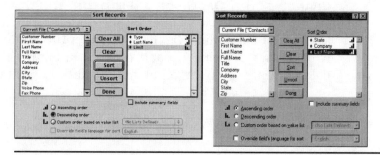

FIGURE 4-18. Examples of multiple field names in the Sort Order list on Mac OS (left) and Windows (right).

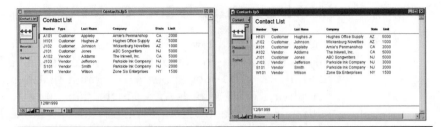

FIGURE 4-19. A columnar report showing records sorted as specified in Figure 4-18 on Mac OS (left) and Windows (right).

INCLUDING A SUMMARY FIELD IN THE SORT ORDER LIST Turn on the Include Summary Fields check box. Then add the summary field to the list after the field by which you want to summarize information. For example, to include a summary field named Total Invoices, first include a Customer Number or Salesperson field by which to summarize the Total Invoices field.

CHANGING THE ORDER OF A FIELD ON THE SORT ORDER LIST Position your mouse pointer on the double-headed arrow to the left of the field name. The mouse pointer turns into a double line with arrows pointing up and down (see Figure 4-20). Drag the field name up or down to put it in the desired position.

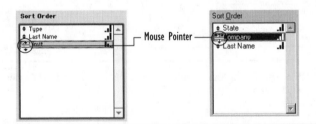

FIGURE 4-20. The mouse pointer when positioned over the arrows to the left of a field name on Mac OS (left) and Windows (right).

TIP *Another way to move a selected field name up or down in the list is to hold down the Command (Mac OS) or Control (Windows) key and press the Up or Down Arrow key.*

REMOVING A FIELD FROM THE SORT ORDER LIST Click the name of the field that you want to remove to select it, then click the Clear button. The field name is removed from the Sort Order list.

REMOVING ALL FIELDS FROM THE SORT ORDER LIST Click the Clear All button. All field names are removed from the Sort Order list.

CHANGING THE SORT ORDER FOR A SPECIFIC FIELD Click the name of the field that you want to change to select it. Then click the option for the sort order that you want the field to use. The icon beside the field name in the sort order list changes.

SAVING A SORT ORDER LIST WITHOUT SORTING Click the Done button. The sort order you specified is saved with the file, but the records are not sorted.

About Sort Status

The sort status appears in the status area (see Figure 4-17 and Figure 4-19). It tells you whether the records are sorted. There are three possible statuses:

UNSORTED This means the records are in the order in which they were entered into the database file.

SORTED This means the records have been sorted. FileMaker Pro maintains the records in the sorted order until you perform a find, use the Find All command, or add records to the database.

SEMI-SORTED This means the records were sorted, but after sorting them you added at least one new record.

Unsorting Records

To return records to the order in which they were entered into the database file, choose Sort from the Records menu (see Figure 4-14) or press Command-S (Mac OS) or Control-S (Windows). In the Sort Records dialog box that appears (see Figure 4-18), click the Unsort button. The records return to their original order in Browse mode.

Step-by-Step

Ready to give finding and sorting records a try?

In this section, I provide step-by-step instructions for finding and sorting the records you entered into the Contacts.fp5 database at the end of Chapter 3. If you didn't enter any data (shame on you!) or you're interested in working with a copy of the file that has a few more records, you can find Contacts.fp5 at the companion Web site for this book, http://www.gilesrd.com/fmprocomp/.

Finding Records

Here are instructions for performing a handful of find requests. As you work through each exercise in this section, be sure to check the records that were found to make sure they meet the criteria you enter. When you're finished, come up with a few of your own examples.

Just to refresh your memory, here are two additional instructions used throughout these exercises:

TO SWITCH TO FIND MODE...   Choose Find from the View menu or press Command-F (Mac OS) or Control-F (Windows).

TO CREATE A NEW FIND REQUEST...   Choose New Request from the Requests menu or press Command-N (Mac OS) or Control-N (Windows).

A Few Simple Finds

Here are a few simple finds. In each instance, you'll enter only one criterion in a single field of a single find request. Simple find requests are discussed in the section titled "Creating a Find Request" on page 136.

FIND ALL CUSTOMERS   Switch to Find mode. Enter *Customer* in the Type field. Click the Find button.

FIND ALL CONTACTS IN NEW JERSEY   Switch to Find mode. Enter *NJ* in the State field. Click the Find button.

FIND ALL CONTACTS WITH A CREDIT LIMIT OF $2000 OR MORE Switch to Find mode. Enter *>=2000* in the Limit field. (You can use the Symbols menu if you like to enter the >= symbol or simply type it in.) Click the Find button.

FIND ALL CONTACTS WITHOUT AN E-MAIL ADDRESS   Switch to Find mode. Enter = by itself in the Email field. Click the Find button.

FIND ALL CONTACTS EXCEPT THOSE IN NEW JERSEY   Switch to Find mode. Enter *NJ* in the State field. Turn on the Omit check box. Click the Find button.

A Few Complex Finds

Here are a few more complex finds. In these examples, you'll enter multiple criteria, either in the same find request or multiple find requests. Complex find requests are discussed in the section titled "Performing Complex Searches" on page 147.

FIND ALL CUSTOMERS IN NEW JERSEY   Switch to Find mode. Enter *NJ* in the State field. Enter *Customer* in the Type field. Click the Find button.

FIND ALL CUSTOMERS WITH A CREDIT LIMIT OF $2000 OR MORE Switch to Find mode. Enter *Customer* in the Type field. Enter >=2000 in the Limit field. Click the Find button.

FIND ALL CONTACTS WHO ARE CUSTOMERS OR WHO ARE LOCATED IN NEW JERSEY Switch to Find mode. Enter *Customer* in the Type field. Create a new find request. Enter *NJ* in the State field. Click the Find button.

FIND ALL CONTACTS WHO ARE VENDORS OR WHO ARE LOCATED IN ARIZONA EXCEPT THOSE WITH THE LAST NAME SMITH Switch to Find mode. Enter *Vendor* in the Type field. Create a new find request. Enter *AZ* in the State field. Create another new find request. Enter *Smith* in the Last Name field and turn on the Omit check box. Click the Find button.

Finding All Records

Choose Find All from the Records menu or press Command-J (Mac OS) or Control-J (Windows).

Sorting Records

Here are instructions for sorting records a number of ways. You can sort either all the records or the records in the found set after performing one or more of the find exercises in the previous sections. After each sort, check the records to make sure they were sorted the way you expect them to be. When you're finished, come up with a few of your own examples.

Just to refresh your memory, here are additional instructions used throughout these exercises:

OPENING THE SORT RECORDS DIALOG BOX Choose Sort from the Records menu or press Command-S (Mac OS) or Control-S (Windows).

A Few Simple Sorts

In each of the following exercises, you'll sort the records by only one field as discussed in "Setting Sort Order" on page 153 and "Sorting" on page 156.

SORT BY CUSTOMER NUMBER   In the Sort Records dialog box, move the Customer Number field to the Sort Order list. Make sure Ascending order is selected for the field. Click the Sort button.

SORT BY CREDIT LIMIT IN DESCENDING ORDER   In the Sort Records dialog box, if necessary, clear the contents of the Sort Order list. Move the Limit field to the Sort Order List. Make sure Descending order is selected for the field. Click the Sort button.

A Few Multiple-Level Sorts

In these exercises, you'll sort by more than one field. All fields after the first field in the Sort Order list act as tie-breakers. This is discussed in the section titled "Adding More Fields to the Sort Order List" on page 157.

SORT BY CREDIT LIMIT IN DESCENDING ORDER AND CUSTOMER NUMBER IN ASCENDING ORDER   In the Sort Records dialog box, if necessary, move the Limit field to the Sort Order list. Make sure Descending order is selected for the field. Move the Customer Number field to the Sort Order list. Make sure Ascending order is selected for the field. Click the Sort button.

SORT BY STATE, TYPE, AND CREDIT LIMIT   In the Sort Records dialog box, if necessary, clear the contents of the Sort Order list. Move the State, Type, and Limit fields to the list. Make sure Ascending order is set for all three fields. Click the Sort button.

Unsorting Records

In the Sort Records dialog box, click the Unsort button.

Developing Layouts and Reports

This part of the book provides detailed information about using one of FileMaker Pro's most powerful features: layouts. Its four chapters are:

Chapter 5: Understanding Layouts

Chapter 6: Creating New Layouts

Chapter 7: Arranging Layout Objects

Chapter 8: Polishing Layout Appearance and Functionality

Understanding Layouts

Although it's true that FileMaker Pro is a great tool for gathering, organizing, and storing information, it's also an excellent tool for viewing information on screen or in printed reports. Its layout feature is both easy to use and flexible. Whether you want to create onscreen data entry forms, columnar reports, mailing labels, or form letters, FileMaker Pro has you covered.

In this chapter, I introduce you to FileMaker Pro's powerful layout feature by telling you more about Layout mode and its tools and commands.

NOTE *There's a lot of reference information in this chapter, some of which may not make a lot of sense as you read it. Don't worry. It will all come together in Chapters 6, 7, and 8 when I tell you how to create and modify layouts.*

Layout Basics

A *layout* is an arrangement of fields, labels, and other objects that is used to display database contents on screen or printed documents. A FileMaker Pro database can have any number of layouts, each for a different purpose. Each layout can include any combination of fields.

In this section, I tell you more about Layout mode and describe the various layout components and types.

Layout Mode Revisited

Layout mode (see Figure 5-1) is the mode you use to view, create, modify, and delete layouts. It includes a number of tools and menu commands that you can use to move or modify each layout object—fields, text, and graphic elements. I provide more Layout mode basics in the section titled "Layout Mode" on page 12.

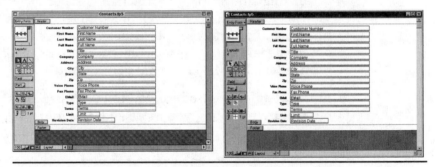

FIGURE 5-1. Layout mode on Mac OS (left) and Windows (right).

To switch to Layout mode, choose Layout from the View menu (see Figure 5-2) or press Command-L (Mac OS) or Control-L (Windows).

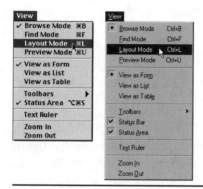

FIGURE 5-2. Choosing Layout from the View menu on Mac OS (left) and Windows (right).

Layout Parts

The most basic component of a layout is the layout *part*. A part is a portion of a layout that performs specific functions:

- A part determines the position of the objects it contains relative to the objects in other parts.

- A part can determine the position of page breaks and/or the restarting of page numbers in printed reports.

- A summary or sub-summary part can instruct FileMaker Pro to calculate the values in summary fields for all records in the found set or each group of records when sorted by a specific field.

You can include eight different kinds of parts in a layout. Each part can be sized to accommodate its contents. Here's a list, in the order in which they can appear in a layout:

TITLE HEADER A title header appears at the top of just the first page of a printed report.

HEADER   A header appears at the top of every page of a printed report—unless there is a title header, in which case the header does not appear.

LEADING GRAND SUMMARY   A leading grand summary appears before database records and normally is used to display summary fields for the found set.

BODY   The body is repeated for each record in the found set. It is the most commonly used part; it will appear in almost every layout that you create. When you enter data into a database field, that field is most likely in the body of the layout.

SUB-SUMMARY   A sub-summary is repeated for each group of records when the records are sorted by a specific field. It normally is used to display summary fields for groups of records. You can have more than one sub-summary part in a layout. Sub-summary parts only appear in Preview mode or printed reports.

NOTE   *Summary and sub-summary parts have been known to cause confusion among FileMaker Pro users. That's why I included an expanded discussion of them in the section titled "Creating a Columnar Report with Summaries" on page 277.*

TRAILING GRAND SUMMARY   A trailing grand summary appears after database records and any sub-summaries and normally is used to display summary fields for the found set.

FOOTER   A footer appears at the bottom of every page of a printed report—unless there is a title footer, in which case the footer does not appear.

TITLE FOOTER   A title footer appears at the bottom of the first page of a printed report.

NOTE   *By default, most layouts include a header, body, and footer.*

TIP *The gray part labels at the far left side of the layout identify each layout part. You can see the part labels in Figure 5-1 and other Layout mode figures throughout this chapter.*

Layout Objects

Everything you see within the document window while in Layout mode—fields, field labels, text objects, and graphics—is a *layout object*. The arrangement of layout objects determines how data appears when browsed or printed.

NOTE *Layout objects are positioned on layout parts—never on the dark gray area that represents the nonprinting area of the layout.*

Fields

Fields, which are another kind of layout object, display the information stored in the database. As far as FileMaker Pro layouts are concerned, there are two kinds of fields:

FIELD A field is a data holder. In Browse and Find modes, a field typically resembles an edit box into which you can enter data. In Layout mode, it looks like a rectangle that may or may not have dotted baselines (see Figure 5-1). This is the type of field that you'll use in data entry forms, columnar reports, and most other types of layouts. It can be resized as necessary to accommodate its contents, and formatted in a variety of ways.

MERGE FIELD A merge field is designed to incorporate database information into text objects. You cannot enter data into a merge field or use it to create a find request. Instead, it simply displays field contents (see Figure 5-4). Merge fields are usually used in form letters (see Figure 5-3, left) and mailing labels (see Figure 5-3, right). In Layout mode, they appear as field names enclosed within pairs of less than (<<) and greater than (>>) symbols and can be formatted a number of ways.

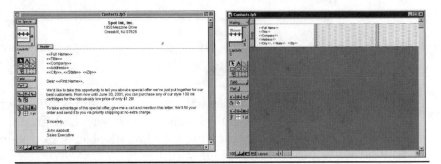

FIGURE 5-3. Merge fields in a form letter on Mac OS (left) and in mailing labels on Windows (right).

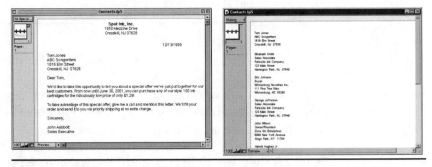

FIGURE 5-4. The layouts in Figure 5-3 when viewed in Preview mode on Mac OS (left) and Windows (right).

TIP   *The best part about merge fields is that they blend seamlessly with the text with which they are used. No matter how long a field's contents are, text with embedded merge fields maintains perfect word wrap. There's no reason to use the mail merge feature of a word processor with the excellent built-in text editing and merge field features available in FileMaker Pro's Layout mode.*

Field Labels or Text Objects

A *field label* or *text object* is text on a layout that can be formatted a variety of ways. Labels and text objects can be used to accomplish several things:

- Field labels identify fields (see Figure 5-1). This helps ensure that you enter information into the appropriate field!

- Text objects can display static text, such as letterhead information or text that appears for every record (see Figures 5-3 and 5-4, left).

- Text objects can be used to enter symbols that display dynamic information, such as the current date (see Figures 5-3 and 5-4, left), time, or page number, in Browse or Preview mode or printed reports.

Graphic Elements

A *graphic element* is a drawn object or image on a layout. It is normally used to make the layout more visually appealing or separate or group other layout objects. Here are some examples of graphic elements and how they can be used:

- Use lines to separate items in a columnar report.

- Use colored boxes to group items in an entry form.

- Use a logo to show company identity.

- Use patterned boxes or circles to liven up a layout.

NOTE *Don't confuse a graphic element on a layout with a picture in a container field. A graphic element appears on the layout no matter what record is displayed. A picture in a field appears only when its field is included on a layout and its record is displayed.*

Layout Types

The arrangement of layout objects determines the appearance and purpose of the layout. Although you can build any kind of layout you need from scratch, FileMaker Pro's New Layout/Report dialog box offers six predefined types of layouts, each offering a variety of formatting and sorting options.

TIP   *I tell you how to create layouts in the section titled "Using the New Layout/Report Dialog Box" on page 201.*

Standard Form

A standard form layout places the database fields you select, along with corresponding field labels, in the body of a layout that also includes a header and footer. It displays only one record at a time on screen. Layout #1, which is automatically created when you create a new database and define fields, is an example of a standard form layout with all fields selected.

Columnar List/Report

A columnar list/report layout (see Figures 5-5 and 5-6) places the fields that you select in a row across the body of a layout with field labels in the header above them. If you select more fields than will fit across a page, you have the option of placing them in the same row or in a second row of the body, with corresponding labels in a second row in the header (see Figures 5-5, right, and 5-6, right). This type of layout, which also includes a footer, displays many records on a screen or page.

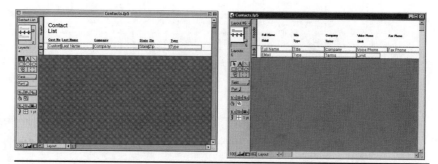

FIGURE 5-5. A columnar report layout with only a few fields on Mac OS (left) and with more fields than will fit across a page on Windows (right).

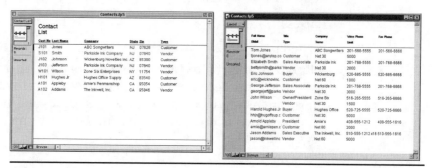

FIGURE 5-6. The layouts in Figure 5-5 when viewed in Browse mode on Mac OS (left) and Windows (right).

Table View

A table view layout displays the fields you select in a grid. Each record appears in a row; each field appears in a column. Although this layout looks like a standard form layout when viewed in Layout mode (see Figure 5-7, left), it looks like a table when viewed in Browse mode (see Figure 5-7, right).

TIP   *You can choose View as Table from the View menu to view any layout as a table. It is not necessary to create a special layout.*

FIGURE 5-7. A Table view layout in Layout mode on Mac OS (left) and in Browse mode on Windows (right).

Labels

A label layout (see Figure 5-3, right) uses the merge fields that you select to arrange fields for printing on mailing label stock. You can specify standard Avery brand label stock or provide the dimensions for custom label stock. This type of layout includes a blank header, which is used to set spacing between the top of the label page and the first label.

Envelope

An envelope layout uses the merge fields that you select to display fields on a standard business envelope. It includes a blank header, which is used to set spacing so the envelope prints properly with your printer's envelope feeder.

Blank Layout

A blank layout is a layout with an empty header, body, and footer. You must manually add all fields and other layout objects and resize the layout parts to create the layout you want.

TIP *Start with a blank layout when you want to create a layout that is completely different from the other predefined layout types—like the form letter shown on the left side of Figure 5-3.*

Layout Options

As you'll see in Chapter 6, the New Layout/Report dialog box offers a variety of options you can take advantage of to fine-tune your layout during the initial creation process. Here's a quick look at each of these options so you know what to expect.

NOTE *I provide lots more information about each of these options in Chapter 6.*

Field Selection

When creating most layout types, you'll be given an opportunity to select the fields you want to appear in the layout. The order in which you select the fields is the order in which they appear.

Theme

FileMaker Pro 5's new theme feature enables you to add professioal-looking formatting to your layouts without hiring a professional to create them. Simply select one of the predefined themes, which include font formatting and color.

Sorting and Scripting

For some layout types, you can specify sorting options while creating the layout. This feature is particularly useful when used with the scripting option, which can create a script that automatically sorts the records in the found set and displays them in the layout.

Display Mode

The last option you'll be offered is the mode in which you want to display the completed layout. Choose Preview or Browse mode (whichever is offered) if you want to view or modify the data with the brand new layout. Choose Layout mode if you plan to make changes to the layout right away.

Layout Mode Tools and Commands

When in Layout mode, FileMaker Pro offers a variety of tools and commands that enable you to create, modify, and organize the layouts in your database. In this section, I introduce all the Layout mode status area tools and menu commands.

Status Area Tools

In Layout mode, the status area (see Figure 5-8) displays a variety of tool buttons and menus that you can use to work with database layouts. I provide a brief overview of these tools in the section titled "The Status Area in Layout Mode" on page 22; now I'll identify and describe them in detail.

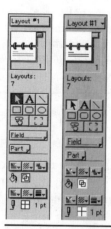

FIGURE 5-8. The status area in Layout mode on Mac OS (left) and Windows (right).

TIP   *If the status area is not displayed, click the status area control button at the bottom of the window (see Figure 5-9).*

FIGURE 5-9. The status area control button on Mac OS (left) and Windows (right).

Layouts Pop-up Menu

The Layouts pop-up menu provides a quick way to switch from one layout to another (see Figure 5-10).

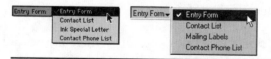

FIGURE 5-10. The Layouts pop-up menu on Mac OS (left) and Windows (right).

Tip   *Although the Layouts pop-up menu lets you switch from one layout to another in all FileMaker Pro modes, it only displays a complete list of database layouts in Layout mode. I explain how to exclude layouts from the Layouts pop-up menu in the section titled "Excluding a Layout from the Layouts Pop-up Menu with the Layout Setup Dialog Box" on page 333.*

Book

In Layout mode, the book is another tool for switching from one layout to another. For more information about using the book, refer to the section titled "Book Icon" on page 18.

Tool Panel

The eight buttons on the tool panel change the function of the mouse pointer so you can use it to work with a layout. There are three ways to select a tool panel button:

- Click the button once to select the tool for one-time use. When you are finished using it, the mouse pointer returns to the pointer tool.

- Double-click the button to select the tool for multiple uses. The tool remains active until you click or double-click another tool.

- Press the Enter key on the numeric keypad (not the Return or Enter key with the letter keys) to toggle between the pointer tool and the last tool you used.

Here's a description of each tool.

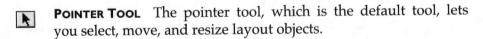 **POINTER TOOL**   The pointer tool, which is the default tool, lets you select, move, and resize layout objects.

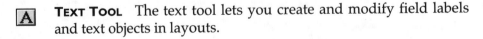 **TEXT TOOL**   The text tool lets you create and modify field labels and text objects in layouts.

LINE TOOL The line tool lets you draw straight lines.

RECTANGLE TOOL The rectangle tool lets you draw rectangles and squares.

ROUNDED RECTANGLE TOOL The rounded rectangle tool lets you draw rectangles and squares with rounded corners.

OVAL TOOL The oval tool lets you draw ovals and circles.

BUTTON TOOL The button tool lets you draw buttons that can be linked to button commands or FileMaker Pro scripts. I tell you about buttons and scripting in Chapter 12.

PORTAL TOOL The portal tool lets you create portals that display fields from related databases. I tell you about related files in Chapter 11.

Field Tool

The field tool lets you add an existing field to the layout. To use it, drag it onto the layout, then select a field in the Specify Field dialog box that appears. I tell you all about using the field tool to add fields in the section titled "Adding Layout Objects" on page 234.

NOTE *The field tool does not let you create fields—it only lets you add existing fields to a layout. To create a field, you must use the Define Fields dialog box, which you can read more about in the section titled "Using the Define Fields Dialog Box" on page 60.*

Part Tool

The part tool offers one way to add a part to the layout. To use it, drag it onto the layout where you want to insert the part. Use the Part Definition dialog box that appears to select the type of part that you want. I explain how to use the part tool in the section titled "Adding a Part" on page 258.

Color, Pattern, and Width Palettes

Five palettes or menus let you set the color, pattern, and line thickness of objects you draw or select.

FILL COLOR AND PATTERN   The fill area (see Figure 5-11) displays a color palette (see Figure 5-12) and pattern palette (see Figure 5-13). You can use them to select the color and pattern of the interior of enclosed layout objects, such as shapes and fields.

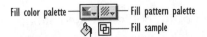

FIGURE 5-11. The fill color and pattern area.

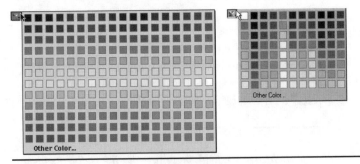

FIGURE 5-12. The color palette on Mac OS (left) and Windows (right) with different palette options selected in the Application Preferences dialog box.

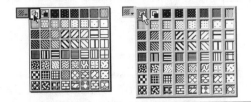

FIGURE 5-13. The pattern palette on Mac OS (left) and Windows (right).

NOTE *The number of colors that appear in the color palettes depends on the Color Palette option selected in the Layout tab of the Application Preferences dialog box. Figure 5-12 shows the Web palette (right) and System subset palette (left). I cover the Color Palette option in the section titled "Color Palette" on page 37.*

 EFFECTS   The Effects button beside the fill area displays a menu of special effects (see Figure 5-14) that you can apply to a selected layout object. This is a quick and easy way to make your layouts more interesting.

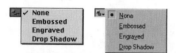

FIGURE 5-14. The Effects button menu on Mac OS (left) and Windows (right).

PEN COLOR, PATTERN, AND THICKNESS   The pen area (see Figure 5-15) displays a color palette (see Figure 5-12), pattern palette (see Figure 5-13), and line thickness palette (see Figure 5-16). You can use them to select the color, pattern, and line thickness of lines, shape borders, and field borders.

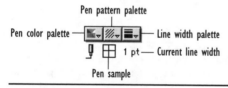

FIGURE 5-15. The pen color, pattern, and line width area.

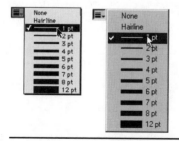

FIGURE 5-16. The line width palette on Mac OS (left) and Windows (right).

Part Label Control

The part label control isn't exactly in the status area, but since it's like so many other status area buttons and appears only in Layout mode, I'll tell you about it here.

The part label control, which is at the bottom of the document window, toggles the part labels between a horizontal and vertical position. As shown in the examples in Figure 5-17, this changes your view of the part label's contents.

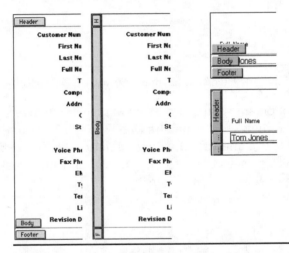

FIGURE 5-17. Part label examples on Mac OS (left) and Windows (right): horizontal part labels (left and top-right) and vertical part labels (center and bottom-right).

TIP   *Although the horizontally displayed part labels are easy to read, they sometimes hide layout objects from view. You can see this in the top-right illustration in Figure 5-17.*

Insert Menu Commands

In Layout mode, the Insert menu (see Figure 5-18) displays a number of commands you can use to modify a layout's structure and contents.

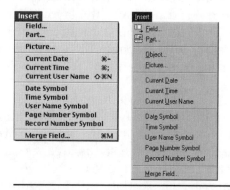

FIGURE 5-18. The Insert menu in Layout mode on Mac OS (left) and Windows (right).

 I tell you about using the Insert menu in Browse mode in the section titled "Using Insert Menu Commands" on page 101.

You can use these commands two ways:

• Choose the command to insert the information or symbol into the layout as a text object, then move the object into the desired position in the layout.

• Position the insertion point inside an existing text object and choose the command to insert the information or symbol at the insertion point.

The Insert menu commands available in Layout mode can be broken down into four categories: layout formatting components, static text, dynamic text symbols, and merge fields.

Layout Formatting Components

The first three commands under the Insert menu enable you to insert layout formatting components into the existing layout.

FIELD   The Field command displays the Specify Field dialog box, which you use to insert a field into the layout. This is the menu equivalent of the Field tool in the status area, as discussed in the section titled "Field Tool" on page 181. I explain how to insert fields into layouts in the section titled "Adding a Standard Field" on page 234.

PART   The Part command displays the Part Definition dialog box, which you use to insert a part into the layout. This is the menu equivalent to the Part tool in the status area, as discussed in the section titled "Part Tool" on page 181. I tell you how to insert parts into layouts in the section titled "Adding a Part" on page 258.

PICTURE   The Picture command displays the Insert Picture dialog box, which you use to insert a picture into the layout. I explain how to insert a picture into a layout in the section titled "Adding an Image" on page 241.

Static Text

The static text commands enter information as text that does not change. There are three options:

CURRENT DATE   The Current Date command enters the current date, as determined by your computer's clock.

CURRENT TIME   The Current Time command enters the current time, as determined by your computer's clock.

CURRENT USER NAME   The Current User Name command enters the current user name, as determined by settings in the Application Preferences dialog box.

Dynamic Text Symbols

The dynamic text symbols commands enter character combinations that display as information, when viewed in Browse or Preview mode or on a printed report. The information displayed by the symbols can change based on the type of information. There are five options:

TIP *You don't need to use the Insert menu's commands to enter these symbols. If you know what a symbol is, simply type it into a text object.*

DATE SYMBOL The Date Symbol command enters two forward slashes (//) that display as the current date, as determined by your computer's clock.

TIME SYMBOL The Time Symbol command enters two colons (::) that display as the current time, as determined by your computer's clock.

NOTE *Don't expect to see live time changes in Browse and Preview mode when you view the time symbol. The time changes only when switching to a different record or page.*

USER NAME SYMBOL The User Name Symbol command enters two vertical lines (| |) that display as the user name, as determined by settings in the Application Preferences dialog box.

PAGE NUMBER SYMBOL The Page Number Symbol command enters two pound signs (##) that display as the page number. This symbol is normally used in a header or footer of a layout, which is displayed only once on each printed or previewed page. The page number symbol appears as a question mark (?) when viewed in Browse mode.

RECORD NUMBER SYMBOL   The Record Number Symbol command enters two at signs (@@) that display as the number of the current record. This symbol normally is used in the body of a layout, which is displayed for each record in the found set.

Merge Fields

The Merge Fields command displays the Specify Field dialog box, which you can use to enter a merge field. I explain what a merge field is in the section titled "Merge Field" on page 171, and how to enter merge fields into a layout in "Adding a Merge Field" on page 236.

TIP   *If you know the name of a field that you want to enter as a merge field, simply type two less than signs (<<) followed by the exact field name and two greater than signs (>>). You may find this a lot quicker than using the Specify Field dialog box if you need to enter more than just one or two merge fields.*

View Menu and Show Submenu Commands

The View menu (see Figure 5-19) and its Show submenu (see Figure 5-20) offer commands to display or hide what I think of as layout aids. These items help you see and work with layout objects.

To display or hide an item, choose its command from the View menu or Show submenu. An item with a check mark to its left is displayed.

Here's a description of what each command does. Pay close attention—most of these options are not discussed elsewhere in this book.

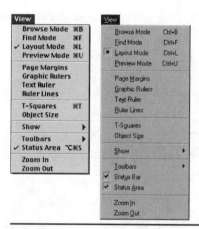

FIGURE 5-19. The View menu in Layout mode on Mac OS (left) and Windows (right).

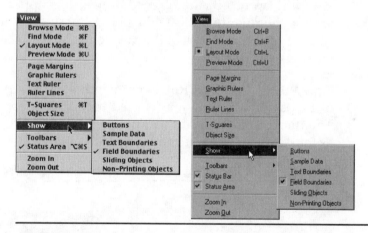

FIGURE 5-20. The Show submenu under the View menu on Mac OS (left) and Windows (right).

PAGE MARGINS   The Page Margins command displays the unusable area around the edge of the page in gray (see Figure 5-21). (Normally, this area doesn't show at all.) FileMaker Pro does not allow you to place layout objects within the margin area.

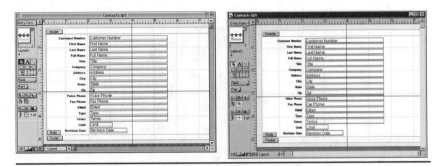

FIGURE 5-21. Graphic ruler, page margins, T-squares, and ruler lines displayed on Mac OS (left) and Windows (right).

GRAPHIC RULERS   The Graphic Rulers command displays a ruler at the top and left side of the layout window (see Figure 5-21). As you drag an object, the object's dimensions appear as a shaded area on the ruler to indicate the object's position. You can use this ruler to get a rough idea of the position or size of a layout object as you move or resize it.

TEXT RULER   The Text Ruler command displays a ruler at the top of the layout window for selected text objects (see Figure 5-22). The ruler offers character and paragraph formatting options such as font, size, style, justification, and tab settings.

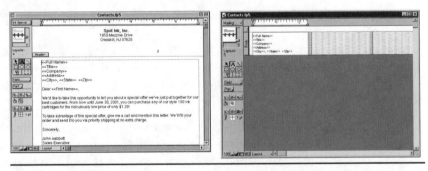

FIGURE 5-22. The text ruler displayed for a text object on Mac OS (left) and Windows (right).

RULER LINES   The Ruler Lines command displays a grid of lines that correspond to the unit measurements on the graphic rulers (see Figure 5-21). You can use these lines to help you align layout objects as you move them.

TIP   *The Set Alignment command, although not entirely intuitive, offers a more exact way to align objects. I explain how to use the Set Alignment and Align commands in the section titled "Aligning Objects" on page 323.*

T-SQUARES   The T-Squares command displays a horizontal and vertical line across the center of the layout (see Figure 5-21). You can drag these lines into desired positions, then use them to line up objects, which "snap" to the lines when you drag them close.

OBJECT SIZE   This command displays the Size window (see Figure 5-23), which provides location and dimension information for one or more selected items. The Size window stays on top of all other windows, even when it is inactive. You can move and close it like any other window.

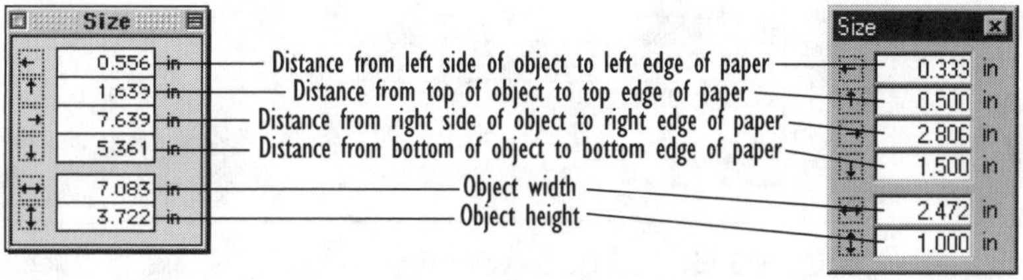

FIGURE 5-23. The Size window on Mac OS (left) and Windows (right).

BUTTONS   The Buttons command puts a gray border around any button or other layout object formatted as a button. I tell you about buttons in Chapter 12.

SAMPLE DATA   The Sample Data command fills fields with data from the current record (see Figure 5-24). If a field in the current record is empty, FileMaker Pro puts phrases such as "Customizable buttons" and random numbers, dates, and times in the fields. This helps you determine the correct size to display a field's contents.

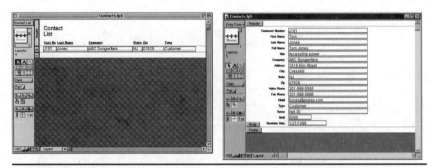

FIGURE 5-24. Sample data displayed on Mac OS (left) and Windows (right).

TEXT BOUNDARIES The Text Boundaries command puts a box around text objects on a layout (see Figure 5-25). This box does not print; it merely indicates the area occupied by the text object.

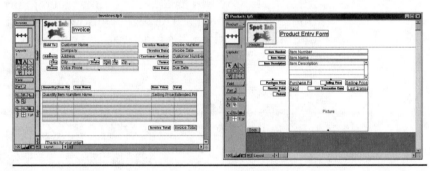

FIGURE 5-25. Text boundaries, field boundaries, sliding objects, and nonprinting objects displayed on Mac OS (left) and Windows (right).

FIELD BOUNDARIES The Field Boundaries command, which is selected by default, puts a box around fields on a layout. This box does not print; it just shows you the area occupied by the field. You can see field boundaries in all layout illustrations in this chapter.

TIP *To print boxes around fields, use the Field Borders command under the Format menu. I tell you how in the section titled "Applying Field Formats" on page 313.*

SLIDING OBJECTS The Sliding Objects command displays arrows on any objects that are set to slide up or to the left (see Figure 5-25). This makes it easy to identify sliding objects at a glance. I tell you more about sliding objects in the section titled "Sliding Layout Objects" on page 538.

NON-PRINTING OBJECTS The Non-printing Objects command displays gray boxes around any object that will not appear in Preview mode or on a printed report (see Figure 5-25). I explain nonprinting objects in the section titled "Preventing Layout Objects from Printing" on page 536.

Layouts Menu Commands

In Layout mode, the Records menu is replaced with a Layouts menu (see Figure 5-26). This menu is full of commands for working with the layouts in your database file.

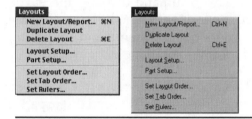

FIGURE 5-26. The Layouts menu on Mac OS (left) and Windows (right).

NEW LAYOUT/REPORT This command displays the New Layout/ Report dialog box, which you can use to create—you guessed it— a new layout or report.

DUPLICATE LAYOUT The Duplicate Layout command makes an exact copy of the current layout and names it by appending the word "copy" to the end of the current layout's name. The duplicate becomes the current layout.

TIP *If you want to make major changes to a layout, use the Duplicate Layout command to make a copy of the layout before you change the original. Then, if you like the changes, delete the copy. Why bother? Because FileMaker Pro automatically saves all changes that you make to a layout. If you didn't make a copy you'd be stuck with your changes, whether you liked them or not.*

DELETE LAYOUT The Delete Layout command deletes the current layout. Don't worry—FileMaker Pro displays a confirmation dialog box first, just in case you choose the command or use its shortcut key by mistake.

NOTE *Deleting a layout does not delete the fields on the layout from the database. The fields and the data they contain remain in the database. The only way to delete data is to delete a record or a field from the database.*

LAYOUT SETUP This command displays the Layout Setup dialog box, which you can use to change the layout's name, toggle its display on the Layouts pop-up menu, and set print options such as the number of columns and page margin widths.

PART SETUP This command displays the Part Setup dialog box, which you can use to create, modify, and delete parts from the layout.

SET LAYOUT ORDER This command displays the Set Layout Order dialog box, which you can use to specify the order in which layout names appear on menus and in dialog boxes. You can also use this dialog box to toggle the display of a layout on the Layouts pop-up menu.

SET TAB ORDER This command displays the Set Tab Order dialog box, which you can use to specify the order in which fields are activated when you press the Tab key in Browse mode.

SET RULERS This command displays the Set Rulers dialog box, which you can use to specify the units and grid spacing options for the ruler and ruler lines that you can display in Layout mode.

Arrange Menu Commands

The Arrange menu (see Figure 5-27) is another menu that appears only in Layout mode. It offers commands for working with selected layout objects.

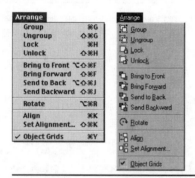

FIGURE 5-27. The Arrange menu on Mac OS (left) and Windows (right).

Group/Ungroup

The Group and Ungroup commands are opposites that work on selected objects.

GROUP The Group command joins multiple selected objects (see Figure 5-28, left) into one object (see Figure 5-28, right). This makes it easy to work with multiple objects together. Once grouped, selection handles appear around the group rather than each individual object in the group. You must have at least two objects or groups selected to use this command.

UNGROUP The Ungroup command separates members of a group (see Figure 5-28, right) into individual objects or groups (see Figure 5-28, left). This makes it possible to work with a member of a group without changing the entire group. You must have a group selected to use this command.

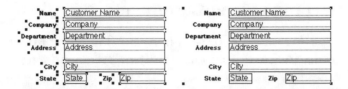

FIGURE 5-28. Individual selected layout objects (left) and the same objects after using the Group command (right).

Lock/Unlock

The Lock and Unlock commands are also opposites that work on selected layout objects.

LOCK The Lock command makes a selected object unmovable until it is unlocked. This command usually is used to prevent an object from being moved accidentally while modifying a layout. Locked items appear with gray selection handles rather than black ones (see Figure 5-29).

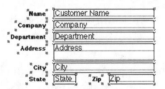

FIGURE 5-29. The layout objects from the left side of Figure 5-28 after using the Lock command.

UNLOCK The Unlock command makes a selected item moveable again. A locked item must be selected to use the Unlock command.

Stacking Order Commands

Every object that you place on a layout is on a different layer of the layout. The stacking order commands—Bring to Front, Bring Forward, Send to Back, and Send Backward—let you change a selected object's layer.

If the concept of layered objects is new to you, here's an analogy to help you understand it. Think of each object on a layout being drawn on a separate sheet of clear overhead transparency. If one object is drawn in the same space as another, the one on the top-most transparency is the one that is clearly visible; the other one is blocked. Using the stacking order commands is like shuffling the stack of transparencies so different items are visible. Since the stacking order also determines the order in which objects are drawn, these commands can also change how things appear on screen.

Figure 5-30 shows an example of three overlapping objects, each on a different level. In the left illustration, the striped box, which is in the middle layer, is selected. In the center illustration, the selected box has been moved to the bottom layer. In the right illustration, the selected box has been moved to the top layer.

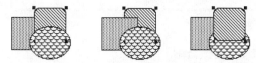

FIGURE 5-30. Stacking order example with the selected box in the middle layer (left), bottom layer (center), and top layer (right).

There are four stacking order commands, each of which works on the selected layout object(s).

BRING TO FRONT The Bring to Front command moves the selected object to the top layer.

BRING FORWARD The Bring Forward command moves the selected object up one layer.

SEND TO BACK The Send to Back command moves the selected object to the bottom layer.

SEND BACKWARD The Send Backward command moves the selected object down one layer.

Rotate

The Rotate command rotates a selected layout object 90° clockwise around its center axes—each time you select it. Selecting this command repeatedly can display the object at 90°, 180° (upside-down), and 270°. You can see all this in Figure 5-31.

FIGURE 5-31. Rotated text example.

TIP   *To rotate a field label and field together, group them first, then rotate them.*

Alignment Commands

The alignment commands enable you to align selected objects with each other. I provide detailed instructions for using these commands in the section titled "Aligning Objects" on page 323. Here's a quick overview.

ALIGN   The Align command applies the alignment options set in the Set Alignment dialog box. If the Top to Bottom and Left to Right alignment options are both set to None in the Set Alignment dialog box, the Align command will be gray.

SET ALIGNMENT   This command displays the Set Alignment dialog box, which you use to specify vertical (Top to Bottom) and horizontal (Left to Right) alignment options.

NOTE   *To align text within selected fields or text objects, use the Align Text submenu under the Format menu. I tell you more about formatting options in Chapter 8.*

Object Grids

The Object Grids command, which is turned on by default, restricts the movement of layout objects so they must "snap" to an invisible grid. Although this feature can be a nuisance at times, it certainly can help you align layout objects as you move them.

 You can override the Object Grids feature temporarily by holding down the Command key (Mac OS) or Alt key (Windows) while you drag an object.

Step-by-Step

Since this chapter was filled primarily with reference material, there's no real step-by-step tutorial. But if you're interested in reviewing the information I provided, follow these steps.

1. Use Finder (Mac OS) or Windows Explorer (Windows) techniques to duplicate any one of the step-by-step tutorial files you created or modified at the end of previous chapters. If you haven't been working on these files, duplicate any File-Maker Pro database file or download the files from the companion Web site for this book, http://www.gilesrd.com/fmprocomp/.

2. Open the duplicate file.

3. Browse this chapter to review the concepts it discusses. Try different menu commands, open various dialog boxes. Don't be afraid to experiment! The file is a duplicate so messing it up won't hurt a thing.

Creating New Layouts

Chapter 5 told you all about Layout mode, layout objects, and layout tools and commands. But the first step to working with a layout is creating it. In this chapter, I explain how you can use FileMaker Pro's New Layout/Report dialog box to create a wide variety of layouts in your databases.

NOTE *All the instructions in this chapter must be performed in Layout mode. To switch to Layout mode, choose Layout from the View menu or press Command-L (Mac OS) or Control-L (Windows). I tell you more about Layout mode in the section titled "Layout Mode" on page 12 and throughout Chapter 5.*

Using the New Layout/Report Dialog Box

The first step to creating a new layout from scratch is to open the New Layout/Report dialog box. Choose New Layout/Report from the Layouts menu (see Figure 6-1) or press Command-N (Mac OS) or Control-N (Windows). The New Layout/Report dialog box appears (see Figure 6-2).

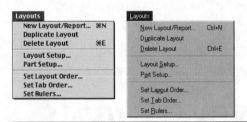

FIGURE 6-1. The Layouts menu on Mac OS (left) and Windows (right).

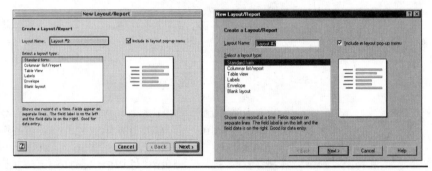

FIGURE 6-2. The New Layout/Report dialog box on Mac OS (left) and Windows (right).

Naming the Layout

When you first open the New Layout dialog box, the Layout Name box contains a default layout name created by appending a number to *Layout #*. This name is boring and doesn't say much about the layout. Fortunately, you're not stuck with it.

To enter a preferred name for the new layout, type it into the Layout Name box. You can name a layout anything you like. Make it short but descriptive so you and others who access the database know what the layout is for.

Setting the Layout Pop-up Menu Display Option

The Include in Layout pop-up menu check box, which is turned on by default, determines whether the layout will appear on the Layout pop-up menu in the status area. To exclude the layout from this menu in Browse, Find, and Preview modes, turn this check box off. The layout name will always appear in the Layout pop-up menu in Layout mode.

TIP *You can change this setting in the Layout Setup and Set Layout Order dialog boxes. I discuss both of these dialog boxes in the section titled "Managing Layouts" on page 331.*

Selecting the Layout Type

Next, select the type of layout that you want to create. As I discuss in the section titled "Layout Types" on page 174, FileMaker Pro offers six preset layout types, each of which is best suited for a particular purpose. The layout type you select determines what happens when you click Next:

STANDARD FORM OR TABLE VIEW The Specify Fields screen, which you use to select the fields that you want on the layout, appears (see Figure 6-5). Continue reading in the section titled "Selecting Fields" on page 205.

COLUMNAR LIST/REPORT The Choose Report Layout screen appears (see Figure 6-4). Continue reading in the section titled "Choosing a Report Layout" on page 204.

LABELS The label setup screen, which you use to set label size options, appears. Continue reading in the section titled "Setting Label Size Options" on page 218.

ENVELOPE The Specify Envelope Contents screen (see Figure 6-20, right), which you use to select and place merge fields for an envelope layout, appears. Continue reading in the section titled "Specifying Label or Envelope Contents" on page 219.

BLANK Instead of a Next button, you'll click a Finish button. The layout appears (see Figure 6-3). Blank layouts do not include any fields—just a header, body, and footer—so there are no additional options to set.

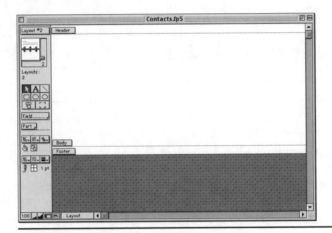

FIGURE 6-3. A blank layout on Mac OS.

Choosing a Report Layout

The Choose Report Layout screen of the New Layout/Report dialog box (see Figure 6-4) enables you to select a format for your columnar report.

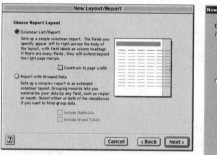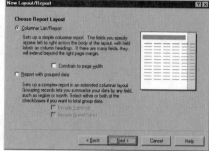

FIGURE 6-4. The Choose Report Layout screen of the New Layout/Report dialog box on Mac OS (left) and Windows (right).

You have two options:

- **Columnar List/Report** enables you to create a simple list of records in a table-like format. If you select this option, you can turn on the Constrain to page width check box to prevent the fields you select later from extending past the right margin of the page.

- **Report with Grouped Data** also enables you to set up a list of records in a table-like format. But records can be grouped and summarized by a field. If you select this option, you can turn on check boxes to specify whether you want to include subtotals and/or grand totals.

Select options as desired and click Next. The Specify Fields screen (see Figure 6-5), which I discuss next, appears.

Selecting Fields

The Specify Fields screen (see Figure 6-5) enables you to select the fields that you want to appear on a standard form, columnar list/ report, or table view layout.

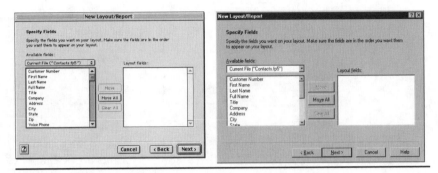

FIGURE 6-5. The Specify Fields screen of the New Layout/Report dialog box on Mac OS (left) and Windows (right).

Adding Field Names to the Field Order List

There are several ways to copy field names from the Available fields list (on the left side of the dialog box) to the Layout fields list (on the right side of the dialog box):

- Click once on the name of a field to select it. Then click the Move button to copy it to the Layout fields list.

- Double-click the name of a field to select it and move it to the Layout fields list all at once.

- Click the Move All button to copy all fields to the Layout fields list.

Modifying the Field Order List

Before you click Next, make sure that the Layout fields list includes all the fields you want to see on the layout, in the order in which you want them to appear. You can modify the Layout fields list to fine-tune your selection before saving it.

- To remove a field from the Layout fields list, click the name of the field once to select it and click the Clear button. Or just double-click the name of the field.

- To move a field up or down in the Layout fields list, begin by positioning the mouse pointer on the double-headed arrow to the left of the field name. The mouse pointer turns into a pair of horizontal lines with arrows pointing up and down (see Figure 6-6). Press the mouse button down and drag to move the field name. Or click once on the field name to select it and then press Command-Up-Arrow or Command-Down-Arrow (Mac OS) or Control-Up-Arrow or Control-Down-Arrow (Windows) to move it.

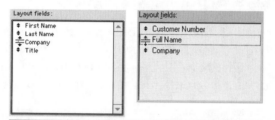

FIGURE 6-6. Preparing to drag a field name on Mac OS (left) and Windows (right).

- To remove all fields from the Layout fields list, click the Clear All button.

Saving the Field Selections

When you are finished selecting the fields to appear in the layout, click the Next button. What happens next depends on what type of layout you are creating:

STANDARD FORM OR TABLE VIEW The Select a Theme screen appears (see Figure 6-13). Continue reading in the section titled "Selecting a Theme" on page 213.

STANDARD COLUMNAR LIST/REPORT The Sort Records screen appears (see Figure 6-8). Continue reading in the section titled "Specifying a Sort Order" on page 209.

COLUMNAR LIST/REPORT WITH GROUPED DATA If you specified that the report should include subtotals (with or without grand totals), the Organize Records by Category screen (see Figure 6-7), which I discuss next, appears. If you specified that the report should include grand totals but not subtotals, the Sort Records screen appears (see Figure 6-8). Continue reading in the section titled "Specifying a Sort Order" on page 209.

Selecting a Grouping Category

If you specified that your columnar list or report should be grouped with subtotals, the Organize Records by Category screen appears (see Figure 6-7). Use this screen to select the fields by which you want to group information for subtotals.

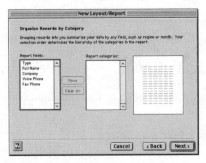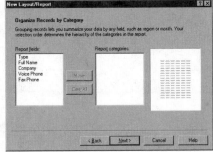

FIGURE 6-7. The Organize Records by Category screen of the New Layout/Report dialog box on Mac OS (left) and Windows (right).

In the Report fields list, select the field by which you want to summarize. Click the Move button to add the field to the Report categories list. You can add as many fields as you like; each one you add will become a subgroup under the first field.

For example, say you're working with Contacts.fp5 and want to group records by type. You'd add the Type field to the Report categories list. Within each type, say you want to group the records by state. You'd add the State field to the Report categories list under the Type field. Of course, you must first include these fields on the report by specifying them in the Specify Fields screen (see Figure 6-5).

TIP   *My advice is to keep things simple here. The more grouping fields you select, the more complex the report will be.*

When you're finished selecting grouping fields, click the Next button. The Sort Records screen (see Figure 6-8), which I discuss next, appears.

Specifying a Sort Order

The next step in creating a columnar list/report layout is to specify a desired sort order for the report. This is a brand new feature in FileMaker Pro 5 that enables you to associate a sort order with a layout. You do this with the Sort Records screen of the New Layout/Report dialog box (see Figure 6-8).

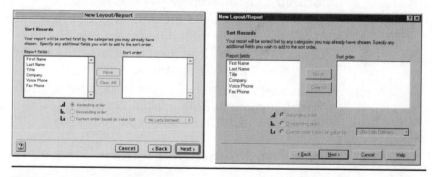

FIGURE 6-8. The Sort Records screen of the New Layout/Report dialog box on Mac OS (left) and Windows (right).

As you may have noticed, the Sort Records screen looks very much like the Sort Records dialog box, which I discuss in Chapter 4. It works the same way, too. For detailed instructions on using this dialog box to set a sort order, consult the section titled "Setting Sort Order" on page 153.

If you're creating a columnar list/report with subtotals, the fields you specified in the Organize Records by Category screen () are automatically included in the Sort Order list. A padlock icon indicates that they cannot be removed. This is because you must sort a columnar report with subtotals in order to see the totals. I tell you more about this in the section titled "Creating a Columnar Report with Summaries" on page 277.

NOTE   *You don't have to set a sort order when creating a standard columnar list/report. As discussed in Chapter 4, you can sort the records in a layout at any time.*

When you're finished setting the sort order, click Next. The screen that appears depends on the type of layout you are creating:

STANDARD COLUMNAR LIST/REPORT The Select a Theme screen appears (see Figure 6-13). Continue reading in the section titled "Selecting a Theme" on page 213.

COLUMNAR LIST/REPORT WITH GROUPED DATA If you specified that the report should include subtotals (with or without grand totals), the Specify Subtotals screen (see Figure 6-9), which I discuss next, appears. If you specified that the report should include grand totals but not subtotals, the Specify Grand Totals screen appears (see Figure 6-12). Continue reading in the section titled "Specifying Grand Total Fields" on page 212.

Specifying Subtotal Fields

To include subtotals in a columnar report, you must specify which summary fields should be used for the subtotals. You do this with the Specify Subtotals screen of the New Layout/Report window (see Figure 6-9).

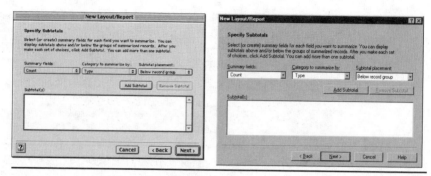

FIGURE 6-9. The Specify Subtotals screen of the New Layout/Report dialog box on Mac OS (left) and Windows (right).

Here's how it works. First select a summary field from the Summary fields menu. Then choose one of the grouping fields from the Category to summarize by menu. Then select a location from the Subtotal placement menu. Finally, click the Add Subtotal button to add the information to the Subtotal(s) list (see Figure 6-10). Repeat this process for each subtotal you want.

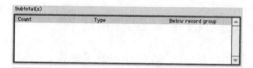

FIGURE 6-10. The Subtotal(s) list with one subtotal added.

If you haven't created the summary field you need yet, choose Create Summary Field from the menu and use the Options for Summary Field dialog box that appears (see Figure 6-11) to create a new summary field. When you click OK, you'll be returned to the Specify Subtotals screen and the new field will appear in the Summary fields menu.

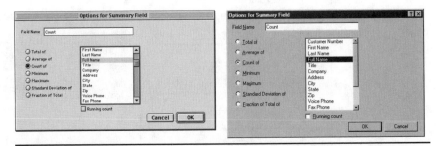

FIGURE 6-11. The Options for Summary Field dialog box on Mac OS (left) and Windows (right).

When you're finished setting up subtotals, click Next. If you specified that the report should include subtotals but not grand totals, the Select a Theme screen appears (see Figure 6-13). Continue reading in the section titled "Selecting a Theme" on page 213. If you specified that the report should include grand totals, the Specify Grand Totals screen, which I discuss next, appears (see Figure 6-12).

Specifying Grand Total Fields

The Specify Grand Totals screen looks and works very much like the Specify Subtotals screen (see Figure 6-9), so I won't go into detail here. The only thing you don't have to do when setting up a grand total is to specify a category. Otherwise, just follow the instructions in the section titled "Specifying Subtotal Fields" on page 210 to add as many grand totals as desired.

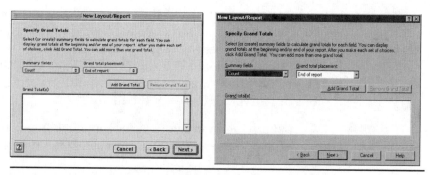

FIGURE 6-12. The Specify Grand Totals screen of the New Layout/Report dialog box on Mac OS (left) and Windows (right).

When you're finished, click Next to display the Select a Theme screen (see Figure 6-13), which I discuss next.

Selecting a Theme

The next step in creating a standard form, columnar list/report, or table view layout is to select a theme. This feature enables you to include attractive formatting in your reports without a lot of manual formatting work. You select a theme with the Select a Theme screen (see Figure 6-13).

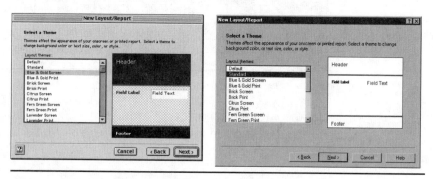

FIGURE 6-13. The Select a Theme screen of the New Layout/Report dialog box on Mac OS (left) and Windows (right).

Click to select one of the themes in the Layout themes scrolling list. When you select a theme, a preview of it appears in the right side of the dialog box. *Default* uses currently defined text and object formatting for the theme. *Standard* uses the preset File-Maker Pro formatting—the same formatting used in previous versions of FileMaker Pro—for the theme.

When you have made your selection, click Next. Again, the type of layout you are creating determines what happens:

STANDARD FORM   Instead of a Next button, you'll click a Finish button. The layout appears (see Figure 6-14). Although a standard form layout includes a header and footer, you cannot set them within the New Layout/Report dialog box.

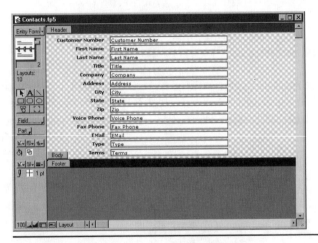

FIGURE 6-14. A standard form layout on Windows.

COLUMNAR LIST/REPORT OR TABLE VIEW   The Header and Footer Information screen appears (see Figure 6-15). I discuss that next.

Setting the Header and Footer

The ability to set a header and footer while creating a report is another new feature of FileMaker Pro version 5. And the Header and Footer Information screen (see Figure 6-15) makes it very easy to do.

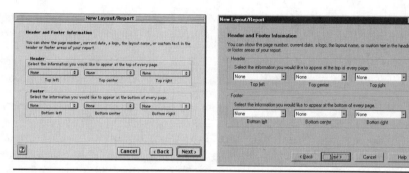

FIGURE 6-15. The Header and Footer Information screen of the New Layout/ Report dialog box on Mac OS (left) and Windows (right).

A *header* is content (text, graphics, etc.) that appears on the top of each page of a report. A *footer* is content that appears at the bottom of each page. The Header and Footer Information screen offers six locations for placing content: Top left, Top center, and Top right for the header; and Bottom left, Bottom center, and Bottom right for the footer.

To set a header or footer, use the menus within the dialog box to select an option for each location in which you want to place header or footer content. Here are your options:

- **None** leaves the location blank.

- **Page Number** places the page number symbol in the location. When the report is previewed or printed, this number will be different for each page.

- **Current Date** places the date symbol in the location. When the report is browsed, previewed, or printed, the current date appears.

- **Layout Name** places the name of the layout in the location.

- **Large Custom Text** displays the Custom Text dialog box (see Figure 6-16), which you can use to enter text you want to appear in the location. The text will be formatted with a large font size.

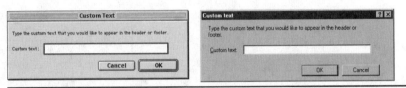

FIGURE 6-16. The Custom Text dialog box on Mac OS (left) and Windows (right).

- **Small Custom Text** also displays the Custom Text dialog box (see Figure 6-16), which you can use to enter text you want to appear in the location. The text will be formatted with a small font size.

- **Logo** displays the Insert Picture dialog box (see Figure 6-17), which you can use to locate, select, and open a picture file to place in the location.

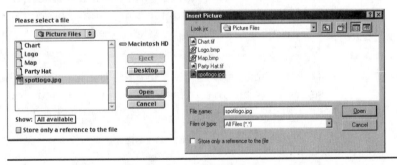

FIGURE 6-17. The Insert Picture dialog box on Mac OS (left) and Windows (right).

When you are finished making selections, click the Next button. What appears next depends on the type of layout you are creating:

COLUMNAR LIST/REPORT The Create a Script for this Report screen appears (see Figure 6-18). I discuss that in the next section.

TABLE VIEW The You are Finished screen appears (see Figure 6-23). Continue reading in the section titled "Selecting a Layout Viewing Mode" on page 222.

Creating a Script for a Report

The Create a Script for this Report screen of the New Record/Layout report dialog box enables you to specify whether FileMaker Pro should create a script to automate the display of the layout. Although scripting is not new to FileMaker Pro, the ability to create a script when you create a layout is. This feature is especially useful if your layout includes sorting instructions and you always want to view the report with the records sorted as specified.

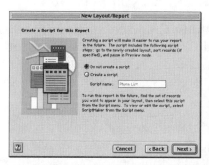

FIGURE 6-18. The Create a Script for this Report screen of the New Layout/Report dialog box on Mac OS (left) and Windows (right).

If you elect to create a script, FileMaker Pro creates a script that automatically switches to the layout, sorts records (if sort instructions were provided), and displays the layout in Preview mode. Once the layout and script have been created, displaying the layout is as easy as choosing a command from the Scripts menu.

NOTE *I discuss FileMaker Pro's scripting feature, including how to create, modify, and run scripts, in Chapter 12.*

The dialog box has two options:

• **Do not create a script** does not create a script for the layout.

• **Create a script** creates a script for the layout with the name you specify in the Script name box.

When you click Next, the You are Finished! screen (see Figure 6-23) appears. Continue reading in the section titled "Selecting a Layout Viewing Mode" on page 222.

Setting Label Size Options

When you click Next in the New Layout/Report dialog box to create labels, the label setup screen appears (see Figure 6-19). Use it to set the size of the label stock on which you will print the labels.

FileMaker Pro includes a bunch of predefined label templates for popular Avery and CoStar brand labels. Using one of these templates is the easiest way to create properly sized and spaced labels—provided, of course, that you're using one of the supported label stocks.

Specifying a custom label size is a bit more work, but the results should be satisfactory—that is, if you can use a ruler and count. You see, to create custom labels, you need to know the label dimensions and the number of labels across a sheet. But this may be necessary if FileMaker Pro does not include predefined measurements for your labels.

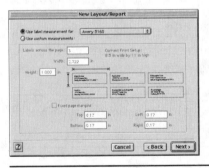 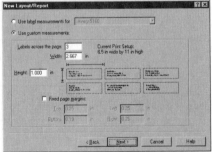

FIGURE 6-19. The label setup screen in the New Layout/Report dialog box on Mac OS (left) and Windows (right).

Choosing One of the Predefined Label Measurements

Select the Use label measurement for option (see Figure 6-19, left), then choose the label stock you are using from the menu beside it.

Specifying Custom Label Measurements

Select the Use custom measurements option (see Figure 6-19, right), then enter information about your labels in the boxes in the bottom half of the dialog box:

- **Labels across the page** is the number of labels across each label sheet.

- **Width** is the width of the label from its left edge to the left edge of the label beside it. If there is no label beside it, just enter the width of the label.

- **Height** is the height of the label from its top edge to the top edge of the label below it.

- **Fixed page margins** options enable you to enter the size of the Top, Bottom, Left, and Right margins. You must turn on the check box to set the options.

Once you've made your measurement selection or entries, click Next. The Specify Label Contents screen, which I discuss next, appears (see Figure 6-20, left).

Specifying Label or Envelope Contents

The next step for creating labels or envelopes is to select and arrange fields. You do this with the Specify Label Contents screen (see Figure 6-20, left) or the Specify Envelope Contents screen (see Figure 6-20, right) of the New Layout/Report dialog box. The appropriate dialog box appears automatically as part of the envelope or label creation process.

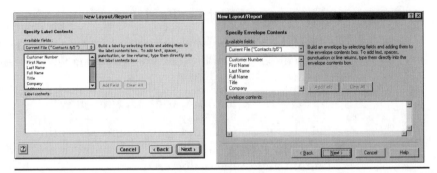

FIGURE 6-20. The Specify Label Contents screen of the New Layout/Report dialog box on Mac OS (left) and the Specify Envelope Contents screen of the New Layout/Report dialog box on Windows (right).

Labels and envelope layouts both take advantage of the merge fields feature of FileMaker Pro, which I tell you about in the section titled "Merge Field" on page 171. This enables you to merge field contents with spaces, punctuation, text, and other characters that you may want to include on labels or envelopes.

Your job is to enter fields and other text (if desired) into the Layout contents box. Here's how.

Adding a Merge Field

Double-click the field name in the Available fields scrolling list. It appears in the Label contents or Envelope Contents box with a pair of less-than signs on its left and a pair of greater-than signs on its right (see Figure 6-21). If you prefer, you can type in the field name, but don't forget the less-than and greater-than signs around it.

FIGURE 6-21. A merge field in the label contents box.

Adding Text, Punctuation, or Spaces

Type the text, punctuation, or space character that you want to include. It appears at the insertion point in the Label contents or Envelope contents box.

Starting a New Line

Press the Return (Mac OS) or Enter (Windows) key at the end of a line.

Removing a Merge Field

Use your mouse pointer to select the field, including the less-than and greater-than signs that surround it. Then press Delete (Mac OS) or Backspace (Windows).

Removing Text or Other Characters

Use your mouse pointer to select the characters that you want to remove. Then press Delete (Mac OS) or Backspace (Windows). To remove all fields and characters, click the Clear All button.

Figure 6-22 shows an example of a field arrangement with spacing and punctuation that's appropriate for mailing labels or envelopes.

FIGURE 6-22. An example of fields arranged for labels or envelopes.

When you're finished setting up the layout contents, click the Next button to display the You are Finished! screen (see Figure 6-23).

Selecting a Layout Viewing Mode

The very last step to creating a columnar list/report, table view, labels, or envelopes layout is to specify the mode in which you want to view the layout. You do this in the You are Finished! screen of the New Layout/Report dialog box (see Figure 6-23).

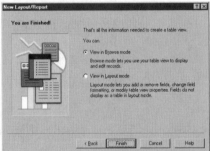

FIGURE 6-23. The You are Finished! screen of the New Layout/Report dialog box on Mac OS for a columnar list/report (left) and on Windows for a table view layout (right).

NOTE *Standard form and blank layouts are displayed automatically in layout mode at the conclusion of the creation process.*

The options that appear in this screen vary depending on the type of layout you are creating:

COLUMNAR LIST/REPORT, LABEL, OR ENVELOPE Your options are Preview mode and Layout mode. Choose Preview if you want to see the data. Choose Layout if you want to fine-tune the layout before you view it. These options are illustrated in Figure 6-24 through Figure 6-27.

TABLE VIEW Your options are Browse mode and Layout mode. Choose Browse if you want to see the data in table view. Choose Layout if you want to modify the layout; it will look like a standard view layout. These options are illustrated in Figure 6-28.

Select the option you want and click the Finish button. The new layout appears in the mode you specified (see Figure 6-24 through Figure 6-28).

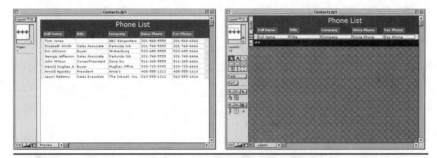

FIGURE 6-24. A standard columnar list/report on Mac OS in Preview mode (left) and Layout mode (right).

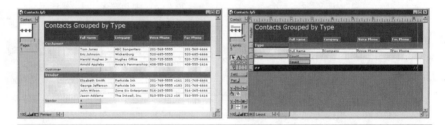

FIGURE 6-25. A columnar list/report with subtotals and grand totals on Windows in Preview mode (left) and Layout mode (right).

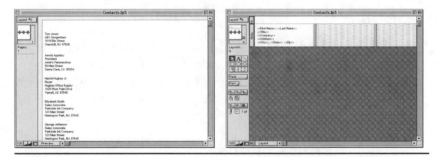

FIGURE 6-26. A label layout on Mac OS in Preview mode (left) and Layout mode (right).

FIGURE 6-27. An envelope layout on Windows in Preview mode (left) and Layout mode (right).

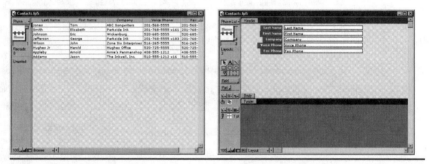

FIGURE 6-28. A table view layout on Windows in Browse mode (left) and Layout mode (right).

Setting Other Layout Options

There are a few additional layout options that you may want to set right after you create a layout, before you start fine-tuning and working with it: print columns, margins, and views. All three are set in the Layout Setup dialog box (see Figure 6-30).

Print Columns

The labels layout shown on the right side of Figure 6-26 works by printing database contents with a multiple-column layout. In that example, the label template accommodates three labels across a sheet. The fields are arranged once in the first column. They are repeated automatically in the second and third columns, which are represented by the light gray area on the right side of the body.

You can create multiple-column layouts for any purpose, not just labels. Just tell FileMaker Pro that the layout should print with multiple columns. Then arrange the layout objects so they fit into the body.

Two Examples

Figure 6-29 shows two examples. The illustration on the right is for a phone list created by including two fields in a columnar list/report layout. The illustration on the right is for a catalog created by removing and rearranging fields on a standard layout. (I explain how to manipulate layout objects in the section titled "Step-by-Step" on page 230.) Since neither of these layouts needs an entire page width, I can print them in two columns to save paper.

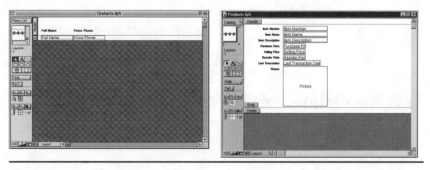

FIGURE 6-29. Two examples of multiple column layouts—one on Mac OS (left) and the other on Windows (right)—*before* applying multiple columns.

Setting It Up

Start by choosing Layout Setup from the Layouts menu (see Figure 6-1). The General tab of the Layout Setup dialog box for the current layout appears (see Figure 6-30).

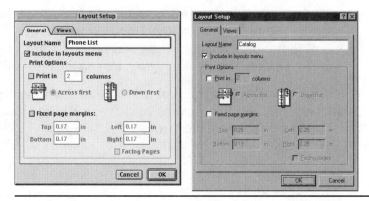

FIGURE 6-30. The General tab of the Layout Setup dialog box on Mac OS (left) and Windows (right).

Turn on the Print in check box in the Print Options area. Then enter the number of columns that you want in the box beside it. To specify the print order of records, select one of the options:

- **Across first** prints records across all columns of the page before starting a new row. This is the default selection.

- **Down first** prints records down the first column of the page before starting a new column.

Click OK to save your settings.

Checking the Result

The current layout changes to reflect the number of columns you selected. The usable area within the body narrows to indicate the amount of space required for each column. The light gray area represents the space required by the other columns. None of the layout objects have been moved. Figure 6-31 shows what the layout looks like in Layout mode, and Figure 6-32 shows what it looks like in Preview mode. (As you can see, both layouts need a little more work; I tell how to fine-tune them in Chapter 7.)

FIGURE 6-31. The examples from Figure 6-29, *after* setting the layout to print in two columns.

FIGURE 6-32. The layouts from Figure 6-31 in Preview mode.

NOTE *To see what a multiple-column layout looks like, you must view it in Preview mode (or print it). Browse mode shows the records in a single column, no matter how many columns are set in the Layout Setup dialog box.*

Margins

By default, FileMaker Pro creates layouts with the narrowest margins supported by your printer driver. This maximizes the amount of space available for the placement of objects on your layout.

Although this may sound like a great feature, it does have a major drawback. Since the margin size is determined by the printer driver, the margins may change depending on the printer driver selected for the computer on which the database is being viewed.

An Example

Here's a real-life example. I have an old Hewlett-Packard LaserJet 4MP printer. Its printer driver supports really tiny margins, enabling me to get a lot on a page. But when I pass my file to someone with, say, a LaserWriter 8 driver, the margins are resized so they're wider. The result? The layout objects on the far right side of the page don't print!

Fortunately, FileMaker Pro enables you to set the exact size for all four page margins. This prevents the margins in a database file from shifting when it's used on various computers.

Setting It Up

Choose Layout Setup from the Layouts menu (see Figure 6-1) to display the General tab of the Layout Setup dialog box for the current layout (see Figure 6-30). Turn on the Fixed page margins check box in the Print Options area of the dialog box. Then enter measurements in the Top, Bottom, Left, and Right boxes (see Figure 6-33). Click OK to save your settings.

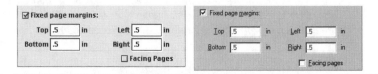

FIGURE 6-33. Setting fixed margins on Mac OS (left) and Windows (right).

Tip *If you plan to take advantage of the fixed margins feature, set the margins when you first create your layouts. This enables you to design your layouts with the final margin sizes set.*

NOTE   *I tell you lots more about printing in Chapter 14.*

Views

FileMaker Pro's views feature enables you to view a layout in a number of different ways: as a form, list, or table. I tell you all about views in the section appropriately titled "Views" on page 15.

In FileMaker Pro version 5, you can now specify which views are available in Browse and Find mode. You do this with the Views tab of the Layout Setup dialog box (see Figure 6-34).

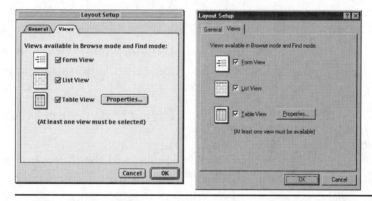

FIGURE 6-34. The Views tab of the Layout Setup dialog box on Mac OS (left) and Windows (right).

Choose Layout Setup from the Layouts menu (see Figure 6-1) to display the Layout Setup dialog box for the current layout. Click the Views tab to display its options (see Figure 6-34). Then turn on the check boxes for each view you want available for the layout in Browse and Find modes. By default, all three views are set to display. Click OK to save your settings.

Step-by-Step

Ready to give layout creation a whirl? Here are step-by-step instructions for creating layouts in Contacts.fp5, one of the databases you've been working on at the end of each chapter. If you've been skipping around in the book and don't have the completed exercise files from Chapter 4 (*not* Chapter 5), you can download them from the companion Web site for this book, http://www.gilesrd.com/fmprocomp/.

Creating a Columnar Report

Spot wants a phone list that includes the customer's full name, title, company name, and phone numbers. Here are the instructions to create the layout.

1. Open the New Layout/Report dialog box, enter *Phone List* in the Layout Name box, select Columnar list/report, and click Next.

2. In the Choose Report Layout screen, select Columnar List/Report. Click Next.

3. In the Specify Fields screen, add the following fields to the Layout fields list: Full Name, Title, Company, Voice Phone, and Fax Phone. Click Next.

4. In the Sort Records screen, add Company to the Sort order list and click Next.

5. In the Select a Theme screen, select Standard from the Layout themes list. Click Next.

6. In the Header and Footer Information screen, use the Logo option on the Top left menu to insert spotlogo.jpg (or any other logo-sized image file on your computer) into the header. Set a centered, Large Custom Text header that says *Contact Phone List*. Set the footer so the Current Date is in

the bottom left and the Page Number is in the bottom right. Click Next.

7. In the Create a Script for this Report screen, select the Create a Script option. If necessary, enter *Contact Phone List* in the Script name box. Click Next.

8. In the You are Finished! screen, select the View the report in Layout mode option and click Finish.

9. Change the layout's margins to a fixed measurement of 0.50 for each side.

You'll make modifications to this layout at the end of Chapter 7.

Creating Mailing Labels

Spot Ink does a lot of advertising by mail and needs mailing labels for its contacts. Here are the instructions for creating a labels layout. When you're finished, your layout should look like the one in Figure 6-35.

1. Open the New Layout/Report dialog box, enter *Mailing Labels* in the Layout Name box, select Labels, and click Next.

2. In the label setup dialog box, choose Avery 5261 from the label measurements menu and click Next. (If you prefer, you can select a label size for labels you have on hand.)

3. In the Specify Label Contents screen, add merge fields, spaces, and punctuation so the Label contents box looks like the one in Figure 6-22. Click Next.

4. In the You are Finished! screen, select View in Layout mode and click Finish.

5. Compare your layout to the one in Figure 6-35. Then view the layout in Browse and Preview modes to see how it looks.

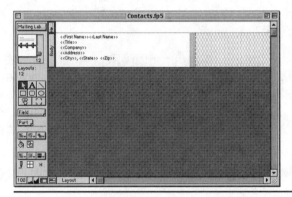

FIGURE 6-35. The completed Mailing Labels layout on Mac OS.

Arranging Layout Objects

In Chapter 6, I explain how to use the New Layout/Report dialog box to create new layouts. But in most cases, the layout you end up with will not be exactly the way you want it to be. That's when it's time to fine-tune it, using the layout tools and commands available in Layout mode.

In this chapter, I explain how you can modify the structure of layouts to meet your needs.

NOTE   *All the instructions in this chapter must be performed in Layout mode. To switch to Layout mode, choose Layout from the View menu or press Command-L (Mac OS) or Control-L (Windows). I tell you more about Layout mode in the section titled "Layout Mode" on page 12 and throughout Chapter 5.*

Working with Layout Objects

Once you've created a layout, you can add and manipulate layout objects to fine-tune it for your specific needs. In this section, I tell you how to work with layout objects such as fields, text objects, drawn objects, and images.

Adding Layout Objects

When you create any type of layout except a blank layout, File-Maker Pro automatically places fields and field labels or merge fields on the appropriate layout part(s). You can modify a layout at any time to add more fields, as well as text objects, drawn objects, and images.

 NOTE   *You can also add portals and buttons, which I discuss in Chapters 11 and 12, respectively.*

Adding a Standard Field

You can use the field tool to add a field, with or without a field label, to a layout. Simply drag the field tool onto the layout and select the field that you want.

Start by positioning your mouse pointer over the field tool in the status area. Press the mouse button down and drag the tool onto the layout. As you drag, a dotted line border indicates where the field will go when you release the mouse button (see Figure 7-1).

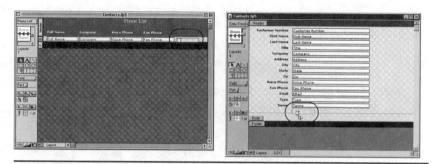

FIGURE 7-1. Dragging the field tool onto a layout on Mac OS (left) and Windows (right).

When you have the field in position, release the mouse button. The Specify Field dialog box appears (see Figure 7-2).

TIP   *Another way to add a field is to choose Field from the Insert menu (see Figure 7-4). This also displays the Specify Field dialog box (see Figure 7-2). After inserting a field this way, however, you must move the field (and its label, if necessary) into the desired position on your layout.*

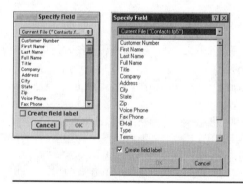

FIGURE 7-2. The Specify Field dialog box on Mac OS (left) and Windows (right).

In the scrolling list of field names, click once on the name of the field that you want to add to select it. To include a field label in the layout to the left of the field, make sure the Create field check box is turned on; otherwise, turn it off. Click OK. The field you specified (with its label, if appropriate) appears on the layout (see Figure 7-3).

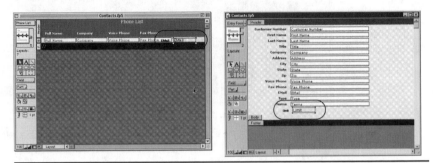

FIGURE 7-3. Newly added fields with field labels on Mac OS (left) and Windows (right).

NOTE *As shown in Figure 7-3, newly added fields and field labels don't always appear exactly where you want them to. I tell you how to move them in the section titled "Moving Objects" on page 251. If your layout uses a FileMaker Pro theme, newly added fields are not formatted to match.*

Adding a Merge Field

Merge fields are added as text objects on layouts. You can either add a merge field as a new text object on the layout or add the merge field within an existing text object on the layout.

ADDING A MERGE FIELD AS A NEW TEXT OBJECT Choose Merge Field from the Insert menu (see Figure 7-4) or press Command-M (Mac OS) or Control-M (Windows). The Specify Field dialog box appears (see Figure 7-2). Select the name of the field that you want to add and click OK. The field appears on the layout (see Figure 7-5).

NOTE *The << and >> characters around merge field names are what identifies them as merge fields. Do not delete these characters!*

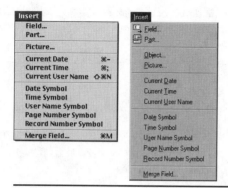

FIGURE 7-4. The Insert menu on Mac OS (left) and Windows (right).

FIGURE 7-5. Merge field added as a text object.

ADDING A MERGE FIELD WITHIN AN EXISTING TEXT OBJECT Click the text tool to select it, then click within the text object to position the blinking insertion point (see Figure 7-6, left). Choose Merge Field from the Insert menu (see Figure 7-4) or press Command-M (Mac OS) or Control-M (Windows). The Specify Field dialog box appears (see Figure 7-2). Select the name of the field that you want to add and click OK. The field appears at the insertion point (see Figure 7-6, right). Click anywhere else on the layout or press the Enter key on the numeric keypad to deselect the text object.

FIGURE 7-6. Two steps to adding a merge field to an existing text object: position the insertion point (left) and insert the field (right).

WARNING *Do not insert a merge field within another merge field in an existing text object. Doing so will prevent FileMaker Pro from recognizing one or both of the fields as merge fields.*

Adding a Text Object

A text object is text that you add to a layout and format as desired. Here are some examples of text objects that you may want to include on your layouts:

- **Field labels**, which can be created automatically by File-Maker Pro when you create a layout or add a field, identify fields. Field labels normally appear in the body to the left of a field name in a standard or single-page form layout or in the header above a field name in a columnar report or extended columnar layout.

- **Report titles**, which normally appear in the header of a layout, identify the purpose of the layout.

- **Instructional text**, which normally appears in the header or footer of the layout, explains how to enter data or work with a layout.

- **Informational text**, which normally appears in the title header, header, footer, or title footer, can explain where the database information comes from, who maintains it, whether it is copyrighted—or anything else you need to communicate. Informational text can also include a date, time, user name, or other information that can be entered as static or dynamic text.

How you add a text object depends on the type of text object that you want to add and where you want to put it.

ADDING A TEXT OBJECT ANYWHERE IN THE LAYOUT Click the text tool to select it. The mouse pointer turns into an I-beam pointer. Click in the layout window where you want the text to appear. A box with a blinking insertion point appears. Type the text. When you are finished, click anywhere else on the layout or press the Enter key on the numeric keypad to complete the entry. Figure 7-7 shows each of these steps.

FIGURE 7-7. Four steps to entering a field label: Position I-beam pointer on layout (left), click to display box and insertion point (left-center), type text in box (right-center), and click elsewhere to accept entry (right).

ADDING A TEXT OBJECT WITHIN AN EXISTING TEXT OBJECT Click the text tool to select it, then click within the text object to position the blinking insertion point. Type the text. When you are finished, click anywhere else on the layout or press the Enter key on the numeric keypad to complete the entry and deselect the text object.

PASTING STATIC OR DYNAMIC INFORMATIONAL TEXT Click the text tool to select it, then click to position the blinking insertion point in the layout window or within an existing text object where you want the text to appear. Choose an option from the Insert menu (see Figure 7-4). The item or symbol for the item appears. Click anywhere else on the layout or press the Enter key on the numeric keypad to complete the entry and deselect the text object. I discuss the options available in Layout mode under the Insert menu in the section titled "Insert Menu Commands" on page 185.

TIP

If you prefer, you can choose an option from the Insert menu without first positioning an insertion point with the text tool. The text or symbol will appear as a text object on the layout and can be moved into position as desired. I tell you how to move objects in the section titled "Moving Objects" on page 251.

WARNING *When entering symbols for dynamic text, the size of the text object must be sufficient to display all characters of the dynamic information being displayed. Otherwise, characters may be lost. I explain how to resize text objects in the section titled "Resizing Objects" on page 248.*

Drawing a Line or Shape

You can use the drawing tools on the tool panel, which I describe in the section titled "Tool Panel" on page 180, to add a drawn object such as a line, box, or circle. These simple graphic elements, when added tastefully and imaginatively, can improve the overall appearance of a layout.

NOTE *I tell you how to change the color, pattern, and line thickness of drawn objects in the section titled "Changing the Appearance of an Existing Drawn Object" on page 330.*

ADDING A LINE Click the line tool to select it. The mouse pointer turns into a crosshair pointer. Position the pointer where you want the line to begin. Press the mouse button down and drag. As you drag, a dotted line appears. When the line is the desired length, release the mouse button to complete it. You can see these steps in Figure 7-8.

FIGURE 7-8. Three steps to adding a line: position the crosshairs pointer at the start of the line (left), drag to the end of the line (center), and release the mouse button (right).

ADDING A PERFECTLY HORIZONTAL, VERTICAL, OR DIAGONAL LINE
Follow the instructions in the previous paragraph to add a line,
but hold down the Shift (Mac OS) or Control (Windows) key
while dragging. This constrains the angle of the line.

ADDING A SHAPE Click one of the shape tools to select it. The
mouse pointer turns into a crosshairs pointer. Position the pointer
where you want a corner of the shape to appear. Press the mouse
button down and drag diagonally. As you drag, a dotted line of the
shape appears. When the shape is the desired size, release the
mouse button to complete it. You can see these steps in Figure 7-9.

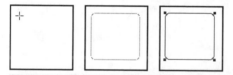

FIGURE 7-9. Three steps to adding a closed shape: position the crosshairs pointer
at the corner of the shape (left), drag to the opposite corner of the shape
(center), and release the mouse button (right).

**ADDING A SQUARE, A SQUARE WITH ROUNDED CORNERS, OR A
CIRCLE** Follow the instructions in the previous paragraph to add
a shape, but hold down the Option (Mac OS) or Control (Windows) key while dragging. This constrains the proportions of the
shape.

Adding an Image

You can also include an image in a layout by either pasting it in
from another document or inserting it from a file on disk. This is a
great way to add a company logo or other graphic element that
would be impossible to draw with FileMaker Pro's drawing tools.

NOTE   *Adding an image to a layout is not the same as entering an image into a container field. An image on a layout appears no matter what record is displayed. An image in a container field appears only when its record and field are displayed. I tell you about entering images into container fields in the section titled "Inserting Data into Container Fields" on page 102.*

PASTING IN AN IMAGE   Open the document that contains the image that you want to use and select the image. Choose Copy from the Edit menu to copy the image. Switch to the FileMaker Pro database layout in which you want to paste the image. Choose Paste (Mac OS) or Paste Layout Object(s) (Windows) from the Edit menu (see Figure 7-10). The image appears in the layout (see Figure 7-11).

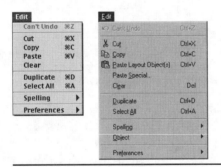

FIGURE 7-10. The Edit menu in Layout mode on Mac OS (left) and Windows (right).

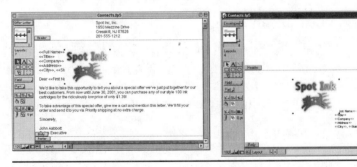

FIGURE 7-11. An image pasted or inserted onto a layout on Mac OS (left) and Windows (right).

IMPORTING AN IMAGE FILE Choose Picture from the Insert menu (see Figure 7-4). The Insert Picture dialog box appears (see Figure 7-12). Use it to locate and select the image file that you want to use in the layout. To save disk space and to store only a reference to the image file in the database rather than the whole image, turn on the Store only a reference to the file check box. When you click the Open button, the image file appears in the layout (see Figure 7-11).

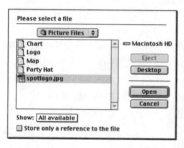

FIGURE 7-12. The Insert Picture dialog box on Mac OS (left) and Windows (right).

WARNING *If you store only a reference to the file in the database, the image will not appear on the layout if the original image file is deleted or otherwise inaccessible.*

Changing a Field

If you add the wrong field to a layout or change your mind about a field you added, you can change it.

Changing a Regular Field

To change a field, simply double-click the field that you want to change to display the Specify Field dialog box (see Figure 7-2). The name of the currently selected field will be highlighted. Click the name of the field that you really want and then click OK. The field you originally double-clicked is replaced with the field you selected.

You can also use this technique to add a field label for an existing field. Double-click the field for which you want to add a label, then turn on the Create field label check box in the Specify Field dialog box without changing the field selection. When you click OK, the field label appears.

Changing a Merge Field

Changing a merge field requires a bit more effort. Because a merge field is part of a text object, you have to change the text object.

Click the text tool to select it, then click inside the text object containing the merge field to position the blinking insertion point. Use your mouse pointer to select the entire merge field, including the less than and greater than signs that enclose it. Now choose Merge Field from the Insert menu (see Figure 7-4) or press Command-M (Mac OS) or Control-M (Windows). In the Specify Field dialog box that appears (see Figure 7-2), select the name of the field that you really want and click OK. The merge field you originally selected is replaced (see Figure 7-13).

```
<<First Name>> <<Last Name>>      <<First Name>> <<Last Name>>
<<Full Name>>                     <<Title>>
<<Company>>                       <<Company>>
<<Address>>                       <<Address>>
<<City>>, <<State>> <<Zip>>       <<City>>, <<State>> <<Zip>>
```

FIGURE 7-13. Two steps to replacing a merge field: select the entire field that you want to replace (left) and replace it (right).

 If you know the exact name of the merge field that you want to use, you can type it in. Select the name of the field that you want to replace without selecting its less-than and greater-than signs, then type in the name of the field you want to replace it with.

Modifying a Text Object

You can modify a text object to change what it says by either replacing it or editing it.

REPLACING A TEXT OBJECT Select the text object that you want to replace (see Figure 7-14, left). Now type the text that you want to replace it with. The selected text object disappears and a new text object appears in the same place as you type (see Figure 7-14, center). Press the Enter key on the keypad or click anywhere in the layout other than in the text object to complete the entry (see Figure 7-14, right).

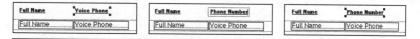

FIGURE 7-14. Three steps to replacing a text object: select the object (left), type the new text (center), and press Enter (right).

NOTE *When you replace a text object, the new text object appears in the same place and with the same formatting as the one you replaced.*

EDITING A TEXT OBJECT Click the text tool to select it. Then click to position the insertion point within the text object that you want to edit (see Figure 7-15, left). Use standard Mac OS or Windows editing techniques to insert (see Figure 7-15, center) or delete characters. When you're finished making changes, press the Enter key on the keypad or click anywhere on the layout other than in the text object to complete the entry (see Figure 7-15, right).

FIGURE 7-15. Three steps to editing a text object: position the insertion point (left), make changes (center), and press Enter (right).

Selecting Layout Objects

Selecting one or more layout objects is often the first step to performing other tasks. Here are some examples:

• Select a layout object to resize, move, or delete it.

- Select several layout objects to resize, move, or delete them together.

- Select one or more layout objects to Copy or Cut them for use in another layout or elsewhere in the same layout.

- Select one or more layout objects to change their formatting options. (I tell you about formatting layout objects in Chapter 8.)

You can use the group command to group items that you always want to work with together. I explain the Group and Ungroup commands in the section titled "Group/Ungroup" on page 195.

Selecting an object is easy. Just click it once. Selection or resizing *handles*, which look like little black boxes, appear in its corners (see Figure 7-16).

Customer Number | Customer Number ....

FIGURE 7-16. A selected field.

Here are some more object selection techniques:

SELECTING A SHAPE THAT HAS NO FILL COLOR OR PATTERN Click the edge of the shape. Handles appear in its corners.

SELECTING MULTIPLE OBJECTS BY CLICKING Hold down the Shift key and click once on each object that you want to select. Handles appear in the corners of each object as you click it.

SELECTING MULTIPLE ADJACENT OBJECTS BY DRAGGING Position the mouse pointer above and to the left of the first object that you want to select. Hold down the mouse button and drag. A selection box grows as you drag (see Figure 7-17). When all of the objects that you want to select are completely enclosed in the selection box, release the mouse button. The selection box disappears and handles appear in the corners of each object (see Figure 7-18).

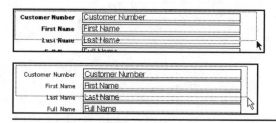

FIGURE 7-17. Dragging a selection box around layout objects on Mac OS (top) and Windows (bottom).

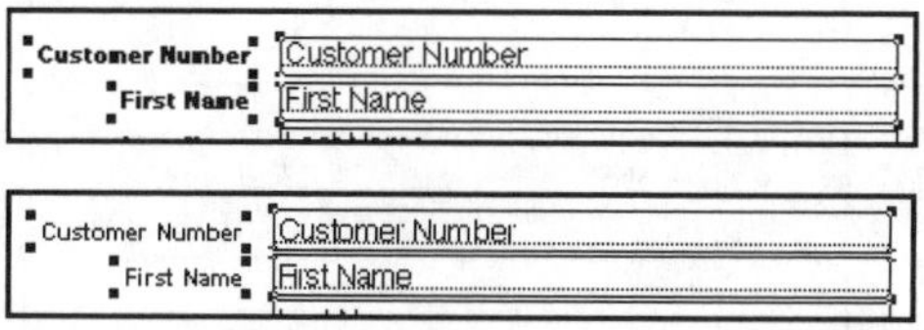

FIGURE 7-18. Objects selected after releasing the mouse button in Figure 7-17.

TIP *To select objects that are touched by the selection box as well as those inside it, hold down the Command (Mac OS) or Control (Windows) key while dragging.*

SELECTING ALL OBJECTS ON THE LAYOUT Choose Select All from the Edit menu (see Figure 7-10) or press Command-A (Mac OS) or Control-A (Windows). Handles appear in the corners of all objects on the layout.

TIP *Once you've selected all the objects on a layout, you can hold down the Shift key and click on each object that you want to deselect. This is a quick way to select almost* all *the objects on a layout.*

DESELECTING AN OBJECT Click anywhere else in the window other than on the object. The handles disappear.

Resizing Objects

You can change an object's dimensions by dragging one of its handles or entering new measurements in the Size palette, which I describe in the section titled "Object Size" on page 191.

RESIZING AN OBJECT BY DRAGGING A HANDLE   Select the object that you want to resize to display its handles. Position the mouse pointer on one of the handles. Press the mouse button down and drag in the appropriate direction to stretch or shrink the object. As you drag, a dotted line indicates the new border of the object (see Figure 7-19). When the border shows the desired final size, release the mouse button. The object resizes (see Figure 7-20).

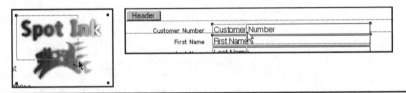

FIGURE 7-19. Dragging to resize an image on Mac OS (left) and a field on Windows (right).

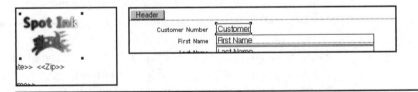

FIGURE 7-20. The resized image and field from Figure 7-19.

Here are a few things to keep in mind when resizing an object by dragging:

• The mouse pointer must be positioned on a handle when you drag. If it is positioned within the object's boundaries, the object will be moved rather than resized. I tell you about moving objects in the section appropriately titled "Moving Objects" on page 251.

- If the object grid feature is turned on, object boundaries will be restricted to the grid. To override the grid positions, either turn off the Object Grid option by selecting it from the Arrange menu or temporarily disable the object grid feature by holding down the Command (Mac OS) or Control (Windows) while dragging the object's corner. I tell you about the object grid feature in the section titled "Object Grids" on page 199.

- If more than one object is selected, all selected objects are resized by the same amount. This is a handy way to keep multiple objects like fields the same size without resizing them individually.

- You cannot drag an object's handle off the layout parts.

RESIZING AN OBJECT WITH THE SIZE PALETTE Select the object that you want to resize. If the Size palette is not already showing, choose Object Size from the View menu (see Figure 7-21) to display it (see Figure 7-22). Now double-click the value in one of the bottom two boxes to select the object's width or height. Enter a new value and press Enter. The object resizes.

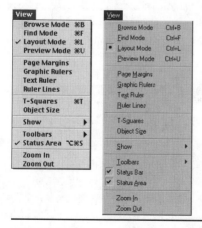

FIGURE 7-21. The View menu on Mac OS (left) and Windows (right).

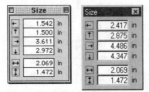

FIGURE 7-22. The Size palette on Mac OS (left) and Windows (right).

NOTE   *If you enter a new, larger size that would cause the item to extend off the bottom of the layout, a dialog box like the one in Figure 7-23 appears. If you click Yes, the part in which the object resides is enlarged to accommodate the object. If you click No, the object is not resized.*

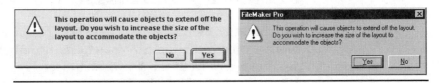

FIGURE 7-23. The dialog box that appears on Mac OS (left) and Windows (right) when you make an object too big.

SETTING AN IMAGE SO IT MAINTAINS ITS PROPORTIONS WHEN RESIZED

Double-click the image to display the Graphic Format dialog box (see Figure 7-24). Turn on the Maintain original proportions check box. Then click OK.

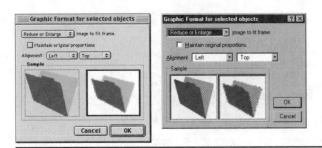

FIGURE 7-24. The Graphic Format dialog box on Mac OS (left) and Windows (right).

You can also open the Graphic Format dialog box by selecting the image and then choosing Graphic from the Format menu.

Moving Objects

You can move an object anywhere within a layout part—even onto another layout part—by dragging it, using the arrow keys on the keyboard, or entering new measurements in the Size palette, which I describe in the section titled "Object Size" on page 191.

Before I provide detailed instructions for these three techniques, here are a few additional things you should keep in mind when moving objects:

- If more than one object is selected when you move one of them, all selected objects are moved together. If you always want to move certain objects together, select them and use the Group command to group them. I explain the Group and Ungroup commands in the section titled "Group/Ungroup" on page 195.

- To prevent an object from being moved, select it and choose Lock from the Arrange menu. I explain the Lock and Unlock commands in the section titled "Lock/Unlock" on page 196.

- If an object spans two parts, it will appear on the uppermost part in Browse, Find, and Preview modes. For example, if you position a field so close to the top of the body that its top handles are in the header, the field will appear in the header—that means it won't repeat for every record in the database!

MOVING AN OBJECT BY DRAGGING Position the mouse pointer in the center of the object (*not* on one of its handles!), press the mouse button down, and drag. As you drag, a dotted outline of the object moves with the mouse pointer (see Figure 7-25). When the object's outline is in the desired position, release the mouse button. The object appears in its new position (see Figure 7-26).

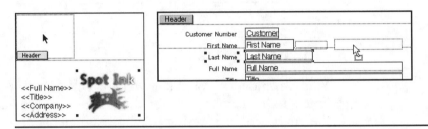

FIGURE 7-25. Dragging to move an image on Mac OS (left) and a pair of selected objects on Windows (right).

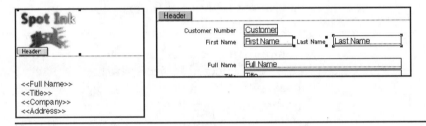

FIGURE 7-26. The moved objects from Figure 7-25.

Here are three things to keep in mind when moving an object by dragging:

- The mouse pointer must be positioned *inside* the object's boundaries when you drag. If it is positioned on one of the object's handles, the object will be resized rather than moved. I tell you how to resize objects in the section titled "Resizing Objects" on page 248.

- If the object grid feature is turned on, object movement will be restricted to the grid. To override the grid positions, either turn off the Object Grid option by selecting it from the Arrange menu or temporarily disable the object grid feature by holding down the Command (Mac OS) or Control (Windows) while dragging the object. I tell you about the AutoGrid feature in the section titled "Object Grids" on page 199.

- A dotted text baseline appears for the first line of a text object as you drag it. You can use this baseline to line up a text object with the baseline of a field.

MOVING AN OBJECT WITH THE ARROW KEYS Select the object(s) that you want to move. Press one of the arrow keys to move the selected object(s) one pixel at a time in the direction of the arrow.

TIP *Using the arrow keys is an excellent way to get an object exactly where you want it—especially with the object grid feature turned on or when your mouse hand is shaky from too much coffee.*

MOVING AN OBJECT WITH THE SIZE PALETTE Select the object(s) that you want to move. If the Size palette is not already showing, choose Object Size from the View menu (see Figure 7-21) to display it (see Figure 7-22). Double-click the value in one of the top four boxes to select the distance between an object's edge and the left, top, right, and bottom of the page. Enter a new value and press Enter. The object shifts to the new position.

NOTE *If you enter a measurement that would cause the item to extend off the bottom of the layout, a dialog box like the one in Figure 7-23 appears. If you click Yes, the part in which the object resides is enlarged to accommodate the object. If you click No, the object is not moved.*

Copying, Cutting, and Pasting Objects

You can copy, cut, and paste layout objects using the Copy, Cut, and Paste (Mac OS) or Copy, Cut, and Paste Layout Object(s) (Windows) commands under the Edit menu (see Figure 7-10). If you've been using Mac OS or Windows for a while, this shouldn't be a surprise to you.

To use the Copy or Cut command, begin by selecting the object(s) that you want to copy. Then copy or cut them. If necessary, switch to the layout in which you want to paste the selected object(s). Then paste them in.

I tell you more about the Copy, Cut, and Paste commands way back in the section titled "Edit Menu Commands" on page 27.

Duplicating Objects

As you may have surmised, the Duplicate command under the Edit menu enables you to duplicate one or more selected objects. But did you know you could also use it to step and repeat an object? Or that you can also duplicate an object by dragging it? Read on to learn more.

DUPLICATING AN OBJECT WITH THE DUPLICATE COMMAND Select the object(s) that you want to duplicate (see Figure 7-27, left). Choose Duplicate from the Edit menu (see Figure 7-10) or press Command-D (Mac OS) or Control-D (Windows). A copy of the selected item appears beside it (see Figure 7-27, right).

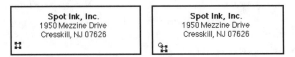

FIGURE 7-27. A selected object (left) and its newly created duplicate (right).

STEPPING AND REPEATING AN OBJECT Follow the steps in the previous paragraph to duplicate an object. Now move the object copy into the desired position on the layout (see Figure 7-28, left). Choose Duplicate from the Edit menu again. Another copy of the item appears, this time the same distance and direction from the first copy as the first copy is from the original (see Figure 7-28, center). Repeat this process until you have as many duplicates as you want (see Figure 7-28, right).

FIGURE 7-28. A moved (and still selected) duplicate (left), a new duplicate automatically positioned an equal distance away (center), and a row of duplicates automatically positioned (right).

DUPLICATING AN OBJECT BY DRAGGING Hold down the Option (Mac OS) or Control (Windows) key while dragging an object. When you release the mouse button, a copy of the object appears at the mouse pointer.

Deleting Objects

Deleting an object is easy. Simply select it and press Delete (Mac OS) or Backspace (Windows), or choose Clear from the Edit menu (see Figure 7-10). The object disappears.

Here are three things to keep in mind:

- As you might expect, you can delete a bunch of objects at once if you select them all, then delete them.

- FileMaker Pro does not confirm layout object deletions. You can, however, use the Undo command under the Edit menu to recover an item immediately after you delete it.

- Deleting a field from a layout is not the same as deleting a field from a database. When you delete a field from a layout, its data remains in the database. You can still add the field back to that layout or to another layout. When you delete a field from a database, however, you remove all traces of the field—including its data—from the database and from all layouts on which it appears.

Using Layout Parts

All of the objects on your layouts are placed on layout parts. As I explain in the section titled "Layout Parts" on page 169, layout parts determine the position and functionality of the layout objects on them.

In this part of the chapter, I explain how to use layout parts to organize and summarize database information, both on screen and in printed reports.

Working with Layout Parts

Every layout you create starts with at least one part on which you place layout objects. In this section, I tell you how to add, remove, and modify layout parts.

Default Layout Parts

Before I tell you how to work with layout parts, let me review the parts that are created by default on each kind of layout and how they are used on that layout. Each of these layout types is illustrated in Chapter 6.

STANDARD FORM A standard form layout includes three parts: a header, body, and footer. The body is sized large enough to accommodate all the fields you select for the layout, one above the other, which are automatically placed when you create the layout.

COLUMNAR LIST/REPORT This type of layout includes a header, body, and footer. The body is sized large enough to place the fields you select side by side across the page. A second row of fields appears on a columnar report if the Constrain to page width check box is turned off in the Choose Report Layout screen of the New Layout/Report dialog box and if you add more fields than will fit on a single row. The header contains field labels for the fields placed within the body, along with any other header information you specify in the Header and Footer Information screen of the New Layout/Report dialog box. The footer contains any footer information you specify in the Header and Footer Information screen.

TABLE VIEW   A table view layout is the same as a standard form in Layout mode, but appears in Table view when in Browse mode.

NOTE   *You can set layout options for table view in the Table View Properties dialog box, which I discuss in the section titled "Setting Table View Properties" on page 270.*

LABELS   A labels layout includes a header and a body. The header is sized to act as a margin for positioning the first label on the label stock when printed. The body contains the merge fields that you specified in a text object. If there is more than one label across the page, the layout is automatically set up for multiple-column printing, which I tell you about in the section titled "Print Columns" on page 224.

ENVELOPE   An envelope layout also includes a header and a body. The header is sized to act as a top margin for positioning the envelope for printing. Like the labels layout, the body contains the merge fields that you specified in a text object.

BLANK   A blank layout includes a header, body, and footer. The body is roughly 3.25 inches tall. No fields are placed by FileMaker Pro when you create a blank layout. You must place all fields and other layout objects manually following the instructions I provide in the section titled "Adding Layout Objects" on page 234.

TIP   *Blank layouts are excellent for creating form letters using FileMaker Pro merge fields in text objects.*

Adding a Part

FileMaker Pro offers two ways to add a part to a layout: with the Part Setup dialog box and with the part tool.

NOTE *You can have only one of each type of part—except a sub-summary part—on a layout.*

ADDING A PART WITH THE PART SETUP DIALOG BOX Choose Part Setup from the Layouts menu (see Figure 7-29) to display the Part Setup dialog box (see Figure 7-30). Click the Create button. The Part definition dialog box appears (see Figure 7-31). Select the option for the part that you want to create. If you choose Sub-Summary, select one of the fields in the scrolling list of fields; I tell you more about that in the section titled "Using Summary Parts and Fields" on page 265. Click OK to accept your settings. If you created a sub-summary part, a dialog box like the one in Figure 7-32 appears. Click the Print Above or Print Below button to determine the position of the sub-summary in relation to the body. Then click the Done button in the Part Setup dialog box. The part appears on the layout (see Figure 7-33).

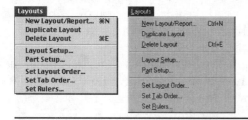

FIGURE 7-29. The Layouts menu on Mac OS (left) and Windows (right).

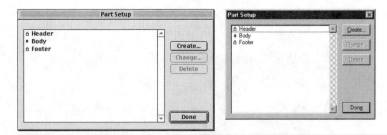

FIGURE 7-30. The Part Setup dialog box on Mac OS (left) and Windows (right).

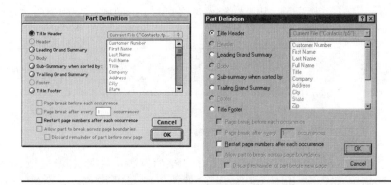

FIGURE 7-31. The Part Definition dialog box on Mac OS (left) and Windows (right).

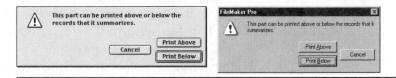

FIGURE 7-32. The dialog box that appears on Mac OS (left) or Windows (right) when you create a sub-summary part.

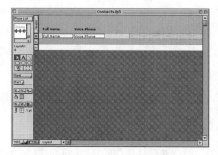

FIGURE 7-33. A title footer added to a multiple-column columnar report on Mac OS (left) and a title header added to a columnar report on Windows (right).

NOTE   As shown in Figure 7-33, newly added parts appear in white, no matter what FileMaker Pro theme was used to create the layout. I explain how to change the background color of a layout part in the section titled "Other Object Formatting Options" on page 329.

ADDING A PART WITH THE PART TOOL   Position the mouse pointer on the part tool in the status area. Press the mouse button down and drag it into the layout window. As you drag, a dotted outline of a part label and its bottom border appear (see Figure 7-34). When the outline is in the desired position for the part, release the mouse button. The Part Definition dialog box appears (see Figure 7-31). Select the option for the type of part that you want to create. If you choose Sub-Summary, select one of the fields in the scrolling list of fields; I tell you more about that in the section titled "Using Summary Parts and Fields" on page 265. Click OK to accept your settings and dismiss the dialog box. The part appears on the layout (see Figure 7-35).

TIP   Another way to display the Part Definition dialog box is to choose Part from the Insert menu (see Figure 7-4).

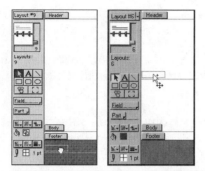

FIGURE 7-34. Dragging the part tool beneath the footer on Mac OS (left) and in the middle of the body on Windows (right).

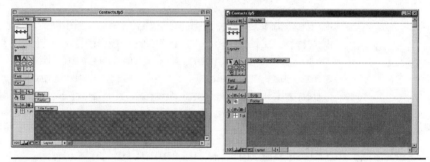

FIGURE 7-35. A title footer added on Mac OS (left) and a leading grand summary added on Windows (right).

NOTE *When you use the part tool to create a part, the Part Definition dialog box only lets you create a part that would appear where you released the part tool on your layout. This limits the type of part you can create. In addition, if you release the part tool in the middle of another part, that part's size is reduced. You can see this on the right side of Figure 7-35.*

Changing a Part

You can change a part's type, depending on the parts on your layout. For example, you can turn a summary part into a sub-summary part or, if you don't already have a title footer, you can turn a footer into a title footer.

To change a part's type, use the Part Definition dialog box (see Figure 7-31). Use one of these two methods to open it for an existing part:

- Choose Part Setup from the Layouts menu (see Figure 7-29). In the Part Setup dialog box that appears (see Figure 7-30), select the part that you want to change. Then click the Change button.

- Double-click the part label on the left or bottom of the part that you want to change.

Once the Part Definition dialog box is open, select the option for the type of part you want to change to. Your choices are restricted based on the position of the part. If you choose Sub-Summary, you'll have to select a break field in the scrolling list of fields. Then click OK. If you opened the Part Setup dialog box, click Done to dismiss it, too.

Changing the Arrangement of Parts

Although some parts must have a certain position in the part order, other parts can be rearranged. You rearrange parts in the Part Setup dialog box.

Choose Part Setup from the Layouts menu (see Figure 7-29) to display the Part Setup dialog box (see Figure 7-30 and Figure 7-36). Position your mouse pointer over the double-headed arrow to the left of a part that you want to move up or down in the part order. Press the mouse button down and drag. When you release the mouse button, the part moves. Click OK to dismiss the dialog box and see the change on the layout.

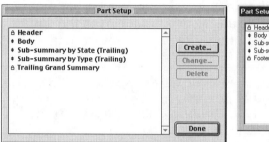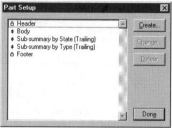

FIGURE 7-36. The Part Setup dialog box, showing parts that can be rearranged on Mac OS (left) and Windows (right).

 NOTE *You can move only the parts with the double-arrow icon before them. You cannot rearrange any of the parts that display a padlock icon. Figure 7-36 shows both.*

Resizing a Part

FileMaker Pro doesn't always create parts in the size you want them. Fortunately, you can change a part's size to meet your needs.

TIP *You may have to move a part's contents higher in the part before you can make a part smaller. I tell you how to move layout objects in the section titled "Moving Objects" on page 251.*

CHANGING A PART'S SIZE BY DRAGGING ITS BORDER Position your mouse pointer on the lower border of the part. Press the mouse button down—it turns into a pair of horizontal lines with arrows (see Figure 7-37, left)—and drag up or down. As you drag, a dotted border moves with the mouse pointer. When the border is in the desired position, release the mouse button. The part resizes (see Figure 7-38, left).

CHANGING A PART'S SIZE BY DRAGGING ITS LABEL Position your mouse pointer on the part label, press the mouse button down, and drag up or down. As you drag, a dotted outline of the part label and bottom border move with the mouse (see Figure 7-37, right). When the tag and border are in the desired position, release the mouse button. The part resizes (see Figure 7-38, right).

NOTE *This technique works only if the part labels are displayed horizontally; you can toggle the part label display by clicking the part label control, which I discuss in the section titled "Part Label Control" on page 184.*

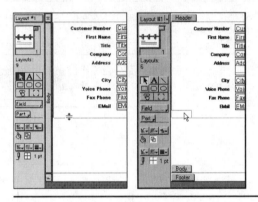

FIGURE 7-37. Resizing a part by dragging the border on Mac OS (left) and the part label on Windows (right).

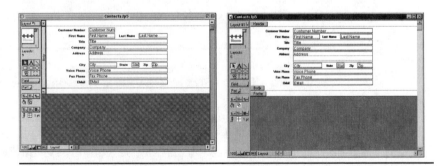

FIGURE 7-38. The resized body from Figure 7-37.

Moving Objects into a Part

I already told you all you need to know to move objects into a part—whether those objects are already in another part or haven't even been added to the layout yet. Check the sections titled "Moving Objects" on page 251 and "Adding Layout Objects" on page 234 for details.

Deleting a Part

Deleting a part is easy. Click its part label to select it and press the Delete (Mac OS) or Backspace (Windows) key. If the part is empty, it'll simply disappear. But if the part contained one or more layout objects, a dialog box like the one in Figure 7-39 appears. Click Delete to delete the part and its objects or click Cancel to leave the part right where it is.

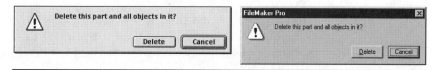

FIGURE 7-39. The dialog box that appears on Mac OS (left) and Windows (right) when you try to delete a part that contains layout objects.

NOTE *When you delete a part and its objects, the data in the database remains. It's just the objects on the layout that are removed from the layout.*

Using Summary Parts and Fields

Summary parts are special parts. They're designed primarily to work with summary fields. You create a summary part, then move one or more summary fields into it. FileMaker Pro automatically calculates summary information and displays it in the summary field.

NOTE *I explain what a summary field is and how to define one in Chapter 2, in the sections titled "Summary" on page 59 and "Completing the Definition for a Summary Field" on page 67.*

TIP *You can use the New Report/Layout dialog box to create complex summary reports with ease. I explain how throughout the section titled "Using the New Layout/Report Dialog Box" on page 201.*

Types of Summary Parts

There are two kinds of summary parts and, although they're similar, they do have important differences.

- **Grand summaries** summarize all the information for the records being browsed. There are two kinds of grand summary parts: a leading grand summary, which appears above or before the body, and a trailing grand summary, which appears below or after the body. You can have only one of each of these kinds of summaries in a layout.

- **Sub-summaries** summarize all the information for a group of records. When you create the sub-summary part, you specify a *break field*, which is used to group the records. When you sort the records by the break field, FileMaker Pro displays a summary for each group of records with the same entry in the break field. You can have as many sub-summaries in a layout as you have fields, but normally you'll have only one or two. Sub-summaries appear only in Preview mode or on printed reports—you can't see them in Browse mode.

The Importance of the Break Field in a Sub-Summary Part

The break field that you select when you create a sub-summary part is vitally important to the operation of the part. It tells File-

Maker Pro how the records should be grouped when calculating summary fields in the part.

Sub-summary parts require a bit more effort when it comes to viewing or printing a summarized report, too. You see, if you don't sort the records by the break field, the summary fields in a sub-summary part won't be calculated at all.

NOTE   *I explain how to use the Sort dialog box to sort records in the section titled "Sorting Records" on page 153.*

Using Summary Parts—Two Examples

Sometimes the best way to explain something as complex as summary and sub-summary parts is to provide an example. Here are two of them.

Figure 7-40 illustrates the first example. The left side shows a layout with header, body, sub-summary, and trailing grand summary parts set up like this:

- The header includes the report title, a funky dividing line, and the field names for column headings.

- The body includes a few fields that will be repeated for each record.

- The sub-summary, which is set up with the State field as the break field, includes a summary field that counts the entries in the Full Name field. There's also a text object that includes the State merge field and a line to separate the sub-summary from the next group of records.

- The trailing grand summary includes the same summary field found in the sub-summary, along with a descriptive text object and a line to mark the end of the report.

The right side of Figure 7-40 shows the same layout after sorting by the State and Last Name fields and switching to Preview mode. See how FileMaker Pro displays a summary for each group of records in the same state? That's what the sub-summary field does. The total at the bottom of the page was created with the trailing grand summary.

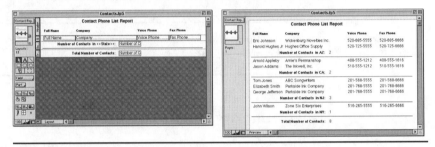

FIGURE 7-40. A layout with header, body, sub-summary, and trailing grand summary parts (left) and the same layout in Preview mode after sorting by State (right).

Let's take this example a step further.

You can have more than one sub-summary part. If you do, each sub-summary part should be set with a different break field. Then, when you sort the records to view the report, list the break fields in the Sort Order list of the Sort dialog box in the reverse order that they are used on the layout.

The layout on the right side of Figure 7-41 is the same as the one in Figure 7-40, with a second sub-summary field added. The second sub-summary field uses the Type field as a break field. It includes the same summary field, as well as a text object that includes the Type merge field. The left side of Figure 7-41 shows what the layout looks like after sorting by Type, State, and Last Name, and switching to Preview mode.

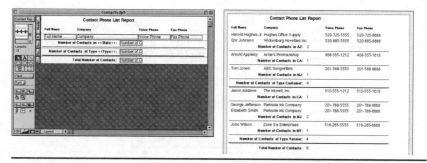

FIGURE 7-41. The same layout as the one in Figure 7-40 with an additional sub-summary part and field.

TIP *There's no rule stating that a layout must include a body. If you're only interested in summary information and don't care about the details provided by including fields in the body, delete the body. What's left is a summary report.*

Viewing a Layout with a Sub-Summary

If you haven't been paying very close attention, you probably missed an important trick to viewing a report that includes one or more sub-summary parts.

Sorting records by the sub-summary part's break field enables FileMaker Pro to calculate summary field contents. But to view the results on screen, you must switch to Preview mode, which shows you what the layout will look like when printed. In Browse mode, sub-summary parts don't show at all (see Figure 7-42).

FIGURE 7-42. The layout from the left side of Figure 7-41 when viewed in Browse mode.

So remember these two steps when viewing layouts with sub-summary parts:

1. Sort the records.

2. Switch to Preview mode.

TIP *If you'd like FileMaker Pro to perform these two steps automatically for you, check out Chapter 12, where I tell you about scripting.*

Setting Table View Properties

FileMaker Pro 5's new Table view enables you to view data as a table with column headings for each field. There are two ways to use this feature:

• Choose View as Table from the View menu (see Figure 7-21).

• Use the New Layout/Report dialog box to create a table view layout, then view it in Browse mode.

Either way, the data is displayed in table format. You can switch to a different view—list or form—by choosing its option from the

View menu. The data appears in its regular layout or standard form layout.

You can customize the appearance and functionality of Table view by setting options in the Table View Properties dialog box. Choose Layout Setup from the Layouts menu to display the General tab of the Layout Setup dialog box. Click the Views tab to display its options, then click the Properties button beside the Table View option. The Table View Properties dialog box appears (see Figure 7-43).

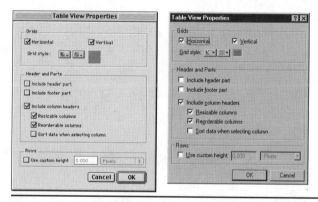

FIGURE 7-43. The Table View Properties dialog box on Mac OS (left) and Windows (right).

SETTING GRID OPTIONS   The Grids area of the dialog box enables you to set options that control the appearance of grids in table view. *Grids* are the horizontal and vertical lines that appear between records and fields.

- **Horizontal** toggles the display of horizontal grid lines between records.

- **Vertical** toggles the display of vertical grid lines between fields.

- **Grid style** offers two menus you can use to specify the color and pattern of the grid lines. The sample box to the right of the menus show what the grid lines will look like. (They're gray by default.)

NOTE *I explain how to use the Color and Pattern menus in the section titled "Color, Pattern, and Width Palettes" on page 182*

SETTING HEADER AND PART OPTIONS The Header and Parts area of the dialog box offer options you can use to set up various parts of a Table view layout.

- **Include header part** displays a header in the Table view layout. You can modify the contents of the header in Layout mode.

- **Include footer part** displays a footer in the Table view layout. You can also modify the contents of the footer in Layout mode.

- **Include column headers** displays the field names as column headings.

- **Resizable columns** enables you to change the width of a column in Table view by dragging its right border. This option is available only if the Include column headers option is turned on.

- **Reorderable columns** enables you to change the order of columns in Table view by dragging them to the right or left of other columns. This option is available only if the Include column headers option is turned on.

- **Sort data when selecting column** enables you to sort records by a field by simply selecting that field's column. This option is available only if the Include column headers option is turned on.

SETTING ROW OPTIONS The Rows area of the Table View Properties dialog box enables you to set custom row height for each row in the table. To take advantage of this feature, turn on the Use custom height checkbox and enter a measurement in the box beside it. You can use the menu beside the box to select a unit of measurement for the value you enter; the default is Pixels.

When you're finished setting Table View Properties options, click the OK button to save them. Then click OK in the Layout Setup dialog box to dismiss it. Your changes take effect immediately.

Step-by-Step

Whew! This was a long chapter, full of information that you'll use over and over as you refine databases with FileMaker Pro. But it's not done yet.

In this section, I provide step-by-step instructions for modifying layouts in Contacts.fp5—most of which you created at the end of Chapter 6. If don't have the completed exercise files from Chapter 6, you can download them from the companion Web site for this book, http://www.gilesrd.com/fmprocomp/.

Fine-Tuning a Data Entry Layout

Layout #1, which is the standard layout created by FileMaker Pro when you created Contacts.fp5, can easily be modified to serve as a data entry form to enter new records into the database. Here are the instructions to modify the layout. When you're finished, it should look like the layout in Figure 7-44.

1. In Layout mode, switch to Layout#1.

2. Choose Graphic Rulers from the View menu to display the graphic rulers.

3. Change the layout's margins to a fixed measurement of 0.50 for each side.

4. Resize the header so it is approximately 1 inch tall. You can use the graphic ruler to estimate the size.

5. In the header, add a text object that says *Spot Ink, Inc.* on the first line and *Data Entry Form* on the second line. You will have to press Return (Mac OS) or Enter (Windows) to finish the first line and start a second one within the text object.

6. Reduce the width of the following fields as indicated:

Field Name	Approximate Width
Customer Number	1″
First Name	1″
Last Name	1.5″
City	1.5″
State	0.5″
Zip	1.5″
Voice Phone	1.25″
Fax Phone	1.25″
Terms	1″
Limit	1″
Revision Date	1″

7. Delete the field labels for Full Name, City, State, and Zip, and the Full Name field.

8. Arrange the remaining fields and field labels to match Figure 7-44.

9. Reduce the size of the body so it ends just beneath the last field on the layout.

10. Change the second line of text in the header to read *Contact Entry Form.*

11. **Extra Credit:** If you have access to the Internet, download the file named spotlogo.jpg from the book's companion Web site (http://www.gilesrd.com/fmprocomp/). If not, select any image file on your computer. Add the image to the layout header, just to the left of the text label you

added in Step 5. If necessary, resize the image so it completely fits in the header.

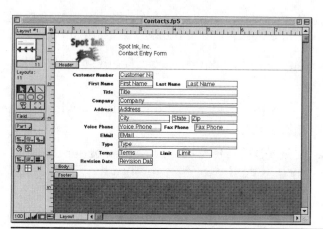

FIGURE 7-44. The completed entry form layout on Mac OS.

Creating a Columnar Report

Remember the Phone List layout you created at the end of Chapter 6? It's time to modify it a bit to meet Spot's needs. Here are the instructions to modify the layout. When you're finished, it should look like the one in Figure 7-45.

1. In Layout mode, switch to the Phone List layout.

2. If necessary, choose Graphic Rulers from the View menu to display the graphic rulers.

3. Decrease the size of the two phone number fields so they're approximately 1.25" wide, and increase the size of the Company field to almost 2" wide.

4. Shift the fields and their corresponding field labels so they line up one beside the other without any overlap, as shown in Figure 7-45. Make sure that the last field does not cross over the dashed page break line on the far right side

of the layout; you may have to scroll the window's contents to see it.

5. If necessary, shift the page number symbol (##) to the left of the dashed page break line in the footer.

6. If necessary, reduce the size of the inserted logo so it's only about 1" tall.

7. Move the header text so it's aligned with the middle of the logo.

8. Use the Part tool to add a title header that ends about 1/2 inch after the logo in the header. (This splits the header into two parts: a title header and a header).

9. Duplicate all of the field labels in the header and move the duplicates into the title header, immediately above the originals.

10. Compare your finished layout to the one in Figure 7-45. Then choose Contact Phone List from the Scripts menu to look at the report in Preview mode.

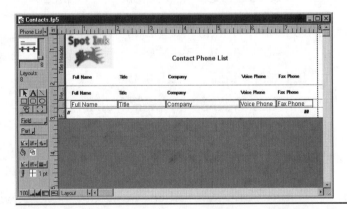

FIGURE 7-45. The completed Phone List layout on Windows.

Creating a Columnar Report with Summaries

Spot also wants a report like the Phone List layout, but he wants it to display the Limit field instead of the Fax Phone field and show the average limit grouped by the type of contact. Although that sounds tough, it really isn't. All you need to do is add a summary part with a summary field to the layout. Here are the instructions for duplicating the layout and modifying it to add the summary. When you're finished, your layout should look like the one in Figure 7-46.

1. With the Phone List layout showing, choose Duplicate Layout from the Layouts menu. A copy of the layout becomes the current layout.

2. Replace the *Contact Phone List* text object in the title header with one that says *Contact Credit Limits*.

3. Change the Fax Phone field to the Limit field.

4. Replace the *Fax Phone* field labels with ones that say *Credit Limit*.

5. Add a sub-summary part with Type as the break field and position it below the body.

6. Resize the sub-summary part so it's approximately 1/2" tall.

7. Define a summary field named Limit Average that averages the Limit field.

8. If preferences are set to add newly defined fields to the current layout automatically, the new field appears in the body; move it into the sub-summary part and reduce the body to its original size. If the Limit Average field did not automatically appear on the layout, add it and its field label to the sub-summary part.

9. Edit the *Limit Average* field label in the sub-summary part so it says *Average Credit Limit for Contact Type <<Type>>*. This includes a merge field that will identify the group.

10. In the sub-summary part, add a line above and another line below the summary field and its label.

11. Compare your finished layout to the one in Figure 7-46. Then switch to Preview mode and sort the records by Type and Last Name to see how the summary part works.

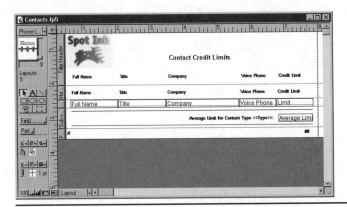

FIGURE 7-46. The completed Contact Credit Limits layout on Windows.

Extra Credit: Two More Layouts

Layout #1 in the Products.fp5 and Invoices.fp5 file could each use some work. Use the techniques I share throughout this chapter to modify them so they look like the ones in Figure 7-47 and Figure 7-48.

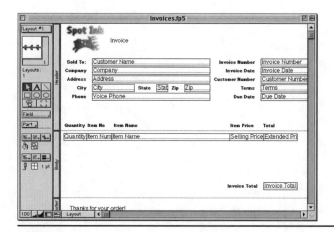

FIGURE 7-47. Layout #1 in Invoices.fp5 after modification on Mac OS.

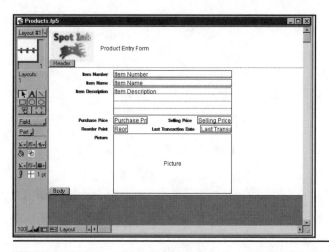

FIGURE 7-48. Layout #1 in Products.fp5 after modification on Windows.

8

Polishing Layout Appearance and Functionality

Chapter 7 provides a wealth of information about adding, positioning, resizing, and removing layout objects and parts. In this chapter, I build on that information by telling you how to format fields and other layout objects so they look and work just the way you want. I also provide some instructions for managing the layouts that you create.

Text Formatting

Although FileMaker Pro's layout theme feature can apply some interesting (or at least colorful) formatting to fields, field labels, and text objects on the layouts you create, these formatting options may not meet your needs. Fortunately, you can change a wide range of formatting options for text characters and paragraphs in layout objects to make them more visually appealing and easier to read.

In this section, I explain what you need to do to apply text formatting, then tell you all about the text formatting options that FileMaker Pro offers by looking at the different menus, submenus, dialog boxes, and other tools you can use to apply formatting changes.

Applying Text Formatting

You can apply text formatting to both text objects and fields. To do so, you must first switch to the correct mode and select the text or object that you want to format.

Pick a Mode

To apply formatting to a text object, you must be in Layout mode. There's no choice. Once in Layout mode, you can select all or part of a text object, then apply the formatting. The formatting options that are available vary depending on what is selected.

To apply text formatting to a field, however, you can be in either Layout or Browse mode. There is an important difference, however. When you apply formatting in Layout mode, the formatting is applied to the entire field for every record in the database on that particular layout. When you apply formatting in Browse mode, the formatting is applied to the selected text in the field entry, thus overriding the formatting options set for that field in Layout Mode for all layouts.

Here's an example. If you select the First Name field in Layout mode and apply bold formatting to it, the contents of the First Name field will appear in bold type for every record when viewed on that layout. But instead, if you select the name *Tom* in the First Name field in a layout in Browse mode and apply bold formatting to it, the word *Tom* will appear in bold type for every layout for that record.

See the difference?

Most of the formatting you do will be in Layout mode. This ensures that the contents of fields are consistently formatted within each individual layout and enables you to specify different formatting for the same fields in different layouts.

Selecting What You Want to Format

Once you've switched to the correct mode, your next step to formatting something is to select what you want to format.

 To change the formatting of a bunch of text objects or fields in Layout mode quickly, select them all at once before applying the formatting changes. I explain how to select multiple objects in Layout mode in the section titled "Selecting Layout Objects" on page 245.

SELECTING FIELD CONTENTS IN BROWSE MODE   Drag over the text that you want to select to highlight it.

SELECTING A TEXT OBJECT OR FIELD IN LAYOUT MODE   Use one of the following procedures:

- To select an entire text object, click it. Handles appear in its corners.

- To select all the text in a field, click the field. Handles appear in its corners.

- To select part of a text object with the pointer tool, click the entire text object to select it. Then click within the text object to position an insertion point within it and drag over the text that you want to select to highlight it.

- To select part of a text object with the text tool, click the Text tool button in the status area, then drag over the text that you want to select to highlight it.

Formatting a Selection

The last step is to use FileMaker Pro's menu commands, dialog boxes, or other options to apply text formatting to your selection:

- Choose a command from one of the submenus under the Format menu. This enables you to change the font, size, style, alignment, line spacing, and text color. Consult the section titled "Format Menu Options" on page 285 for details.

- Set options in the Text Format dialog box. This enables you to change character formatting options such as font, size, and style. When you're finished making changes, click OK to apply them. I tell you about this dialog box in the section titled "Text Format Dialog Box" on page 291.

- Set options in the Paragraph dialog box. This enables you to set paragraph formatting options such as alignment, indentation, and line spacing. I explain Paragraph dialog box options in the section titled "Paragraph Dialog Box" on page 292.

- Set tabs with the Tabs dialog box. This enables you to specify exact tab positions. I tell you more about the Tabs dialog box in the section titled "Tabs Dialog Box" on page 294.

- Set formatting options with the Text Formatting toolbar. This enables you to set character formatting options such as font, size, and some styles, as well as paragraph formatting options such as alignment. I explain how to display and use the Text Formatting toolbar in the section titled "Text Formatting Toolbar" on page 296.

- Set formatting options with the text ruler. This enables you to set paragraph formatting options such as tabs and indentation. I describe the text ruler and explain how to use it in the section titled "Text Formatting Toolbar" on page 296.

NOTE *If no layout objects are selected when you use a formatting option, the formatting option you select becomes a default option, which is applied to all new layout objects. If you want to format an object, make sure it is selected before you apply formatting.*

Format Menu Options

The Format menu (see Figure 8-1) includes a number of submenus with commands for applying formatting options. If you only need to make one quick change to a selection, choosing a command from one of these submenus might just be the quickest way.

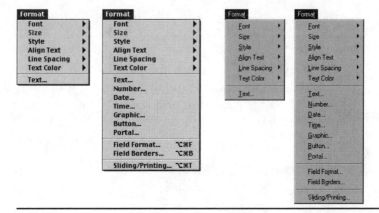

FIGURE 8-1. The Format menu in Browse and Layout modes on Mac OS (far left and center-left) and Windows (center-right and far right).

Font Submenu

The Font submenu (see Figure 8-2) enables you to select a font or typeface to apply to a selection.

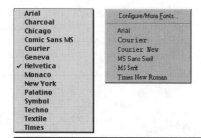

FIGURE 8-2. The Font submenu under the Format menu on Mac OS (left) and Windows (right).

The options listed on the Font submenu vary depending on your operating system and installed fonts:

MAC OS The Font submenu lists all fonts properly installed in the system.

WINDOWS The Font submenu lists the most commonly used fonts. You can edit the menu by choosing Configure/More Fonts from the Font submenu and using the Configure Font Menu dialog box that appears (see Figure 8-3) to add or remove installed fonts.

FIGURE 8-3. The Configure Font Menu dialog box on Windows.

Size Submenu

The Size submenu (see Figure 8-4) enables you to select a font size to apply to a selection.

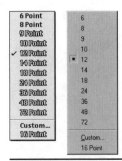

FIGURE 8-4. The Size submenu under the Format menu on Mac OS (left) and Windows (right).

APPLYING A COMMONLY USED SIZE   Choose the size that you want to apply from the Size submenu.

CREATING AND APPLYING A CUSTOM SIZE   Choose Custom from the Size submenu to display the Custom Font Size dialog box (see Figure 8-5). Enter the desired font size and click OK. The size you enter is applied and is listed on the Size submenu beneath the Custom command.

FIGURE 8-5. The Custom Font Size dialog box on Mac OS (left) and Windows (right).

Style Submenu

The Style submenu (see Figure 8-6) enables you to apply standard style options to a selection. If you've been using Mac OS or Windows for a while, these options should be familiar to you because they appear in most other programs.

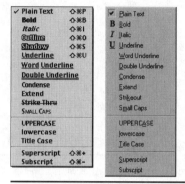

FIGURE 8-6. The Style submenu under the Format menu on Mac OS (left) and Windows (right).

- **Plain Text** removes all styles from the selection.

- **Bold** applies bold formatting to the selection.

- **Italic** applies italic formatting to the selection.

- **Underline** places an underline under the entire selection.

- **Word Underline** places an underline under each individual word in the selection. It does not underline spaces.

- **Double Underline** places a double underline under the entire selection.

- **Condense** tightens the spacing between characters in the selection.

- **Extend** loosens the spacing between characters in the selection.

- **Strikeout** places a line through the selection.

- **Small Caps** displays lowercase characters in the selection as small uppercase characters and uppercase characters as regular uppercase characters.

- **UPPERCASE** displays all characters in the selection as uppercase characters.

- **lowercase** displays all characters in the selection as lower-case characters.

- **Title Case** displays the first letter of each word in the selection as uppercase characters and the remaining characters as lowercase characters.

- **Superscript** shrinks and raises all characters in the selection.

- **Subscript** shrinks and lowers all characters in the selection.

Align Text Submenu

The Align Text submenu (see Figure 8-7) enables you to set the horizontal and vertical alignment of text in a selection.

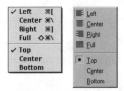

FIGURE 8-7. The Align Text submenu under the Format menu on Mac OS (left) and Windows (right).

- **Left** aligns all text in the selected field or paragraph against the left side of the text boundary.

- **Center** centers all text in the selected field or paragraph between the left and right text boundaries.

- **Right** aligns all text in the selected field or paragraph against the right side of the text boundary.

- **Full** aligns all text in the selected field or paragraph against both the left and right text boundaries.

- **Top** aligns all text in the selection against the top text boundary.

- **Center** aligns all text in the selection between the top and bottom text boundaries.

- **Bottom** aligns all text in the selection against the bottom text boundary.

NOTE   *The Top, Center, and Bottom options are available only in Layout mode.*

Line Spacing Submenu

The Line Spacing submenu (see Figure 8-8) enables you to set the spacing between lines in a field or selected paragraph.

FIGURE 8-8. The Line Spacing submenu under the Format menu on Mac OS (left) and Windows (right).

- **Single** applies single spacing to a selected field or paragraph.

- **Double** applies double spacing to a selected field or paragraph.

- **Custom** displays the Paragraph dialog box (see Figure 8-11), which you can use to set alignment, indentation, and line spacing for the selected field or paragraph. I tell you more about the Paragraph dialog box in the section titled "Paragraph Dialog Box" on page 292.

Text Color Submenu

The Text Color submenu (see Figure 8-9) enables you to select a color to apply to the selection. The colors that appear on this menu vary depending on the setting in the Layout tab of the

Application Preferences dialog box, which is covered in the section titled "Layout" on page 36.

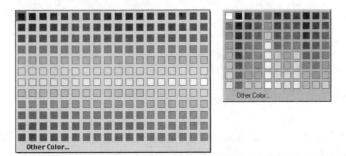

FIGURE 8-9. The Text Color submenu under the Format menu on Mac OS with the Web palette selected (left) and on Windows with the System subset palette selected (right).

Text Format Dialog Box

The Text Format dialog box (see Figure 8-10) puts a bunch of text formatting options all in one place. To open it, choose Text from the Format menu (see Figure 8-1). You can set options as desired and click OK to apply them.

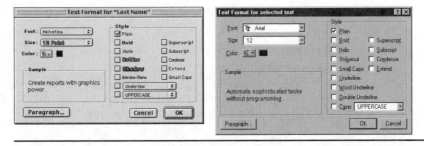

FIGURE 8-10. The Text Format dialog box for a field selected in Layout mode on Mac OS (left) and for selected field contents in Browse mode on Windows (left).

FORMATTING OPTIONS Menus and check boxes offer options from the Font, Size, Text Color, and Style submenus under the Format menu. To learn more about these options, consult the section titled "Format Menu Options" on page 285.

SAMPLE The sample area displays some sample text with the selected formatting options applied. This enables you to preview your changes before you click OK to apply them.

PARAGRAPH BUTTON Clicking the Paragraph button displays the Paragraph dialog box (see Figure 8-11). You can use this dialog box to set alignment, indentation, and line spacing options and to access the Tabs dialog box (see Figure 8-13).

Paragraph Dialog Box

The Paragraph dialog box appears when you choose Custom from the Line Spacing submenu (see Figure 8-8) or click the Paragraph button in the Text Format dialog box (see Figure 8-10). You can use it to set a number of paragraph formatting options. When you're finished, click OK to accept them.

FIGURE 8-11. The Paragraph dialog box on Mac OS (left) and Windows (right).

Alignment

The alignment area lets you select from Left, Center, Right, and Justified (or Full) alignment. I explain these alignment options in the section titled "Align Text Submenu" on page 289).

Indentation

Indentation options enable you to set paragraph indentation—the distance between the text characters and the text boundaries.

- **Left** is the amount of space between text characters at the left end of a line and the left text boundary.

- **Right** is the amount of space between text characters at the right end of a line and right text boundary.

- **First** is the amount of space between text characters at the left end of the first line and the left indent.

Figure 8-12 shows an example of indentation set for two paragraphs of a large text object. The text ruler, which I discuss in the section titled "Text Formatting Toolbar" on page 296, is displayed to show the positions of the indentation markers.

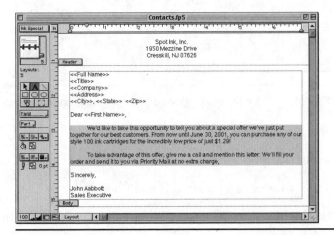

FIGURE 8-12. Indentation set for two paragraphs within a large text object on Mac OS.

Line Spacing

Line spacing lets you set the spacing between both lines and paragraphs. Enter a measurement in the box and use the menu to select units—lines, pixels, inches, or cm.

- **Height** is the amount of space taken up by a single line. Typographers refer to this as *leading*.

- **Above** is the amount of space above the paragraph.

- **Below** is the amount of space below the paragraph.

Tabs Dialog Box

The Tabs dialog box (see Figure 8-13) appears when you click the Tabs button in the Paragraph dialog box (see Figure 8-11) or double-click a tab on the text ruler. You can use it to set tabs for the selected field or paragraph.

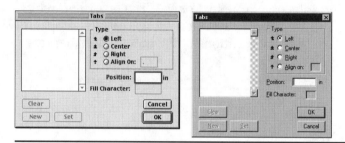

FIGURE 8-13. The Tabs dialog box on Mac OS (left) and Windows (right).

There are four types of tabs:

- **Left** aligns the left side of tabbed text at the tab marker.

- **Center** centers tabbed text at the marker.

- **Right** aligns the right side of tabbed text at the marker.

- **Align on** lets you specify a character to align text with the tab marker. Normally, you'll enter a period or decimal point in the box to create what is called a decimal tab. This aligns the decimal point in numbers with the tab marker.

Figure 8-14 shows an example of how tabs can be used with merge fields in a text object to create a columnar report. In the illustration, the text ruler is displayed to show you the positions of the tab markers. I tell you about the text ruler in the section titled "Text Formatting Toolbar" on page 296.

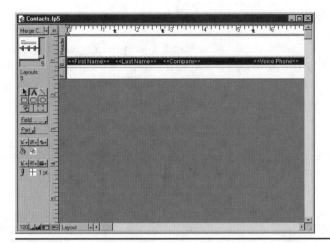

FIGURE 8-14. Tab settings for a selected text object to display a columnar report with merge fields on Windows.

Here's how to use the Tab dialog box to add, change, and remove tabs:

ADDING A TAB   Select the option for the type of tab that you want. Enter a measurement for the tab position in the Position box. Then click New. The tab appears in the list within the dialog box.

CHANGING A TAB   In the scrolling list of tabs, click once on the tab that you want to change. Select a different Type option or enter a new position for the tab. Then click Set. The information in the list is revised.

DELETING A TAB   In the list of tabs, click once on the tab that you want to delete. Then click Clear. The tab disappears from the list.

TIP   *You can include tabs in fields. Normally, when you press the Tab key while in a field in Browse mode, FileMaker Pro activates the next field. To insert a tab character within a field, hold down the Option (Mac OS) or Control (Windows) key while pressing Tab.*

Text Formatting Toolbar

FileMaker Pro's new Text Formatting toolbar (see Figure 8-15) puts buttons for commonly used formatting options well within mouse pointer reach. You simply select what you want to format and either click a button or choose a menu command to apply formatting to it.

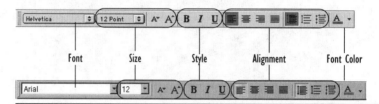

FIGURE 8-15. The Text Formatting toolbar on Mac OS (top) and Windows (bottom).

To display the Text Formatting toolbar, choose Text Formatting from the Toolbars submenu under the View menu (see Figure 8-16).

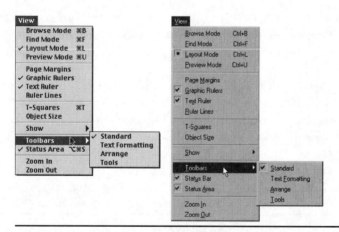

FIGURE 8-16. The Toolbars submenu under the View menu in Layout mode on Mac OS (left) and Windows (right).

Here's a quick list of the formatting options included on the Text Formatting toolbar.

Font

The Font menu (see Figure 8-17) displays the same list of fonts available in the Font submenu under the Format menu (see Figure 8-2). I tell you about these options in the section titled "Font Submenu" on page 285.

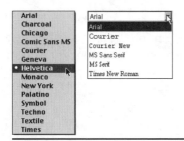

FIGURE 8-17. The Font menu on the Text Formatting toolbar on Mac OS (left) and Windows (right).

Size

The Size menu (see Figure 8-18) displays the same size selection as the Size submenu under the Format menu (see Figure 8-4). I tell you about size options in the section titled "Size Submenu" on page 286.

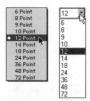

FIGURE 8-18. The Size menu on the Text Formatting toolbar on Mac OS (left) and Windows (right).

You can also click one of the two buttons to the right of the Size menu on the toolbar to decrease or increase font size one point at a time.

Styles

Three style buttons enable you to apply bold, italic, and underline formatting to selected fields or text. If you don't know what those options do, check the section titled "Style Submenu" on page 287.

Alignment

Seven alignment buttons enable you to apply horizontal or vertical alignment to selections. I explain alignment options in the section titled "Align Text Submenu" on page 289.

Text Color

The Text color button displays a menu of colors (see Figure 8-19) that can be applied to selected fields or text objects. This works just like the Text Color submenu under the Format menu, which I discuss in the section titled "Text Color Submenu" on page 290.

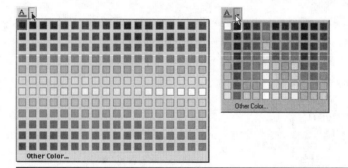

FIGURE 8-19. The Text Color button's menu on the Text Formatting toolbar on Mac OS with the Web palette selected (left) and on Windows with the System subset palette selected (right).

Text Ruler

The Text Ruler (see Figure 8-20), which can be displayed at the top of the document window in Layout or Browse mode, also has a few formatting options. Use it to apply formatting to field contents in Layout or Browse mode and to text objects in Layout mode.

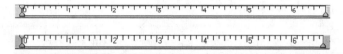

FIGURE 8-20. The Text Ruler on Mac OS (top) and Windows (bottom).

To display the Text Ruler, choose Text Ruler from the View menu (see Figure 8-21).

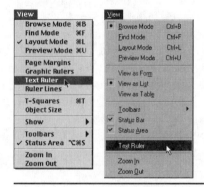

FIGURE 8-21. Choosing Text Ruler from the View menu in Layout mode on Mac OS (left) and in Browse mode on Windows (right).

Tabs

You can use the Text Ruler to set tabs for selected paragraphs of text.

 You can set tabs on the ruler only when a blinking insertion point is within a text object in Layout mode (see Figure 8-22) or within a field in Browse mode.

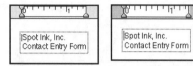

FIGURE 8-22. The text ruler in Layout mode with the insertion point blinking in a text object on Mac OS (left) and Windows (right).

SETTING A TAB Click the ruler where you want to place the tab. A Left tab marker appears.

MOVING A TAB Drag the tab marker for the tab that you want to move to a new place on the ruler.

CHANGING A TAB'S SETTINGS Double-click the tab marker to display the Tabs dialog box (see Figure 8-13). Make changes as desired and click OK. I tell you more about setting tab options in the section titled "Tabs Dialog Box" on page 294.

DELETING A TAB Drag the tab marker on the ruler into the document window. When you release the tab marker, it disappears.

Indentation

When the insertion point is blinking within a text object in Layout mode or within a field in Browse mode, indent markers appear on the text ruler (see Figure 8-22). You can use these markers to set indentation for a selected paragraph.

SETTING FIRST LINE INDENTATION Drag the top-left indent marker to where you want to set first line indentation. This setting affects only the first line in each selected paragraph.

SETTING LEFT INDENTATION Drag the bottom-left indent marker to where you want to set left indentation for all lines of the selected paragraph(s) other than the first line(s).

SETTING RIGHT INDENTATION Drag the right indent marker to where you want to set right side indentation for all lines of the selected paragraph(s).

 TIP *I tell you more about setting indentation in the section titled "Paragraph Dialog Box" on page 292.*

Changing the Default Text Formatting

FileMaker Pro's default formatting (which is used in the Standard layout theme) applies the following text formatting to the fields, field labels, and text objects that you add to layouts:

Layout Object	Mac OS Formatting	Windows Formatting
Field	12-point Helvetica	12-point Arial
Field Label	9-point, bold Helvetica	9-point, bold Arial
Field Label for Columnar Report	9-point, bold, underlined Helvetica	9-point, bold, underlined Arial
Text Object	12-point Helvetica	12-point Arial

You can change the default font formatting while in Layout mode. First make sure that nothing in the document window is selected. Then choose the desired options to set the text formatting the way you want it. From that point forward, all items that you add to the layout will be added with the text formatting you specified.

Other Field Formatting Options

In addition to text formatting options, there are a number of other formatting options that can be applied to fields.

- Change the formatting of a field's contents to display numbers, dates, times, and graphics the way you want them to, no matter how they were entered.

- Apply field formats that specify the appearance and functionality of fields.

- Set field borders to make your fields stand out.

I cover all of these options next.

NOTE *You must be in Layout mode to set the field formatting options I discuss in this part of the chapter.*

Formatting Field Contents

The text formatting options I discuss in the first part of this chapter can be applied to virtually any kind of field to modify the appearance of characters within the field. Other formatting options, however, work with specific types of fields and determine some of the characters that display.

Number Formatting

Number formatting determines the appearance of numbers in number, calculation, summary, or global fields or text objects. For example:

- Display numbers as Boolean values, where 0 displays as No and any number other than 0 displays as Yes.

- Display numbers as decimal numbers, with or without a fixed number of decimal points, separators, and notation that you specify.

- Display negative numbers with special characters or color.

You can set many combinations of these options in the Number Format dialog box (see Figure 8-23).

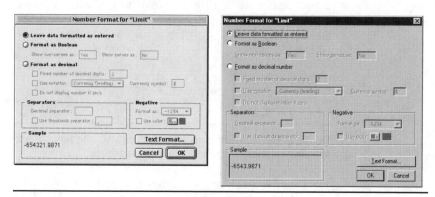

FIGURE 8-23. The Number Format dialog box on Mac OS (left) and Windows (right).

OPENING THE NUMBER FORMAT DIALOG BOX Select a field or text object that contains or can contain a number. Then choose Number from the Format menu (see Figure 8-1).

KEEPING A NUMBER FORMATTED AS ENTERED OR CALCULATED Select the Leave data formatted as entered option (see Figure 8-23). This is the default setting.

FORMATTING A NUMBER AS BOOLEAN Select the Format as Boolean option (see Figure 8-24). If desired, enter the values you want to appear for nonzero values and zero values in the boxes. The default options are Yes and No.

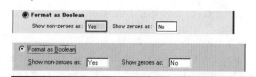

FIGURE 8-24. Number formatting options with the Format as Boolean option selected on Mac OS (top) and Windows (bottom).

FORMATTING A NUMBER AS A DECIMAL NUMBER Select the Format as decimal number option (see Figure 8-25). Then turn on check boxes and enter values as desired to utilize related options.

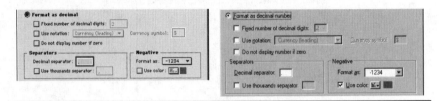

FIGURE 8-25. Number formatting options with the Format as decimal option selected on Mac OS (left) and Windows (right).

- **Fixed number of decimal digits**, when turned on, displays numbers with the number of decimal digits that you specify in the box.

- **Use notation**, when turned on, lets you select a type of notation from its menu (see Figure 8-26). If you select one of the Currency options, you can enter whatever mark you have a yen for in the Currency symbol box. (OK, I'll stop the bad puns.)

FIGURE 8-26. The Use notation menu in the Number Format dialog box on Mac OS (left) and Windows (right).

- **Do not display number if zero**, when turned on, tells File-Maker Pro not to show zero values.

- **Separators** enables you to specify a decimal separator character and, if you turn on the Use thousands separator option, a thousands separator character. You might find this handy if you have to create financial reports for use in Europe—Europeans use a period as a thousands separator and a comma as a decimal separator.

- **Negative** lets you set formatting for negative numbers. Choose an option from the Format as menu (see Figure 8-27). To display negative numbers in a special color, turn on the Use color check box and choose a color from the menu beside it (see Figure 8-28).

FIGURE 8-27. The Format as menu in the Number Format dialog box on Mac OS (left) and Windows (right).

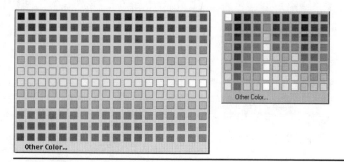

FIGURE 8-28. The Use color menu in the Number Format dialog box on Mac OS with the Web palette selected (left) and on Windows with the System subset palette selected (right).

PREVIEWING YOUR SETTINGS   Check the Sample area at the bottom of the dialog box (see Figure 8-23). It displays a negative number formatted to your specifications.

APPLYING YOUR SETTINGS   Click the OK button. Your changes are applied to the selected object(s).

Date Formatting

Date formatting determines the appearance of dates in date, calculation, summary, or global fields or text objects. For example:

- Display dates using one of several built-in date formats.

- Display dates with a custom date format you specify.

- Display dates with or without leading characters in front of day or month numbers.

You can set these options in the Date Format dialog box (see Figure 8-29).

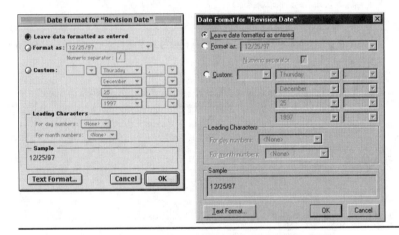

FIGURE 8-29. The Date Format dialog box on Mac OS (left) and Windows (right).

OPENING THE DATE FORMAT DIALOG BOX Select a field or text object that contains or can contain a date. Then choose Date from the Format menu (see Figure 8-1).

KEEPING A DATE FORMATTED AS ENTERED OR CALCULATED Select the Leave data formatted as entered option (see Figure 8-29). This is the default setting.

FORMATTING A DATE USING ONE OF THE BUILT-IN DATE FORMATS Select the Format as option (see Figure 8-30), then choose a format from its menu (see Figure 8-31). If desired, you can enter a different separator character in the Numeric separator box.

FIGURE 8-30. Date formatting options with the Format as option selected on Mac OS (left) and Windows (right).

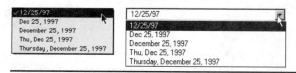

FIGURE 8-31. The Format as menu in the Date Format dialog box on Mac OS (left) and Windows (right).

FORMATTING A DATE WITH A CUSTOM DATE FORMAT Start by selecting the Custom option to display the custom formatting options (see Figure 8-32). Use the menus (see Figure 8-33) to choose the date format components to make up your custom format. As you choose options, the format of the date in the Sample area changes to show the effects of your choices.

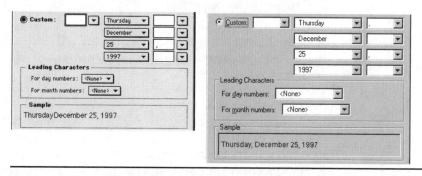

FIGURE 8-32. Date formatting options with the Custom option selected on Mac OS (left) and Windows (right).

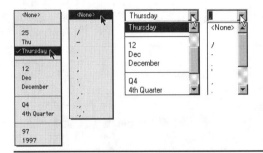

FIGURE 8-33. Custom date component menus on Mac OS (left) and Windows (right). The menus offer formats for date information (far left and center-right) and separators or punctuation (center-left and far right).

SETTING LEADING CHARACTERS   If you select the Format as or Custom options, you can use the menus in the leading characters area (see Figure 8-34) to specify whether a character should appear before single-digit day or month numbers. Your options are None, Zero, or Space. None is the default.

FIGURE 8-34. Leading character menus in the Date Format dialog box on Mac OS (left) and Windows (right).

PREVIEWING YOUR SETTINGS   Check the Sample area at the bottom of the dialog box (see Figure 8-29). It displays a date formatted to your specifications.

APPLYING YOUR SETTINGS   Click the OK button. Your changes are applied to the selected object(s).

Time Formatting

Time formatting determines the appearance of times in time, calculation, summary, or global fields or text objects. For example:

• Display times using one of several built-in time formats.

- Display times with a 12- or 24-hour clock and specify the before-noon and afternoon notation characters and their location.

- Display times with or without leading characters in front of hour, minute, or second numbers.

You can set these options in the Time Format dialog box (see Figure 8-35).

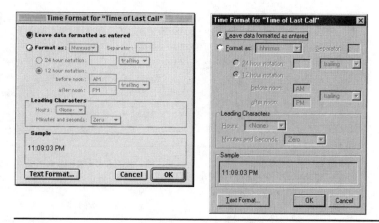

FIGURE 8-35. The Time Format dialog box on Mac OS (left) and Windows (right).

OPENING THE TIME FORMAT DIALOG BOX Select a field or text object that contains or can contain a time. Then choose Time from the Format menu (see Figure 8-1).

KEEPING A TIME FORMATTED AS ENTERED OR CALCULATED Select the Leave data formatted as entered option (see Figure 8-35). This is the default setting.

FORMATTING A TIME USING ONE OF THE BUILT-IN TIME FORMATS Select the Format as option (see Figure 8-36), then choose a format from its menu (see Figure 8-37). Your options are:

- **hhmmss** displays the time with hours, minutes, and seconds.

- **mmss** displays the time with hours and minutes.

- **hh** displays just the hour portion of the time.

- **mm** displays just the minute portion of the time.

- **ss** displays just the seconds portion of the time.

If desired, you can enter a different separator character in the Separator box.

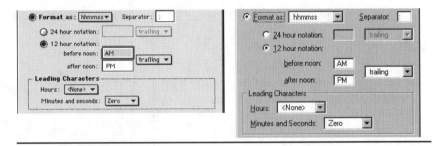

FIGURE 8-36. Time formatting options with the Format as option selected on Mac OS (left) and Windows (right).

FIGURE 8-37. The Format as menu in the Date Format dialog box on Mac OS (left) and Windows (right).

FORMATTING A TIME WITH 12-HOUR OR 24-HOUR NOTATION Make sure the Format as option is selected. Then select the option beneath it to specify whether you want 24-hour or 12-hour notation. For each option, you can specify characters to appear before (leading) or after (trailing) the time; just enter the characters in the boxes and select the location from the menu nearby (see Figure 8-38).

FIGURE 8-38. The Notation location menu in the Date Format dialog box on Mac OS (left) and Windows (right).

SETTING LEADING CHARACTERS   If you select the Format as option, you can use the menus in the leading characters area (see Figure 8-34) to specify whether a character should appear before single-digit hour, minute, or second numbers. Your options are None, Zero, or Space. None is the default setting for Hours, and Zero is the default setting for Minutes and Seconds.

PREVIEWING YOUR SETTINGS   Check the Sample area at the bottom of the dialog box (see Figure 8-35). It displays a time formatted to your specifications.

APPLYING YOUR SETTINGS   Click the OK button. Your changes are applied to the selected object(s).

Graphic Formatting

Graphic formatting determines the appearance of graphics in container, calculation, or global fields or layout objects. For example:

- Change the size of a graphic to fit within the field or object boundaries.

- Maintain original proportions no matter how the graphic is resized.

- Set horizontal and vertical alignment of a graphic within its boundaries.

You can set these options in the Graphic Format dialog box (see Figure 8-39).

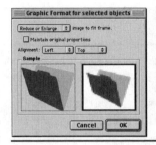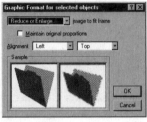

FIGURE 8-39. The Graphic Format dialog box on Mac OS (left) and Windows (right).

OPENING THE GRAPHIC FORMAT DIALOG BOX Select a field or object that contains or can contain a graphic. Then choose Graphic from the Format menu (see Figure 8-1).

SETTING GRAPHIC RESIZING OPTIONS Choose an option from the menu at the top of the dialog box (see Figure 8-40). Your options are:

- **Crop** cuts away the portion of the graphic that does not fit within its boundaries.

- **Reduce**, which is the default choice, reduces the size of the graphic if it does not fit within its boundaries.

- **Enlarge** increases the size of the graphic if it is smaller than its boundaries.

- **Reduce or Enlarge** reduces the size of the graphic if it does not fit within its boundaries and increases the size of the graphic if it is smaller than its boundaries.

FIGURE 8-40. The menu that appears at the top of the Graphic Format dialog box on Mac OS (left) and Windows (right).

ENSURING THAT A GRAPHIC MAINTAINS ITS PROPORTIONS Turn on the Maintain original proportions check box. This ensures that the graphic maintains its proportions no matter how it is resized.

SETTING A GRAPHIC'S ALIGNMENT WITHIN ITS BOUNDARIES Choose options from the two Alignment menus (see Figure 8-41).

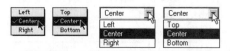

FIGURE 8-41. The Alignment menus in the Graphic Format dialog box on Mac OS (left) and Windows (right). One menu handles horizontal alignment (far left and center-right) while the other handles vertical alignment (center-left and far right).

PREVIEWING YOUR SETTINGS Check the Sample area at the bottom of the dialog box (see Figure 8-39). It displays two images—a File-Maker Pro graphic and a reduced version of the same graphic—with your formatting selections applied.

APPLYING YOUR SETTINGS Click the OK button. Your changes are applied to the selected object(s).

Applying Field Formats

The Field Format dialog box (see Figure 8-42) offers special formatting options that can be applied to selected fields. These options specify a field's style or appearance, repetitions, and behavior.

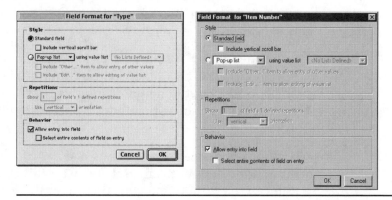

FIGURE 8-42. The Field Format dialog box on Mac OS (left) and Windows (right).

To open the Field Format dialog box, choose Field Format from the Format menu (see Figure 8-1) or press Option-Command-F (Mac OS only). When you're finished setting options, click OK to apply them to selected fields.

Tip   *You can set the default field format for all fields subsequently added to the layout by setting options in the Field Format dialog box when no fields are selected.*

Style

The field's Style options determine its appearance and functionality. Select one of two options to choose the format, then use menus and/or check boxes to set other options.

There are five field styles, each of which are illustrated in Figure 8-43.

- **Standard field** displays the field as an edit or text box, with or without a vertical scroll bar.

- **Pop-up list** displays the field as an edit or text box that displays a menu of options from a specified value list when you select or activate it. You can select an item from the list by clicking with the mouse pointer or by pressing an arrow key and the Return (Mac OS) or Enter (Windows) key.

- **Pop-up menu** displays the field as a menu of options from a specified value list. Mac OS users must use a mouse pointer to display the menu; Windows users can display the menu with a mouse pointer or by activating it with the Tab key.

- **Check boxes** displays the field as a series of check boxes with options from a specified value list. With check boxes, a user can select more than one option for the field.

WARNING   *Do not use check boxes for fields that are calculated with the SUM function or included in subtotals.*

- **Radio buttons** displays the field as a series of radio buttons with options from a specified value list. With radio buttons, a user can normally select only one option for the field, however, a user can make multiple selections by holding down the Shift key while clicking on each option.

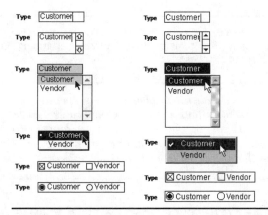

FIGURE 8-43. The field styles supported by FileMaker Pro—standard, standard with vertical scroll bar, pop-up list, pop-up menu, check boxes, and radio buttons—on Mac OS (left) and Windows (right).

FORMATTING A FIELD AS AN EDIT OR TEXT BOX   Select the Standard field option.

FORMATTING A FIELD AS AN EDIT OR TEXT BOX WITH A VERTICAL SCROLL BAR   Select the Standard field option, then turn on the Include vertical scroll bar check box beneath it.

FORMATTING A FIELD AS A POP-UP LIST, POP-UP MENU, CHECK BOXES, OR RADIO BUTTONS   Select the second option in the Style area, then choose a formatting option from the menu beside it (see Figure 8-44). Finally, choose a value list from the value list menu (see Figure 8-45).

FIGURE 8-44. The field style menu in the Field Format dialog box on Mac OS (left) and Windows (right).

FIGURE 8-45. The value list menu in the Field Format dialog box on Mac OS (left) and Windows (right). The items on this menu vary depending on the value lists that exist within the database file.

NOTE *You must select a value list to display a field as a pop-up menu, pop-up list, check boxes, or radio buttons. If an appropriate value list does not exist, choose Define Value Lists from the value list menu (see Figure 8-45) and use the dialog box that appears to create a value list. I explain how to create and modify value lists in the section titled "Value List" on page 353.*

INCLUDING AN "OTHER" OPTION IN A FIELD FORMATTED AS A POP-UP MENU, CHECK BOXES, OR RADIO BUTTONS Follow the instructions in the section titled "Formatting a Field as a Pop-up List, Pop-up Menu, Check Boxes, or Radio Buttons" on page 315 to set up the field as a pop-up menu, check boxes, or radio buttons. Then turn on the Include "Other..." item to allow entry of other values check box. The "Other" option appears with the items from the value list (see Figure 8-46). When a you select it in Browse mode, the Other dialog box appears (see Figure 8-47). Enter a value in the box and click OK to enter it in the field.

FIGURE 8-46. A field formatted as a pop-up menu, check boxes, and radio buttons with an "Other" option on Mac OS.

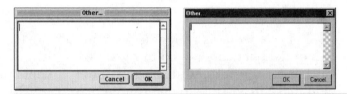

FIGURE 8-47. The Other dialog box on Mac OS (left) and Windows (right).

INCLUDING AN "EDIT" OPTION IN A FIELD FORMATTED AS A POP-UP LIST OR POP-UP MENU Follow the instructions in the section titled "Formatting a Field as a Pop-up List, Pop-up Menu, Check Boxes, or Radio Buttons" on page 315 to set up the field as a pop-up list or pop-up menu. Then turn on the Include "Edit…" item to allow editing of the value list check box. The "Edit" option appears with the items from the value list (see Figure 8-48). When you select it in Browse mode, the Edit Value List dialog box appears (see Figure 8-49). Edit the value list as desired and click OK. Choose a value from the edited pop-up list or pop-up menu to enter data in the field.

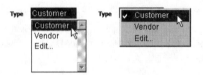

FIGURE 8-48. A field formatted as a pop-up list and a pop-up menu with an "Edit" option on Windows.

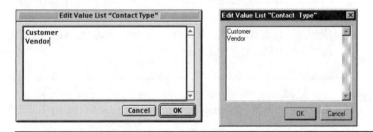

FIGURE 8-49. The Edit Value List dialog box on Mac OS (left) and Windows (right).

Repetitions

A field's Repetitions options (see Figure 8-50) determine the number of field containers—edit or text boxes, menus, etc.—that will appear for the field. By displaying multiple containers for a field, you make it possible to enter more than one field value. Repetitions options in the Field Format dialog box are used in conjunction with the repetitions option in the Entry Options dialog box. I explain the concept of repeating fields in detail in the section titled "Storage Options" on page 363.

FIGURE 8-50. Repetitions options in the Field Format dialog box on Mac OS (top) and Windows (bottom).

NOTE *The Repetitions options in the Field Format dialog box are available only if the field has been defined with repetitions. Otherwise, the options will appear gray (see Figure 8-42).*

SETTING THE NUMBER OF DISPLAYED REPETITIONS FOR A FIELD Use the Entry Options dialog box for the field to specify a number of field repetitions greater than 1. Then select the field and open the Field Format dialog box. Enter the number of repetitions you want to display in the Show box.

NOTE *If you attempt to enter a value greater than the number of defined repetitions for the field, a dialog box like the one in Figure 8-51 appears. Click OK to dismiss it and enter a different value within the range.*

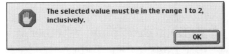
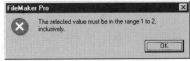

FIGURE 8-51. The dialog box that appears on Mac OS (left) and Windows (right) when you attempt to display more repetitions than are defined for a field.

SETTING THE ORIENTATION OF DISPLAYED REPETITIONS With a value greater than 1 in the Show box, choose an option from the orientation menu beneath it (see Figure 8-52).

- **Vertical** displays the repetitions one above the other (see Figure 8-53, right).

- **Horizontal** displays the repetitions one beside the other (see Figure 8-53, left).

FIGURE 8-52. The orientation menu in the Repetitions area of the Field Format dialog box on Mac OS (left) and Windows (right).

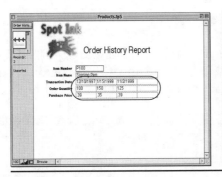
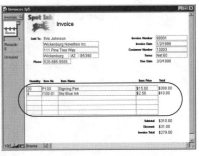

FIGURE 8-53. Four repetitions of three fields displayed horizontally on Mac OS (left) and five repetitions of five fields displayed vertically on Windows (right).

Behavior

A field's Behavior options determine whether it can be activated in Browse mode and what happens when it is.

PREVENTING DATA FROM BEING ENTERED INTO A LAYOUT'S FIELD Select the field for which you want to disable entry. In the Field Format dialog box, turn off the Allow entry into field check box. This prevents the field from being activated in Browse mode.

SELECTING A FIELD'S CONTENTS AUTOMATICALLY WHEN THE FIELD IS ACTIVATED If necessary, turn on the Allow entry into field check box for the field. Then turn on the Select entire contents of field on entry check box. In Browse mode, when you select the field, all of its contents will be selected.

 TIP   *Turn this option on for any field you expect to edit regularly. This saves time when you need to change the field's contents—you won't have to manually select everything in the field before you type in replacement text.*

Setting Field Borders

The Field Borders dialog box (see Figure 8-54) enables you to display borders, text baselines, and fill for fields. These formatting options appear both on screen and in printed reports.

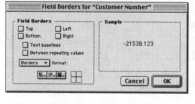

FIGURE 8-54. The Field Borders dialog box on Mac OS (left) and Windows (right).

To open the Field Borders dialog box, choose Field Borders from the Format menu (see Figure 8-1) or press Option-Command-B (Mac OS only). Set options as desired; you can view the effect of your changes in the Sample area of the dialog box. When you're finished, click OK to apply your settings to the selected field(s).

*T**ip*** *You can set the default field border options for all fields subsequently added to the layout by setting options in the Field Borders dialog box when no fields are selected.*

DISPLAYING BORDERS OR TEXT BASELINES Turn on the desired check boxes in the Field Borders area of the dialog box:

- **Top** displays the top border of the field.

- **Bottom** displays the bottom border of the field.

- **Left** displays the left border of the field.

- **Right** displays the right border of the field.

- **Text baselines** displays the lines on which text appears within the field box.

- **Between repeating values** displays borders between each displayed repetition. (I tell you how to display a field's defined repetitions in the section titled "Repetitions" on page 318.)

Figure 8-55 shows two examples of field border options set for fields.

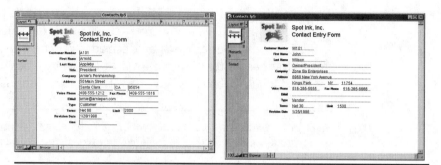

FIGURE 8-55. Left and bottom field borders set for fields on Mac OS (left) and text baselines set for fields on Windows (right).

MODIFYING THE APPEARANCE OF FIELD BORDERS, TEXT BASELINES, OR FIELD FILL Choose the type of item that you want to modify from the format menu in the Field Borders dialog box (see Figure 8-56). Then use the menus at the bottom of the dialog box to set options:

- **Color** (see Figure 8-57, left) sets the color of the border, text baseline, or fill.

- **Pattern** (see Figure 8-57, center) sets the pattern of the border, text baseline, or fill. The first option removes pattern or fill; the second option (beside it) sets a solid fill.

- **Line** thickness (see Figure 8-57, right) sets the thickness of the border or text baseline.

FIGURE 8-56. The format menu in the Field Borders dialog box on Mac OS (left) and Windows (right).

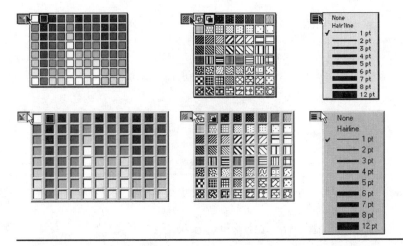

FIGURE 8-57. The color (left), pattern (center), and line thickness (right) menus in the Field Borders dialog box on Mac OS (top) and Windows (bottom).

Other Layout Formatting Options

In this section, I provide details on two more commonly used layout options: setting alignment and tab order. I also explain how to use miscellaneous options discussed in Chapter 5 to format selected objects.

NOTE *You must be in Layout mode to set the formatting options I discuss in this part of the chapter.*

Aligning Objects

The Arrange menu (see Figure 8-58) offers two commands you can use to align and distribute space between multiple objects on a layout—Align and Set Alignment. Here's how they work.

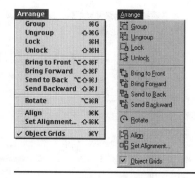

FIGURE 8-58. The Arrange menu on Mac OS (left) and Windows (right).

Selecting Objects to Align

Before you use the Align or Set Alignment commands, you must select at least two layout objects to align. In most cases, the objects will be aligned vertically or horizontally, with space between them. Figure 8-59 shows two examples of fields selected for alignment.

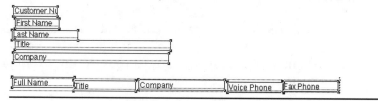

FIGURE 8-59. Unaligned fields selected on Mac OS (top) and Windows (bottom).

Setting Alignment

To set alignment options, choose Set Alignment from the Arrange menu (see Figure 8-58) or press Shift-Command-K (Mac OS) or Control-Shift-K (Windows). The Set Alignment dialog box appears (see Figure 8-60).

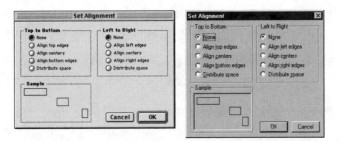

FIGURE 8-60. The Set Alignment dialog box on Mac OS (left) and Windows (right).

SETTING VERTICAL ALIGNMENT Select one of the options in the Top to Bottom area of the dialog box:

- **None** does not set any vertical alignment.

- **Align top edges** places the top edges of all selected objects along the same invisible line.

- **Align centers** places the vertical center of all selected objects along the same invisible line.

- **Align bottom edges** places the bottom edges of all selected objects along the same invisible line.

- **Distribute space** adds up the vertical space between each object and redistributes it evenly.

SETTING HORIZONTAL ALIGNMENT Select one of the options in the Left to Right area of the dialog box:

- **None** does not set any horizontal alignment.

- **Align left edges** places the left edges of all selected objects along the same invisible line.

- **Align centers** places the horizontal center of all selected objects along the same invisible line.

- **Align right edges** places the right edges of all selected objects along the same invisible line.

- **Distribute space** adds up the horizontal space between each object and redistributes it evenly (see Figure 8-61).

SETTING VERTICAL AND HORIZONTAL ALIGNMENT AT THE SAME TIME Choose an option from the Top to Bottom and Left to Right areas.

PREVIEWING ALIGNMENT SETTINGS Check the illustration in the Sample area of the dialog box. If it does not align the sample boxes the way you want selected objects aligned, something's not set right.

ACCEPTING ALIGNMENT SETTINGS Click OK. The selected objects are aligned according to settings in the Set Alignment dialog box.

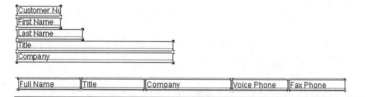

FIGURE 8-61. The selected fields from Figure 8-59 after aligning them. For the top five fields, the Set Alignment dialog box options were set to Distribute space and Align left edges. For the bottom five fields, the Set Alignment dialog box options were set to Align bottom edges and Distribute space.

WARNING   *If you use the Set Alignment or Align command and get unexpected results, immediately choose Undo Alignment from the Edit menu. You can then try again. If you attempt to fix an incorrect alignment by using the Set Alignment dialog box again without first undoing the error, there's a good chance you'll make it worse! I know—I've been there!*

Repeating an Alignment

Once you've set options in the Set Alignment dialog box, you can perform the same alignment on different selected objects without reopening the dialog box. Simply select Align from the Arrange menu (see Figure 8-58) or press Command-K (Mac OS) or Control-K (Windows).

NOTE *If the Top to Bottom and Left to Right alignment options are both set to None in the Set Alignment dialog box, the Align command will be gray.*

Setting Tab Order

By far, the quickest way to advance from field to field in Browse or Find mode is by pressing the Tab key. But what if the Tab key doesn't advance you to fields in the order in which you want to work with them?

Don't worry. FileMaker Pro has you covered. You can use the Set Tab Order command under the Layouts menu (see Figure 8-62) to specify the exact order in which fields should be activated when you press the Tab key in Browse mode. Here's how.

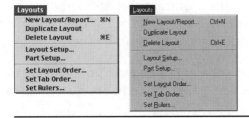

FIGURE 8-62. The Layouts menu on Mac OS (left) and Windows (right).

EDITING AN EXISTING TAB ORDER Choose Set Tab Order from the Layouts menu (see Figure 8-62). Tab markers appear on the layout and the Set Tab Order dialog box appears (see Figure 8-63). Make sure the Edit tab order option is selected in the Set Tab Order dialog box. Then click a tab marker that you want to change and type in a new order number. Repeat the click-type process until you've changed all the markers you want to change. Then click OK to apply the revised tab order.

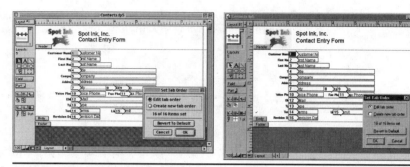

FIGURE 8-63. Setting tab order on Mac OS (left) and Windows (right). Note: The illustration on the right includes repeating fields.

CREATING A NEW TAB ORDER Choose Set Tab Order from the Layouts menu (see Figure 8-62). Tab markers appear on the layout and the Set Tab Order dialog box appears (see Figure 8-63). Select the Create new tab order option in the Set Tab Order dialog box to remove all the numbers from the tab markers. Then click the tab markers in the order you wish to set the tabs. When you're finished, click OK to apply the new tab order.

OMITTNG FIELDS FROM A TAB ORDER Follow the instructions in one of the previous sections to edit or create a tab order. Then:

- To omit a field from a tab order that you are editing, select the number in the field's tab marker box and press Delete (Mac OS) or Backspace (Windows) to remove it. Do not assign a new tab number.

- To omit a field from a new tab order, simply skip over it when clicking tab markers.

When you click OK to apply the revised or new tab order, a dialog box like the one in Figure 8-64 appears. Click the Omit button to omit the fields from the tab order. In Browse mode, those fields will be skipped over when you press the Tab key.

FIGURE 8-64. The dialog box that appears on Mac OS (left) and Windows (right) when you omit fields from a tab order.

RESETTING THE TAB ORDER TO THE DEFAULT ORDER Choose Set Tab Order from the Layouts menu (see Figure 8-62). Then click the Revert to Default button in the Set Tab Order dialog box (see Figure 8-63). Click OK to apply the default tab order.

 By default, when you press the Tab key in Browse mode, fields are activated from left to right in the same row across the screen, then down to the next row. Use the alignment commands, which I discuss in the section titled "Aligning Objects" on page 323, to assure that objects that appear in the same row across the screen are properly aligned if you want to use the default tab order to tab across a row of fields.

Other Object Formatting Options

The Arrange menu (see Figure 8-58) and status area offer a number of other commands and tools for formatting selected objects. They're pretty straightforward and easy to use, so I'll just discuss them briefly here. You can find more information about these options in Chapter 5.

Using Arrange Menu Options

The Arrange menu options (see Figure 8-58) can group, ungroup, lock, unlock, change stacking order, align, or rotate one or more selected objects. To use one of these commands, select one or more objects and choose the command.

You can learn more about each command and see illustrations of them in action in the section titled "Layouts Menu Commands" on page 193. I tell you about the alignment commands earlier in this chapter, in the section titled "Aligning Objects" on page 323.

Formatting Drawn Objects

The status area offers a number of palettes you can use to change the appearance of drawn objects. There are two ways to use these palettes.

DRAWING AN OBJECT WITH SPECIFIC FORMATTING Make sure no object on the layout is selected. Then use the appropriate palette(s) to set formatting as desired. (This sets default formatting for the drawing tools.) When you use a drawing tool to create an object, the object is created with the formatting options you set.

CHANGING THE APPEARANCE OF AN EXISTING DRAWN OBJECT Select the object(s) that you want to format. Then use the appropriate palette(s) to change the formatting as desired. This changes only the selected objects; it does not affect default settings.

I provide specific details and illustrations of each formatting palette in the status area in the section titled "Color, Pattern, and Width Palettes" on page 182.

TIP   *You can also use the Fill Color and Pattern palettes to assign a color and/or pattern to the background of a layout part. Click to select the part tag (see Figure 8-65), then use the appropriate palette to make the change.*

FIGURE 8-65. Four part tags on Mac OS; the Body tag, which appears here in dark gray, is selected.

Managing Layouts

At this point, you have enough information about working with FileMaker Pro layouts to create dozens of layouts in your database files. You might be wondering how you can take control of all those layouts.

That's what this part of the chapter is all about. It provides layout management techniques that you can use to organize the layouts you've created.

Renaming a Layout

One of the things you'll probably want to do sooner or later is rename a layout. Layout #1 is a good candidate. After all, if *you* were going to name it, would you name it *that*? I think you have more imagination than FileMaker Pro has.

You change a layout's name with the Layout Setup dialog box (see Figure 8-66), which I introduced in the section titled "Setting Other Layout Options" on page 224. If you recall, you can open the Layout Setup dialog box by choosing Layout Setup from the Layouts menu (see Figure 8-62).

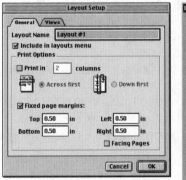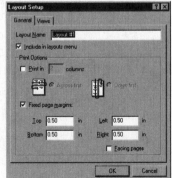

FIGURE 8-66. The Layout Setup dialog box on Mac OS (left) and Windows (right).

To rename a layout, enter a new name in the Layout Name box. Then click OK to accept the change. The new name appears in the layouts menu at the top of the status area. It also changes in any buttons or scripts within the file.

Changing Layout Order

You can use the Set Layout Order dialog box (see Figure 8-67) to change the order in which layouts appear on the layouts menu in the status area and any other list of layouts within the file.

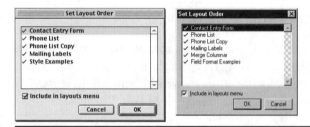

FIGURE 8-67. The Set Layout Order dialog box on Mac OS (left) and Windows (right).

Open the Set Layout Order dialog box by choosing Set Layout Order from the Layouts menu (see Figure 8-62). Then use your mouse pointer to drag layout names up or down in the list to change their order. Click OK to save your changes.

Excluding a Layout from the Layouts Menu

You can exclude a layout from the Layouts menu at the top of the status area. This is particularly helpful if you have a lot of layouts and want to keep the Layouts menu as short as possible.

NOTE   *When you exclude a layout from the Layouts menu, the only way to view that layout is to switch first to Layout mode or to use a button or script that switches to the layout.*

FileMaker Pro offers two ways to exclude a layout from the layouts menu: with the Layout Setup dialog box (see Figure 8-66) and with the Set Layout Order dialog box (see Figure 8-67).

EXCLUDING A LAYOUT FROM THE LAYOUTS POP-UP MENU WITH THE LAYOUT SETUP DIALOG BOX   Switch to the layout that you want to exclude from the layouts pop-up menu in the status area. Then choose Layout setup from the Layouts menu (see Figure 8-62) to open the Layout Setup dialog box (see Figure 8-66). Turn off the Include in layouts menu check box and click OK.

EXCLUDING ONE OR MORE LAYOUTS FROM THE LAYOUTS MENU WITH THE SET LAYOUT ORDER DIALOG BOX   Choose Set Layout Order from the Layouts menu (see Figure 8-62) to open the Set Layout Order dialog box (see Figure 8-67). Click on the check mark to the left of a layout that you want to exclude from the layouts menu to remove the check mark. Repeat this step for every layout that you want to exclude from the menu. When you're finished, click OK.

NOTE   *As you've probably guessed, you can use the same two techniques to include a previously excluded layout on the layouts menu. Simply turn on the check box or check mark in the Layout Setup or Set Layout Order dialog box.*

Duplicating a Layout

When you want to create a layout that is very similar to an existing layout, you can save a lot of time and trouble by simply duplicating the existing layout first, then making necessary modifications. Duplicating a layout is also a great way to experiment with a layout if you're not sure whether you'll want to keep your changes.

To duplicate a layout, switch to the layout that you want to duplicate and choose Duplicate Layout from the Layouts menu (see Figure 8-62). A copy of the layout appears. Its name is the same as the original layout with the word *copy* appended to it. I tell you how to rename a layout in the section titled "Renaming a Layout" on page 331.

Deleting a Layout

Got a layout you never use anymore? Or perhaps you experimented so much with a copy of a layout that it's a huge mess you never want to see again? Delete it!

NOTE *Deleting a layout does not delete data. The only way to delete data in FileMaker Pro is to delete records or fields from the database.*

To delete a layout, switch to the layout that you want to delete and choose Delete Layout from the Layouts menu (see Figure 8-62) or press Command-E (Mac OS) or Control-E (Windows). A dialog box like the one in Figure 8-68 appears. To permanently delete the layout, click the Delete button.

FIGURE 8-68. The dialog box that appears on Mac OS (left) and Windows (right) when you attempt to delete a layout.

WARNING *When I say "permanently delete," I'm not kidding. You cannot undo the Delete Layout command.*

Step-by-Step

This chapter covered all kinds of formatting options you can use to fine-tune the appearance of the layouts you create in your File-Maker Pro databases. Ready to give some of those options a try?

In this section, I provide step-by-step instructions for modifying the layouts in the database files you've been working on at the end of each chapter. If you've been skipping around in the book and don't have the completed exercise files from Chapter 7, you can download them from the companion Web site for this book, http://www.gilesrd.com/fmprocomp/.

Formatting Text and Fields

The data entry form you modified in Chapter 7 can use some additional modifications. Here are the instructions to get you started. If there are other changes you want to make, please do!

1. Open the file named Contacts.fp5 and switch to Layout #1.

2. Switch to Layout mode.

3. Use the Layout Setup dialog box to rename the layout *Contact Entry Form*.

4. Select the text *Spot Ink, Inc.* in the header and make it 24 points and bold.

5. Select the text *Contact Entry Form* in the header and make it 18 points.

6. Select the entire text object in the header and horizontally center its contents.

7. Select both objects in the header and use the Set Alignment dialog box to align their vertical centers.

8. Select all fields on the layout and use the Field Borders dialog box to display text baselines.

9. Use the Field Format dialog box to format all the fields so their entire content is selected on entry.

10. Select the Limit field and use the Number Format dialog box to format it as a decimal number with two decimal places, currency notation, and thousands separator.

11. Select the Revision date field and use the Date Format dialog box to format it with standard mm/dd/yy formatting. Make sure a zero appears as a leading digit for single-digit month and day numbers.

12. Switch to Browse mode to see the effect of your changes.

Formatting Text and Fields, Take 2

Now repeat some of the steps in the previous section to make similar modifications to Layout #1 in the Products.fp5 file. If you'd like to make other changes, feel free to do so.

1. Open the file named Products.fp5 and switch to Layout mode.

2. Rename the layout to *Product Entry Form*.

3. Format the text object in the header so it's 18 points.

4. Align the vertical centers of the two objects in the header.

5. Use the Number Format dialog box to Format the Purchase Price and Selling Price fields as currency with two decimal points and a thousands separator.

6. Use the Number Format dialog box to Format the Reorder Point field with zero decimal points and a thousands separator.

7. Use the Field Format dialog box to format all the fields so their entire content is selected on entry.

8. Use the Field Format dialog box to display a vertical scroll bar in the Product Description field.

9. Switch to Browse mode to see the effect of your changes.

Formatting Text and Fields, Take 3

Guess what? The Invoices.fp5 file can also use some modifications. Repeat some of the steps in the previous two sections to make modifications to Layout #1 in this file. If you'd like to make other changes, feel free to do so.

1. Open the file named Invoices.fp5 and switch to Layout mode.

2. Rename the layout to *Invoices*.

3. Format the *Invoice* text object in the header so it's 18 points.

4. Align the vertical centers of the company logo and *Invoice* text object in the header.

5. Use the Field Borders dialog box to display dark gray Left and Bottom borders and light gray fill for all fields.

6. Use the Number Format dialog box to format the Selling Price, Extended Price, and Invoice Total fields as currency with two decimal places and a thousands separator.

7. Use the Number Format dialog box to format the Quantity field with zero decimal places and thousands separator.

8. Use the Set Tab Order dialog box to create a new tab order as follows: Customer Name, Company, Address, City, State, Zip, Voice Phone, Invoice Number, Invoice Date, Customer Number, Terms, Due Date, Quantity, Item Number, Item Name, and Selling Price. Omit any fields that are not listed here.

9. Switch to Browse mode to see the effect of your changes.

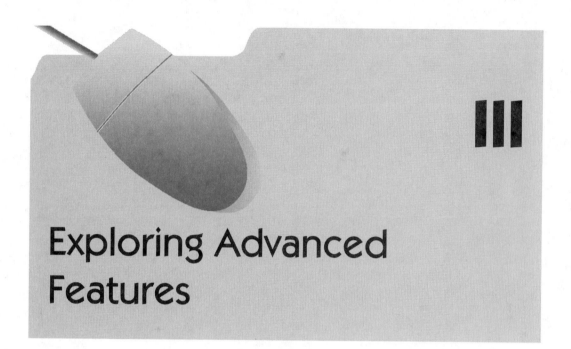

Exploring Advanced Features

This part of the book begins to go beyond the basics of using File-Maker Pro by covering more advanced topics. Its four chapters are:

Chapter 9: Using Field Entry Options

Chapter 10: Tapping into the Power of Calculations

Chapter 11: Developing Relationships between Files

Chapter 12: Working with Scripts and Buttons

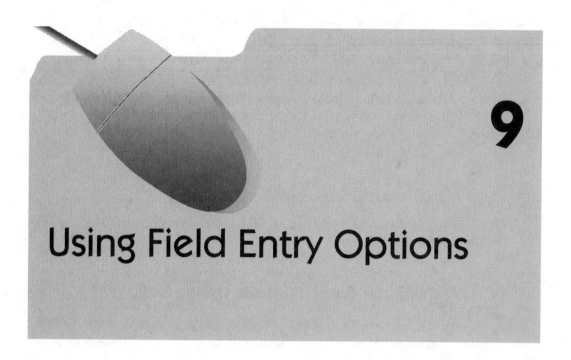

Using Field Entry Options

9

Back in Chapter 2, I explain how to define fields. But there's one important concept I left out: *field entry options*. That's what this chapter is all about.

About Field Entry Options

Field entry options are additional settings within a field's definition that affect the way data is entered or accepted in a field.

Types of Field Entry Options

There are two main categories of field options:

- **Auto Enter** options instruct FileMaker Pro to enter certain data into a field automatically.

- **Validation** options instruct FileMaker Pro to check that the value entered into a field matches certain criteria before accepting the entry.

Field entry options also include the number of repetitions for a field, which I discuss briefly in the section titled "Repetitions" on page 318, and storage options.

In this chapter, I tell you about all entry options available for File-Maker Pro fields.

Using the Entry Options Dialog Box

You can use the Entry Options dialog box (see Figure 9-1) to set many different combinations of field entry options for text, number, date, and time fields.

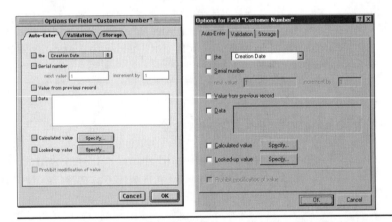

FIGURE 9-1. The Auto Enter options of the Entry Options dialog box on Mac OS (left) and Windows (right).

OPENING THE ENTRY OPTIONS DIALOG BOX If necessary, choose Define Fields from the File menu to open the Define Fields dialog box. Then use one of the following techniques:

- Click once on the name of the field for which you want to set entry options to select it. Then click the Options button.

- Double-click the name of the field for which you want to set entry options.

DISPLAYING AUTO ENTER, VALIDATION, OR STORAGE OPTIONS Click the tab for the type of option you want to display.

SAVING SETTINGS IN THE ENTRY OPTIONS DIALOG BOX After setting options as desired in all tabs of the dialog box, click OK.

Auto Enter Options

Auto enter options (see Figure 9-1) tell FileMaker Pro to enter data into the field as you create it. This saves you the bother of entering data manually.

NOTE *Auto enter options apply only to new records as they are created. Setting auto enter options for a field does not affect the contents of the field in existing records.*

To select one of the auto enter options, turn on its check box. Then, if necessary, specify additional information for the option.

Here are the details for each type of auto enter option, along with some suggestions on how you can use them.

Creation/Modification Information

The first auto enter option displays a menu of six different pieces of information that FileMaker Pro can enter automatically in the field (see Figure 9-2):

FIGURE 9-2. The menu for the first auto enter option in the Entry Options dialog box on Mac OS (left) and Windows (right).

- **Creation Date** is the date the record was created.

- **Creation Time** is the time the record was created.

- **Modification Date** is the date the record was last modified.

- **Modification Time** is the time the record was last modified.

- **Creator Name** is the active user name when the record was created.

- **Modifier Name** is the active user name when the record was modified.

NOTE *FileMaker Pro gets the creation and modification date and time from the computer's system clock. It gets the creator and modifier name from the User Name option in the General Application Preferences dialog box; I tell you more about that in the section titled "General" on page 35.*

NOTE *The options that are available for selection from this menu vary depending on the type of field. I describe field types in the section titled "Types of Fields" on page 55.*

Use these options in separate fields within a database to automatically track when a record was created and modified and who was responsible for the changes.

Serial Number

A serial number is a number that automatically increments each time a new record is added to the database. As the name suggests, it's commonly used to enter serial numbers like invoice, item, or customer numbers.

Creating Serial Numbers

To create serial numbers, turn on the Serial number check box and enter values in the two boxes beneath it:

- **Next value** is the value that you want to appear in the field for the next new record that you create.

- **Increment by** is the value by which you want to increment the serial numbers. This is normally 1, but can be any number you like.

Figure 9-3 shows two examples of how the serial number option can be used to enter invoice numbers automatically.

FIGURE 9-3. Setting up serial numbers on Mac OS (left) and Windows (right).

 You can include text characters in the next value box if desired. For example, if you enter INV001 in the next value box, the following values will be entered into each new record: INV001, INV002, INV003, etc.

WARNING *The value in the next value box automatically changes each time you create a new record. If you change this value to a lower value already used, duplicate serial numbers may result! I tell you how to prevent duplicate entries in a field in the section titled "Unique" on page 353.*

Reserializing Records

Occasionally, you might want to enter serial numbers either in a field that does not already contain them or in a field that contains other data. You can perform this task, which is often referred to as *reserializing*, with the Replace dialog box.

NOTE   *The Replace dialog box is used to replace the contents of a field in all records being browsed. I tell you more about the Replace dialog box in the section titled "Replacing Field Contents" on page 112 and "Replacing Field Contents with Calculated Results" on page 378.*

Start by using the Find or Find All command to Browse the records that you want to reserialize. In the first record, click inside the field in which you want to enter serial numbers. Then choose Replace from the Records menu (see Figure 9-4) or press Command-= (Mac OS) or Control-= (Windows) to display the Replace dialog box (see Figure 9-5).

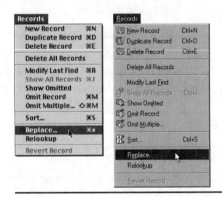

FIGURE 9-4. Choosing Replace from the Records menu on Mac OS (left) and Windows (right).

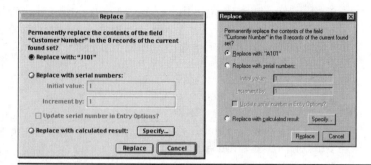

FIGURE 9-5. The Replace dialog box on Mac OS (left) and Windows (right).

Select the Replace with serial number option. Then enter values in the two boxes beneath it:

- **Initial value** is the value that you want to appear in the field for the first record being browsed.

- **Increment by** is the value by which you want to increment the serial numbers.

If you want subsequently created records to continue numbering where the reserialized numbers end, turn on the Update serial number in Entry Options? check box. This option, which only appears if the field already has the serial number option entry option turned on, resets the serial number values in the Entry Options dialog box (see Figure 9-3) for the field.

When you're finished setting options, click Replace. The field's values change according to your settings.

  You cannot undo the Replace command!

Value from Previous Record

The Value from Previous Record option tells FileMaker Pro to copy the value in the same field of the previous record to the field in the new record. It's the same as activating the field and choosing From Last Record from the Insert menu—except that File-Maker Pro does all the work automatically for you.

Data

The Data option enables you to specify a value that you want File-Maker Pro to enter automatically into the field.

To use this option, turn on the Data check box, then enter the value that you want FileMaker Pro to enter. That value appears automatically in that field for every new record that you create.

TIP   *I often use this feature to specify a default value in conjunction with a value list when a particular option is usually the one selected by a user. I tell you how to create and use value lists in the section titled "Value List" on page 353.*

Calculated Value

The Calculated value option tells FileMaker Pro to enter a value based on a calculation you specify.

To use this option, turn on the Calculated value check box. The Specify Calculation dialog box (see Figure 9-6) should open automatically; if it doesn't, click the Specify button. Then use the dialog box to enter the calculation that should be evaluated to enter data into the field. When you're finished, click OK to save the calculation.

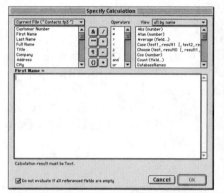

FIGURE 9-6. The Specify Calculation dialog box on Mac OS (left) and Windows (right).

TIP *The Specify Calculation dialog box appears when creating calculation fields and in other places throughout FileMaker Pro. I tell you all about it—including how to use it to create simple and complex calculations—in Chapter 10.*

NOTE *You might be wondering what the difference is between setting this option for a text, number, date, or time field, and creating a calculation field. Here are the two main differences. First, a field using this option to enter data can be edited in Browse mode; a calculation field cannot. Second, a field using this option to enter data will not automatically change if the contents of a field referenced by its formula change; a calculation field changes automatically each time the contents of a field referenced by its formula changes.*

Looked-Up Value

The Looked-up value option instructs FileMaker Pro to look up a value in another database file and copy that value to the field. For example, you can use a lookup to get an item's description or price from an inventory database when you enter the item number in an invoices database. This feature works in conjunction with the related files feature, which I discuss in detail throughout Chapter 11.

To use this option, turn on its check box. Then use the Lookup dialog box that appears to set the lookup options. Since this feature requires a relationship between the current file and another file, I won't say any more about it here. Instead, check Chapter 11, especially the section titled "Looking Up Values in a Related File" on page 426.

Prohibiting Modification

If you select any of the auto enter options, you can also turn on the Prohibit modification of value check box. If you do, the field's contents cannot be modified. If you try to enter a value in the field manually, a dialog box like the one in Figure 9-7 appears.

FIGURE 9-7. The dialog box that appears on Mac OS (left) and Windows (right) when you attempt to change the contents of a field that cannot be modified.

 TIP *If you want to allow some users to enter values into a field but prevent others, use FileMaker Pro's access privileges features. I tell you all about them in Chapter 17.*

Validation Options

Validation options (see Figure 9-8) tell FileMaker Pro to check the values you enter into a field as you enter it. If the data you enter into the field does not pass validation, FileMaker Pro displays a warning dialog box similar to the ones in Figure 9-9 to provide more information about the data that is expected. This helps ensure that data is correctly entered.

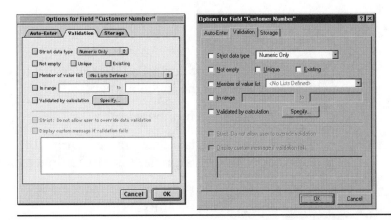

FIGURE 9-8. The Validation options of the Entry Options dialog box on Mac OS (left) and Windows (right).

FIGURE 9-9. Examples of the kinds of dialog boxes that appear on Mac OS (left) and Windows (right) if an entry fails validation.

NOTE *Validation options apply only to a field as data is entered into it. Setting validation options for a field does not affect existing field entries.*

TIP *By default, you can override the validation feature; I tell you how to prevent overriding the feature in the section titled "Allowing Overrides" on page 362.*

To select one of the validation options, turn on its check box. Then, if necessary, specify additional information for the option.

Here are the details for each type of validation option, along with some suggestions on how you can use them.

Strict Data Type

The Strict data type option tells FileMaker Pro to verify that the field's value is one of the following types:

- **Numeric Only** is a number entry.

- **4-Digit Year Date** is a date entered with all four digits of the year. This helps prevent confusion over dates in the 1900s or 2000s.

- **Time of Day** is a time entry.

With the Strict data type option turned on, if you enter the wrong type of data, a warning dialog box appears (see Figure 9-9).

To use this option, turn on the Strict data type check box, then choose an option from its menu (see Figure 9-10).

FIGURE 9-10. The Strict data type menu in the Entry Options dialog box on Mac OS (left) and Windows (right).

Not Empty

The Not empty option tells FileMaker Pro to make sure the field is not empty. With this option turned on, if you leave the field empty, a warning dialog box appears (see Figure 9-9).

Unique

The Unique option tells FileMaker Pro to make sure the value in the field does not already exist in the same field in another record of the database. With this check box turned on, if you enter an existing value, a warning dialog box appears (see Figure 9-9).

TIP   *Use this option in conjunction with the serial number auto entry option to prevent duplicate serial numbers from being entered. I tell you about the serial number option in the section titled "Serial Number" on page 345.*

Existing

The Existing option is the opposite of the Unique option. It tells FileMaker Pro to make sure the value in the field already exists in the same field in another record of the database. With this check box turned on, if you enter a unique value, a warning dialog box appears (see Figure 9-9).

TIP   *This is a great option to help ensure consistent data entry. To learn why that should interest you, read the section titled "The Importance of Consistent Data Entry" on page 89.*

NOTE   *Are you wondering how FileMaker Pro knows whether an entry is unique or existing? It uses an automatic indexing feature to keep track of field contents. I tell you more about that in the section titled "Indexing" on page 367.*

Value List

The Value list feature, which I discuss briefly in the section titled "Style" on page 314, enables you to create a list of valid values for the field. You can then tell FileMaker Pro to make sure the field's contents matches one of the values in the value list.

The value list feature is one of the more powerful features of File-Maker Pro. Here are some of the ways you can use it:

- Use the Field Format dialog box to display a list of possible values for a field as a pop-up list, pop-up menu, radio buttons, or check boxes. This enables users to select one of the values when entering data in the field or using the field to enter find criteria. I explain how to format a field using one of these options in the section titled "Style" on page 314.

- Specify a custom sort order based on the order of items in a list of values for the field. This enables you to sort records in an order other than ascending or descending. For example, if a Size field used a value list containing the values X-Small, Small, Medium, Large, and X-Large, you could sort in that order. I tell you how to set sort order in the section titled "Selecting the Field's Sort Order" on page 155.

- Check the field's entry against a list of values to ensure that the entry is valid. I tell you how to validate an entry with a value list in the section titled "Using a Value List for Entry Validation" on page 360.

Creating a Value List

Before you can use a value list, you must create it. That's what the Define Value Lists dialog box (see Figure 9-11) is for.

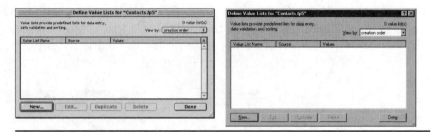

FIGURE 9-11. The Define Value Lists dialog box on Mac OS (left) and Windows (right).

OPENING THE DEFINE VALUE LISTS DIALOG BOX Use one of the following techniques:

- Choose Define Value Lists from a value list menu (see Figure 9-12) within a dialog box, such as the Member of value list menu in the Entry Options dialog box (see Figure 9-8).

FIGURE 9-12. A value list menu in a dialog box on Mac OS (left) and Windows (right).

- Choose Define Value Lists from the File menu (see Figure 9-13).

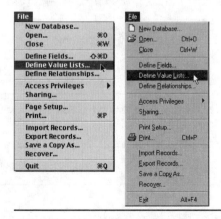

FIGURE 9-13. Choosing Define Value Lists from the File menu on Mac OS (left) and Windows (right).

CREATING A VALUE LIST Click the New button in the Define value Lists window. In the Edit Value List dialog box that appears (see Figure 9-14), enter a name for the value list and specify value list contents as discussed in the next few sections.

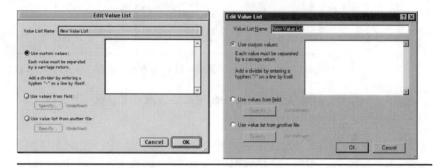

FIGURE 9-14. The Edit Value List dialog box on Mac OS (left) and Windows (right).

ADDING CUSTOM VALUES TO A VALUE LIST In the Edit Value List dialog box (see Figure 9-14), make sure the Use custom values option is selected. Then enter the items that you want to include in the value list in the large list box. Press the Return (Mac OS) or Enter (Windows) key after each entry. Figure 9-15 shows two examples of custom value lists.

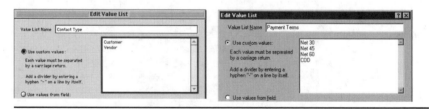

FIGURE 9-15. Examples of custom value lists in the Edit Value List dialog box on Mac OS (left) and Windows (right).

TIP *To include a separator in the value list, enter a hyphen or dash on a line by itself.*

USING VALUES FROM A FIELD IN THE SAME DATABASE FILE In the Edit Value List dialog box (see Figure 9-14), select the Use values from field option. The Specify Fields for Value List dialog box (see Figure 9-16) should appear automatically; if it does not, click the Specify button. Make sure the All values option is selected and that the name of the current database file appears beside the Specify File button. Then select the field that contains the values that you want to use in the list. Click OK to save your settings and return to the Edit Value List dialog box.

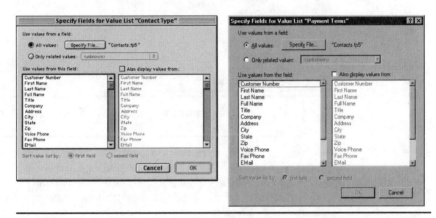

FIGURE 9-16. The Specify Fields for Value List dialog box on Mac OS (left) and Windows (right).

T*IP*   *If desired, you can also display values from a second field in the value list. The two values will appear side by side, although only the first value is stored in the field when selected. To include a second field, turn on the Also display values from check box and select one of the fields beneath it. You can then select one of the Sort value list by options at the bottom of the dialog box to determine in which order the value list items appear.*

USING VALUES FROM A FIELD IN A DIFFERENT DATABASE FILE   Follow the instructions in the previous section, but when the Specify Fields for Value List dialog box appears (see Figure 9-16), click the Specify File button. Use the Open File dialog box that appears (see Figure 9-17) to select and open the file containing the field with the values you want to appear in the value list. Then continue following the instructions in the previous section to select a field and click OK to save your settings and return to the Edit Value List dialog box.

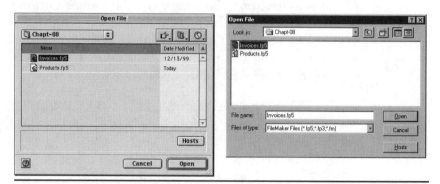

FIGURE 9-17. The Open File dialog box on Mac OS (left) and Windows (right).

Tip *This is a great way to relate one file to another without creating a formal relationship. For example, in the Step-by-Step section of this chapter, you'll use this feature to create a value list in the Invoices.fp5 file that displays item numbers from the Products.fp5 file. I tell you more about developing relationships between files in Chapter 11.*

SAVING A VALUE LIST   When you're finished setting or modifying value list contents in the Edit Value List dialog box, click the OK button. Your value list appears in the Define Value Lists dialog box (see Figure 9-18).

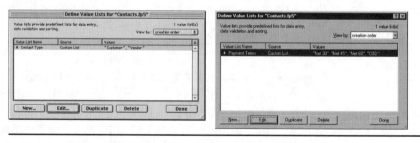

FIGURE 9-18. A newly defined value list in the Define Value Lists dialog box on Mac OS (left) and Windows (right).

CLOSING THE DEFINE VALUE LISTS DIALOG BOX When you are finished defining value lists, click the Done button to save your changes and dismiss the Define Value Lists dialog box.

Editing, Duplicating, or Deleting a Value List

You use the Define Value Lists dialog box (see Figure 9-18) to edit, duplicate, or delete existing value lists, too.

RENAMING A VALUE LIST Select the name of the value list that you want to rename. Click the Edit button to display the Edit Value List dialog box (see Figure 9-15). Enter a new name in the Value List Name box, then click OK to save your change.

CHANGING THE VALUES IN A VALUE LIST Select the name of the value list for which you want to change values. Click the Edit button to display the Edit Value List dialog box (see Figure 9-15). Either edit the list of values (see "Adding Custom Values to a Value List" on page 356) or choose a different field containing the values you want to use (see "Using Values from a Field in the Same Database File" on page 356 or "Using Values from a Field in a Different Database File" on page 357). Click the OK button to save your changes.

TIP   *You can also edit the values in a value list while in Browse mode if a field that is formatted to display the value list as a pop-up list or pop-up menu includes an Edit item. I tell you how to include this option in a field's format in the section titled "Including an "Edit" Option in a Field Formatted as a Pop-up List or Pop-up Menu" on page 317.*

DUPLICATING A VALUE LIST Select the name of the value list that you want to duplicate. Click the Duplicate button. A new value list, which was named by appending the word *Copy* to the originally selected value list's name, appears in the list of value lists. Rename and/or edit the duplicate value list as desired.

DELETING A VALUE LIST Select the name of the value list that you want to delete. Click the Delete button. A warning dialog box like the one in Figure 9-19 appears. Click the Delete button to confirm that you want to remove the value list.

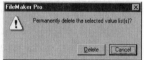

FIGURE 9-19. The dialog box that appears on Mac OS (left) and Windows (right) when you delete a value list.

WARNING *If you delete a value list, it will be removed from any FileMaker Pro option that references it. For example, if you use a value list to display a field's options as a pop-up list, the value list will no longer appear.*

Using a Value List for Entry Validation

Once you've created a value list, you can use it to validate the entry in a field. With this feature enabled, if you enter a value that is not included on the value list, a warning dialog box appears (see Figure 9-9).

To use this feature, in the Entry Options dialog box (see Figure 9-8), turn on the Member of value list check box. Then choose the appropriate value list from the menu beside it (see Figure 9-20).

FIGURE 9-20. A value list menu in a dialog box on Mac OS (left) and Windows (right) after two value lists have been created.

Range

The In range option tells FileMaker Pro to make sure that the value entered in the field falls within a range of values. With this feature enabled, if you enter a value outside the range, a warning dialog box appears (see Figure 9-9).

To set up this option, turn on the In range check box. Then enter a minimum value and maximum value in the boxes beside it. The values you enter can be numbers, text, dates, or times. Figure 9-21 shows two examples of the In range option in action.

FIGURE 9-21. Examples of the In range option on Mac OS (left) and Windows (right).

Validated by Calculation

The Validated by calculation option tells FileMaker Pro to check a field's entry against the results of a calculation. Unlike other calculations that result in numbers, text, dates, or times, a validation calculation's result must be Boolean—Yes or No, True or False, etc.

To use this feature, turn on the Validated by calculation check box. If the Specify Calculation dialog box does not automatically appear, click the Specify button to display it. Then enter the calculation in the large list box. If you want the field's entry validated only when it is modified, turn on the Validate only if field has been modified check box. Then click OK to save the calculation.

Figure 9-22 shows two examples. The illustration on the left simply requires that the entry in the Limit field be greater than 500. The illustration on the right is more complex. It compares the contents of an Entry Date field with today's date. If less than 180 days have passed, the entry in the Limit field must be less than 1000. Otherwise, the entry in the limit field must be more than 0.

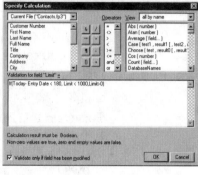

FIGURE 9-22. Examples of validation calculations in the Specify Calculation dialog box on Mac OS (left) and Windows (right).

 The Specify Calculation dialog box appears when creating calculation fields and in other places throughout FileMaker Pro. I tell you all about it—including how to use it to create simple and complex calculations—in Chapter 10.

Allowing Overrides

If you select any of the validation options, you can also turn on the Strict: Do not allow user to override validation check box. If you do, the warning dialog box that appears when the entry fails validation (see Figure 9-9) will not include a Yes button, thus making it impossible to enter an invalid value in the field.

 If you want to allow some users to enter override validation but prevent others, use FileMaker Pro's security features. I tell you all about them in Chapter 17.

Custom Message If Validation Fails

If desired, you can create a custom message that appears in the dialog box when an entry fails validation. This message can include additional information to help users enter valid data.

To use this feature, turn on the Display custom message if validation fails check box. Then enter the message that you want to appear in the dialog box. Figure 9-23 shows two examples of custom messages you can display.

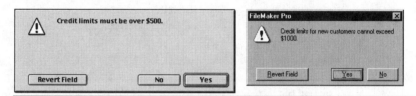

FIGURE 9-23. Examples of custom messages you can display on Mac OS (left) and Windows (right) if an entry does not pass validation.

Storage Options

Several *storage options* are available for certain types of FileMaker Pro fields:

- **Repeating**, which is available for all types of fields, enables you to input more than one entry for a field.

- **Indexing**, which is available for text, number, date, time, and calculation fields, keeps track of every value entered in the field.

- **Storing calculation results**, which is available for calculation fields, performs the calculation when the calculation's definition or a field it references changes, then stores the result for display as needed.

In most instances, you'll set storage options in the Storage tab of the Entry Options dialog box (see Figure 9-24), but there are other dialog boxes that may appear depending on the type of field and the type of storage option you want to set.

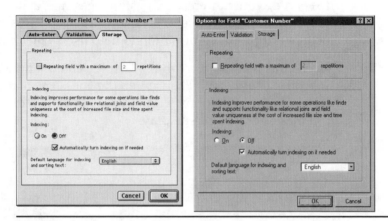

FIGURE 9-24. The Storage tab of the Entry Options dialog box on Mac OS (left) and Windows (right).

In this part of the chapter, I explain what each storage option is for and how you can set them up for your fields.

Repeating Fields

FileMaker Pro's repeating field feature enables you to specify the number of possible repetitions for a field. You can use this feature to allow more than one value in a field.

I've always thought that this was a weird feature of FileMaker Pro, but I can't deny that it's useful. For example, consider Invoices.fp5, the invoicing file you've been working on at the end of each chapter. If each field could hold only one piece of information (see Figure 9-25, left), you could enter only one item on each invoice. But if the Quantity, Item Number, Item Name, Selling Price, and Extended Price fields could hold multiple values (see Figure 9-25, right), you could enter multiple items on each invoice. That makes more sense, doesn't it?

FIGURE 9-25. An invoice example without repeating fields on Mac OS (left) and with repeating fields on Windows (right).

Creating a layout like the one on the right side of Figure 9-25 is a two-step process:

1. Use the Entry Options, Specify Calculation, or Options for Global Field dialog box to define the field(s) as having multiple repetitions. I tell you how in this section.

2. Switch to layout mode and use the Field Format dialog box to display multiple repetitions for the field(s). I tell you how in the section titled "Repetitions" on page 318.

SPECIFYING MULTIPLE REPETITIONS FOR A TEXT, NUMBER, DATE, TIME, OR CONTAINER FIELD   In the Define Fields dialog box, double-click the name of the field for which you want to set repeating field options. Click the Storage tab of the Entry Options dialog box that appears (see Figure 9-24). Turn on the Repeating field with a maximum of check box, then enter the maximum number of values for the field in the repetitions box beside it. Click OK to save your settings.

SPECIFYING MULTIPLE REPETITIONS FOR A CALCULATION FIELD   In the Define Fields dialog box, double-click the name of the calculation field for which you want to set repeating field options. In the Specify Calculations dialog box that appears (see Figure 9-26), turn on the Repeating field with a maximum of check box. Then enter the maximum number of values for the field in the values box beside it. Click OK to save your settings.

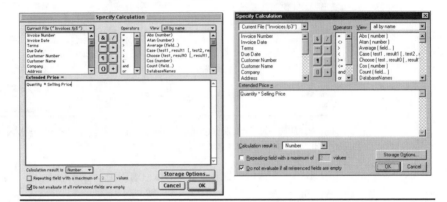

FIGURE 9-26. The Specify Calculation dialog box on Mac OS (left) and Windows (right).

SPECIFYING MULTIPLE REPETITIONS FOR A GLOBAL FIELD In the Define Fields dialog box, double-click the name of the global field for which you want to set repeating field options. In the Options for Global Field dialog box that appears (see Figure 9-27), turn on the Repeating field with a maximum of check box. Then enter the maximum number of values for the field in the repetitions box beside it. Click OK save your settings.

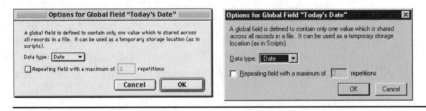

FIGURE 9-27. The Options for Global Field dialog box on Mac OS (left) and Windows (right).

Indexing

By default, FileMaker Pro automatically keeps track of the values entered into fields that are used to validate fields (see "Validation Options" on page 350) or match fields in a related, lookup, or master file (see "Looking Up Values in a Related File" on page 426). You can turn a field's automatic indexing setting on or off or set up a field so that it is always or never indexed.

The Pros and Cons

Why mess with indexing? Indexing fields can improve the performance of FileMaker Pro for tasks such as finding records. The drawback, however, is that indexed fields take up more space on disk and, in the case of very large database files, can slow down performance of operations that don't use the index.

TIP   *My advice? Don't mess with a field's indexing setting unless you often use the field for finding records. FileMaker Pro is smart enough to index a field if it needs to.*

Setting the Indexing Option

There are three indexing options:

- **Indexing** is the main option, which can be enabled (on) or disabled (off). If enabled, FileMaker Pro always indexes the field. If disabled, and the automatic indexing option below it is turned on, FileMaker Pro only indexes the field when it needs to.

- **Automatic indexing** is available when indexing is turned off. It tells FileMaker Pro to index a field automatically if it needs to. With this option turned off, FileMaker Pro will never index the field.

- **Default language for indexing and sorting text** (see Figure 9-28) is the language FileMaker Pro uses when indexing and sorting a field's text contents. This option is useful when a field contains information in a different language.

FIGURE 9-28. The Default language for indexing and sorting pop-up menu on Mac OS (left) and Windows (right).

You set the indexing option in the Storage tab of the Entry Options dialog box (see Figure 9-24) or the Storage Options dialog box (see Figure 9-29).

SETTING INDEXING OPTIONS FOR A TEXT, NUMBER, DATE, OR TIME FIELD In the Define Fields dialog box, double-click the name of the field for which you want to set indexing options. Click the Storage tab of the Entry Options dialog box that appears (see Figure 9-24) and set options in the Indexing area as desired. Click OK to save your settings.

SETTING INDEXING OPTIONS FOR A CALCULATION FIELD In the Define Fields dialog box, double-click the name of the calculation field for which you want to set indexing options. In the Specify Calculations dialog box that appears (see Figure 9-26), click the Storage Options button to display the Storage Options dialog box (see Figure 9-29). Set options in the Indexing area as desired and click OK to save your settings.

FIGURE 9-29. The Storage Options dialog box for a calculation field on Mac OS (left) and Windows (right).

Storing Calculation Results

FileMaker Pro usually evaluates the result of a calculation field's formula whenever the formula is modified or a field that is referenced by the formula is modified. The result of the calculation is then stored within FileMaker Pro so it can be quickly displayed when necessary. If desired, however, you can prevent FileMaker Pro from storing the results of a calculation, thus forcing it to evaluate the formula every time it needs to display its results.

NOTE   *The only time FileMaker Pro doesn't automatically store calculation field results is when the formula refers to a global field, an unstored calculation field, a related field, or a calculation that includes a summary field.*

Pros and Cons

What can changing the storage setting do for you? Storing values can speed up the calculation of formulas and the display of layouts that include calculation fields. Like indexing, however, storing calculation results takes up more disk space.

Setting the Storing Calculation Results Option

You set the storing calculation results option in the Storage Options dialog box (see Figure 9-29). To open this dialog box, double-click the calculation field for which you want to set storage options, to display the Specify Calculation dialog box (see Figure 9-26). Then click the Storage Options button.

PREVENTING A CALCULATION FIELD'S RESULTS FROM BEING STORED
Turn on the Do not store calculation results -- calculate only when needed check box. Neither the results of that calculation field nor the results of calculation fields that reference it will be stored. Keep in mind, however, that setting this option may cause performance problems in databases with many records.

ALLOWING A CALCULATION FIELD'S RESULTS TO BE STORED Turn off the Do not store calculation results -- calculate only when needed check box. This instructs FileMaker Pro to store the results of the calculation field whenever possible.

Step-by-Step

Ready to try out some of the techniques I covered in this chapter? In this section, I provide step-by-step instructions for modifying fields in the Contacts.fp5 and Invoices.fp5 files you've been working on at the end of each chapter to improve them for data entry. If you've been skipping around in the book and don't have the completed exercise files from Chapter 8, you can download them from the companion Web site for this book, http://www.gilesrd.com/fmprocomp/.

Modifying the Contact Database

In this section, you'll make two kinds of changes:

- Modify fields to take advantage of auto enter and validation options.

- Modify the data entry layout to display value lists for selection.

As you'll see, the techniques in this exercise aren't just from Chapter 9—they're from previous chapters as well.

1. Open the file named Contacts.fp5.

2. Define a value list named Contact Type with the following values: *Customer, Vendor,* and *Employee.*

3. Define a value list named Payment Terms with the following values: *Net 30, Net 45, Net 60, COD.*

4. Set the following entry options for the Customer Number field:

   - Use the Serial number option to set up serial numbers starting at 10001 and incrementing by 1.

   - Use the Unique and Strict options to ensure that all entries are unique and cannot be overridden by users.

5. Set the following entry options for the Type field:

   - Use the validation by value list feature to specify the Contact Type value list.

   - Use the Not empty and Strict options to ensure that the field is not left empty and cannot be overridden by users.

6. Set the following entry options for the Terms field:

   - Use the validation by value list feature to specify the Payment Terms value list.

   - Use the auto-enter data feature to specify a default value of *Net 30.*

7. Set the following entry options for the Limit field:

    - Use the range validation feature to ensure that the field's entry is between 0 and 5000.

    - Set up a custom message that says *The credit limit must be between $0 and $5,000.*

8. Set the following entry options for the Revision Date field:

    - Use the auto-entry feature to enter the modification date automatically.

    - Use the Prohibit modification value option to prevent users from modifying the field's contents.

9. If necessary, switch to Browse mode, choose Find All from the Select menu, and switch to the Contact Entry Form layout.

10. Replace the contents of the Customer Number field with serial numbers starting at 10001 and incrementing by 1. Be sure that the options in the Replace dialog box are set to update the serial number in Entry Options automatically.

11. Switch to Layout mode.

12. Format the Type field as Radio Buttons using the Contact Type value list.

13. Format the Terms field as a pop-up list using the Payment Terms value list.

14. Switch back to Browse mode. Create a new record. Experiment with entries to the fields you modified to see how the Auto-Entry and Validation options work.

TIP   *If the radio buttons do not appear after step 12, use the pen pattern and pen thickness menus in the status area to set a 1-point line. Check the section titled "Pen Color, Pattern, and Thickness" on page 183 for details.*

Modifying the Invoices Database

In this section, you'll also make field definition and layout changes using techniques from Chapters 7 and 8.

1. Open the file named Invoices.fp5.

2. Create a value list named Payment Terms that uses values in the Terms field of the Contacts.fp5 file. Then set entry options for the Terms field so it uses the Payment Terms value list for validation and is not empty.

3. Create a value list named Item Numbers that uses values in the Item Number and Item Name fields of the Products.fp5 file. Then set entry options for the Item Number field so it uses the Item Numbers value list for validation.

4. Set entry options for the Invoice Number field to automatically enter a serial number starting with 98001 and incrementing by 1, prohibit modification by users, and be unique.

5. Set entry options for the Invoice Date field to automatically enter the creation date.

6. Set the Quantity, Item Number, Item Name, Selling Price, and Extended Price fields so they each display a maximum of six repetitions.

7. Switch to Layout mode.

8. Select the Quantity, Item Number, Item Name, Selling Price, and Extended Price fields. Then use the Field Format dialog box to display all six repetitions for these fields in a vertical layout.

9. Select just the Item Number field and use the Field Format dialog box to display it as a pop-up list using the Item Numbers value list.

10. Switch back to Browse mode. Create a new record. Experiment with entries to the fields you modified to see how the Auto-Entry and Validation options work. Be sure to try entering more than one item in the repeated fields.

Tapping into the Power of Calculations

10

In Chapter 2, I introduce you to calculation fields, which you can use to fill in a field with the result of a formula you specify. In that chapter, I provide some simple examples of formulas to get you started.

In this chapter, I expand my discussion of calculations. Not only do I provide more complex formula examples, but I tell you how you can use calculations for other tasks in FileMaker Pro—such as replacing the contents of a field with a calculated value, using calculations in field entry options, and including calculations in scripts.

Using Calculations

You can use calculations to perform a variety of tasks throughout FileMaker Pro. In this section, I discuss the features that offer access to the Specify Calculation dialog box.

Creating Calculation Fields

The most obvious place to specify a calculation is in the Specify Calculation dialog box that appears when you define or edit a calculation field (see Figure 10-1). This enables you to create a field that is filled in automatically by FileMaker Pro based on other database fields and the formula you specify.

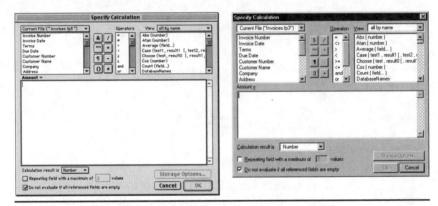

FIGURE 10-1. The Specify Calculation dialog box that appears when you define a calculation field on Mac OS (left) and Windows (right).

You open this dialog box from within the Define Fields dialog box, which I discuss in detail in the section titled "Using the Define Fields Dialog Box" on page 60. Either create a new calculation field, double-click an existing calculation field, or select an existing calculation field and click the Options button.

NOTE   *When you define a calculation field, the contents of the field always display the results of the formula you enter in the Specify Calculation dialog box. You cannot edit the field's contents in Browse mode. The only way to change the contents of a calculation field is to change its formula.*

I provide basic information about using the Specify Calculation dialog box to define a calculation field in the section titled "Completing the Definition for a Calculation Field" on page 63. I tell you exactly how to use the Specify Calculation dialog box to write a formula later in this chapter.

Using Calculations as Field Entry Options

Another way a calculation can be used within FileMaker Pro is as an auto enter option for a text, number, date, or time field. You can set this up with the Entry Options dialog box (see Figure 10-2), which I discuss in detail throughout Chapter 9.

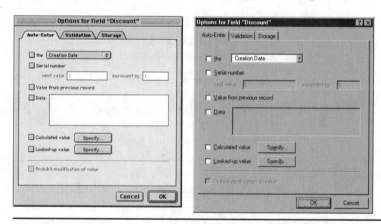

FIGURE 10-2. The Auto Enter options of the Entry Options dialog box on Mac OS (left) and Windows (right).

In the Define Fields dialog box, either double-click a field name, or click once on a field name and click the Options button. The Entry Options dialog box appears. If necessary, click the Auto-Enter tab at the top of the dialog box to display the Auto Enter options (see Figure 10-2). Turn on the Calculated value check box. The Specify Calculation Dialog box (see Figure 10-3) should appear automatically; if it does not, click the Calculated value option's Specify button to display it.

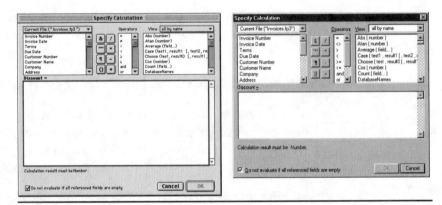

FIGURE 10-3. The Specify Calculation dialog box that appears when you specify a formula as an auto enter option on Mac OS (left) and Windows (right).

NOTE *If you use the Auto Enter feature to enter the results of a calculation in a field automatically, the field's contents can still be modified in Browse mode. This option works only on new records created after the option has been set up; it does not change information in existing records.*

I tell you more about working with the Define Fields dialog box in the section titled "Using the Define Fields Dialog Box" on page 60. I explain how to use Auto Enter options in the Entry Options dialog box in the section titled "Auto Enter Options" on page 343. I tell you exactly how to use the Specify Calculation dialog box to write a formula later in this chapter.

Replacing Field Contents with Calculated Results

You can also use a calculation in conjunction with the Replace dialog box (see Figure 10-4) to replace the contents of a field in one or more records with the result of a calculation. This gives you the ability to change entered data, including calculated results entered automatically as part of a field entry option (see "Using Calculations as Field Entry Options" on page 377).

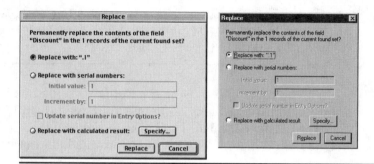

FIGURE 10-4. The Replace dialog box on Mac OS (left) and Windows (right).

If necessary, use the Find or Find All command to browse the records for which you want to replace a field's entry. Then choose Replace from the Records menu or press Command-= (Mac OS) or Control-= (Windows) to display the Replace dialog box (see Figure 10-4). Select the Replace with calculated result option. The Specify Calculation dialog box (see Figure 10-5) should open automatically; if it does not, click the Specify button.

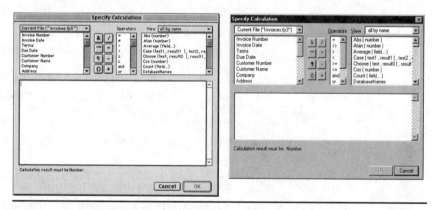

FIGURE 10-5. The Specify Calculation dialog box that appears when you replace a field's entry with a calculated result or specify a calculation as part of a script step on Mac OS (left) and Windows (right).

NOTE *If you use the Replace feature to change the contents of a field, the field's contents can still be modified in Browse mode. You cannot use the Replace feature to change the contents of a calculation field.*

I tell you more about using the Replace dialog box in the sections titled "Replacing Field Contents" on page 112 and "Reserializing Records" on page 346. I tell you exactly how to use the Specify Calculation dialog box to write a formula later in this chapter.

Using Calculations in Scripts

Finally, you can use calculations within FileMaker Pro scripts. This powerful combination of features extends the automation capabilities of FileMaker Pro, enabling you to incorporate if/then logic in scripts, write scripts that enter or change data based on the contents of fields, and, with a little imagination and know-how, push FileMaker Pro scripting to its limits.

The Specify Calculation dialog box (see Figure 10-5) appears when you select one of the following script steps on the right side of the Script Definition dialog box and click the Specify button.

- **If** requires that you enter a formula with a Boolean (True or False) result. The result of the formula determines the branching of the script's operations.

- **Exit Loop If** has basically the same formula requirement and use as If.

- **Set Field** requires that you enter a formula with an appropriate type—text, number, date, or time—of result. The formula's result is pasted into a field.

- **Paste Result** has basically the same formula requirement and use as Set Field.

- **Replace** displays the Replace dialog box (see Figure 10-4). You may select the Replace with calculated result option to display the Specify Calculation dialog box. The formula requirement and use is the same as it is for Set Field or Paste Result.

I tell you more about using the Script definition dialog box to write scripts throughout Chapter 12. I tell you exactly how to use the Specify Calculation dialog box to write a formula next.

Specifying Calculations

No matter what you're using a calculation for, you create its formula in the Specify Calculation dialog box. The exact appearance of the dialog box varies depending on what you're using it for, but its main features—the lists and buttons in the top part of the dialog box that enable you to compose your formula—are always the same. Figure 10-1 shows an example.

The object of the game is to use the Specify Calculation dialog box's buttons and lists to write a formula in the big box in the middle of the window. In this section, I explain how.

T*IP* *You don't have to use the lists and buttons in the Specify Calculation dialog box to enter fields in your formula. If you know what you want the formula to say, simply type it in. Just be careful! If you make a mistake, the formula won't work the way you expect—or it just won't work at all.*

About the Big Box

The big box is just that—a big edit or text box. You enter information into it the same way you enter information into any other edit or text box. There's an insertion point that indicates where the information you enter will appear. All keyboard keys work just the way you expect them to when you're composing or editing a formula.

Here are a few pointers to keep you on track.

ENTERING TEXT   Either type the text that you want to enter or use one of the lists or buttons in the dialog box to enter it.

DELETING TEXT   Press the Delete (Mac OS) or Backspace (Windows) key to delete the character to the left of the insertion point. Press the Del key to delete the character to the right of the insertion point. Any of these keys will also delete selected text.

MOVING THE INSERTION POINT   Use one of the arrow keys to move the insertion point left, right, up, or down. Or use your mouse pointer to click where you want to move the insertion point.

SELECTING TEXT   Use your mouse pointer to drag over the text that you want to select.

COPYING OR CUTTING SELECTED TEXT   Choose Copy or Cut from the Edit menu.

PASTING COPIED OR CUT TEXT   Position the insertion point where you want the text to appear, then choose Paste from the Edit menu.

Fields

In many cases, a formula will be based on the contents of one or more other fields in the same database or in another database. Here are some examples:

- To calculate the value for a Total Amount field on an invoice, you may want to multiply the Quantity field by the Item Price field. (This is similar to a calculation you defined for the Invoices.fp5 file at the end of Chapter 2.)

- To calculate the value for an Invoice Total field on an invoice, you may want to add the Item Total, Sales Tax, and Shipping Cost fields.

- To calculate the value for a Discount field based on an Item Total field, you may want to use a logical function to evaluate the value of the Item Total field and return one percentage if the value is higher than a set amount and a different percentage if the value is lower than a set amount. (I tell you about using functions in the section titled "Functions" on page 390.)

Inserting a Field

The field list in the upper-left corner of the dialog box lists all the fields that you can include in your formula. It makes it easy to insert any field into the big box.

INSERTING THE NAME OF A FIELD WITHIN THE SAME DATABASE Position the insertion point where you want the field name to appear. Then locate the name of the field in the field list and double-click it. The field name is inserted at the insertion point.

WARNING *Do not insert the name of the field you are defining or modifying in the formula. If you do, when you click the OK button to save the formula, FileMaker Pro will display a dialog box like the one in Figure 10-6. You must click OK and correct the formula to continue.*

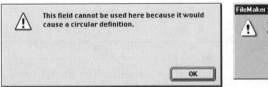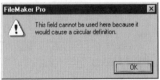

FIGURE 10-6. The dialog box that appears on Mac OS (left) and Windows (right) when you include the name of a field in its own formula.

INSERTING THE NAME OF A FIELD IN A RELATED DATABASE Position the insertion point where you want the field name to appear. Then use the menu above the field list (see Figure 10-7) to choose the relationship for the file that includes the field that you want to use. The field list changes to show the names of fields in the related file (see Figure 10-8). Locate the name of the field that you want to enter and double-click it. The name of the relationship, followed by a pair of colons (::), and the field name are inserted at the insertion point (see Figure 10-9).

FIGURE 10-7. The relationship menu above the field list in the Specify Calculation dialog box on Mac OS (left) and Windows (right).

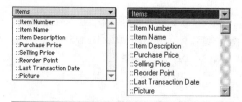

FIGURE 10-8. The field list with a relationship selected from the menu above it on Mac OS (left) and Windows (right).

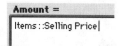

FIGURE 10-9. A related field inserted into a formula.

NOTE *To use a field from a related file in a formula, you must first create a relationship between the current file and the file containing the field that you want to use. I tell you all about creating relationships between files in Chapter 11.*

Operators

Operators tell FileMaker Pro how to work with the other formula components. Some of them perform basic mathematical operations like addition, subtraction, and multiplication. Others perform comparisons like equals, not equals, and less than. Still others perform text operations and logical operations.

A Closer Look at Operators

Here's a complete rundown of the types of operators, along with descriptions and examples of each individual operator.

TEXT OPERATORS Text operators are used to concatenate text within a formula. You can find all text operators on buttons in the Specify Calculation dialog box.

NOTE *Text operators are throwbacks from earlier versions of FileMaker Pro that did not include the merge field feature. Those versions required complex calculations to combine literal text with FileMaker Pro fields. If you need to concatenate text, consider using merge fields instead of calculation fields. I tell you how to add merge fields to text objects in your layouts in the section titled "Adding a Merge Field" on page 236.*

- & is used to concatenate text. For example: *Last Name & " " & First Name* puts the Last Name and First Name fields together with a space between them.

- " " (double-quotes) are used to enclose text constants or literal text. In the previous example, they enclose a space character. Here's another example: *"Your credit limit is " & Limit* appends the text constant *Your credit limit is* to the value in the Limit field.

TIP   *To include a double-quote character (") inside a text string, enter two dou-*
       ble-quote characters ("").

- ¶ ends a paragraph in a text string. Here's an example of how it might be used in a formula: *"Dear " & First Name & ",¶Here is the information you requested..."* This formula results in the text constant *Dear* followed by the value in the First Name field on one line. The next line displays the text constant *Here is the information you requested....* The ¶, which must be enclosed within the double-quote characters, does not display. It merely signals the end of a paragraph.

TIP   *On Mac OS, you can type the ¶ symbol by pressing Option-7.*

MATHEMATICAL OPERATORS Mathematical operators are used to perform standard mathematical operations within a formula. You can find most mathematical operators on buttons in the Specify Calculation dialog box.

TIP   *Not sure how FileMaker Pro and other computer programs evaluate formula*
       components utilizing mathematical operators? You're not alone. Most people
       don't have the foggiest idea. Here's my trick to remember calculation order:
       remember the sentence Please Excuse My Dear Aunt Sally. *Each letter in the*
       sentence stands for a type of operation: Parentheses, Exponentials, Multipli-
       cation, Division, Addition, and Subtraction. Computer programs like File-
       Maker Pro work through formulas by evaluating the contents of parentheses
       first, then exponentials, then multiplication and division, and finally addition
       and subtraction. If you can't remember that, just remember to politely excuse
       my dear Aunt Sally. That's what I do.

- ( ) (parentheses) are used to surround portions of a formula. They determine the order in which formula components are evaluated. For example, consider the following two formulas: 5+4*2 and (5+4)*2. In the first example, File-

Maker Pro evaluates 4*2 first, resulting in 8, then adds it to 5 for a final result of 13. In the second example, FileMaker Pro evaluates 5+4 first, resulting in 9, then multiplies it by 2 for a final result of 18. See the difference?

NOTE *In addition to changing the order in which formula components are evaluated, parentheses are also used to enclose function parameters. I tell you about functions in the section titled "Functions" on page 390.*

- / divides the value on the left of the slash by the value on the right. For example *10 / 2* divides 10 by 2 for a result of 5.

- * multiplies the value on the left of the asterisk by the value on the right. For example, *10 * 2* multiplies 10 by 2 for a result of 20.

- - subtracts the value on the right of the hyphen from the value on the left. For example *10 - 2* subtracts 2 from 10 for a result of 8.

- + adds the value on the left of the plus to the value on the right. For example, *10 + 2* adds 10 and 2 together for a result of 12.

- ^ raises the value on the left of the caret to the power of the value on the left. For example *10^2* raises 10 to the 2nd power for a result of 100.

 TIP *Having trouble finding the ^ operator? Scroll to the end of the Operator's list to find it. I guess it doesn't rate a button.*

COMPARISON OPERATORS Comparison operators compare the values on the left and right side of the operator to return Boolean results—true (1) or false (0). You can find all comparison operators in the Operators list in the Specify Calculation dialog box.

- = checks the values for equality. For example *10=2* checks to see if 10 is equal to 2. Since they're not equal, the result is false.

- ≠ **(Mac OS) or <> (Windows)** checks the values for inequality. For example *10≠2* checks to see if 10 is not equal to 2. Since they're not equal, the result is true.

TIP *Mac OS users can type the ≠ symbol by pressing Option-=.*

- \> checks whether the value on the left of it is greater than the value on the right. For example *10>2* checks to see if 10 is greater than 2. Since 10 is greater than 2, the result is true.

- < checks whether the value on the left of it is less than the value on the right. For example *10<2* checks to see if 10 is less than 2. Since 10 is not less than 2, the result is false.

- ≥ **(Mac OS) or >= (Windows)** checks whether the value on the left of it is greater than or equal to the value on the right.

TIP *Mac OS users can type in the ≥ symbol by pressing Option-. (period).*

- ≤ **(Mac OS) or <= (Windows)** checks whether the value on the left of it is less than or equal to the value on the right.

TIP *Mac OS users can type in the ≤ symbol by pressing Option-, (comma).*

LOGICAL OPERATORS Logical operators evaluate multiple comparison expressions and return a Boolean result—true (1) or false (0). You can find all logical operators in the Operators list in the Specify Calculation dialog box.

- **and** returns true only when *all* conditions are true. If at least once condition is false, the result is false. For example, the expression *10>2 AND 2>1* results in true but the expression *10>2 AND 1>2* results in false.

- **or** returns true when *any* condition is true. For example, both the expression *10>2 OR 2>1* and the expression *10>2 OR 1>2* result in true.

- **xor** returns true when *one* condition is true. If both conditions are true, the result is false. For example, the expression *10>2 XOR 2>1* results in false but the expression *10>2 XOR 1>2* results in true.

- **not** reverses the result of the expression that follows it in parentheses. For example, *NOT (10>2)* reverses the result of 10>2 (which is true) to result in false.

Inserting an Operator

Now that you know what the operators are, here's how you can insert them into your formulas.

INSERTING AN OPERATOR FROM A BUTTON Position the insertion point where you want the operator to appear, then click the operator's button once. The operator is inserted at the insertion point.

NOTE *When you click the double-quotes or parentheses operator button, the insertion point automatically appears between the characters, making it easy to insert literal text or formula components.*

INSERTING AN OPERATOR FROM THE OPERATORS LIST Position the insertion point where you want the operator to appear, then double-click the operator's name in the Operator list. The operator is inserted at the insertion point.

Functions

Functions are predefined mathematical formulas. Each function is designed to perform a specific type of calculation based on parameters included in parentheses after the function name.

 TIP   *Do you use spreadsheet software such as Microsoft Excel? If so, you may already be familiar with FileMaker Pro's functions. Spreadsheet software uses many of the same functions, although it usually refers to parameters as arguments.*

About Function Syntax

To use a function, you must understand its *syntax*. Syntax is like grammar—it deals with the organization and punctuation used to enter functions and their parameters. But there's a big difference between syntax and grammar. If you have poor grammar, people will probably still understand what you're trying to say. But if you enter a function with incorrect syntax, FileMaker Pro probably won't understand what you're trying to calculate.

In FileMaker Pro, functions use the following syntax:

FunctionName (parameter1, parameter2, etc.)

Here's a closer look at each component of a function's syntax:

- *FunctionName* is the name of the function. It determines the type of calculation and the number and purpose of each of its parameters.

- **Parentheses** are used to enclose all parameters that work with a function.

- **Parameters** are values, fields, or expressions that work with the function. The number of parameters a function requires varies from one function to another.

- **Commas** are used to separate parameters.

You can find complete syntax information for each of FileMaker Pro's functions in Appendix B.

Types of Functions

FileMaker Pro has dozens of functions, each of which is listed and described in Appendix B. Here's a quick description of each type of function just to give you an idea of the kinds of things you can do with them.

- **Text functions** return information about or perform operations on text. For example, Length (*text*) returns the number of characters in *text*. The *text* parameter can be constant text enclosed in double-quote characters or the name of a text field.

- **Number functions** return information about or perform operations on single numbers. For example, Int (*number*) returns the integer or whole portion of *number*. The *number* parameter can be a number or a number field.

- **Date functions** return information about or perform operations on dates. For example, Month (*date*) returns the month number of *date*. The *date* parameter can be a date or a date field.

- **Time functions** return information about or perform operations on times. For example, Hour (*time*) returns the hour number of *time*. The *time* parameter can be a time or a time field.

- **Aggregate functions** perform calculations on nonblank values in one or more repeating fields or related fields. For example, Sum (*field*) returns the sum of all values in *field*. The *field* parameter can be a number or a field.

- **Summary functions** perform calculations on summary fields. For example, GetSummary (*summary field, break field*) returns the value of *summary field* when records are sorted by *break field*. The *summary field* parameter must be a summary field; the *break field* parameter must be the field by which you want to summarize information.

- **Repeating functions** return information about or perform operations on repeating fields. For example, Last (*repeating field*) returns the last nonblank value in *repeating field*. The *repeating field* parameter must be a field.

- **Financial functions** perform financial calculations on numbers. For example, PV (*payment, interest rate, periods*) returns the net present value of a series of equal *payments* made at regular *periods* using a fixed *interest rate*. Each parameter can be a constant number or a number field.

- **Trigonometric functions** perform trigonometric calculations on a single number. For example, Cos (*number*) returns the cosine of the angle of *number*. The *number* parameter can be a constant number of a number field.

- **Logical functions** perform a test, then return a value based on the result of the test. For example, If (*test, result one, result two*) evaluates the expression in *test*, then returns *result one* if the expression is true or *result two* if the expression is false. The parameters of logical functions vary from one function to another.

- **Status functions** return information about the state of the database file or your computer. For example, Status (CurrentFieldName) returns the name of the current field. Status functions have predefined parameters; they are not based on constant values, fields, or expressions.

- **Design functions** return information about the structure of any database file that is currently open on your computer. For example, FieldNames (*database name, layout name*) returns the names of all the fields in *layout name* of *database name*. The parameters of design functions vary from one function to another.

- **External functions** work with FileMaker Pro Web Companion and other FileMaker Pro plug-ins. For more information about these functions, consult the documentation that came with the plug-in.

Inserting a Function

Here's how you can work with the Specify Calculation dialog box's function list, insert functions, and replace parameter names with appropriate parameters.

DISPLAYING ONLY ONE TYPE OF FUNCTION IN THE FUNCTION LIST Choose the type of function that you want to view from the View menu above the function list (see Figure 10-10). The list changes to display only the type of function you chose (see Figure 10-11).

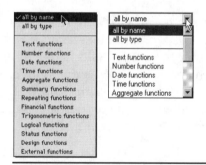

FIGURE 10-10. The View menu above the function list in the Specify Calculation dialog box on Mac OS (left) and Windows (right).

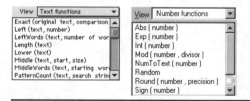

FIGURE 10-11. Examples of the function list displaying only one type of function: text functions on Mac OS (left) and number functions on Windows (right).

DISPLAYING ALL FUNCTIONS IN THE FUNCTION LIST SORTED BY NAME OR BY TYPE Choose all by name or all by type from the View menu above the function list (see Figure 10-10). The list changes to display all the functions sorted in the order you specified.

INSERTING A FUNCTION Position the insertion point where you want the function to appear. Locate the name of the function in the function list and double-click it. It is inserted at the insertion point with its parameter names selected. Figure 10-12 shows two examples.

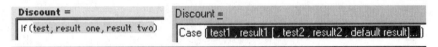

FIGURE 10-12. Examples of inserted functions on Mac OS (left) and Windows (right).

REPLACING A PARAMETER NAME WITH AN APPROPRIATE PARAMETER Select the entire name of the parameter that you want to replace (see Figure 10-13). Enter the value, field name, or expression that you want to use for the parameter. Whatever you enter overwrites the selected parameter name in the formula (see Figure 10-14). Repeat this process until all parameter names have been replaced with appropriate parameters (see Figure 10-15).

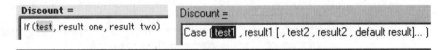

FIGURE 10-13. Selected parameter name on Mac OS (left) and Windows (right).

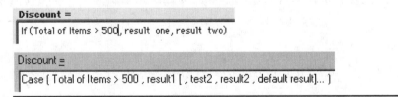

FIGURE 10-14. Parameter name replaced with an expression on Mac OS (top) and Windows (bottom).

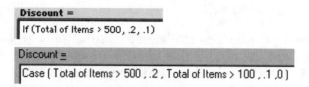

FIGURE 10-15. Completed function on Mac OS (top) and Windows (right).

INSERTING A FUNCTION WITHIN A FUNCTION Select the parameter or parameter name that you want to replace with a function (see Figure 10-16). Locate the name of the function in the function list and double-click it. It appears in place of the selected parameter or parameter name with its parameter names selected (see Figure 10-17). Follow instructions in the previous section to replace the inserted function's parameter names with parameters (see Figure 10-18).

If (Total of Items > 500, .2, result two)

FIGURE 10-16. Selecting a parameter name within a function.

If (Total of Items > 500, .2, If (test, result one, result two))

FIGURE 10-17. Function inserted to replace a parameter name within a function.

If (Total of Items > 500, .2, If (Total of Items > 100, .1, 0))

FIGURE 10-18. Completed nested function.

 Inserting a function within a function is often known as nesting functions.

Other Options in the Specify Calculation Dialog Box

Other options may appear at the bottom of the Specify Calculation dialog box, depending on your use of the calculation.

Calculation Result

If you're creating a formula for a calculation field, you can use the Calculation result is menu (see Figure 10-19) at the bottom of the Specify Calculation dialog box (see Figure 10-1) to choose the type of result for the formula.

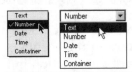

FIGURE 10-19. The Calculation result is menu on Mac OS (left) and Windows (right).

If you're using the Specify Calculation dialog box to create a calculation for another purpose, a note at the bottom of the dialog box (see Figure 10-3 and Figure 10-5) tells you exactly what type of result your formula should have.

Repeating Field

If you're creating a calculation for a calculation field, you can also specify the number of repetitions that the field should have. In the Specify Calculation dialog box (see Figure 10-1), turn on the Repeating field with a maximum of check box and enter a value in the values box beside it.

This option is not available when using the Specify Calculation dialog box for any other purpose (see Figure 10-3 and Figure 10-5).

I tell you more about repeating fields in the section titled "Repeating Fields" on page 364.

Evaluation Option

The Specify Calculation dialog box for a calculation field (see Figure 10-1) and auto-enter options for a text, number, date, or time field (see Figure 10-3) includes the Do not evaluate if all referenced fields are empty check box, which is turned on by default. When turned on, FileMaker Pro will leave the field empty if all the fields referenced by the formula are blank.

TIP   *Some features of FileMaker Pro distinguish between an empty field and a field containing a zero value. This option enables you to set a value the way you want it to appear when referenced values are not available.*

This option is not available when using the Specify Calculation dialog box in conjunction with the Replace dialog box or when creating a script (see Figure 10-5).

Saving the Formula

When you're finished entering your formula, click OK in the Specify Calculation dialog box to save it. One of two things will happen:

IF YOU ENTERED AN ACCEPTABLE FORMULA... The Specify Calculation dialog box disappears so you can get on with other work.

IF YOU ENTERED AN UNACCEPTABLE FORMULA... A dialog box appears, informing you that your formula contains an error. Click OK to dismiss the dialog box and go back to the Specify Calculation dialog box. In many cases, the offensive formula component will be highlighted so you can see it. Make the correction (if you can!) and try clicking OK again.

Calculation Examples

I won't deny it—creating useful calculations can be tough. Since I think one of the best ways to learn something is by example, here are a few calculation examples that go far beyond the simple

*Quantity * Selling Price* formula in Invoices.fp5. Read through them to get an idea of how calculations can be used.

If there's an example here that you think you might want to explore in detail, take a few moments to create an appropriate sample database file with its fields. Or download the files I created from the companion Web site for this book, http://www.gilesrd.com/fmprocomp/.

Getting Logical with the IF and CASE Functions

Figures 9-12 through 9-15 show two examples of functions used to return values based on the contents of another field. Figures 9-16 through 9-18 take one of those examples a step further to create a nested function.

The idea behind all three of these examples is to create a formula that returns a discount amount (Discount) based on the value in another field (Total of Items). In this section, I explain how all three of these examples work.

Using the IF Function

In the first example, the IF function determines whether Total of Items is greater than 500. If it is, the Discount field's value is .2. If it is not, the Discount field's value is set to 0. The formula is:

If (Total of Items > 500 , .2 , 0)

The IF function's syntax is as follows:

If (*test , result one , result two*)

Here's how the formula works:

- The *test* parameter is an expression with a Boolean result. In the formula *Total of Items > 500* is either true or false.

- *Result one* is returned if *test* is true. In the formula, *.2* is returned if *Total of Items > 500* is true.

- The *result two* parameter is returned if *test* is false. In the formula, *0* is returned if *Total of Items > 500* is false.

That's all there is to it.

Using the CASE Function

In the second example, the CASE function makes two tests. First, it determines whether Total of Items is greater than 500. If it is, the Discount field's value is .2 and the formula stops testing. If Total of items is not greater than 500, however, it determines whether the Total of Items is greater than 100. If it is, the Discount field's value is .1 and the formula stops. If Total of Items is not greater than 100 either, the Discount field's value is the default result of 0. The formula is:

> Case (Total of Items > 500 , .2 , Total of Items > 100 , .1 , 0)

As you can see, the CASE function is a bit more tricky, but also more flexible. Its syntax is as follows:

> Case (*test 1* , *result 1* [, *test 2* , *result 2* , *default result*]...)

Here's how the formula works:

- The *test 1* parameter is an expression with a Boolean result. In the formula, *Total of Items > 500* is either true or false.

- The *result 1* parameter is returned if *test 1* is true. In the formula, *.2* is returned if *Total of Items > 500* is true.

- The *test 2* parameter is an expression with a Boolean result. It is only evaluated if *test 1* is false. In the formula, *Total of Items > 100* is either true or false.

- The *result 2* parameter is returned if *test 2* is true. In the formula, *.1* is returned if *Total of Items > 100* is true.

- The *default result* parameter is returned if none of the previous tests are true. In the formula, *0* is returned if *Total of Items > 500 is false* and *Total of Items > 100* is false.

TIP *You can include as many* test *,* result *pairs as CASE function parameters as you like. Just be sure to follow them up with a default result in case all the tests are false.*

Using a Nested IF Function

In the third example, two IF functions are used together to achieve the same results as the CASE function in the second example. The formula is:

If (Total of Items > 500 , .2 , If (Total of Items > 100 , .1 , 0))

Remember the syntax for an IF function:

If (*test , result one , result two*)

Now expand that function like this:

If (*test , result one ,* If (*test , result one , result two*))

Here's how this formula works:

- The *test* parameter is an expression with a Boolean result. In the formula, *Total of Items > 500* is either true or false.

- The *result one* parameter is returned if the test is true. In the formula, *.2* is returned if *Total of Items > 500* is true.

- The *result two* parameter is returned if the expression is false. The formula in the example, however, performs another test if *Total of Items > 500* is false by nesting another IF function expression within the *result two* parameter.

- The *test* parameter in the nested IF function is an expression with a Boolean result. In the formula, *Total of Items > 100* is either true or false.

- The *result one* parameter in the nested IF function is returned if the test is true. In the formula, *.1* is returned if *Total of Items > 500* is false and *Total of Items > 100* is true.

- The *result two* parameter is returned if the expression is false. In the formula, *0* is returned if *Total of Items > 500* and *Total of Items > 100* are false.

Calculating Dates

The following three examples use date and logical functions to calculate a person's age in years; the number of days, months, and years between two dates; and the number of weekdays between two dates.

NOTE *Because these formulas use the TODAY function, they recalculate automatically each time the database file is opened. If you prefer, you can replace the TODAY function in each formula with the name of a field containing an end date.*

TIP *You can find these formulas and more like them among the Tech Info articles on the FileMaker, Inc. Web site, http://www.filemaker.com/.*

Calculating a Person's Age

This example uses a field named Birthdate, along with the YEAR, MONTH, DAY, TODAY, and IF functions. Here's the formula:

Year (Today) - Year (Birthdate) - If (Today < Date (Month (Birthdate), Day (Birthdate), Year (Today)) , 1 , 0)

Here's the syntax for each of these functions:

Year (*date*)
Month (*date*)
Day (*date*)

Date (*month* , *day* , *year*)
Today
If (*test* , *result one* , *result two*)

Here's a quick explanation of the parameters for each function:

- In the YEAR, MONTH, and DAY functions, the *date* parameter should be a date or a date field.

- In the DATE function, the *month, day,* and *year* parameters should be month, day, and year numbers.

- The TODAY function has no parameters; it simply returns today's date.

- In the IF function, the *test* parameter is an expression with a Boolean result, the *result one* parameter is returned if the test is true, and the *result two* parameter is returned if the test is false.

Here's how the formula works:

- *Year (Today) - Year (Birthdate)* subtracts the year in the Birthdate field from today's year.

- *If (Today < Date (Month (Birthdate), Day (Birthdate), Year (Today)) , 1 , 0)* determines whether the current month and day is before the month and day in the Birthdate. If it is, 1 is subtracted from the first part of the formula; otherwise, 0 is subtracted from the first part of the formula.

It may seem confusing, but it's not that tough. If you deconstruct the formula to look at its individual parts, you can see how each function is used to come up with a value.

Calculating the Number of Days, Months, and Years between Two Dates

This next example takes the previous one a step further. Rather than using a Birthdate field, however, it uses a Start Date field. The same basic formula calculates years, and two additional formulas using the same functions plus the MOD function calculate Months and Days. Here are the three formulas:

Years:

Year (Today) - Year (Start Date) - If (Today < Date (Month (Start Date), Day (Start Date), Year (Today)) , 1 , 0)

Months:

Mod (Month (Today) - Month (Start Date) + 12
- If (Day (Today) < Day (Start Date) , 1, 0), 12)

Days:

Day (Today) - Day (Start Date) + If (Day (Today) >= Day (Start Date) , 0 , If (Day (Today - Day (Today)) < Day (Start Date) , Day (Start Date), Day (Today - Day (Today))))

I already described most of the functions in the previous example. Here's the syntax and parameter information for one more:

Mod (*number* , *divisor*)

The MOD function returns the remainder after the *number* parameter is divided by the *divisor* parameter.

Here's how the formula for the Months calculation works:

- *Month (Today) - Month (Start Date) + 12* subtracts the month number in the Start Date field from the month number of the current date and adds 12 to the result.

- *- If (Day (Today) < Day (Start Date) , 1, 0)* determines whether the current day is before the day in the Start Date field. If it is, 1 is subtracted from the previous part of the formula; otherwise, 0 is subtracted from the previous part of the formula.

- *Mod (Month (Today) - Month (Start Date) + 12 - If (Day (Today) < Day (Start Date) , 1, 0), 12)*, which is the entire formula, calculates the remainder after the two previously discussed parts of the formula are evaluated and divided by 12.

If you think that one's tough, here's how the formula for the Days calculation works:

- *Day (Today) - Day (Start Date)* subtracts the day number in the Start Date field from the day number of the current date.

- *- If (Day (Today) >= Day (Start Date) , 0 ,* determines whether the day number in today's date is greater than or equal to the day number in the Start Date field. If it is, it returns 0, which is subtracted from the previous part of the formula. If it isn't, the following IF function is evaluated.

- *If (Day (Today - Day (Today)) < Day (Start Date) , Day (Start Date), Day (Today - Day (Today))))* determines whether the day number of a date calculated by taking the numeric value of today's date and subtracting it from the day number of today's date is less than the day number of the start date. If it is, it subtracts the day number of today's date from the first part of the formula. If it isn't, it subtracts the day number of a date calculated by taking the numeric value of today's date and subtracting it from the day number of today's date.

NOTE *I can't explain exactly how the logic that makes these two formulas work came about, but I do know that they work. I calculated all the individual values by hand and, when I put them together as instructed in the formula, I came up with the right answers.*

Calculating the Number of Weekdays between Two Dates

This final date example calculates the number of weekdays (Mondays, Tuesdays, Wednesdays, Thursdays, and Fridays) between a Start Date and today's date. Here's the formula:

Int ((Today - Start Date) / 7) * 5 + Mod (Today - Start Date , 7)
   - If (DayofWeek (Today) < Day of Week (Start Date) , 2, 0)

I discussed the TODAY and IF functions in the age example ("Calculating a Person's Age" on page 401) and the MOD function in the days, months, and years example ("Calculating the Number of Days, Months, and Years between Two Dates" on page 402). Here are the other two functions that this example uses:

Int (*number*)
DayofWeek (*date*)

- The INT function returns the integer or whole number value of *number*.

- The DAYOFWEEK function returns the day number of *date* where Sunday = 1 and Saturday = 7.

Here's how the formula works:

- *Int ((Today - StartDate) / 7) * 5* subtracts the Start Date field from today's date, divides the result by 7, chops off any decimal places, and multiplies the result by 5.

- *+ Mod (Today - Start Date , 7)* subtracts the Start Date field from today's date, divides the result by 7, and takes the remainder. This is added to the previous part of the formula.

- *- If (DayofWeek (Today) < Day of Week (Start Date) , 2, 0)* determines whether the number of today's day of the week is less than the number of the Start Date's day of the week. If it is, it subtracts 2 from the results of the rest of the formula; if not, it subtracts 0.

T*IP* *For a much more complex version of this formula that takes holidays into consideration, check the Tech Info note called "Calculating Number of Weekdays (Work Days) Between Dates. You can find it on FileMaker Inc.'s Web site, http://www.filemaker.com/.*

Using Calculations to Format Telephone Numbers

Not everyone enters telephone numbers the way you might want them to appear in a report. This example uses text functions to test the length of a Phone field, then formats the field's contents using (###) ###-#### format.

Testing Phone Number Length

The length of the phone number entry often determines how the number is entered. Here are some examples, along with the number of characters each uses:

Phone Number Entry	Characters
(800) 555-1212	14
800-555-1212	12
8005551212	10
555-1212	8

As you can imagine, there are other possibilities. To keep it simple, the formula in this example will just test for and handle these.

NOTE   *For this example to work properly, the Phone field must be a text field.*

Writing the Formula

Here's the formula to format the preceding examples:

If (Length (Phone) = 8 , "(800) " & Left (Phone , 3) & "-"
& Right (Phone , 4),
If (Length (Phone) = 10 , "(" & Left (Phone , 3) & ") " & Middle
(Phone, 4 , 3) & "-" & Right (Phone , 4),
If (Length (Phone) = 12 , "(" & Left (Phone , 3) & ") " & Middle
(Phone, 5 , 3) & "-" & Right (Phone , 4),
If (Length (Phone) = 14 , Phone , Phone))))

TIP   *In the previous example, Returns have been added to improve legibility; you can include Returns in the Specify Calculation dialog box without affecting the outcome of your formulas.*

This formula uses a bunch of text functions:

Length (*text*)

Left (*text* , *number*)

Middle (*text* , *start* , *size*)

Right (*text* , *number*)

Here's some information about each function and its parameter(s):

- The LENGTH function returns the number of characters in *text*.

- The LEFT function returns the first *number* characters in *text*. For example, *Left (Phone , 3)* returns the first three characters in the Phone field.

- The MIDDLE function returns the middle *size* characters starting at character *start* in *text*. For example, *Middle (Phone , 4, 3)* returns the middle three characters in the Phone field, starting with character number 4.

- The RIGHT function returns the last number characters in text. For example *Right (Phone , 4)* returns the last four characters in the Phone field.

How It Works

The formula uses four nested IF functions to perform four different tests on the contents of the Phone field. Each test checks to see if the field contains a certain number of characters. If the Phone field passes a test, the formatting instructions right after the test are used to format the field; if it fails the test, the next test is applied. If it fails all tests, the field is displayed as already formatted.

Six Calculation Hints

This is only one of the many helpful articles you can find at the FileMaker, Inc. Tech Info library at http://www.filemaker.com/support/techinfo.html. This article has been edited for space and is reprinted with permission.

1. You can use Return characters within a calculation to help you organize the calculation. FileMaker Pro ignores returns within formulas (unless they are surrounded by quotes). For example, organize an If statement like this:

    If (test,
    Result if true,
    Result if false)

    In complicated formulas, this can help a great deal.

2. Create and test each component of a long, complex calculation in separate fields. Then use field names in a temporary calculation. When the component fields all work, copy and paste their calculations into a final calculation.

    For example, you can set up a main calculation as:

    If (test, result if true, result if false)

    then create fields called *test*, *result if true*, and *result if false*. When you have those fields working correctly, you will see the result in your main calculation.

3. Even though you can't use the Edit menu to copy, cut, paste, and select all in the Specify Calculation dialog box, you can still use the corresponding shortcut keys for these commands. This enables you to copy formulas between files or other formulas.

4. Use the mouse, rather than typing, as much as possible. This prevents you from misspelling or mistyping the functions, operators, and field names and helps keep the commas and parentheses in the correct locations.

5. If you want to change the data in a non-calculation field using a calculation function, you can create a calculation field with a formula to make the change, then change the calculation field to a non-calculation field. When you change a calculation field to a different type of field, it retains the data generated by the calculation.

6. Here's a way to include comments in a calculation without interfering with the calculation.

    Consider the following calculation:

    Left ("How does this thing work, anyway?",0)

    This formula instructs FileMaker Pro to return 0 characters, starting from the left, from the string "How does this thing work, anyway?" The result is nothing.

    You can use this technique in any type of FileMaker formula. Since it evaluates to nothing, it does not affect the outcome of the formula. To make comments easier to find and read, enter them in uppercase. Here is an example:

    If (Date 2 - Date 1 > 14 & left ("ARE THEY MORE THAN 14 DAYS APART?",0),"It took two weeks" & left ("TELLS THEM IT TOOK TWO WEEKS",0),"" & left ("LEAVE THE FIELD BLANK",0))

The formatting instructions extract portions of the Phone field's contents and concatenate them with parentheses, spaces, and dashes as required.

Tip *This formula can't handle all input formats. It can be expanded, however, to test for other input formats by replacing the final Phone field in the formula with yet more nested IF functions.*

Stripping Quotation Marks from a Field

Is your head spinning from the previous examples? If so, grab hold of something firm and get ready to relax. This example is much easier. It shows off how calculations can be used with the Replace command.

The Premise

Sometimes, when you import text from a spreadsheet or word processor into FileMaker Pro, double-quote characters are included in fields containing commas or tabs. In most cases, you don't want those characters. You can use the SUBSTITUTE function with the Replace command to strip them out. This example strips quotes out of a field creatively named Text.

Performing the Striptease

In Browse mode, browse all the records that include the offensive double-quote characters in the text field. Click in the field to activate it. Then choose Replace from the Mode menu to display the Replace dialog box (see Figure 10-4). Select the Replace with calculated result option. In the Specify Calculation dialog box that appears (see Figure 10-5), enter the following formula:

Substitute (Text , """" , "")

Click OK to save the formula and dismiss the Specify Calculation dialog box. Click Replace to dismiss the Replace dialog box and strip out the double-quote characters.

How It Works

The SUBSTITUTE function has the following syntax:

Substitute (*text* , *search string* , *replace string*)

It works by looking through *text* for *search string* and replacing it with *replace string*.

The formula in this example searches through a field named Text for a double-quote character. To search for any text—including a double-quote character—it must be enclosed between a pair of double-quote characters. That gives you three double-quote characters. But FileMaker Pro won't let you create a formula with an uneven number of quote characters, so you have to add one more to make FileMaker Pro happy. That's why the formula has four double-quote characters for the *search string* parameter. When it finds the double-quote character, it replaces it with nothing. The replacement text string—even if it's nothing—must be enclosed within a double-quote character. That's why the formula has two double-quote characters with nothing between them in the *replace string* parameter.

Step-by-Step

Ready to try a few more advanced calculations in one of your files? In this section, I provide step-by-step instructions for adding calculations to the Invoices.fp5 file you've been working on at the end of each chapter. If you've been skipping around in the book and don't have the completed exercise files from Chapter 9, you can download them from the companion Web site for this book, http://www.gilesrd.com/fmprocomp/.

Calculating the Due Date

Right now, the Invoices file is set up so you have to enter a due date manually for every invoice. But the file already contains all the information FileMaker Pro needs to calculate the due date for you. Here's how you can revise the Due Date field to calculate the date that an invoice is due.

1. Open the Invoices.fp5 file.

2. Use the Define Fields dialog box to change the Due Date field's type from Date field to Calculation.

3. In the Specify Calculation dialog box that appears, enter the following formula:
   If (Terms = "Net 30", Invoice Date + 30 , If (Terms = "Net 45", Invoice Date + 45, If (Terms = "Net 60", Invoice Date + 60, Invoice Date))).

4. Choose Date from the Calculation result is menu and save the calculation.

5. Back in Browse mode, change the entry in the Terms field of the invoice. The Due Date field should change automatically.

6. **Extra Credit:** Write a formula using the CASE function and use that in step 3.

Creating a Discount Field

Spot Ink, Inc. likes to reward its best customers by offering big discounts for big purchases. In these steps, you'll rename a field, then create a new calculation field and arrange and format it on the layout using techniques I discuss in Chapters 7 and 8.

1. If necessary, open the Invoices.fp5 file.

2. Use the Define Field dialog box to change the Invoice Total field's name to Subtotal.

3. Create a new calculation field named Discount (see "Adding a Field" on page 62).

4. In the Specify Calculation dialog box that appears, enter the following calculation:
For Mac OS: *Subtotal * Case (Subtotal ≥ 500, .2 , Subtotal ≥ 100, .1, 0)*
Or for Windows: *Subtotal * Case (Subtotal >= 500, .2, Subtotal >= 100, .1, 0)*

5. Make sure the Calculation result is menu is set to Number and save the calculation.

6. If necessary, use techniques in Chapter 7 to add the newly created field and a corresponding field label to the layout, right beneath the Subtotal field.

7. Use techniques in Chapter 8 to format the newly added field so it has the same shading, borders, and number format as the Subtotal field.

8. Switch back to Browse mode and experiment with the values in the Quantity or Item Price field. See how the discount amount changes for subtotals less than $100, between $100 and $499, and over $500?

Adding a New Invoice Total Field

The invoice is now missing an invoice total field. In these steps, you'll create a new calculation field, then arrange and format it on the layout using techniques I discuss in Chapters 7 and 8.

1. If necessary, open the Invoices.fp5 file.

2. Use the Define Field dialog box to create a new calculation field named Invoice Total.

3. In the Specify Calculation dialog box that appears, enter the following calculation:
Subtotal - Discount.

4. Make sure the Calculation result is menu is set to Number and save the calculation.

5. If necessary, use techniques in Chapter 7 to add the newly created field and a corresponding field label to the layout, right beneath the Discount field.

6. Use techniques in Chapter 8 to format the newly added field so it has the same shading, borders, and number format as the Discount field.

7. Switch back to Browse mode to test and admire your work.

Developing Relationships between Files

FileMaker Pro is a *relational database*. That means you can create relationships between records in one database—such as a customer database—with records in another—such as an invoice database.

In this chapter, I tell you more about relationships and explain how to create and use relationships in your database files.

How Relationships Work

Before you can use relationships in your database files, you should have a complete understanding of what a relationship is, how it works, and how it can be used. I tackle all of these issues next.

What Is a Relationship?

A relationship is a set of instructions that tells FileMaker Pro how to match records in one database file (the *master file*) with records in another (the *related file*). To do this, both files must have at least one field in common. This field is referred to as the *match field*.

Here's How It Works

When you enter a value in the match field of the master file, File-Maker Pro searches the match field of the related file for a match. It then looks in the appropriate field (the *lookup source field* or *related field*) of the record that contains the match (the *related record*) and returns its value to the appropriate field in the master file (the *lookup destination field* or *related field*).

Here's an example that's illustrated in Figure 11-1. Say you have an Invoice database (the master file) that has a relationship to a Customer database (the related file). Both databases include a Customer Number field (the match field) that contains a unique identifying number for each customer.

1. Enter a value in the match field of the master file. In the illustration, the value 10003 is entered in the Customer Number field of the Invoices file.

2. FileMaker Pro searches the match field of the related file for a related record. In the illustration, FileMaker Pro has found the value 1003 in the Customer Number field of the record for Eric Johnson of Wickenburg Novelties Inc.

3. FileMaker Pro then looks at the value in the lookup source field or related field of the related file. In the illustration, the value in the Customer Name field of the Customer file is Eric Johnson.

4. FileMaker Pro then puts that value in the lookup destination field or related field in the master file. In Figure 11-1,

Eric Johnson is entered in the Customer Name field of the Invoices file.

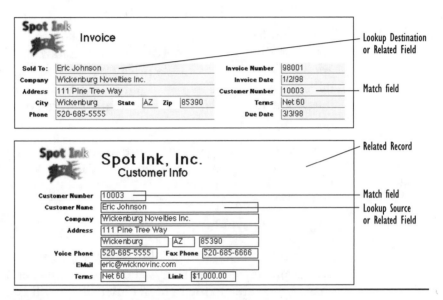

FIGURE 11-1. A master file (top) and related file (bottom).

NOTE *Field names are not important—they don't have to be the same. It's the data that the fields contain that are important when using match, lookup source, lookup destination, and related fields.*

Using Relationships in Database Files

There are two ways that you can use relationships in your database files: lookups and related fields.

About Lookups

A *lookup*, which I discuss very briefly in the section titled "Looked-Up Value" on page 349, copies the lookup source field's value from the related file to a lookup destination field in the master file. This is a static copy that does not change unless you perform a relookup. I tell you about relookups in the section titled "Performing a Relookup" on page 430.

For example, say you have a product database that lists all products and their prices. You could use the lookup feature to copy appropriate values from the price field of the product database to the price field in the invoice database. Then, if the price changes in the product database, the price already entered on the invoice will not change.

You create a lookup with the Entry Options dialog box for a field. I tell you exactly how in the section titled "Looking Up Values in a Related File" on page 426.

About Related Fields

A *related field* is an actual field from the related file. When placed in the master file, it displays the value in the related file. If you change the value in the field in either file, it will change automatically in both files.

Take another look at the Invoices and Customer file example. You can place fields from the Customer file in the Invoice layout of the Invoices file. When you enter a Customer Number, the values in the related fields appear in the layout. If a customer's entry changes in the Customer file, it will change automatically in the Invoices file—in all existing records for that customer. If you change a value in the Invoices file, it automatically changes for the customer in the Customer file.

There are two ways to include related fields in a layout:

INDIVIDUAL RELATED FIELD An individual related field is simply a related field placed on a layout. It displays the value in the field for a single record. The previous example would be a good use for an individual related field. I explain how to include an individual related field on a layout in the section titled "Using Related Fields in a Layout" on page 431.

PORTAL   A *portal* is a specially formatted window on a layout that contains one or more related fields. It enables you to view and work with the values in related fields for multiple records at the same time. An example of this might be a portal in the Customer file that displays all the invoice numbers, dates, and totals for the customer. In this case, the Customer file would be the master file and the Invoices file would be the related file. All the appropriate fields would appear in a portal. I explain how to include a portal on a layout in the section titled "Using a Portal" on page 434.

Setting Up a Relationship

Before you can use either a lookup or a related file in a database, you must define the relationships. And before you define a relationship, you should think things out so the relationship you create works the way you want it to. Those are the next two topics on this chapter's agenda.

Planning a Relationship

If you think you may want to take advantage of FileMaker Pro's relational database features, you should start thinking about your databases and the data they will contain before you create a single file. By planning the structure of your database files and relationships between them, you can prevent a lot of duplicate data entry without omitting any data from the file or layout that needs to display it.

An Example

The trio of database files you've been working on at the end of each chapter make a good example. (It's no coincidence that they were selected for this book.) Here's a table that lists the fields that these files have in common:

Contacts.fp5	Invoices.fp5	Products.fp5
Customer Number	Customer Number	
Full Name	Customer Name	
Company	Company	
Address	Address	
City	City	
State	State	
Zip	Zip	
Voice Phone	Phone	
Terms	Terms	
	Item Number	Item Number
	Item Name	Item Name
	Selling Price	Item Price

The way the files are currently set up, when you create an invoice in the Invoices.fp5 file, you must manually re-enter 12 pieces of information that already exist in other files!

Develop a Plan

When you create a database, take a moment to think about any other existing database files that may already contain some of the information that you need in the new file. You may find it helpful to create a table like the one above that lists fields that are the same in both files. Then ask yourself the following important question: Is there a field in the related (existing) database that can be used to uniquely identify a record?

Look at the example again. Say that Contacts.fp5 is an existing file and Invoices.fp5 hasn't been created yet. You can see that the existing file includes many fields that can be used in the new file. But are any of the existing fields unique for every record? The answer is yes. The Customer Number field is different for every record in Contacts.fp5. That's good news. It means you can use that field as a match field.

Create the Database and Define the Relationship

Once you have identified a potential match field in the existing file, you're ready to create the new database and define the relationship between it and the existing one. With a relationship established, you can use the lookup and/or related field features to display data from the existing file in the new file, saving a lot of repetitive data entry.

Defining a Relationship

You define a relationship in the master file—remember, that's the file that will obtain information from the related file. Make sure that file is open and active before you begin.

Opening the Define Relationships Dialog Box

You can create and edit relationships in the Define Relationships dialog box. Choose Define Relationships from the File menu (see Figure 11-2). The Define Relationships dialog box (see Figure 11-3) appears.

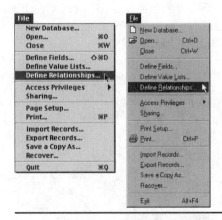

FIGURE 11-2. Choosing Relationships from the Define submenu under the File menu on Mac OS (left) and Windows (right).

FIGURE 11-3. The Define Relationships dialog box on Mac OS (left) and Windows (right).

TIP *You can also define a relationship as you create a lookup or add a related field or portal to a layout. Choose Define Relationships from the menu at the top of the Lookup dialog box (see Figure 11-10), Specify Field dialog box (see Figure 11-16), or Portal Setup dialog box (see Figure 11-20) to display the Define Relationships dialog box (see Figure 11-3).*

Creating a New Relationship

In the Define Relationships dialog box (see Figure 11-3), click the New button. An Open File dialog box appears (see Figure 11-4) with a message above it telling you to specify a file to relate to the current database. Select the database that you want to use as a related file and click the Open button.

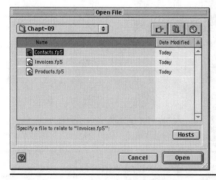
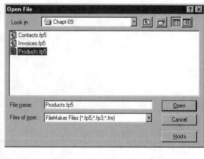

FIGURE 11-4. The Open File dialog box on Mac OS (left) and Windows (right).

The Edit Relationships dialog box appears next (see Figure 11-5). This is where you provide the instructions FileMaker Pro needs to use the relationship.

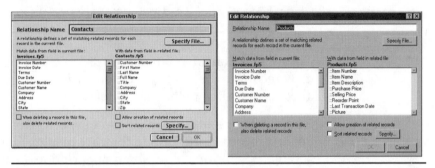

FIGURE 11-5. The Edit Relationship dialog box on Mac OS (left) and Windows (right).

Start by entering a name for the relationship in the Relationship Name box. By default, this box contains the name of the file that you selected as a related file, but you can name it anything you like.

TIP

I usually name a relationship with the related database name and the match field name—like To Contacts on Customer Number. *This helps keep the relationships straight in my mind when my files use multiple relationships.*

Next, choose the name of the match field in both scrolling lists. Remember, the field names do not have to be the same. It's the contents of the fields that determine whether a match will be found.

The bottom part of the dialog box is a bit trickier. It enables you to set options that determine the behavior of the relationship when related files are displayed in the master file. (These options do not affect lookups.) There are three options:

- **When deleting a record in this file, also delete related records** tells FileMaker Pro to delete related records in the related file automatically when you delete a record in the master file.

WARNING   *Use this option with care! It can cause data to be permanently lost.*

- **Allow creation of related records** enables you to add a new record to the related file from within the master file if there is no match to the match field.

- **Sort related records** enables you to specify how you want related records sorted when they are displayed in the master file. I tell you more about this option in the section titled "Sorting Portal Contents" on page 441.

Set options as desired. (Figure 11-6 shows two examples of the Edit Relationship dialog box with options set.) Then click the OK button to save your settings. The Edit Relationship dialog box disappears. The name of the relationship you just created appears in the Define Relationships dialog box (see Figure 11-7).

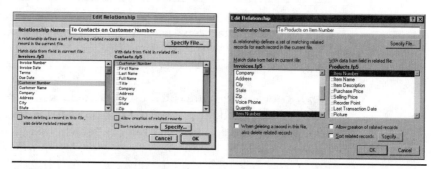

FIGURE 11-6. The Edit Relationship dialog box with relationship options set on Mac OS (left) and Windows (right).

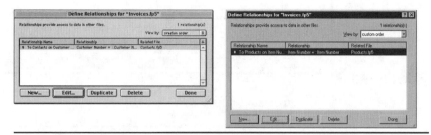

FIGURE 11-7. The Define Relationship dialog box after creating a relationship on Mac OS (left) and Windows (right).

Working with Existing Relationships

You can also use the Define Relationships dialog box (see Figure 11-7) to edit, duplicate, or delete an existing relationship.

EDITING A RELATIONSHIP Select the name of the relationship that you want to edit and click the Edit button, or simply double-click the name of the relationship that you want to edit. The Edit Relationship dialog box appears (see Figure 11-6). Make changes as desired; see the section titled "Creating a New Relationship" on page 422 for details. To change the related file, click the Specify File button, then use the Open File dialog box that appears (see Figure 11-4) to select a different file. When you're finished, click OK.

DUPLICATING A RELATIONSHIP Select the name of the relationship that you want to duplicate. Click the Duplicate button. A new relationship appears in the Define Relationships dialog box. Its name is the same as the relationship that you duplicated with the word *copy* appended to it. Follow the instructions in the previous paragraph to change the duplicate's name and/or settings.

DELETING A RELATIONSHIP Select the name of the relationship that you want to delete. Click the Delete button. A warning dialog box like the one in Figure 11-8 appears. Click Delete to delete the relationship.

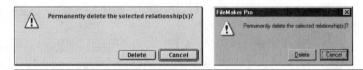

FIGURE 11-8. The dialog box that appears on Mac OS (left) and Windows (right) when you delete a relationship.

WARNING *When you delete a relationship, any lookups or related fields in the master database will no longer function.*

Closing the Define Relationships Dialog Box

When you're finished using the Define Relationships dialog box, click its Done button. The relationship(s) you created are saved and ready to use in the database file.

Using Relationships

As I discuss earlier in this chapter, once you have a relationship, you can use it to create lookups for fields in the master file, or to display related fields individually or in portals on layouts in the master file. In this section, I tell you how to set up all of these things.

Looking Up Values in a Related File

When you create a lookup, you copy the contents of the lookup source field in the related file to the lookup destination field in the master file. A separate field must exist in each database file. Once copied, the information in the master file does not change if the record changes in the related file—unless you perform a relookup.

Creating the Lookup Destination Field

In the master database, use the Define Fields dialog box to create a field into which the looked-up value should be copied. The field can be a text, number, date, or time field. Check the section titled "Adding a Field" on page 62 if you need complete instructions for creating a field.

Setting Up the Lookup

With the field name selected in the Define Fields dialog box, click the Options button to display the Entry Options dialog box. If necessary, choose Auto Enter from the menu (Mac OS) or click the Auto Enter tab (Windows) at the top of the dialog box to display auto enter options (see Figure 11-9).

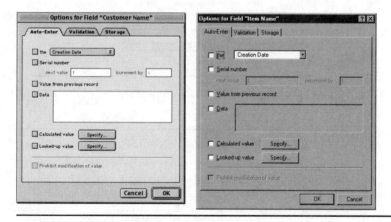

FIGURE 11-9. The Auto-Enter options of the Entry Options dialog box on Mac OS (left) and Windows (right).

Turn on the Looked-up value check box. The Lookup dialog box (see Figure 11-10) should automatically appear. If it does not, click the Specify button to display it.

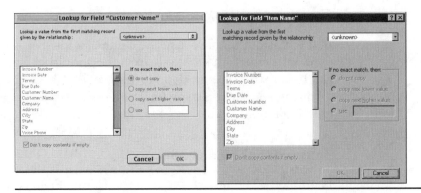

FIGURE 11-10. The Lookup dialog box on Mac OS (left) and Windows (right).

Use the menu at the top of the dialog box to choose the name of the relationship that you want to use for the lookup (see Figure 11-11).

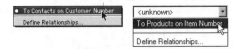

FIGURE 11-11. Choosing a relationship from within the Lookup dialog box on Mac OS (left) and Windows (right).

TIP *If an appropriate relationship does not exist, you can choose Define Relationships from the menu to display the Define Relationships dialog box (see Figure 11-7). I tell you how to define a relationship in the section titled "Creating a New Relationship" on page 422.*

The field names from the related file appear in the scrolling list on the left side of the dialog box. Each field name is preceded by a pair of colons (::)—this is FileMaker Pro's way of indicating that the field resides in another database. Select the name of the field that contains the value you want to copy to the lookup destination field.

Setting Other Lookup Options

There are a two other lookup options that you may want to set:

SPECIFYING WHAT SHOULD HAPPEN IF THE LOOKUP SOURCE FIELD IS EMPTY Turn the Don't copy contents if empty check box on or off. When turned on, FileMaker Pro does not copy the empty value to the lookup destination field. When turned off, an empty value copied to the lookup destination field would remove any value that may already be in that field. This option is turned on by default.

SPECIFYING WHAT SHOULD HAPPEN IF THERE'S NO EXACT MATCH TO THE MATCH FIELD Select one of the If no exact match options. Here's what each of them does:

- **do not copy** does not copy anything from the related file to the master file. This is the default selection.

- **copy next lower** copies the next lower value in the lookup source field to the lookup destination field.

- **copy next higher** copies the next higher value in the lookup source field to the lookup destination field.

- **use** enables you to enter up to 255 characters to copy to the source destination field.

Figure 11-12 shows two examples of how the Lookup dialog box might appear after setting up a lookup.

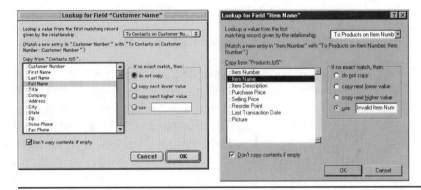

FIGURE 11-12. The Lookup dialog box after setting options on Mac OS (left) and Windows (right).

Saving the Lookup Settings

When you're finished setting options, click OK to save them. The Lookup dialog box disappears. Click OK to dismiss the Entry Options dialog box and, if you're finished working with field definitions, click Done to dismiss the Define Fields dialog box.

Testing the Lookup

The last step to setting up a lookup is testing it. If necessary, switch to Browse mode. Enter a valid value in the match field of the master file and press the Tab key or click in another field. The correct value from the related file should automatically appear in the lookup destination field.

Performing a Relookup

Since the contents of the lookup source field are copied to the lookup destination field, the contents of the lookup destination field will never automatically change. But there may be times when you want to compare values in the two fields and copy any changed value in the lookup source field to the lookup destination field again. That's when it's time to do a relookup.

If desired, use the Find command to Browse only those records in the master file for which you want to perform the relookup. Then select the match field and choose Relookup from the Records menu (see Figure 11-13). A dialog box like the one in Figure 11-14 appears. Click OK to replace the values of lookup destination fields based on that match field with fresh values from the corresponding lookup source fields.

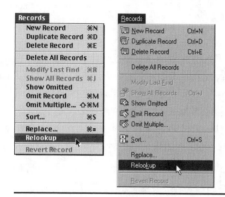

FIGURE 11-13. Choosing Relookup from the Records menu on Mac OS (left) and Windows (right).

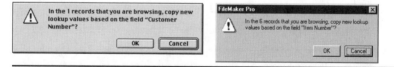

FIGURE 11-14. The dialog box that appears on Mac OS (left) and Windows (right) when you perform a relookup.

Using Related Fields in a Layout

When you use a related field in a master file, you place the related field on a layout, thus making that one field available in both the related and master files. Any changes you make to the contents of the field in either database will change the value in both databases.

Remember, you can add a related field two different ways. When you add a related field directly to a layout, that field displays values from only one record. But when you add a related field to a portal on a layout, the portal can display values for multiple records.

Adding a Related Field

To add a related field to a layout, begin by switching to Layout mode. Then use the field tool in the status area, which I discuss in the section titled "Adding a Standard Field" on page 234, to drag a field onto the layout where you want the related field to appear. When you release the mouse button, the Specify Field dialog box appears. If necessary, use the menu at the top of the dialog box (see Figure 11-15) to choose the relationship for the related file with the field that you want to use.

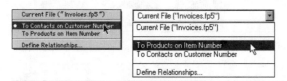

FIGURE 11-15. Choosing a relationship from within the Specify Field dialog box on Mac OS (left) and Windows (right).

Tip *If an appropriate relationship does not exist, you can choose Define Relationships from the menu to display the Define Relationships dialog box (see Figure 11-7). I tell you how to define a relationship in the section titled "Creating a New Relationship" on page 422.*

A list of the related file's fields appears, with a pair of colons before each field (see Figure 11-16). Select the name of the field that you want to display on the layout. Use the Create field label check box to specify whether a field label should also be added. Then click OK. The field appears in the layout (see Figure 11-17).

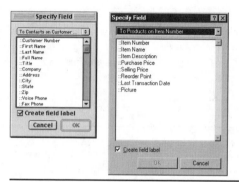

FIGURE 11-16. The Specify Field dialog box displaying related fields on Mac OS (left) and Windows (right).

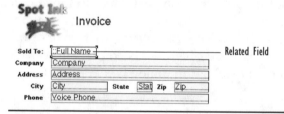

FIGURE 11-17. A related field on a layout in layout mode.

TIP   *You can add as many related fields as you like to a layout. All values in the related fields that you add for a relationship come from the same record in the related file.*

You can format a related field just as you format a field within the same database. I provide details about formatting fields and working in layout mode in Chapters 8 and 9. After formatting a related field to match the formatting of other fields, there's no way to distinguish it from the others once you switch to Browse mode (see Figure 11-18).

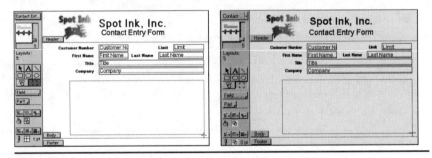

FIGURE 11-18. A related field in Browse mode. With a little formatting, it can look just like any other field.

Using a Portal

To add a portal with related fields to a layout, begin by switching to layout mode. Click the portal tool in the status area to select it. The mouse pointer turns into a crosshair pointer. Drag this pointer to draw a box the approximate size of the portal that you want to create (see Figure 11-19). When you release the mouse button, the Portal Setup dialog box appears (see Figure 11-20).

FIGURE 11-19. Drawing a portal with the portal tool on Mac OS (left) and Windows (right).

FIGURE 11-20. The Portal Setup dialog box on Mac OS (left) and Windows (right).

If necessary, use the menu at the top of the dialog box (see Figure 11-21) to choose the relationship for the related file with the fields that you want to include in the portal.

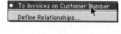

FIGURE 11-21. Choosing a relationship from within the Portal Setup dialog box on Mac OS (left) and Windows (right).

***T*IP** *If an appropriate relationship does not exist, you can choose Define Relationships from the menu to display the Define Relationships dialog box (see Figure 11-7). I tell you how to define a relationship in the section titled "Creating a New Relationship" on page 422.*

Then set other options in the dialog box as desired.

- **Allow deletion of portal records** makes it possible to delete records within the portal. I tell you a little more about this option in the section titled "Deleting Records" on page 438.

***W*ARNING** *Use this option with care! It can cause data to be permanently lost.*

- **Show rows** enables you to enter the number of records to display in the portal at once. Adjusting this number changes the size of the portal.

- **Show vertical scroll bar** displays a vertical scroll bar to the right side of the portal. When there are more records in the portal than can be displayed at once, you can use the scroll bar to scroll through them.

- **Alternate background with** enables you to select a fill color and pattern to alternate with the layout's existing background and color. This can make it easier to read across the rows. These two palettes work just like the fill and pattern palettes in the status area. I tell you about them in the section titled "Color, Pattern, and Width Palettes" on page 182.

When you are finished setting options, the portal dialog box might look like one of the examples in Figure 11-22. Click OK. The portal appears on the layout where you drew it (see Figure 11-23).

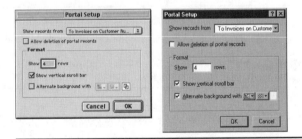

FIGURE 11-22. Two almost identical examples of portal options in the Portal Setup dialog box on Mac OS (left) and Windows (right).

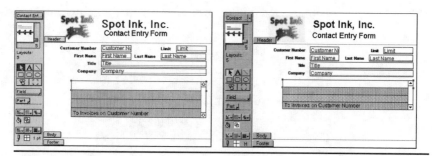

FIGURE 11-23. A portal added to a layout on Mac OS (left) and Windows (right).

Follow the instructions in the section titled "Adding a Related Field" on page 432 to add one or more related fields to the portal. Here are a few additional things to keep in mind.

- You must place the fields on the white area within the portal for them to appear. You can resize the white area if necessary by dragging one of the portal's handles.

- To include field labels, place them outside the portal. Otherwise, they will repeat for every record displayed in the portal.

- You can resize and format fields and field labels any way you like. I tell you about formatting layout objects in Chapters 7 and 8.

Think of the white area at the top of the portal as a tiny layout body part. You can place a portal in any layout part. I tell you more about layout parts in the section titled "Layout Parts" on page 169.

The left side of Figure 11-24 shows an example of a layout with similar portals added. In the example, the portal was resized to fit just the fields within it. The fields and field labels were moved, resized, and formatted. The right side of Figure 11-24 shows what this portal looks like in Browse mode.

FIGURE 11-24. Completed portals, with related fields added, in Layout mode on Mac OS (left) and in Browse mode on Windows (right).

TIP

To summarize the values in a field that appears in a portal—such as the Invoice Total field in the previous example—create a calculation field that uses the appropriate aggregate function with the related Field. For example, the formula Sum (To Invoices on Customer Number::Invoice Total) *would add up all the values in the Invoice Total field in the portal. Place the field on the layout outside the portal to display the value.*

About Related Field Options

Earlier in this chapter, I mention options that add the following capabilities to relationships and related fields:

- Delete related records,
- Create new related records, and
- Sort records in a portal.

Now that you've had a chance to see related fields in action, I can tell you a little more about these options.

Deleting Records

Both the Edit Relationship dialog box (see Figure 11-6), which I discuss in "Defining a Relationship" on page 421, and the Portal

Setup dialog box (see Figure 11-22), which I discuss in "Using a Portal" on page 434, include check boxes that toggle the ability to delete related records. Here's how these two options work.

- **When deleting a record in this file, also delete related records**, which is set in the Edit Relationship dialog box (see Figure 11-6), tells FileMaker Pro to delete related records automatically when you delete the current record in the master file. For example, in the To Contacts on Customer Number example used in the Invoices file in illustrations throughout this chapter, if you delete an invoice, the customer's record will also be deleted. Although this isn't a desirable option for this example, you might find it useful in the relationships you create.

- **Allow deletion of portal records**, which is set in the Portal Setup dialog box (see Figure 11-22), enables you to delete a record displayed in a portal. With this check box turned on for a portal, select any of a record's fields or its row in the portal. Choose Delete Record from the Records menu or press Command-E (Mac OS) or Control-E (Windows). If only a field was selected, a dialog box like the one in Figure 11-25 appears; click the Related button to delete the related record. If the entire portal row was selected, a dialog box like the one in Figure 11-26 appears; click the Delete button to delete the related record.

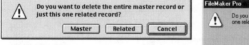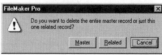

FIGURE 11-25. The dialog box that appears when you select a field in a portal and use the Delete command on Mac OS (left) and Windows (right).

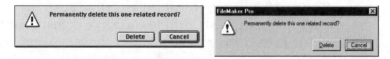

FIGURE 11-26. The dialog box that appears when you select an entire row in a portal and use the Delete command on Mac OS (left) and Windows (right).

Creating Related Records

The Edit Relationship dialog box (see Figure 11-6), which I discuss in "Defining a Relationship" on page 421, includes the Allow creation of related records check box. With this option turned on, you can create a new record in the related file from within the master file.

Here's an example. In the To Contacts on Customer Number example used in the Invoices file in illustrations throughout this chapter, you can enter information in related fields for Customer Name, Company, Address, City, State, Zip, and Phone and File-Maker Pro will create a new record with that information for you automatically.

NOTE *Well, not exactly. The way the Contacts.fp5 file is set up, the Full Name field is a calculation field, which is not modifiable, and the Type field, which does not appear anywhere in the Invoices database, is required to have a value. So if you try this for yourself, it might not work as smoothly as discussed here until you make a few adjustments to field definitions. But you get the idea.*

TIP *The Allow creation of related records check box also enables you to duplicate a related record in a portal. Simply select the record's row and choose Duplicate Record from the Records menu. A copy of the record is added to the related database and appears in the portal.*

Sorting Portal Contents

The Edit Relationship dialog box (see Figure 11-6), which I discuss in "Defining a Relationship" on page 421, also includes the Sort related records check box. When you turn this option on, the Specify Sort dialog box appears. Use it to select one or more fields and sort directions; Figure 11-27 shows two examples. I tell you all about using the Specify Sort dialog box in the section titled "Sorting Records" on page 153.

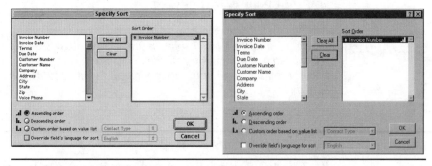

FIGURE 11-27. The Specify Sort dialog box on Mac OS (left) and Windows (right).

Click OK to save your settings and return to the Edit Relationship dialog box. When you use a portal for the relationship in a layout, the records in the portal are sorted in the order you selected.

Step-by-Step

I think the relationships feature of FileMaker Pro offers an excellent way to minimize repetitive data entry. To prove it, in this section I provide step-by-step instructions for turning the three individual databases you've been working on at the end of each chapter—Contacts.fp5, Invoices.fp5, and Products.fp5—into an integrated solution.

If you've been skipping around in the book and don't have the completed exercise files from Chapter 10, you can download them from the companion Web site for this book, http://www.gilesrd.com/fmprocomp/.

Defining the Relationships

In this first series of instructions, you'll define three relationships: two in Invoices.fp5 and one in Contacts.fp5. The steps I provide here are discussed in the section titled "Creating a New Relationship" on page 422.

NOTE *When defining the relationships in this section, make sure the files you select as related databases are in the same folder as the master file. This is especially important if you have multiple versions of the three tutorial databases on your hard disk.*

1. Open the file named Invoices.fp5.

2. Use the Define Relationships dialog box to create a new relationship. In the Open File dialog box that appears, select the file named Contacts.fp5. Name the relationship To Contacts, set the match field to Customer Number in both scrolling lists, and leave all the check boxes turned off. Save the relationship.

3. Follow the instructions in the previous step to create another new relationship to Products.fp5. Name the relationship To Products, set the match field to Item Number in both scrolling lists, and leave all the check boxes turned off.

4. Open the file named Contacts.fp5.

5. Use the Define Relationships dialog box to create a new relationship with the file named Invoices.fp5. Name the relationship To Invoices, set the match field to Customer Number in both scrolling lists, and leave all the check boxes turned off. Save the relationship.

Defining Three Lookups

In this next section, you'll change three existing fields in the Invoices.fp5 file so they automatically look up information from either the Contacts.fp5 file or the Products.fp5 file. The steps I provide here are covered in the section titled "Looking Up Values in a Related File" on page 426.

1. Switch to or open Invoices.fp5.

2. Set up the Terms field so it uses the To Contacts relationship to look up a value from the ::Terms field in the Contacts.fp5 file. If there is no match, the value *Net 30* should be entered.

3. Set up the Item Name field so it uses the To Products relationship to look up a value in the ::Item Name field in the Products.fp5 file. If there is no match, the value *Invalid Number* should be entered.

4. Set up the Selling Price field so that it uses the To Products relationship to look up a value in the ::Selling Price field in the Products.fp5 file. If there is no match, no data should be entered.

Adding Related Fields to a Layout

In this next group of steps, you'll remove a bunch of redundant fields from the Invoices.fp5 file and replace them on the Invoice layout with related fields from the Contacts.fp5 file. I discuss deleting fields in the section titled "Deleting a Field" on page 73 and adding related fields to a layout in the section titled "Adding a Related Field" on page 432.

1. Switch to or open the Invoices.fp5 file.

2. Delete the following fields:
    Customer Name
    Company

Address
City
State
Zip
Voice Phone

3. In Layout mode, use the field tool to place the ::Full Name field from the To Contacts relationship beside the Sold To label. No field label is necessary.

4. Follow the instructions in the previous step to add the following fields to the layout, positioning them appropriately:
::Company
::Address
::City
::State
::Zip
::Voice Phone

5. Use formatting options discussed in Chapter 8 to format the newly added related fields the way the other fields are formatted.

6. Switch back to Browse mode. Change the contents of the Customer Number field to 10003. The related fields you added should automatically fill in with the information from Contacts.fp5.

Adding a Portal to a Layout

In this final set of steps, you'll add a portal to Contacts.fp5 with fields from Invoices.fp5. You'll also create a calculation field that totals information in the portal. When you're done, the layout will look a lot like the one in Figure 11-24.

This section uses Layout building techniques covered in Chapters 7 and 8 as well as portal creation techniques discussed in the section titled "Using a Portal" on page 434, and calculation field creation techniques discussed in the section titled "Completing the Definition for a Calculation Field" on page 63 and Chapter 10.

1. Switch to or open Contacts.fp5.

2. In Layout mode, duplicate the layout named Contact Entry Form and rename it Customer Invoice List.

3. Delete all the fields and associated field labels from the layout except the Customer Number, Company, and Limit fields and their labels.

4. Use the Field tool to add the Full Name field and field label to the layout right beneath the Customer Number field. Change the field label to *Contact Name*.

5. Move the Company field and its label up beneath the Full Name field and its label. Move the Limit field and its label beside the Customer Number field and its label.

6. Click the portal tool in the status area. Use the crosshair pointer to draw a rectangle beneath the Company field.

7. In the Portal Setup dialog box that appears, choose To Invoices from the menu, enter 4 in the Show rows box, and turn on the Show vertical scroll bar check box. Click OK.

8. Use the field tool to place the following fields into the white part of the portal with the field labels positioned above the fields:
   ::Invoice Date
   ::Invoice Number
   ::Invoice Total

9. Resize the portal as necessary to fit the fields. Reposition the portal, fields, and labels as necessary to keep the layout neat. Format the ::Invoice Total field to display as currency with two decimal places and a thousands separator.

10. Switch back to Browse mode. If necessary, switch to the record for Eric Johnson. Invoice information should appear in the portal.

11. Choose Fields from the Define submenu under the File menu. In the Define Fields dialog box that appears, create a calculation field named Customer Total with the following formula: *Sum (To Invoices::Invoice Total)*. Set the Calculation Result is menu to number and click OK. Then click Done to dismiss the Define Fields dialog box.

12. Switch back to Layout mode. If the Customer Total field appeared automatically on the layout, move it into position beneath the ::Invoice Total field just below the portal. If it didn't automatically appear, use the field tool to add it and a field label there. Format the Customer Total field to display as currency with two decimal places and a thousands separator.

13. Switch back to browse mode. The Eric Johnson record should now have a total for its invoices.

Testing Your Work

This is the fun part. In these steps, you'll use the Invoices.fp5 file to create a few invoices for existing customers. Then you can switch to the Contacts.fp5 file and see how the information appears in the Customer Invoice List layout for each customer. This section uses plain old data entry skills covered in Chapter 3, but, as you'll see, there won't be much data to enter!

1. Switch to the Invoices.fp5 file.

2. Create a new invoice. Enter 10001 in the Customer Number field. The terms and customer contact information fill in automatically. Enter 15 in the first Quantity field. Click the Item Number field to display a pop-up list of item numbers in the Products.fp5 file and choose P100. The rest

of the line fills in automatically. Add another item to the invoice if desired.

3. Follow the previous step a few more times to create invoices for a variety of customers with Customer Numbers between 10001 and 10004. Make sure at least one of the customers has at least two invoices.

4. Switch to the Contacts file and browse through the first four customer records. Do the invoices appear? Is the Customer Total correct? Isn't this cool?

Extra Credit

If you're looking for some more work to do on these files, here are a few suggestions. They all involve techniques covered up to this point in the book.

- Modify the tab order of the Invoices layout of Invoices.fp5 so the Customer Number field is the first one selected and only those fields requiring data entry are included (all others are omitted). For instructions, check the section titled "Setting Tab Order" on page 327.

- Modify the relationship named To Invoices in Contacts.fp5 file to sort the portal by Invoice Number in descending order. For instructions, see "Sorting Portal Contents" on page 441.

- Modify the layout named Customer Invoice List in Contacts.fp5 to remove the baselines from fields and adjust the alignment of numbers in the Invoice Total and Customer Total field so the decimal places line up. For help, check out "Setting Field Borders" on page 320 and "Align Text Submenu" on page 289.

- Take a moment to look at the layouts in each of the files. Make any changes that you think they need.

Working with Scripts and Buttons

I think the first ten chapters of this book have provided plenty of examples of the power and flexibility of FileMaker Pro. Its scripting feature takes it a step further by enabling you to automate just about any task you can perform. From creating simple scripts that find, sort, and print records to creating complex end-user solutions, FileMaker Pro's scripting feature makes it possible.

In this chapter, I introduce FileMaker Pro scripting. I explain how it works and how you can use it to create scripts that automate everyday tasks. I also tell you about buttons and how you can include them in layouts to make it even easier to use the scripts that you write.

How Scripts Work

A FileMaker Pro *script* is a series of commands that FileMaker Pro can execute automatically. Most of the commands are right off

FileMaker Pro's menus. Others offer additional capabilities, such as the ability to display a custom dialog box or to loop though a series of steps until a condition is met.

Automating Repetitive Tasks

Don't be intimidated by the idea of writing a script. It really isn't that tough. The more you know about basic FileMaker Pro operations, the easier it is to write a script. And just about any procedure that you do over and over is a perfect candidate for automation. Here are some examples:

- Creating a report that requires you to find a group of records, sort, and print on a certain layout.

- Creating a report that performs a relookup, then finds the records with changed values, sorts them by three different fields, and prints them on two different layouts.

- Creating the report from hell: import records from a tab-delimited text file, strip out unwanted double-quote characters, delete records with an empty Name field, sort by Name, print on Layout #1, sort by Account Number, print on Layout #2 , sort by Date, print on...well, you get the idea. Of course, the report from hell is always prepared *daily*. (I won't tell you what they call the report like this that's printed hourly. I'd just be censored anyway.)

No matter how quickly you can perform the steps in each of these examples, I guarantee that a script can instruct FileMaker Pro to perform them faster. The minutes you spend writing a script to perform a repetitive task is a small price to pay for the minutes you save letting a FileMaker Pro script do the work for you. And the more often you have to perform the task, the more time a script can save you.

Creating a Script When You Create a Layout

Back in Chapter 6, where I explain how to create a new layout or report, I tell you about how FileMaker Pro can automatically create a simple script to display the layout. (To refresh your memory, consult the section titled "Creating a Script for a Report" on page 217). The script FileMaker creates includes the following steps: go to the layout, sort records (if a sort order is specified when the layout is created), and display the layout in Preview mode. Although limited, this is a good example of a basic script that automates a series of tasks.

ScriptMaker and Script Steps

You create a script with *ScriptMaker*, a built-in scripting utility. ScriptMaker enables you to "write" scripts by selecting from a list of available script *steps* and setting options for the steps that you include. This minimizes the possibility of typos that, in other scripting environments, could cause syntax errors. In fact, although I've seen plenty of errors in FileMaker Pro scripts, I've *never* seen a syntax error.

Script steps are organized by category. Here's a brief summary of the categories from which you can choose steps. You can find a complete list of script steps in Appendix C.

- **Control** steps give you control over the flow of the script's execution of steps. This category includes steps to run other scripts, to pause and resume script execution, to use if/then logic, and to create loops.

- **Navigation** steps let you navigate through your database file. This category includes steps to switch to a different layout, record, find request, page, field, portal row, or mode.

- **Sort/Find/Print** steps, as the name implies, let you sort or unsort, find, find all, omit, and print records.

- **Editing** steps let you edit database contents. This is where you'll find commands to copy, cut, paste, clear, and undo—the same commands that are under the Edit menu.

- **Fields** steps let you work with the contents of fields. This category includes commands to change field contents based on a variety of different options.

- **Records** steps let you work with records and find requests. This category includes commands to create, duplicate, delete, revert, and copy records or requests. It also includes the replace and relookup commands and the import and export records commands.

- **Windows** steps let you work with document windows. This is where you'll find commands to refresh, scroll, toggle, and set the zoom magnification of windows.

- **Files** steps let you work with database files. This category includes commands to create, open, close, or save a copy of a file, as well as set password and networking options.

- **Spelling** steps let you include spelling commands in your scripts, such as check selection, record, or found set and access spelling options and dictionaries.

- **Open Menu Item** steps let you include commands to open certain dialog boxes, such as the Preferences, Define Fields, and Help dialog boxes.

- **Miscellaneous** steps let you perform a variety of other tasks that don't fit in any other category. This category includes steps to display a custom dialog box, add comments to a script, send e-mail, open a URL, send Apple Events (Mac OS only) or DDE commands (Windows only), and quit or exit FileMaker Pro.

Running Scripts

Once a script has been created, it is saved as part of the database file. You can run it by choosing its name from the Script menu. If you prefer, you can keep the script off the menu and provide a button that a user can click to run the script. As you'll see when you get more familiar with FileMaker Pro scripting, a script can run another script—even one in another database file.

Preparing to Create a Script

Before you actually create a script, there are a two things you need to do: plan the script and prepare the database file.

Planning a Script

Before I start writing a book, I review the material that I have to write about and create an outline. The review gives me a good idea of what I have to work with. The outline tells me what I have to include and the order in which I should include it. The alternative is to go to work blindly, with no plan. Although that would save me some time up front, I'd waste a lot of time organizing and revising my manuscript as I write.

You can apply the same concept to scripting. Before you write a script, you should review the file that the script will work with and note the steps that you want the script to perform. This way, as you begin to build the script, you know what steps you have to include and the order in which you should include them.

The alternative is to fumble around in the Script Definition dialog box, trying to remember the file's fields and layouts. You'll wind up opening and closing the half-defined script a dozen times just to check the database and figure out what you need to do.

Do your homework. Don't be a fumbler.

One more thing: Make no assumptions. For example, say you write a script that displays records in a certain layout. If you assume that the layout will be active when the script is run and you omit the Go to Layout script step, the script won't work properly if that layout is not active when the script is run. This is just another part of the planning process.

Preparing the Database File

Certain script steps store current settings in the database when included in a script. If the current settings are not appropriate for your needs, the script will store the wrong settings and will not perform the steps as desired.

For example, when you include the Perform Find step in a script, it stores the find request that was current when the script was written and uses that request to find records when the script is run. If the find request at the time the script was written contains criteria that differ from what you want the script to use, the script will not find the correct records. You should, therefore, use the Find command to set up an appropriate find request (or multiple requests) *before* you start to build the script.

NOTE *Of course, there are ways to get around this. You can have the script pause in Find mode to allow the user to enter criteria. Or, you can use additional script steps to build a find request within the script. But in many instances, these techniques can be avoided by simply performing the desired find before writing the script.*

Here's a list of the script steps that store current settings, along with the commands that you should use to set their options:

Script Step	Command	Menu
Sort	Sort	Mode
Perform Find	Find	Mode
Page Setup	Page Setup	File (Mac OS Only)
Print Setup	Print Setup	File (Windows Only)
Import Records	Import Records	File
Export Records	Export Records	File

NOTE *It is only necessary to set options for a command if you are including its script step in a script. If none of these script steps will be used in the script, it is not necessary to set options. I explain these commands and their options throughout this book.*

Using ScriptMaker

When you're ready to write your script, it's time to open the Define Scripts dialog box and work with ScriptMaker. In this section, I explain how to use ScriptMaker to create and edit scripts.

Opening the Define Scripts Dialog Box

The Define Scripts dialog box is where you create and modify scripts. To open it, choose ScriptMaker from the Scripts menu (see Figure 12-1). The Define Scripts dialog box appears (see Figure 12-2).

FIGURE 12-1. Choosing ScriptMaker from the Scripts menu on Mac OS (left) and Windows (right).

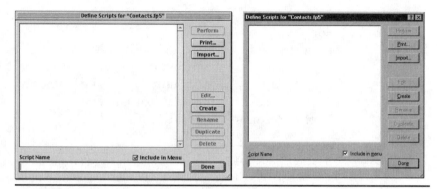

FIGURE 12-2. The Define Scripts dialog box with no scripts defined on Mac OS (left) and Windows (right).

NOTE *The Scripts menu in Figure 12-1 is for a database file with no scripts defined. If you are working with a file that has scripts defined, those scripts may appear on the Scripts menu. I tell you more about running scripts from the Scripts menu in the section titled "Running a Script from the Scripts Menu" on page 468.*

Creating a Script

To create a script, begin by entering a name for the script in the Script Name box. You can name it anything you like; you can include spaces and special characters if desired. When you're finished, click the Create button or press Return (Mac OS) or Enter (Windows). The Script Definition dialog box for the new script appears (see Figure 12-3).

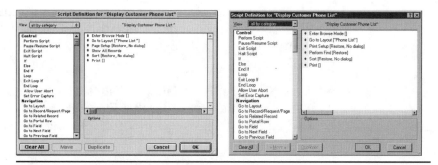

FIGURE 12-3. The default script steps in the Script Definition dialog box on Mac OS (left) and Windows (right).

Understanding the Default Script Steps

When you create a script, FileMaker Pro automatically provides default script steps. You can see these in the scrolling window on the right side of the dialog box (see Figure 12-3). Here's a brief description of each one:

- **Enter Browse Mode [ ]** tells FileMaker Pro to switch to Browse mode.

- **Go to Layout ["Phone List"]** tells FileMaker Pro to switch to the layout named Phone List. This was the active layout when the script was created.

- **Page Setup [Restore, No dialog]** (Mac OS) or **Print Setup [Restore, No dialog]** (Windows) tells FileMaker Pro to restore Page Setup (Mac OS) or Print Setup (Windows) options that were set when the script was created and to do so without displaying the Page Setup (Mac OS) or Print Setup (Windows) dialog box.

- **Show all Records** (see Figure 12-3, left) tells FileMaker Pro to display all records in the database. This step appears if all database records were displayed when you opened the Define Scripts dialog box.

  or

  Perform Find [Restore] (see Figure 12-3, right) tells File-

Maker Pro to perform a find using the find requests that were set when the script was created. This step appears if you performed a find before opening the Define Scripts dialog box.

- **Sort [Restore, No Dialog]** tells FileMaker Pro to perform a sort using the sort order that was set when the script was created and to do so without displaying the Sort dialog box.

- **Print [ ]** tells FileMaker Pro to display the Print dialog box.

Removing Script Steps

Once in a blue moon, you may need to create a script that uses the default script steps exactly as needed. In the ten years I've been working with FileMaker Pro, I've *never* written a script that uses just those steps as written.

NOTE *Do you know what a "blue moon" is? It's the second full moon in a month—an event that happens seldom (although it did happen in both January and March of 1999). "Once in a blue moon" means not very often at all.*

Fortunately, you can delete any or all of the default script steps. Here's how.

DELETING JUST ONE SCRIPT STEP Select the script step you want to delete, then click the Clear button or press Delete (Mac OS) or Backspace (Windows). The step disappears.

DELETING ALL SCRIPT STEPS Click the Clear All button. All steps disappear.

Adding Script Steps

A list of all available script steps appears in a scrolling list on the left side of the Script Definition dialog box (see Figure 12-3). You build a script by adding script steps to the scrolling list on the right side of the dialog box.

TIP *You can narrow down the list of available script steps by choosing an option from the View menu at the top of the dialog box (see Figure 12-4). This may make it easier to find the step you need.*

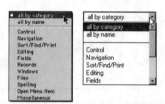

FIGURE 12-4. The View menu at the top of the Script Definition dialog box on Mac OS (left) and Windows (right).

INSERTING A SCRIPT STEP In the scrolling list of steps in your script, select the step after which you want to insert a step. Then, in the list of available steps, select the name of the script step that you want to insert. Click the Move button (see Figure 12-5). The step appears in your script (see Figure 12-6).

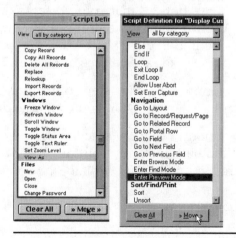

FIGURE 12-5. Clicking the Move button to insert a selected script step on Mac OS (left) and Windows (right).

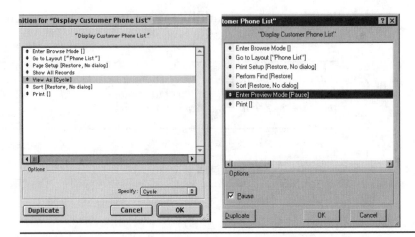

FIGURE 12-6. An inserted script step on Mac OS (left) and Windows (right).

DUPLICATING A SCRIPT STEP In the scrolling list of steps in your script, select the step that you want to duplicate. Click the Duplicate button. The script step is copied and appears immediately below the original.

Setting Script Step Options

Most script steps have options that you can set to determine how the step works. A script step's options appear on the bottom-right side of the Script Definition dialog box when a step in your script is selected. You can see examples of this in Figure 12-6.

The options vary from one script step to another. How you set them depends on the step and what you want it to do for you.

To set a script's options, begin by selecting the step. Then use the check box(es), radio button(s), push button(s), and/or menu(s) at the bottom of the Script Definition dialog box to set options as desired.

Changing the Order of Script Steps

FileMaker Pro executes a script's steps in the order in which they appear in the scrolling window on the right side of the Script Definition dialog box. If the steps are in an incorrect order, you can rearrange them.

Select the script step that you want to move. Position the mouse pointer on the double-headed arrow to the left of the step, press the mouse button down, and drag the step up or down in the window. Release the mouse button to complete the move.

WARNING   *The order in which a script's steps are executed can often determine the successful completion of a script. For example, if a Perform Find step appears after a Sort step, the found set will not be sorted; simply moving the Sort step below the Perform Find step can fix this problem.*

Saving the Script

When you are finished creating a script, click the OK button to save it. The Script Definition dialog box disappears and the name of the new script appears in the Define Scripts dialog box (see Figure 12-7).

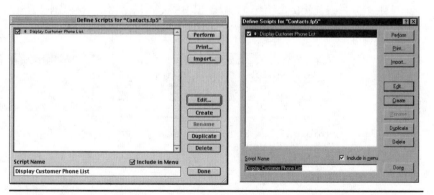

FIGURE 12-7. The Define Scripts dialog box after defining a script on Mac OS (left) and Windows (right).

Duplicating a Script

If you have a script that's almost exactly like another one that you need to create, you can save a lot of time and effort by duplicating the one that's close and modifying its steps to create the new one you need.

TIP   *This is also a good way to save a copy of a script before you experiment with it. If your experiments go wrong and you want to revert to the original script, the duplicate allows you to start fresh.*

Select the script that you want to duplicate and click the Duplicate button. A new script, which is named by taking the original script's name and appending the word *copy* to the end, appears in the Define Scripts dialog box. You can then modify the duplicate script to change its name and steps as instructed in the section titled "Importing a Script" on page 463.

Deleting a Script

You can delete a script from within the Define Scripts dialog box, too. Simply select the script that you want to delete and click the Delete button. A dialog box like the one in Figure 12-8 appears. Click the Delete button to delete the script.

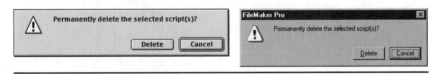

FIGURE 12-8. The dialog box that appears on Mac OS (left) and Windows (right) when you delete a script.

WARNING *If you delete a script that is referenced by another script or a button, the remaining script or the button will no longer function properly. I tell you about using buttons to run scripts in the section titled "Assigning a Command or Script" on page 483.*

Importing a Script

If a script you want to use in the current database file already exists in another database file, you can import it from the other file into the current file.

In the Define Scripts dialog box (see Figure 12-7), click the Import button. Use the Open File dialog box that appears (see Figure 12-9) to locate, select, and open the database file containing the script you want to use. The Import Scripts dialog box appears next (see Figure 12-10). Turn on the check box beside each script you want to import and click the OK button. A dialog box appears, informing you that the scripts import is complete; click the OK button to dismiss it. The scripts you imported are added to the Define Scripts dialog box.

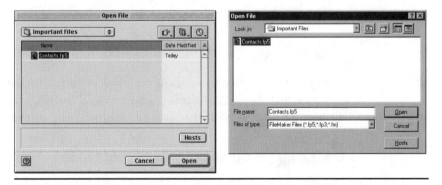

FIGURE 12-9. The Open File dialog box on Mac OS (left) and Windows (right).

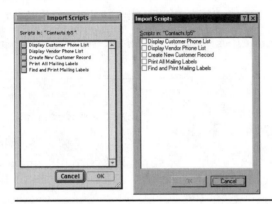

FIGURE 12-10. The Import Scripts dialog box on Mac OS (left) and Windows (right).

After importing a script, check it thoroughly. If it contains references to fields or layouts that are not available in the database file, running the script could cause an error.

Modifying a Script

You can modify a script to change its name or its script steps.

Renaming a Script

In the Define Scripts dialog box, select the name of the script that you want to rename. Enter a new name for the script in the Script Name box and click the Rename button. The name changes.

Editing Script Steps

In the Define Scripts dialog box, select the script that you want to edit and click the Edit button or just double-click the script that you want to edit. The Script Definition dialog box for the script appears. Make changes to the script as discussed in the section titled "Creating a Script" on page 456.

When you click OK to save your changes, a dialog box like the one in Figure 12-11 may appear. This dialog box enables you to change the settings for certain script steps that save settings when the script is created. I told you about these troublemaker steps in the section titled "Preparing the Database File" on page 454.

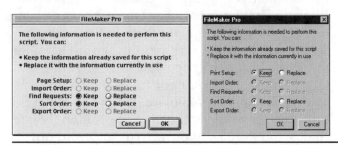

FIGURE 12-11. The Keep/Replace dialog box (for lack of a better name) on Mac OS (left) and Windows (right).

This dialog box confuses more people than the folks at FileMaker, Inc. would like to admit. I think it's because people don't always expect to see it—after all, it didn't appear when the script was created and it doesn't appear for every script. But if you understand what FileMaker Pro is asking in this dialog box, it isn't tough to deal with at all.

Here's the scoop. The dialog box appears when your script includes one or more steps that save settings when the step is created. If you want to change a setting from what it was *then* to what it is *now*, you select its Replace option. If you want to keep the setting the way it was when the step was created, make sure its Keep option is selected.

Here's an example. Say you created one of the scripts in Figure 12-6. Both scripts include a sort command that sorts the records in the found set based on the sort order that was stored when the script was first created.

You decide to change the layout used in the script. You open the Script Definition dialog box for the script and modify the options for the Go to Layout step, then click the OK button. The

Keep/Replace dialog box appears (see Figure 12-11). Since the only change you want to make is to the layout, you want to *keep* all the settings in the dialog box. You click OK and the box goes away. The script includes your layout change, nothing more.

But say that you decide to change the sort order for your script. While in Browse mode, you create a new sort order and sort the records the way you want them in the script. Now you open the Define Script dialog box and the Script Definition dialog box for the script. You don't need to change anything in the Script Definition window, but you need to open it so that when you click OK to close it, the Keep/Replace dialog box appears. (Still with me?) You can then select the Replace button beside Sort Order to change the stored sort order to the new sort order. When you click OK, your change is saved.

Excluding a Script from the Scripts Menu

By default, when you create a new script, it is automatically added to the Scripts menu (see Figure 12-12). It doesn't have to be added to the menu, however.

FIGURE 12-12. The Scripts menu with a script added on Mac OS (left) and Windows (right).

To keep a script's name from appearing on the Scripts menu, turn off the check box to the left of the script name in the Define Scripts dialog box (see Figure 12-7).

Changing the Order of Scripts

The Define Scripts dialog box displays all scripts in the order they were created. The same order is used to display scripts on the Script menu. If desired, you can change the order to display scripts in the order in which you want them to appear.

In the Define Scripts dialog box, select the name of the script that you want to move up or down in the list. Position the mouse pointer on the double-headed arrow to the left of the script name, press the mouse button down, and drag up or down. Release the mouse button to complete the move.

Printing a Script

You can also print a script. This is a great way to document a complex database application or provide information to help you debug a script's steps.

In the Define Scripts dialog box (see Figure 12-7), select the script you want to print and click the Print button. The Print dialog box appears. Set options as desired and click Print to print the script. I tell you more about using the Print dialog box in Chapter 14.

Closing the Define Scripts Dialog Box

When you're finished working with scripts, click the Done button. This dismisses the Define Scripts dialog box so you can work with your database file.

Using Scripts

Once you create a script, it's ready to use. Or at least ready to try.

In this section I tell you how to run FileMaker Pro scripts and how to troubleshoot them if they don't work the way you expect.

Running a Script

FileMaker Pro offers several ways to run a script. The methods available to you vary based on the way you set up the script and the database.

RUNNING A SCRIPT FROM THE SCRIPTS MENU   If a script appears on the Scripts menu (see Figure 12-12), simply choose its name to run it.

RUNNING A SCRIPT WITH A KEYBOARD SHORTCUT   If a script is one of the first ten listed on the Scripts menu, you can run it by pressing its corresponding keyboard shortcut. For example, you can run the first script on the Scripts menu by pressing Command-1 (Mac OS) or Control-1 (Windows). You can learn a script's keyboard shortcut by consulting the Scripts menu (see Figure 12-12).

RUNNING A SCRIPT FROM WITHIN THE DEFINE SCRIPTS DIALOG BOX   Select the script that you want to run (see Figure 12-7) and click the Perform button. The dialog box closes and the script runs.

RUNNING A SCRIPT BY CLICKING A BUTTON   If a script has been assigned to a button on a layout, you can run the script by clicking the button. You must be in Browse or Find mode to use this method. I tell you how to assign a script to a button in the section titled "Assigning a Command or Script" on page 483.

RUNNING A SCRIPT FROM WITHIN A SCRIPT   If a script is referenced by the Perform Script step in another script, the script will run automatically. I tell you more about the Perform Script step in the section titled "Running a Script from within a Script" on page 478.

RUNNING A SCRIPT AUTOMATICALLY WHEN OPENING OR CLOSING THE FILE   Choose Document from the Preferences submenu under the Edit menu (see Figure 12-13). In the Document Preferences dialog box that appears (see Figure 12-14), turn on the appropriate Perform script check box. Then choose a script from the menu beside it and click Done.

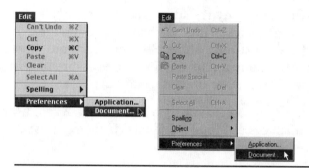

FIGURE 12-13. Choosing Document from the Preferences submenu on Mac OS (left) and Windows (right).

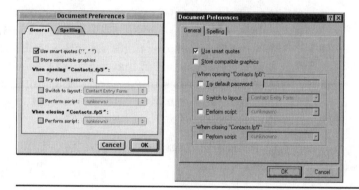

FIGURE 12-14. The Document Preferences dialog box on Mac OS (left) and Windows (right).

Troubleshooting Scripts

If you run a script and it doesn't work the way you expect, it's time to troubleshoot it.

Troubleshooting Theory 101 (or How to Fix Your Golf Swing)

There are three keys to troubleshooting anything—whether it's a problem with your golf swing or a faulty FileMaker Pro script:

- **Know the way it's supposed to work.** The golf ball should go right down the fairway when you hit it with your driver. The FileMaker Pro script should find all records with Customer in the Type field, sort by zip code, and print on the Mailing Label layout.

- **Pay close attention to what's really happening.** The golf ball slices to the left. The FileMaker Pro script prints *all* the records—and they aren't even sorted.

- **Know (or learn) the right procedure to make it work.** Watch videos of professional golfers teeing off and see what they do that you don't (or what they don't do that you do). Manually perform the task you want FileMaker Pro to perform in the script, taking careful notes as you work. Then compare your notes with the script steps to see what you left out (or put in that you don't need). Or, if you have a script that does almost the same thing as the bad one, just compare the two and see how the differences affect the outcome.

If you go through this process and can't find the problem, don't give up. Read on.

Use Script Steps to Help Pinpoint Problems

Now I obviously don't know much about golf, but I do know a little about FileMaker Pro. I know that FileMaker Pro has a few built-in tricks to help you track down exactly *where* a problem occurs within a script.

- **Insert the Pause/Resume Script Step between steps in the script.** Set the options for the step so it pauses indefinitely each time FileMaker Pro reaches it while running the script. Then, as the script runs, FileMaker Pro will pause where you told it to, waiting for you to click a Continue or Cancel button that appears in the status area. By carefully monitoring the script's process as it runs, you may be able to find exactly where things are going wrong.

- **Insert the Beep step between steps in the script.** This is the same idea as the Pause/Resume Script step, but it's noisier and doesn't actually stop the script. Instead, it just beeps where a pause should be. Personally, I don't like this method; it can be tough to keep track of the beeps.

- **Run the script in segments.** Duplicate the script twice, remove half the script steps from one copy and the other half from the other copy. Then run the two halves individually and see which half has the problem. You can repeat this process with the bad half to further narrow down the problem area.

One of these techniques should do the job for you. If it doesn't, read on.

Starting from Scratch

If you still can't find the problem with your script, maybe it's time to start over. Build the script from scratch, but do it a little at a time and test it frequently while you work. If there's an error in your logic, you'll find it right away. Once you know where the problem is, a good review of FileMaker Pro operations and script steps should give you enough information to solve it.

Some More Advanced Scripting Stuff

Most of the scripts that you write—especially when you are first starting out with FileMaker Pro's scripting feature—will perform a series of FileMaker Pro commands to automate repetitive tasks. That's probably one of the best uses of FileMaker Pro's scripting feature. But you can take scripting beyond the basics. In this section, I tell you a little about the script steps you can use to give your scripts decision-making capabilities and enable them to work with other scripts or applications.

Writing Scripts That Think

Performing the same series of steps all the time doesn't take any intelligence. But performing one series of steps in one instance and another series of steps in another instance takes the ability to judge a situation and decide on a course of action. This is something people do all the time, using instinct, intelligence, and experience.

FileMaker Pro includes a number of script steps that you can use to make your scripts think and act. Here are three examples, all of which use If/Then logic.

Trapping Errors

What happens when you perform a find and no records are found? FileMaker Pro displays a dialog box that tells you no records were found and offers to let you modify the find request. You decide what to do and do it.

Now what do you think happens when a script performs a find request and no records are found? The same thing. But if that No Records Found dialog box appears on the screen of a novice user and he clicks the wrong button, the rest of the script may not perform correctly—or at all.

That's what trapping errors is all about—giving a script the ability to see an error condition and act on it.

The following script steps provide an example:

```
Enter Browse Mode [ ]
Go to Layout ["Phone List"]
Set Error Capture [On]
Perform Find [Restore]
If ["Status (CurrentError) <> 0"]
    Show Message ["Oops! There are no records for customers!"]
```

```
      Find All
      Exit Script
End If
Sort [Restore, No Dialog]
```

Now here are those steps again, with line-by-line explanations:

Enter Browse Mode [ ] tells FileMaker Pro to switch to Browse mode.

Go to Layout ["Phone List"] tells FileMaker Pro to switch to the Phone List layout.

Set Error Capture [On] tells FileMaker Pro to look for errors and capture the error code.

Perform Find [Restore] tells FileMaker Pro to perform the stored find request.

If ["Status (CurrentError) <> 0"] tells FileMaker Pro to check to see if an error was received. I don't care which error—if the error occurred right after performing a find request, it's probably an error stating that no records were found. (You can get the actual number if you need it.) The next steps are indented, meaning that they will be performed if the result of the If step is true.

Show Message ["Oops! There are no records for customers!"] tells FileMaker Pro to display an easy-to-understand, if not whimsical, dialog box explaining that no records have been found.

Find All tells FileMaker Pro to find all records.

Exit Script tells FileMaker Pro to stop performing script steps.

End If ends the list of steps to perform if the result of the If step is true. Steps after this one are not indented and will be performed if the result of the If step is false.

Sort [Restore, No Dialog] tells FileMaker Pro to sort the records based on the stored sort order without displaying a dialog box.

There are three things that are vital to the proper operation of this script:

- Turn on error capture before performing a find request. You can turn it on any time before the Perform Find command.

- Check to see if there was an error immediately after performing a find request. If you wait, the standard dialog box will appear.

- Exit the script if an error has been found. Otherwise, the rest of the script steps will be performed anyway!

Logical Branching

Here's a similar example. It prints to a different layout depending on the number of records in the found set. This technique is called branching and, technically, is used in all examples that use If/Then logic.

Here's the script:

```
Enter Browse Mode [ ]
Page Setup [Restore, No Dialog]
Perform Find [Restore]
Sort [Restore, No Dialog]
If ["Status(CurrentFoundCount) >50"]
    Go to Layout ["Phone List for Long Lists"]
    Print [No Dialog]
Else
    Go to Layout ["Phone List for Short Lists"]
    Print [No Dialog]
End If
Find All
Go to Layout ["Contact Entry Form"]
```

Now here's the script again, with comments:

Enter Browse Mode [ ] tells FileMaker Pro to switch to Browse mode.

Page Setup [Restore, No Dialog] tells FileMaker Pro to restore the Page setup options without displaying a dialog box. (This step would read **Print Setup [Restore, No Dialog]** for Windows users.)

Perform Find [Restore] tells FileMaker Pro to perform a find using the stored find request.

Sort [Restore, No Dialog] tells FileMaker Pro to sort using the stored sort order, without displaying a dialog box.

If ["Status(CurrentFoundCount) >50"] tells FileMaker Pro to check to see if more than 50 records were found. The indented steps after this one are performed if this condition is true.

Go to Layout ["Phone List for Long Lists"] tells FileMaker Pro to go to the Phone List for Long Lists layout.

Print [No Dialog] tells FileMaker Pro to print without displaying a dialog box.

Else tells FileMaker Pro to perform the following indented steps if the If condition is false.

Go to Layout ["Phone List for Short Lists"] tells FileMaker Pro to go to the Phone List for Short Lists layout.

Print [No Dialog] tells FileMaker Pro to print without displaying a dialog box.

End If tells FileMaker Pro to perform the following steps whether the If condition was true or false.

Find All tells FileMaker Pro to find all records.

Go to Layout ["Contact Entry Form"] tells FileMaker Pro to switch to the Contact Entry Form layout.

Can you see the similarities between the first example and this one? The main difference is that the Else step specifies what to do if the condition is false, thus making it possible to have the script perform the steps after the End If step under any condition.

Creating Loops

A loop is a series of instructions that repeats itself until a condition is met. Here's an example of a script I wrote a long time ago to go through a file and delete duplicate names as it finds them. If you want to see the actual file, which is called Delete Duplicate Names 1.1 (that's DDN-11.hqx or DDN-11.zip for you folks stuck in the 8+3 era), download it from the companion Web site for this book, http://www.gilesrd.com/fmprocomp/.

Here's the script:

```
Enter Browse Mode [ ]
Go to Layout ["Main Layout"]
Sort [Restore, No Dialog]
Go to Record/Request/Page [First]
Loop
    Copy [Select, "Full Name"]
    Paste [Select, "Test"]
    Go to Record/Request/Page [Exit after last, Next]
    If ["Exact (Full Name, Test)"]
        Delete Record/Request [No Dialog]
        Go to Record/Request/Page [Previous]
    End If
End Loop
```

Now here's the script with explanations:

Enter Browse Mode [ ] tells FileMaker Pro to switch to Browse mode.

Go to Layout ["Main Layout"] 's FileMaker Pro to switch to the layout named *Main Layout*.

Sort [Restore, No Dialog] tells FileMaker Pro to sort using the stored sort order, without displaying a dialog box. (The stored order is by Full Name.)

Go to Record/Request/Page [First] tells FileMaker Pro to go to the first record in the database.

Loop tells FileMaker Pro to repeat the indented instructions beneath this step.

Copy [Select, "Full Name"] tells FileMaker Pro to select and copy the entire contents of the Full Name field.

Paste [Select, "Test"] tells FileMaker Pro to select the contents of the Test field and paste in the contents of the clipboard, thus replacing the contents of the Test field. The test field, by the way, is a global field.

Go to Record/Request/Page [Exit after last, Next] tells FileMaker Pro to go to the next record, but if the next record is the last record, it should exit the loop after this step.

If ["Exact (Full Name, Test)"] tells FileMaker Pro to check to see if the contents of the current record's Full Name field is exactly the same as the contents of the Test field. If the results of this condition are true, perform the indented steps beneath it.

Delete Record/Request [No Dialog] tells FileMaker Pro to delete the current record without displaying a dialog box.

Go to Record/Request/Page [Previous] tells FileMaker Pro to go to the previous record (the one that the full name was copied from).

End If tells FileMaker Pro to perform all steps after this step, whether the If condition was true or false.

End Loop tells FileMaker Pro to perform all steps after this step just once (the loop has ended).

The most important part of this script is the placement of steps. I vaguely remember banging my head against the wall trying to get the script to work. When I switched the order of two of the steps, it worked like a charm, making me feel very stupid. Aspirin and an icepack helped make the headache go away.

Writing Scripts That Work with Other Scripts or Programs

Your FileMaker Pro scripts can also interact with other scripts and with other programs. Here's a little information to get you started.

Running a Script from within a Script

The Perform Script step enables you to perform another script from within a script. The script can be within the same file or in another file.

What's really cool about this step is that when the other script has stopped running, execution of script steps resumes in the original script. Figure 12-15 shows a little diagram of script flow that I threw together in Photoshop—forgive its crudeness; I'm no artist. Follow the arrows to see the flow of steps from Script 1 to Script 2 to Script 3 back to Script 2 and finally back to Script 1.

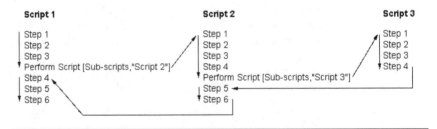

FIGURE 12-15. An example of the flow of script steps from one script to two others.

This is an extremely powerful feature that can do all kinds of wonderful things for you. The trick is to keep track of the flow from one script to another.

To use the Perform Script step, start by adding it to your script. Then set options in the Options area at the bottom of the dialog box (see Figure 12-16). To perform all sub-scripts within another script, make sure the Perform sub-scripts check box is turned on. Then choose a script from the Specify menu (see Figure 12-17).

FIGURE 12-16. The Options area for the Perform Script step on Mac OS (left) and Windows (right).

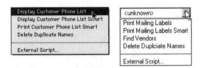

FIGURE 12-17. The Specify menu for the Perform Script step on Mac OS (left) and Windows (right). This menu lists all scripts in the current file, as well as the External Script command.

If you choose External script, a dialog box like the one in Figure 12-18 appears. Click the Change File button to display an Open File dialog box (see Figure 12-9). Select the file containing the script you want to use, and click open. Then use the Script menu in the Specify External Script dialog box (see Figure 12-19) to select the script from within the file that you want to use. Click OK to return to the Script Definition dialog box.

FIGURE 12-18. The Specify External Script dialog box before selecting a file on Mac OS (left) and Windows (right).

FIGURE 12-19. The Specify External Script dialog box and its Script menu on Mac OS (left) and Windows (right).

Communicating with Other Applications

You can also use script steps to instruct FileMaker Pro to communicate with other applications.

- **Send Apple Event** (Mac OS Only) enables FileMaker Pro to send an Apple Event to another application. When you add this script step to a script, click the Specify button in the Options area to display the Specify Apple Event dialog box (see Figure 12-20, left). Set options as desired and click OK.

- **Perform AppleScript** (Mac OS Only) enables FileMaker Pro to run an AppleScript stored in a field or entered into the script step's options. When you add this script step to a script, click the Specify button in the Options area to display the Specify AppleScript dialog box (see Figure 12-20, right). Either specify a field containing the script or enter the script in the big box and click OK.

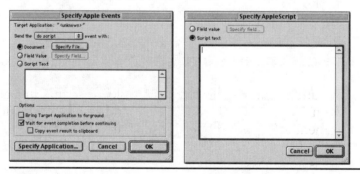

FIGURE 12-20. The Specify Apple Event (left) and Specify AppleScript (right) dialog boxes on Mac OS.

- **Send DDE Execute** (Windows Only) enables FileMaker Pro to send a Dynamic Data Exchange (DDE) command to another program. When you add this script step to a script, click the Specify button in the Options area to display the DDE Execute dialog box (see Figure 12-21, left). Set options as desired and click OK.

- **Send Message** (Windows Only) enables FileMaker Pro to send instructions to another application. When you add this script step to a script, click the Specify button in the Options area to display the Specify Message dialog box (see Figure 12-21, right). Set options as desired and click OK.

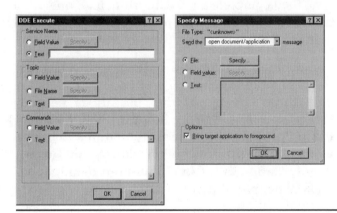

FIGURE 12-21. The DDE Execute (left) and Specify Message (right) dialog boxes on Windows.

Including Buttons in Layouts

Buttons enable you to assign tasks or scripts to a clickable object on a layout. You create buttons and assign commands or scripts to them in Layout mode. Then, when you switch to Browse or Find mode, you can click a button to activate it and perform its assigned task.

Buttons in Real Life

Buttons offer a great way to create user-friendly layouts—the kind a complete novice can use. Rather than give a new user access to FileMaker Pro's menus, you can include buttons that perform menu commands right on the layouts. Not only does this make a custom application, but it protects your database from loss.

Here's a real-life example. One of my clients has a database that is used by the artists in a department. The artists know art, but they don't know FileMaker Pro—heck, it isn't really their job to know it. They simply have to enter information into a database each time they complete a job. Unfortunately, one of the artists tried to delete an incorrectly entered record by using the Delete All command. Hundreds of records were lost.

The solution was to add buttons to the layouts that the artists used. The buttons, which were clearly labeled, offered access to only those commands that the artists needed—New Record, Delete Record, Duplicate Record, Find Record, Quit, etc. Then, using FileMaker Pro's security feature, I removed access to the menus for all the artists. They didn't mind losing the menus and they certainly didn't lose any more data. I tell you more about FileMaker Pro security in Chapter 17.

Creating a Button with the Button Tool

FileMaker Pro's button tool offers a quick and easy way to create nice-looking buttons. Use the button tool to draw a button, use the Specify Button dialog box to assign a command or script, and type in a label. What could be easier?

Drawing the Button

If you're not already in Layout mode, switch to it. Then click the button tool in the status area. The mouse pointer turns into a crosshair pointer. Use this pointer to draw a square or rectangle the size of the button that you want (see Figure 12-22).

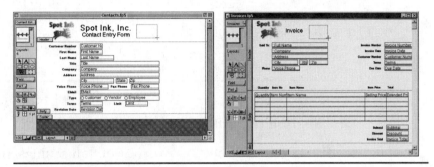

FIGURE 12-22. Using the button tool to draw a button on Mac OS (left) and Windows (right).

Assigning a Command or Script

When you release the mouse button, the Specify Button dialog box appears (see Figure 12-23). It contains the same list of script steps that you'll find in the Script Definition dialog box (see Figure 12-3), but the ones that don't apply to buttons are gray and can't be selected.

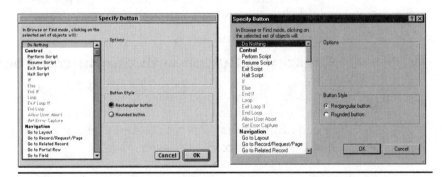

FIGURE 12-23. The Specify Button dialog box on Mac OS (left) and Windows (right).

Scroll through the list to find the step that you want the button to perform and select it. Then, if necessary, set options on the right side of dialog box. You can even specify whether you want rectangular or rounded buttons.

 TIP   *You can assign a script to a button by choosing the Perform Script step and choosing a script from the menu in the options area at the bottom of the Specify Button dialog box.*

Labeling the Button

When you click OK to save your button settings, the button you drew appears on the layout with a blinking insertion point in the middle of it. Enter a name for the button (see Figure 12-24, far-left and center-right) and either press the Enter key on the keypad or click outside the button to complete the entry (see Figure 12-24, center-left and far-right).

FIGURE 12-24. Labeling a button on Mac OS (left) and Windows (right). The finished buttons can be rectangular (center-left) or rounded (far-right).

Formatting a Button

You can change the appearance of a button using the layout tools in the status area (see Figure 12-22) and commands under the Format menu (see Figure 12-25).

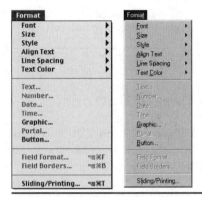

FIGURE 12-25. The Format menu in Layout mode on Mac OS (left) and Windows (right).

CHANGING A BUTTON'S COLOR OR PATTERN Click the button to select it, then use the fill color or pattern palette in the status area to change settings.

ADDING SPECIAL EFFECTS TO A BUTTON Click the button to select it, then choose an option from the Effects menu in the status area to change settings. (The default button setting is Embossed.)

CHANGING A BUTTON BORDER'S COLOR, PATTERN, OR THICKNESS Click the button to select it, then use the pen color, pattern, or thickness palette in the status area to change settings.

CHANGING THE TEXT ON A BUTTON Click the text tool in the status area, then click inside the button to position an insertion point. Edit the button's text as desired. When you're finished, press the Enter key on the keypad or click anywhere outside the button.

CHANGING THE FORMATTING OF TEXT ON A BUTTON Click the button to select it, then use commands under the Format menu to change the font, size, style, text alignment, line spacing, or text color.

NOTE   *I provide details on formatting layout objects in Chapters 5 through 8. All of the techniques in those chapters can be applied to buttons.*

Other Ways to Create Buttons

The button tool makes it easy to create buttons, but it does have its limitations as far as appearance is concerned. Fortunately, there are other ways to create buttons.

Here's a secret: any layout object can be a button. Just select the object and choose Button from the Format menu (see Figure 12-25) to display the Specify Button dialog box (see Figure 12-23). Follow instructions in the section titled "Assigning a Command or Script" on page 483 to specify what the button will do. When you click OK to dismiss the dialog box, the object becomes a button.

Here are some additional tips:

- If you create an object by drawing multiple overlapping objects with (or without) text, group the objects first, then turn the single grouped object into a button. Just remember that if you ungroup the object, it will lose its button settings.

- Buttons can be copied and pasted from one layout to another—even from one document to another.

- A button does not have to be labeled. I occasionally put a "secret button" on a layout to get quick access to other layouts or features. For example, in a database I created for a client, I used the company logo as a button to bypass a lengthy data entry process. Because the logo doesn't look like a button, you can't tell that it is one until you click it.

Changing What a Button Does

To change the command or script that the button performs, either double-click the button or select it and choose Button from the Format menu (see Figure 12-25) to display the Specify button dialog box (see Figure 12-23). Follow the instructions in the section titled "Assigning a Command or Script" on page 483 to reassign a task. When you click OK, the button's function changes.

Disabling a Button

To disable a button, either double-click it or select it and choose Button from the Format menu (see Figure 12-25) to display the Specify Button dialog box (see Figure 12-23). Select the Do Nothing step and click OK. Now the button won't do a thing.

Deleting a Button

You delete a button the same way you delete any other layout object: select it and press the Delete (Mac OS) or Backspace (Windows) key. The button disappears.

Testing a Button

Testing a button is easy. Switch to Browse or Find mode and click the button once. The command or script you assigned to the button should be performed.

If the button doesn't do what you expect it to or it doesn't work at all, switch back to Layout mode and double-click it to display the Specify Button dialog box (see Figure 12-23). Check and, if necessary, change its settings. Click OK and test it again.

Step-by-Step

Ready to create some scripts and buttons? In this section, I provide step-by-step instructions for defining scripts and adding buttons to the Contacts.fp5 and Invoices.fp5 database files you've been working on at the end of each chapter. If you've been skipping around in the book and don't have the completed exercise files from Chapter 11, you can download them from the companion Web site for this book, http://www.gilesrd.com/fmprocomp/.

Display Customer Phone List Script

This script searches Contacts.fp5 for records with Customer in the Type field, then sorts them by the Last Name field and displays them in the Phone List layout. It's a simple script with no error checking that also uses techniques discussed in "Using Script-Maker" on page 455.

1. Open Contacts.fp5, display the Contact Entry Form layout, and switch to Find mode.

2. Select the Customer radio button and click Find.

3. Choose Sort from the Mode menu and use the Sort dialog box to sort the found set by the Last Name field.

4. Choose ScriptMaker from the Script menu to open the Script definition dialog box.

5. Enter *Display Customer Phone List* in the Script Name box and click Create.

6. On the right side of the Script Definition dialog box, select the Go to Layout script step. Choose Phone List from the Specify menu in the Options area.

7. On the right side of the Script Definition dialog box, select the Page Setup (Mac OS) or Print Setup (Windows) script step. Click the Clear button to delete it.

8. On the right side of the Script Definition dialog box, select the Print script step. Click the Clear button to delete it.

9. At this point the script should look like Figure 12-26. Click OK to save it.

♦ Enter Browse Mode []
♦ Go to Layout ["Phone List"]
♦ Perform Find [Restore]
♦ Sort [Restore, No dialog]

FIGURE 12-26. The Display Customer Phone List script.

Display Vendor Phone List Script

This script searches Contacts.fp5 for records with Vendor in the Type field, then sorts them by the Last Name field and displays them in the Phone List layout. It's exactly the same as the previous script—you don't have to edit a thing in the Script Definition dialog box. You do, however, have to change stored settings for the Perform Find step. For details, check "Preparing the Database File" on page 454 and "Editing Script Steps" on page 464.

1. If necessary, open Contacts.fp5, display the Contact Entry Form layout, and switch to Find mode.

2. Select the Vendor radio button and click Find.

3. Choose ScriptMaker from the Script menu to open the Script definition dialog box.

4. Select the Display Customer Phone List script and click the Duplicate button.

5. Change the contents of the Script Name dialog box to *Display Vendor Phone List* and click Rename.

6. Click Edit to display the Script Definition dialog box.

7. Without changing a thing in the dialog box, click the OK button.

8. In the Keep/Replace dialog box that appears, select the Replace option for Find Requests. Click OK.

Create New Customer Record Script

This script switches to the Contact Entry Form layout, creates a new record, enters Customer in the Type field, and positions the insertion point in the First Name field. It uses techniques discussed in "Using ScriptMaker" on page 455.

1. If necessary, open Contacts.fp5 and open the Define Scripts dialog box.

2. Enter *Create New Customer Record* in the Script Name box and click the Create button.

3. On the right side of the Script Definition dialog box, select the Go to Layout step. Select Contact Entry Form from the Specify menu in the Options area.

4. On the left side of the dialog box, double-click the New Record/Request script step. It should appear beneath the Go to Layout step on the right side of the dialog box.

5. On the right side of the dialog box, click the Page Setup (Mac OS) or Print Setup (Windows) step and click the Clear button to delete it.

6. Repeat the previous step to delete the Perform Find, Sort, and Print steps.

7. On the left side of the dialog box, double-click the Paste Literal script step. It should appear beneath the New Record/Request step on the right side of the dialog box. In the Options area, turn on the Specify Field check box, select the Type field in the Specify Field dialog box that appears, and click OK. Then click the Specify button in the Options area, enter *Customer* in the Specify dialog box that appears, and click OK.

8. On the left side of the dialog box, double-click the Go to Field script step. It should appear beneath the Paste Literal step on the right side of the dialog box. In the Options area, turn on the Specify Field check box, select the First Name field in the Specify Field dialog box that appears, and click OK.

9. On the left side of the dialog box, double-click the Pause/ Resume Script script step. It should appear beneath the Go to Field step on the right side of the dialog box.

10. On the left side of the dialog box, double-click the Copy script step. It should appear beneath the Pause/Resume Script step on the right side of the dialog box. Turn on the Specify Field check box in the Options area. In the Specify Field dialog box that appears, select Customer Number and click OK.

11. At this point the script should look like Figure 12-27. Click OK to save the script.

```
♣ Enter Browse Mode []
♣ Go to Layout ["Contact Entry Form"]
♣ New Record/Request
♣ Paste Literal [Select, "Type", "Customer"]
♣ Go to Field ["First Name"]
♣ Pause/Resume Script []
♣ Copy [Select, "Customer Number"]
```

FIGURE 12-27. The Create New Customer Record script.

12. In the Define Scripts dialog box, turn off the Include in Menu check box for this script.

Print All Mailing Labels Script

This first script finds all records in the Contacts.fp5 file, sorts by zip code, and prints on the Mailing Label layout. It uses techniques discussed in "Using ScriptMaker" on page 455.

1. If necessary, open the Contacts.fp5 file.

2. Choose Find All from the Mode menu.

3. Choose Sort from the Mode menu. Use the Sort dialog box that appears to sort all records by the Zip field.

4. If necessary, switch to the Mailing Labels layout.

5. Use the Print command to print the mailing labels. This test ensures that the Page Setup command in the script will have the proper settings.

6. Select ScriptMaker from the Script menu to open the Define Scripts dialog box.

7. Enter *Print All Mailing Labels* in the Script Name box and click the Create button.

8. On the right side of the Script Definition dialog box, select the Go to Layout step. Make sure Mailing Labels is selected from the Specify menu in the Options area.

9. On the right side of the dialog box, select the Print command.

10. On the left side of the dialog box, double-click the Go to Layout script step. The step should appear beneath the Print step on the right side of the dialog box. With the command selected, choose Contact Entry Form from the Specify menu in the Options area.

11. At this point, the right side of the Script Definition dialog box should look like Figure 12-28. Click OK to save the script.

```
◆ Enter Browse Mode []
◆ Go to Layout ["Mailing Labels "]
◆ Page Setup [Restore, No dialog]
◆ Find All
◆ Sort [Restore, No dialog]
◆ Print []
◆ Go to Layout ["Contact Entry Form "]
```

FIGURE 12-28. The Print All Mailing Labels script.

Find and Print Mailing Labels Script

This script modifies a copy of the previous script to enable you to find the records that you want to print as mailing labels. It has built-in error checking to prevent FileMaker Pro from printing all the records if no records are found. This script uses techniques discussed in "Using ScriptMaker" on page 455 and "Some More Advanced Scripting Stuff" on page 471.

1. If necessary, open Contacts.fp5 and open the Define Scripts dialog box.

2. Select the Print All Mailing Labels script and click the Duplicate button.

3. Edit the contents of the Script Name box to Find and Print Mailing Labels. Click the Rename button.

4. Click the Edit button to open the Script Definition dialog box.

5. On the right side of the dialog box, select the first Go to Layout step. Choose Contact Entry Form from the Specify menu in the Options area.

6. On the left side of the dialog box, double-click the Set Error Capture script step. It should appear beneath the Go to Layout step on the right side of the dialog box. Make sure the On option is selected in the Options area.

7. On the left side of the dialog box, double-click the Enter Find Mode script step. It should appear beneath the Set Error Capture step on the right side of the dialog box. Turn off the Restore find requests check box in the Options area.

8. On the left side of the dialog box, double-click the Perform Find script step. It should appear beneath the Enter Find Mode step on the right side of the dialog box. Turn off the Restore find requests check box in the Options area.

9. On the left side of the dialog box, double-click the If script step. Both the If and the End If script steps should appear beneath the Enter Find Mode step on the right side of the dialog box. Click the Specify button in the Options area. In the Specify Calculation dialog box that appears, enter *Status (CurrentError) ≠ 0* (Mac OS) or *Status (CurrentError) <> 0* and click OK.

10. On the left side of the dialog box, double-click the Show Message script step. It should appear indented beneath the If step on the right side of the dialog box. Click the Specify button in the Options area. In the Message Text area of the Specify Message dialog box that appears, enter *No records in this database match your request. No mailing labels will be printed.* Then delete the contents of the Second box and click OK.

11. In the right side of the dialog box, drag the Find All step up so it's right after the Show Message step.

12. On the left side of the dialog box, double-click the Exit Script script step. It should appear beneath the Find All step on the right side of the dialog box.

13. On the right side of the dialog box, select the End If script step.

14. On the left side of the dialog box, double-click the Go to Layout script step. It should appear beneath the End If step on the right side of the dialog box. Select Mailing Labels from the Specify menu in the Options area.

15. At this point, the right side of the Script Definition dialog box should look like Figure 12-29. Click OK to save the script.

```
✦ Enter Browse Mode []
✦ Go to Layout ["Contact Entry Form "]
✦ Set Error Capture [On]
✦ Enter Find Mode [Pause]
✦ Perform Find []
✦ If ["Status(CurrentError) ≠ 0 "]
✦    Show Message ["No records in this database match your request.
✦    Find All
✦    Exit Script
✦ End If
✦ Go to Layout ["Mailing Labels "]
✦ Page Setup [Restore, No dialog]
✦ Sort [Restore, No dialog]
✦ Print []
✦ Go to Layout ["Contact Entry Form "]
```

FIGURE 12-29. The Find and Print Mailing Labels script.

16. In the Keep/Replace dialog box that appears, make sure the Keep options are selected and click OK.

Create Invoice for New Customer Script

This last script, which will be added to the Invoices.fp5 file, will run an external script, then create a new record and paste in some information from the Contacts.fp5 file. It uses techniques discussed in "Running a Script from within a Script" on page 478.

1. If necessary, open Invoices.fp5 and open the Define Scripts dialog box.

2. Enter *Create Invoice for New Customer* in the Script Name box and click Create.

3. On the right side of the Script Definition dialog box, click the Page Setup (Mac OS) or Print Setup (Windows) step and click the Clear button to delete it.

4. Repeat the previous step to delete the Perform Find (or Find All), Sort, and Print steps.

5. On the left side of the dialog box, double-click the Perform Script script step. It should appear beneath the Go to Layout step on the right side of the dialog box. Choose

External from the Specify menu in the Options area. Use the dialog boxes that appear to select the Contacts.fp5 file and the Create New Customer Record script within it, then click OK.

6. On the left side of the dialog box, double-click the New Record/Request script step. It should appear beneath the Perform Script step on the right side of the dialog box.

7. On the left side of the dialog box, double-click the Paste script step. It should appear beneath the New Record/Request step on the right side of the dialog box. Turn on the Specify Field check box. In the Specify Field dialog box that appears, select Customer Number and click OK.

8. At this point, the right side of the Script Definition dialog box should look like Figure 12-30. Click OK to save the script.

```
✚ Enter Browse Mode []
✚ Go to Layout ["Invoices"]
✚ Perform Script [Sub-scripts, External: "Contacts.fp3"]
✚ New Record/Request
✚ Paste [Select, "Customer Number"]
```

FIGURE 12-30. The Create New Customer Record script.

Testing the Scripts

If you haven't been testing as you completed the scripts, test them now. (Don't test the Create New Customer Record script directly; let the Create Invoice for New Customer script run it for you.) If you followed my instructions, they should work. If you feel like experimenting with one of the scripts, duplicate it, make changes in the copy, and test it.

Adding Buttons to the Contacts.fp5 File

In this section, you'll add a few buttons to the Contact Entry Form and Phone List layouts in Contacts.fp5. This section uses techniques covered in "Including Buttons in Layouts" on page 481.

1. If necessary, open Contacts.fp5, display the Contact Entry Form layout, and switch to Layout mode.

2. Click the button tool in the status area to select it, then draw a rectangular button in the header part of the layout.

3. In the Specify Button dialog box that appears when you release the mouse button, select the Perform Script step. Choose Display Customer Phone List from the Specify menu in the Options area and click OK.

4. Enter *Customer List* on the button and press the Enter key on the keypad.

5. Select the button and choose Duplicate from the Edit menu.

6. Move the copy of the button so it does not overlap the original.

7. Double-click the button copy. In the Specify Button dialog box that appears, choose Display Vendor Phone List from the Specify menu and click OK.

8. Click the text tool to select it, then use it to change the button label to *Vendor List*.

9. Switch to the Phone List layout.

10. Click the button tool in the status area to select it, then draw a very small square in the body part of the layout, just to the left of the Full Name field. The entire button must fit within the body.

11. In the Specify Button dialog box that appears when you release the mouse button, select the Go To Layout step.

Choose Customer Invoice List from the Specify menu in the Options area and click OK.

12. Enter $ in the tiny button and press the Enter key on the keypad.

13. Add more navigation buttons as desired. Here are two suggestions:

   • Add buttons on the Contact Entry Form and Customer Invoice List layouts to view the next and previous records.

   • Add buttons on each layout to switch to the other layouts.

Adding a Button to the Invoices.fp5 File

In this section, you'll add a button to the Invoices.fp5 file that will run a script in the Contacts.fp5 file, using techniques covered in "Including Buttons in Layouts" on page 481.

1. Open the Invoices.fp5 file and switch to layout mode.

2. Click the button tool in the status area to select it, then draw a rectangular button in the header part of the layout.

3. In the Specify Button dialog box that appears when you release the mouse button, select the Perform Script step. Choose Create Invoices for New Customer from the Specify menu in the options area.

4. Enter *New Customer* on the button and press the Enter key on the keypad.

Testing the Buttons

Switch back to Browse mode and take a few minutes to check all the buttons you created. Not bad, huh?

Sharing Database Information

IV

This part of the book offers information on sharing database information with others via import/export, printing, networking, and the World Wide Web. Its four chapters are:

Chapter 13: Importing and Exporting Data

Chapter 14: Previewing and Printing Reports

Chapter 15: Sharing Information

Chapter 16: Publishing Data on the Web

Importing and Exporting Data

Way back in Chapter 3, I tell you about how FileMaker Pro can exchange data with documents in other applications using the Copy and Paste commands and drag-and-drop editing. Those techniques are great for exchanging small amounts of information, but when you want to share multiple records, it's time to use the import or export commands.

In this chapter, I tell you all about importing and exporting data between FileMaker Pro and other document formats.

About Importing and Exporting

When you *import* data, you bring it into a FileMaker Pro document from a foreign document or *source file*. When you *export* data, you send it out of FileMaker Pro to a foreign document or *destination file*. Neither importing nor exporting moves records. Instead, they copy records from one file to another.

Two Real-Life Examples

Here are a two examples of how I use the import and export features.

Importing Web Logs

I run a few Web sites, each of which has its own set of activity and error logs. These logs are big text files, with commas separating entry categories (fields) and return characters separating Web page hits (records).

Each month, I import the logs into FileMaker Pro and use its finding, sorting, and summarization fields to analyze the data. I can see which pages get the most hits, which ones are ignored, and which ones generate errors. I can also see visitor IP addresses, which enable me to calculate the number of visitors and see who the repeat visitors are. For a former financial analyst like me, there's no better tool than FileMaker Pro for crunching this kind of data.

Exporting Statistics for Charting

Once I've crunched my log numbers and have created summary reports, I export the summaries to a tab-separated text file and open it with Microsoft Excel. Then I use Excel's Chart Wizard to create all kinds of charts to visualize the data. When they say a picture says a thousand words, they're not kidding. And I know just enough about creating charts to get those pictures to say anything I want them to.

File Formats

FileMaker Pro supports the following file formats for importing and exporting data into text, number, date, and time fields:

Format	Import	Export
FileMaker Pro	X	X
Tab-Separated Text	X	X
Comma-Separated Text (CSV)	X	X
SYLK (Symbolic Linking)	X	X
DIF (Data Interchange Format)	X	X
WKS (Lotus 1-2-3)	X	X
BASIC	X	X
Merge	X	X
ClarisWorks	X	
DBF (dBASE)	X	X
Excel	X	
ODBC	X	
HTML Table		X
Edition File (Mac OS Only)		X

Here's a brief description of each format.

FILEMAKER PRO Database files created with FileMaker Pro version 2.0, 2.1, 3.0, 4.0, 4.1, or 5.0. On Windows, these files have a .FP5, .FP3, or .FM extension.

TAB-SEPARATED TEXT Plain text files with one record per paragraph and tab characters between fields. Most programs can export data to this format. On Windows, these files have a .TXT or .TAB extension.

COMMA-SEPARATED TEXT OR CSV Plain text files with one record per paragraph and commas between fields. This format is also known as Comma-Separated Values (CSV). Many programs can export to this format. If a field contains a comma, the field's contents are usually enclosed in double-quote characters. On Windows, these files have a .TXT or .CSV extension.

SYLK OR SYMBOLIC LINKING A format readable by many spreadsheet programs, including very old ones. On Windows, these files have a .SLK extension.

DIF or Data Interchange Format   A format readable by many spreadsheet and database programs, including very old ones. On Windows, these files have a .DIF extension.

WKS or Lotus 1-2-3   The standard format of the Lotus 1-2-3 spreadsheet program. On Windows, these files have a .WKS and .WK1 extension. FileMaker Pro can import both formats, but can export only to the newer .WK1 format.

BASIC   A Microsoft BASIC format. On Windows, these files have a .BAS extension.

Merge   The data source document format used for mail merge within Microsoft Word. On Windows, these files have an .MER extension.

ClarisWorks   Database files created by ClarisWorks versions 2.0, 3.0, or 4.0. On Windows, these files have a .CWK or .CWS extension. FileMaker Pro can only import from this format.

DBF or dBASE   Database files created by dBASE III and dBASE IV. On Windows, these files have a .DBF extension.

Excel   Worksheet or workbook files created by Excel versions 4.0, 5.0, 97, 98, and 2000. On Windows, these files have a .XLS or .XLW extension. FileMaker Pro can import only from this format.

ODBC   Data source files created or maintained by a ODBC-compliant database application.

HTML Table   An HTML document displaying records in table format. On Windows, these documents have a .HTM extension. FileMaker Pro can export only to this format.

Edition File (Mac OS Only)   A Publish and Subscribe document format.

NOTE *You cannot import data into calculation, summary, or global fields.*

Importing Records

There are two ways to import records into FileMaker Pro:

• Add records in another file to an existing FileMaker Pro file.

• Open another file with FileMaker Pro to create a new File-Maker Pro file.

In this section, I tell you how to use both methods.

Importing Records into an Existing FileMaker Pro File

You can import records from another file into an existing File-Maker Pro file—as long as the file is in a format that FileMaker Pro can import from (see "File Formats" on page 502).

Preparing to Import

Before you start importing records, it's a good idea to know a little about the source file. Get the answers to these questions:

WHAT FIELDS DOES THE SOURCE FILE HAVE? You'll need to match those fields to existing fields in the FileMaker Pro file. Keep in mind, however, that you do not have to import all fields in the source file or fill all fields in the FileMaker Pro file.

IN WHAT ORDER DO THE FIELDS APPEAR? This is especially important to learn in advance if the first record of the source file does not contain field names.

DO ANY OF THE FIELDS CONTAIN IMAGES, MOVIES, OR SOUNDS? Although FileMaker Pro can exchange container field data with other FileMaker Pro files, it cannot do so with files created or maintained with another program. Instead, you'll have to use one of the techniques I discuss in the section titled "Pasting Data" on page 99 or "Inserting Data into Container Fields" on page 102 to import container field data.

HOW MANY RECORDS DOES THE SOURCE FILE HAVE? You might find this number useful after importing the records—to make sure that the right number of records were imported.

IF YOU ARE IMPORTING FROM ANOTHER OPEN FILEMAKER PRO FILE, ARE ALL THE RECORDS YOU WANT TO IMPORT IN THE FOUND SET? Only the records in the found set will be imported, so it's important to either display all records or find the records you want to import before using the Import command.

Once you have information about the source file, take a moment to look at the destination file. Answer these questions and act if necessary:

DOES THE DATABASE HAVE ALL THE FIELDS IT NEEDS TO IMPORT FROM THE SOURCE FILE? If it doesn't, use the Define Fields dialog box to create the fields it needs; see "Using the Define Fields Dialog Box" on page 60 for details.

DO YOU PLAN TO USE THE IMPORT COMMAND TO REPLACE EXISTING RECORDS? If so, use the find feature to browse the records that you want to replace. Then, to play it safe, make a copy of the database file just in case the import doesn't work properly and records are lost. (Remember, FileMaker Pro saves as you work—even if you make a mistake.)

When you've answered all these questions, you're ready to import.

Selecting the Source File

Choose Import Records from the File menu (see Figure 13-1).

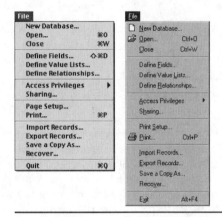

FIGURE 13-1. The File menu on Mac OS (left) and Windows (right).

An Open File dialog box appears (see Figure 13-2). Use it to locate and select the source file for the import. If desired, you can choose an option from the Show (Mac OS) or Files of Type (Windows) menu (see Figure 13-3) to narrow down the list of files to a particular type. Select the file and click the Open button.

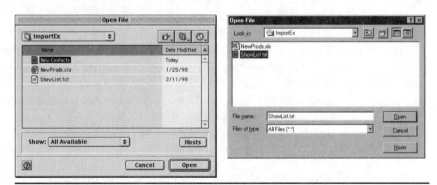

FIGURE 13-2. The Open File dialog box on Mac OS (left) and Windows (right).

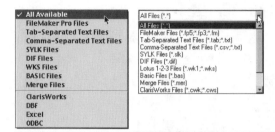

FIGURE 13-3. The Show menu on Mac OS (left) and the Files of Type menu on Windows (right).

NOTE *If the file that you want to import does not appear in this dialog box with All Available or All Files selected from the Show (Mac OS) or Files of Type (Windows) menu and you know you are looking in the right folder, that file may not be in a format supported by FileMaker Pro for importing. Consult the section titled "File Formats" on page 502 for more information.*

Specifying the Import Order

The Import Field Mapping dialog box appears next (see Figure 13-4).

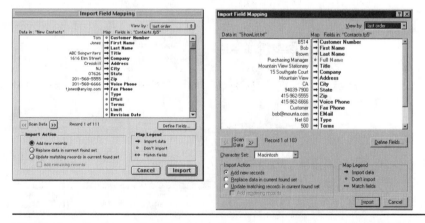

FIGURE 13-4. The Import Field Mapping dialog box on Mac OS (left) and Windows (right).

This is a busy dialog box with a lot going on inside it. Here's what you're looking at:

- The left scrolling list displays all the fields in the source document.

- The right scrolling list displays all the field names in the FileMaker Pro database. A gray field name in the right scrolling list is one that cannot receive data—a calculation, summary, or global field.

- The symbols in the Map column between the two field lists indicate how the field will be processed.

Your job is to map the source document's fields with the File-Maker Pro database's fields. Here's how you do it:

CHANGING THE ORDER OF FIELD NAMES IN THE RIGHT SCROLLING LIST TO A PREDEFINED FIELD ORDER Choose an option from the View By menu (see Figure 13-5) in the top-right corner of the dialog box. Your options are:

- **Matching Names** attempts to match field names in the left scrolling list with field names in the right scrolling list. This option is available only if the left scrolling list displays field names.

- **Last Order** is the last field name order that FileMaker Pro used to import data. This is especially handy if you repeatedly import data from files with the same format and layout.

- **Creation Order** is the order in which fields were created.

- **Field Names** is alphabetical order by field name.

- **Field Types** is in order by type of field.

- **Import Order** is a custom order you create by dragging field names in the right scrolling list. I tell you how next.

FIGURE 13-5. The View By menu at the top of the Import Field Mapping dialog box on Mac OS (left) and Windows (right).

CREATING A CUSTOM IMPORT ORDER Move the field names in the right scrolling list up or down in the list. Position your mouse pointer on a field that you want to move, press the mouse button down, and drag to move it up or down. Release the mouse button to complete the move. Repeat this step for each field name that you need to move until all are lined up with data. You'll probably find that the best way to do this is to start at the top and work your way down.

DISPLAYING DATA FROM ANOTHER RECORD Click one of the Scan Data buttons to view different records in the source file. This is very useful if the source file does not include field names and the first record is missing information from one or more fields (see Figure 13-4, left). By clicking the right Scan Data button, you may be able to find a record that has information in all fields (see Figure 13-6, left). You can then use that record to match fields to field names.

TOGGLING THE MAP SETTING FOR A FIELD Click on the symbol in the Map column between the field and the field name. Here's what each symbol means:

- A right-pointing arrow indicates that data in the source database will be imported into the field.

- A null character (ø) indicates that data in the source database will not be imported into the field. You can see an example of this in Figure 13-6; on the right side illustration, the first field is not imported, even though data is available.

- A double-headed arrow indicates that the field on the left side is a match field for the field on the right. This works with FileMaker Pro's relationship feature to enable you to update data in one FileMaker Pro file (the destination file) with data in another FileMaker Pro file (the source file).

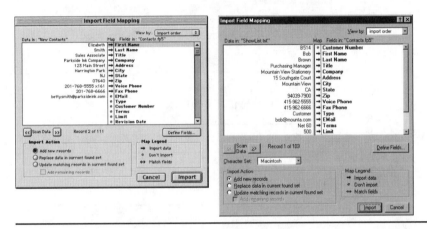

FIGURE 13-6. The Import Field Mapping dialog box with fields properly mapped on Mac OS (left) and Windows (right).

CREATING A NEW FIELD   Click the Define Fields button to display the Define Fields dialog box. Use it to create the field(s) that you need to hold imported data. (I tell you how to use the Define Fields dialog box in the section titled "Using the Define Fields Dialog Box" on page 60.) When you're finished, click the Done button to return to the Import Field Mapping dialog box. The list of fields on the right side of the dialog box is updated to reflect your changes.

Choosing a Character Set for Import (Windows Only)

Windows users can choose a character set for files that they import or export. The character set reflects the operating system on the computer on which the source file was created or on which the destination file will be used.

To select the character set, choose the appropriate option from the Character Set menu (see Figure 13-7).

FIGURE 13-7. The Character Set menu in the Import Field Mapping dialog box on Windows.

TIP   *If you're not sure which character set to choose, don't change it. FileMaker Pro usually gets it right all by itself.*

NOTE   *The character set menu does not appear when you import data from another FileMaker Pro file.*

Adding, Replacing, or Updating Records

The Import Action area of the dialog box (see Figure 13-6) offers three options for specifying how you want imported records added to the database:

- Add new records

- Replace data in current found set

- Update matching records in current found set

Here's how each of these options works.

WARNING   *Always back up your FileMaker Pro database file before using the Replace or Update option. If you fail to do this and something goes wrong with the import, you can lose data.*

ADD NEW RECORDS The Add new records command creates a new record in the FileMaker Pro database for each record imported. After importing with this option turned on, your database has more records than before you imported.

REPLACE DATA IN CURRENT FOUND SET This command replaces the contents of fields in the found set with the contents of imported fields. After importing with this option turned on, your database has the same number of records than before you imported. If you use this option, there are a few things you need to keep in mind:

• If the source file contains more records than the FileMaker Pro database, only the number of records in the database will be replaced with records in the source file. A dialog box like the one in Figure 13-8 appears after the import when this occurs.

FIGURE 13-8. The dialog box that appears on Mac OS (left) and Windows (right) when you attempt to replace the found set with more records than are in the found set.

• If the source file contains less records than the FileMaker Pro database, only the number of records in the source file will be replaced in the database. A dialog box like the one in Figure 13-9 appears after the import when this occurs.

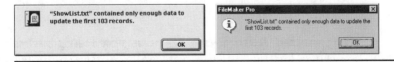

FIGURE 13-9. The dialog box that appears on Mac OS (left) and Windows (right) when you attempt to replace the found set with less records than are in the found set.

UPDATE MATCHING RECORDS IN CURRENT FOUND SET This option instructs FileMaker Pro to use the match fields to find existing records among those in the found set of the destination document that also exist in the source document. It then updates only those destination document records with data from the source documents. This option is especially useful if you have two copies of a database file—say, a copy on your desktop computer and one on your laptop—and you want to update one file with changes you made in the other. To use this option, you must specify a match field in the Map column of the Import Field Mapping dialog box. If you select this option, you can also turn on the Add remaining records check box below it. This instructs FileMaker Pro to add the records that don't match as new records in the database file.

Setting Import Options

When you've made all the necessary changes to settings in the Import Field Mapping dialog box, click the Import button. If your database file has lookups or fields that automatically enter data or you're importing data from a FileMaker Pro file that has repeating fields, the Import Options dialog box appears (see Figure 13-10).

FIGURE 13-10. The Import Options dialog box on Mac OS (left) and Windows (right).

ENABLING AUTO ENTER OPTIONS FOR FIELDS IN IMPORTED RECORDS Turn on the Perform auto-enter options while importing check box. This enables the auto enter options in the Entry Options dialog box for any fields that have them. For example, in the example file called Contacts.fp5, an auto enter option assigns a unique customer number for all new customers. But turning on this check box, customers that are imported will also be assigned unique numbers.

IMPORTING REPEATING FIELDS INTO REPEATING FIELDS Make sure the Keeping them in the original record option is selected. This ensures that repeated fields remain with their original record.

NOTE   *For this option to work properly, the FileMaker Pro destination file must have repeating fields set up for the corresponding fields in the source file.*

SPLITTING REPEATING FIELDS INTO INDIVIDUAL RECORDS Select the Splitting them into separate records option. This creates a new record for every repeating field. The nonrepeating field values are copied for every new record created from values in a repeating field. For example, in the example file named Invoices.fp5, repeating fields exist for items purchased. But selecting this option when importing that file as a source file into another database, each item purchased would be entered into a separate record with the rest of the invoice information repeated for each item's record.

TIP   *Importing a FileMaker Pro file with repeating fields into another FileMaker Pro file with the Splitting them into separate records option selected is a quick and easy way to create separate records for each value in a repeating field.*

Importing the Records

If the Import Options dialog box (see Figure 13-10) appeared, click OK to save your settings and the records are imported. If the dialog box did not appear, the records are imported when you click the OK button in the Import Field Mapping dialog box (see Figure 13-6).

The speed of the import varies based on the number of records and fields being imported and the speed of your computer. If you are importing a large number of records, the Import dialog box (see Figure 13-11) may appear to indicate your progress.

FIGURE 13-11. The Import dialog box on Mac OS (left) and Windows (right).

Checking Imported Records

When the import is complete, the current layout appears in Browse mode with the first of the imported records displayed (see Figure 13-12). The imported records make up the found set.

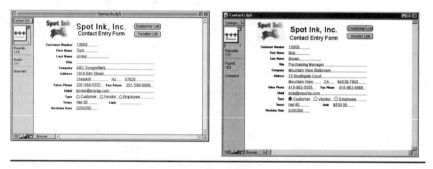

FIGURE 13-12. The current layout in Browse mode immediately after importing 103 records on Mac OS (left) and Windows (right).

Browse through the records to make sure they have imported properly. Here are two things to consider:

IS DATA IMPORTED INTO THE PROPER FIELDS? If data appears in the wrong field, you may have made an error in the Import Field Mapping dialog box.

IS DATA IMPORTED CONSISTENTLY FOR EVERY RECORD? If some records are okay but others aren't, there may be a problem in the source file.

Do Unusual Characters Appear in Fields? If you're a Windows user, you may have selected the wrong option from the Character Set menu in the Import Field Mapping dialog box; see "Choosing a Character Set for Import (Windows Only)" on page 511 for details.

If everything appears okay, you can continue working with the FileMaker Pro file. But if there's a problem, you'll have to redo the import.

Undoing an Import

You may have noticed that the Undo command is not available immediately after importing records. If you need to undo an import, don't panic. There may be a way.

Undoing an Import that Added Records Choose Delete Found Records from the Records menu (see Figure 13-13) to delete the found set. When a confirmation dialog box like the one in Figure 13-14 appears, click its Delete button. The imported records are deleted, returning the database to the way it was before you imported.

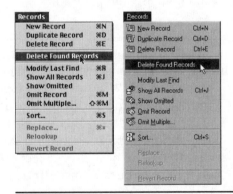

FIGURE 13-13. Choosing Delete Found Records from the Records menu on Mac OS (left) and Windows (right).

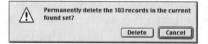 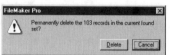

FIGURE 13-14. The dialog box that appears on Mac OS (left) and Windows (right) when you choose the Delete Found Records command.

UNDOING AN IMPORT THAT REPLACED OR UPDATED RECORDS   Close the file and drag its icon to the Trash (Mac OS) or Recycle Bin (Windows). Then duplicate the backup copy that you made before you imported, rename it if desired, and open it up to try again. If you didn't heed my warning and you failed to make a backup, you're out of luck!

Importing Records into a New FileMaker Pro File

You can also import records into a new FileMaker Pro file. It's an easy enough process—just use the Open dialog box to open a document file that has been saved in a format that FileMaker Pro recognizes for importing (see "File Formats" on page 502). This is something I mentioned in the section titled "Opening a File Other Than a FileMaker Pro Database" on page 80.

Opening the Source File

Choose Open from the File menu (see Figure 13-1) or press Command-O (Mac OS) or Control-O (Windows). The Open File dialog box appears (see Figure 13-2). Choose an option from the Show (Mac OS) or Files of Type (Windows) menu (see Figure 13-3); if you're not sure which option to pick, choose All Available or All Files. Then use the dialog box to locate and select the file that you want to import. Click the Open button to continue.

TIP   *You can also open a source file to create a FileMaker Pro database file by dragging its icon onto the FileMaker Pro program icon.*

Importing an Excel Worksheet File

If you are opening an Excel workbook file, the Select Worksheet dialog box (see Figure 13-15) appears next.

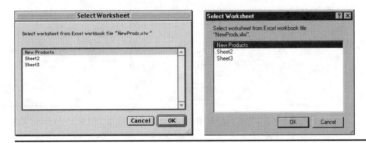

FIGURE 13-15. The Select Worksheet dialog box on Mac OS (left) and Windows (right).

Since FileMaker Pro can import only one worksheet at a time, it displays this dialog box so you can pick one. Select the worksheet that you want to import and click the OK button to continue.

The First Row Option dialog box (see Figure 13-16) may appear next. Use it to specify whether field names or data appear in the first row of the Excel worksheet file. (To select the correct option, you must know how the source file is set up.) Then click OK.

FIGURE 13-16. The First Row Option dialog box on Mac OS (left) and Windows (right).

Naming and Saving the New File

The Name Converted File dialog box (see Figure 13-17) appears next. Use it to enter a name and choose a disk location for the new file. Click the Save button to start the import.

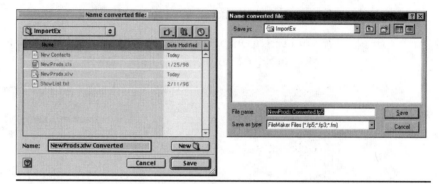

FIGURE 13-17. The Name Converted File dialog box on Mac OS (left) and Windows (right).

About the New File

FileMaker Pro creates a brand new database file based on the contents of the source file (see Figure 13-18).

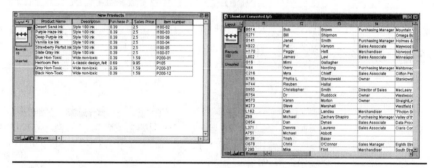

FIGURE 13-18. An Excel worksheet imported into its own FileMaker Pro file on Mac OS (left) and a comma-separated text file imported into its own FileMaker Pro file on Windows (right).

The new file includes the number of fields it needs to store data. The fields are usually text fields, but some formats enable File-Maker Pro to create number, date, and time fields, too. Fields are either named with the letter *f* followed by the number of the field or, if the source file included field names, with the field names of the source file.

FileMaker Pro also creates two layouts:

- **Layout #1** is a standard layout displaying one record at a time.

- **Layout #2** is an columnar list/report layout, displaying multiple records in Table view.

Working with the New File

Once the data has been imported, you can make changes as desired in the file. Here are some suggestions.

- Delete fields that contain information you don't need.

- Rename fields so their names are more descriptive.

- Add calculation and other fields to store additional data.

- Modify, rename, and create layouts to meet your needs.

Exporting Records

Exporting records is like importing—but backwards. Instead of copying records from a source file, you copy records to a destination file. Once in a destination file of an appropriate format (see "File Formats" on page 502), the data can be used by another application.

Preparing to Export

Before you start exporting records from a database, there are a few things you should consider:

WHICH RECORDS DO YOU WANT TO EXPORT? FileMaker Pro exports only the records in the found set. If you want to export all the records, be sure to use the Show All Records command before exporting. If you want to export only some of the records, be sure to use the Find command to locate the records that you want to export. I tell you about using the Find and Show All Records commands in the section titled "Finding Records" on page 133.

DO YOU WANT THE RECORDS EXPORTED IN ANY SPECIAL ORDER? FileMaker Pro exports records in the order in which they are sorted. If you want the records exported in a certain order, be sure to use the Sort command to sort them before exporting. I tell you how to sort records in the section titled "Sorting Records" on page 153.

DO YOU WANT TO INCLUDE SPECIAL FORMATTING FOR EXPORTED DATA? FileMaker Pro can include number, date, and time formats in data exported to all file formats except SYLK and DIF. If you want to take advantage of this option, switch to a layout that displays the fields with the desired formatting before exporting.

DO YOU PLAN TO EXPORT SUB-SUMMARY VALUES IN SUMMARY FIELDS? If you do, the database must be sorted by the break field(s) for the sub-summaries to be calculated. I tell you more about working with sub-summaries in the section titled "Using Summary Parts and Fields" on page 265.

ARE ANY OF THE FIELDS THAT YOU WANT TO EXPORT REPEATING FIELDS? Some export file formats—such as SYLK, WKS, and DBF—can accept only one value per field. If you export to one of these formats, only the value in the first field repetition will be exported. If you want all field contents exported, you must create a separate record for each field repetition. The best way to do this is to import the file's contents into a *clone* (or recordless copy) of the file using the Splitting them into separate records option in the Import Options dialog box. When you're finished, export the contents of the new file. I tell you how to clone a database file in the section titled "Cloning Files" on page 657 and how to use the Import Options dialog box in the section titled "Setting Import Options" on page 514.

Exporting the Records

Once you've prepared the file for export, you're ready to use the Export command. Choose Export from the Import/Export submenu under the File menu (see Figure 13-1) to get started.

Naming and Saving the Destination File

The first thing that appears when you export records is the Export Records to File dialog box (see Figure 13-19).

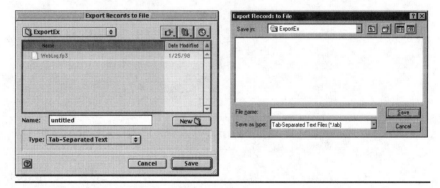

FIGURE 13-19. The Export Records to File dialog box on Mac OS (left) and Windows (right).

Use this dialog box to enter a name and select a disk location for the destination file. Then choose a file format from the Type (Mac OS) or Save as Type (Windows) menu (see Figure 13-20). When you're finished, click the Save button to continue.

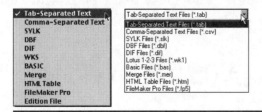

FIGURE 13-20. The Type menu on Mac OS (left) and the Save as Type menu on Windows (right).

Specifying the Export Order

The Specify Field order for Export (Windows) dialog box appears next (see Figure 13-21). The left side of the dialog box lists all the fields in the database. The right side is where you list the fields that you want to export in the order in which you want them exported.

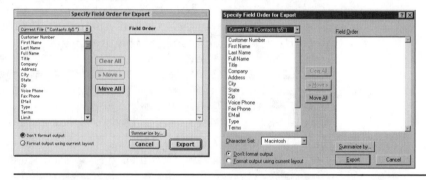

FIGURE 13-21. The Specify Field Order for Export dialog box on Mac OS (left) and Windows (right).

ADDING A FIELD TO THE FIELD ORDER LIST In the list of fields, click the name of a field to select it, then click the Move button. Or simply double-click the field name. The field name appears in the Field Order list.

ADDING A FIELD FROM A RELATED DATABASE TO THE FIELD ORDER LIST Choose a relationship from the menu above the list of fields. A list of fields in the related database appears. Follow the preceding instructions to add a field to the Field Order list. I tell you all about relationships (well, the FileMaker Pro kind anyway) in Chapter 11.

ADDING ALL THE FIELDS IN THE FIELD LIST TO THE FIELD ORDER LIST Click the Move All button.

REMOVING A FIELD FROM THE FIELD ORDER LIST Click the name of the field to select it and click the Clear button, or press Delete (Mac OS) or Backspace (Windows).

REMOVING ALL THE FIELDS FROM THE FIELD ORDER LIST Click the Clear All button.

CHANGING THE ORDER OF FIELDS IN THE FIELD ORDER LIST Position your mouse pointer on the double-headed arrow to the left of a field name that you want to move, press your mouse button down, and drag up or down. Release the mouse button to complete the move. Repeat this process until the fields are in the desired order.

EXPORTING SUB-SUMMARY VALUES Add the summary field containing the values that you want to export to the Field Order list. Then click on the field name in the Field Order list to select it. Click the Summarize by button to display the Summarize By dialog box (see Figure 13-22). Select the break field by which you want to summarize data by clicking to the left of its name to place a check mark there (see Figure 13-22, right). Click OK to close the dialog box. The field name for the sub-summary value appears in italics in the Field Order list and includes the break field name (see Figure 13-23).

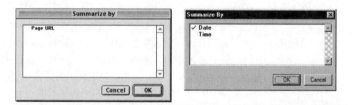

FIGURE 13-22. The Summarize By dialog box on Mac OS (left) and Windows (right).

NOTE *The only fields that appear in the Summarize By dialog box are those by which the database has been sorted.*

Figure 13-23 shows examples of the Specify Field Order for Export dialog box with fields in the Field Order list.

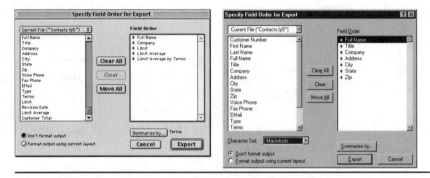

FIGURE 13-23. Examples of field orders set in the Specify Field Order for Export dialog box on Mac OS (left) and Windows (right).

Selecting a Format Option

Select one of the two options at the bottom left of the dialog box (see Figure 13-23) to specify a format option:

- **Don't format output** does not apply any special formatting to numbers, dates, or times.

- **Format output using current layout** includes the symbols and punctuation that are part of the formatting applied to number, date, and time fields on the current layout. Non-numeric characters are exported as text. This option is not available when exporting to SYLK, DBF, or DIF formats.

Choosing a Character Set for Export (Windows Only)

Windows users can use the Character Set menu (see Figure 13-7) to choose an appropriate character set for the exported file. I tell you more about this option in "Choosing a Character Set for Import (Windows Only)" on page 511.

Completing the Export

When you're finished making settings in the dialog box with two names (see Figure 13-21), click the Export button. The records in the found set are exported.

The speed of the export varies based on the number of records and fields being exported and the speed of your computer. If you are exporting a very large number of records, the Export dialog box may appear to indicate your progress. When the export is completed, you can continue working with FileMaker Pro or use the newly exported file with another application.

Step-by-Step

Are you ready to try importing and exporting some data?

Well, you have a choice: You can try a few imports and exports on your own using the techniques discussed in this chapter and some appropriate files sitting around on your hard disk. Or you can obtain the samples files from the companion Web site for this book, http://www.gilesrd.com/fmprocomp/ and follow the instructions in this section.

Importing New Customers from a Text File

The marketing folks at Spot Ink, Inc. have just returned from a trade show where they collected business cards from potential customers and vendors. An overzealous new marketing associate named Steven spent the entire trip back to Spot Ink headquarters entering the names and contact information into a file on his PowerBook for every business card. He even assigned customer numbers using his own numbering scheme. (What a guy!)

Unfortunately, Steven didn't use FileMaker Pro to enter the data. Instead, he created a tab-separated file in his favorite text editor, a shareware program that no one else uses. The file has been saved as plain text, so it can be imported easily into FileMaker Pro. That's your job. If you need help, check "Importing Records into an Existing FileMaker Pro File" on page 505.

1. Open the file named Contacts.fp5.

2. Use the Import Records command and the dialog boxes that appear to import all records in the file named ShowList.txt as new records. All fields should be imported except the Customer Number and Revision date fields. (Steven's numbering scheme, which begins with the same letter of the contact's last name, is all wrong.) In the Import Options dialog box, enable the auto-enter option to generate new customer numbers and revision dates.

3. When the import is complete, scroll through the records in the found set to make sure data is imported into the correct field. If not, delete the found set and try the import again.

Importing Products from an Excel File

Meanwhile, Debbie, the purchasing manager at Spot Ink, Inc., has been busy entering information about new products. For some reason, no one gave her access to the Products.fp5 file—maybe it's because networking is covered in Chapter 15 and you haven't gotten there yet. Debbie entered her information into an Excel 98 workbook file.

Your job is to import the contents of the file into Products.fp5. If you need help, check "Importing Records into an Existing FileMaker Pro File" on page 505.

1. Open the file named Products.fp5.

2. Use the Import Records command and dialog boxes to import the contents of the New Products worksheet within NewProds.xlw as new records.

3. When the import is complete, scroll through the records in the found set to make sure data is imported into the correct field. If field names from the Excel worksheet file are imported as a record, simply delete that record. If there is a problem with the import, use the Delete Found Records command to delete all imported records and try again.

Splitting Repeating Fields

The import feature can also be used to split values in repeated fields into individual records. This might be necessary if you need to export information with repeating fields into a format that can be read by certain other spreadsheet or database software.

In this exercise, you'll create a clone of the Invoices.fp5 file and import the contents of Invoices.fp5 into the clone to split repeating fields. For details on this process, check "Importing Records into an Existing FileMaker Pro File" on page 505, paying close attention to "Setting Import Options" on page 514. I tell you more about cloning database files in the section titled "Cloning Files" on page 657.

1. Open the file named Invoices.fp5.

2. Choose Save a Copy As from the File menu.

3. In the Create Copy dialog box that appears, choose clone (no records) from the Type (Mac OS) or Save as (Windows) menu. For the sake of convenience, use the dialog box to open the same folder in which Invoices.fp5 is stored. Then click the Save button to save the recordless copy.

4. Open the file named Invoices Clone.fp5. This file has no records.

5. Use the Import Records command and the Open File dialog box that appears to begin setting up the import of records from Invoices.fp5.

6. In the Import Field Mapping dialog box, check to be sure that the field names on the right are lined up with the field names on the left. If they aren't, choose Matching Names from the View By menu at the top right of the dialog box to line them up quickly. All fields that can be imported should be imported.

7. In the Import Options dialog box, select the option for Splitting them into separate records. This will create a separate record for every value in a repeating field. Click OK.

8. When the import is complete, scroll through the records in the found set to make sure data is imported into the correct field. Also notice that each individual invoice has only one item listed as sold—that's just one value in each repeating field. If there was a problem with the import, delete the found set and try again.

Exporting Sub-summary Values

Can you do me a favor? I need to have the contents of my WebLog.fp5 file exported so I get a report in tab-separated text format of total hits by page. I'm going to use the file to create a chart with Excel. The WebLog.fp5 file is already set up and can be found in the ExportEx folder. I'll walk you through the export process here. For more information, check "Exporting Records" on page 521.

1. Open the file named WebLog.fp5 in the ExportEx folder.

2. Use the display Hits per URL script under the Script menu to display a report of hits per page. (This automatically sorts the records in the order you need to export the sub-summary values by the Page URL break field; if you prefer, you can manually sort by that field.)

3. Choose Export Records from the File menu.

4. In the Save As dialog box that appears, name the file Page-Hits.txt and select Tab-Separated Text from the Type menu. Click Save.

5. In the Export Field Order dialog box, add Full URL and Count to the Field Order list. Then click the Count field to select it and click the Summarize by button. Click to the left of the Page URL field name to place a check mark there. Then click OK.

6. Count by Page URL should appear beneath the Count field. With the Count field still selected, click the Clear button to remove it. The two remaining items in the Field Order list should be Full URL and Count by Page URL.

7. Click the Export button.

8. When export is finished, open the file named PageHits.txt with a word processor, text editor, or spreadsheet program. It should contain the same basic information shown in the report you displayed in step 2. If not, try again.

Extra Credit

Here are two possible extra credit exercises that you can try on your own.

- Repeat the instructions in "Exporting Sub-summary Values" on page 530 but create an exported file of hits per day called DayHits.txt. A script in WebLog.fp5 will sort the information for you.

- Write a script that does the export for you. For more information, consult Chapter 12.

- Open the file named PageHits.txt as a FileMaker Pro file. Check "Importing Records into a New FileMaker Pro File" on page 518 for details.

- Open the file named PageHits.txt with Excel and create the column chart I need. If you need help, you'll have to pick up one of my Excel books.

Previewing and Printing Reports

Back in Chapters 5 through 8, I tell you all about FileMaker Pro's powerful layout feature and show you how you can create layouts to display information on screen or on paper. In this chapter, I tell you everything you need to know to prepare your layouts for previewing on screen and printing on paper.

Before You Preview or Print

Before you even think about previewing or printing a layout, there are a number of options you should consider:

- Have you set all necessary print-related options for the layout and layout objects? This includes margins, non-printing objects, and sliding objects.

- Are you browsing all the records that you plan to print? Or, if you plan to print only one record, is it the current record?

- Are the records you plan to print in the order that you want them to appear when printed?

I tell you about all these considerations in this section.

Setting Print-Related Options for Layouts and Layout Objects

There are a number of print-related options that you may want to take advantage of for your layout or certain layout objects. You should set these options *before* you preview or print a report.

Setting Margins

Page margins determine the amount of space between layout objects and the edge of the paper. By default, FileMaker Pro sets the maximum margins available based on the capabilities of the default printer. Because this can change from one printer to another, however, you can set fixed margins. This helps ensure consistent output from printer to printer.

I explain how to set margins in the section titled "Margins" on page 227, so I won't repeat it here. If you haven't set margins for your layout and you want to, go back and check that section for instructions.

 TIP   *I highly recommend setting margins before you position objects on a layout. That's why I discuss margins in detail in a layout chapter rather than the printing chapter.*

Setting Page Breaks

Setting page breaks in FileMaker Pro isn't quite as easy as positioning an insertion point and choosing a menu command or pressing a magic keystroke. Instead you use the Part Definition dialog box to specify how page breaks should work with individual layout parts. This determines how much information appears on a printed page.

Switch to Layout mode, then double-click the part tag for the part for which you want to set page breaks. The Part Definition dialog box for that part appears (see Figure 14-1).

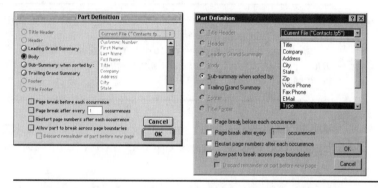

FIGURE 14-1. The Part Definition dialog box on Mac OS (left) and Windows (right).

Set check boxes as desired to set pagination options:

- **Page break before each occurrence** tells FileMaker Pro to start a new page each time this part appears. For example, turning on this option for a body part forces each record to appear on a new page.

- **Page break after every *n* occurrences** tells FileMaker Pro to start a new page after the part has appeared the number of times you specify. If you turn on this option, you must enter a value in the box. For example, turning on this option for a trailing sub-summary part and setting the value to 1 forces a new page after each subtotal.

- **Restart page numbers after each occurrence** tells File-Maker Pro to start renumbering the pages after each time this part appears. For example, turning on this option for a trailing sub-summary restarts page numbering after each subtotal.

- **Allow part to break across page boundaries** tells File-Maker Pro that it's okay to put a page break in the middle of this part. If you turn this option on, the **Discard remainder of part before new page** option also becomes available. Turning this on tells FileMaker Pro not to print the remainder of the part after the page break.

WARNING   *Turning on the Allow part to break across page boundaries option could cause page breaks to occur in the middle of objects. I've seen this happen and it looks awful. If you use this option, be sure to use Preview mode to check every page before printing. I tell you about Preview mode in the section titled "Using Preview Mode" on page 547.*

When you're finished setting options, click the OK button to save them. You can set these options individually for every part on a layout.

I tell you more about parts and the Part Definition dialog box in the section titled "Using Layout Parts" on page 256.

TIP   *If a page break will occur in the middle of a part, you may be able to see it in Layout mode. It appears as a dark, dotted horizontal line like the vertical line that marks the right margin of the page.*

Preventing Layout Objects from Printing

You don't have to print all objects on a layout. Buttons, for example, which can appear on any layout, would look pretty silly if printed on a report. By setting a button (or any other layout object, for that matter) as a non-printing object, the object will not appear in Preview mode or on paper when the layout is printed.

To prevent an object from printing, begin by viewing the layout on which the object appears and switching to Layout mode. Select the object that you don't want to print. Choose Sliding/Printing from the Format menu (see Figure 14-2) or press Option-Command-T (Mac OS only). In the Set Sliding/Printing dialog box that appears (see Figure 14-3), turn on the Do not print the selected objects check box. Click OK to save your settings.

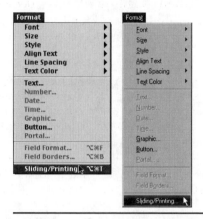

FIGURE 14-2. Choosing Sliding/Printing from the Format menu in Layout mode on Mac OS (left) and Windows (right).

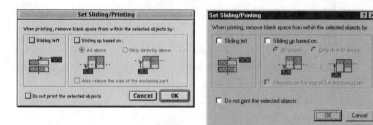

FIGURE 14-3. The Set Sliding/Printing dialog box on Mac OS (left) and Windows (right).

NOTE *If the Non-Printing Objects option on the Show submenu under the View menu is turned on (see Figure 14-4), a thick gray border appears in Layout mode around any layout object that will not print (see Figure 14-5). I tell you about the Non-Printing Objects command in the section titled "Non-printing Objects" on page 193.*

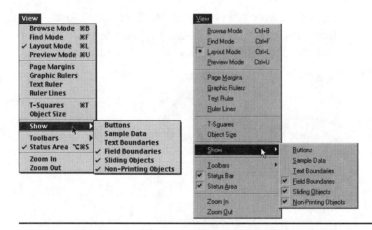

FIGURE 14-4. The Show menu on Mac OS (left) and Windows (right).

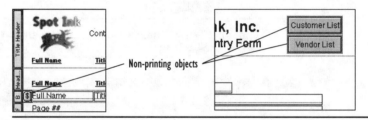

FIGURE 14-5. A thick gray border around non-printing objects on Mac OS (left) and Windows (right).

Sliding Layout Objects

You can set layout objects so they move up or to the left when printed. This shrinks the size of fields to remove empty space after field contents and closes up space left by empty or partially filled fields.

Figure 14-6 shows a good example. In the illustration on the left, the name, address, and type fields are set to print where they were placed on the layout. In the illustration on the right, the same fields are set to slide up and to the left. The result: fields shrink and require less space, there is no empty space between fields, and the body part of the layout is reduced to fit more records on a page.

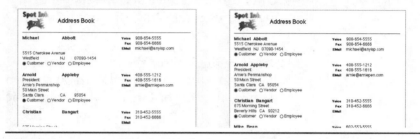

FIGURE 14-6. An example of a layout without sliding objects (left) and one with sliding objects (right).

A good way to get around the need to work with sliding objects is to use merge fields in text objects on your layouts. I tell you how to add merge fields to a layout in the section titled "Adding a Merge Field" on page 236.

To set the sliding options for an object, begin by viewing the layout on which the object appears and switching to Layout mode. Select the object(s) for which you want to set sliding options. Choose Sliding/Printing from the Format menu (see Figure 14-2) or press Option-Command-T (Mac OS only). In the Set Sliding/ Printing dialog box that appears (see Figure 14-3), turn on the appropriate Sliding check boxes:

- **Sliding left** closes up the empty space to the right of the object, enabling objects on the right to slide to the left into the unused space.

- **Sliding up based on** closes up the empty space beneath an object, enabling objects below it to slide up into the unused space. When you turn on this check box, you must also select the appropriate radio button beneath it:

  - **All above** maintains vertical spacing with other columns in the layout. With this option selected, the object does not slide up unless the objects beside it also slide up.

- **Only directly above** allows independent vertical spacing of a column. With this option selected, the object slides up even if the objects beside it don't slide up.

- **Also reduce the size of the enclosing part**, which is only available when the Sliding up based on check box is turned on, reduces the size of the layout part in which the object resides to close up space between parts.

Click OK to save your settings.

In Figure 14-7, the First Name, Last Name, Title, Company, Address, City, State, Zip, and Type fields are set with the Sliding left, Sliding up based on Only directly above, and Also reduce size of the enclosing part options turned on. You can see the results of these settings in the right side of Figure 14-6.

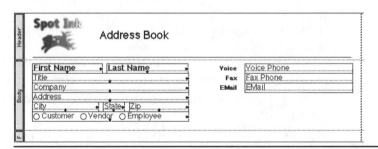

FIGURE 14-7. Fields set to slide up and to the left.

 NOTE   *If the Sliding Objects option on the Show submenu under the View is turned on (see Figure 14-4), arrows appear to indicate the direction in which sliding objects are set to slide. You can see this in Figure 14-7. I tell you about the Sliding Objects command in the section titled "Sliding Objects" on page 193.*

Finding Records

Preview mode displays the records being browsed. The Print command prints either the records being browsed, or the current record. Therefore, before you either Preview or print records, you should use the Find or Show All Records command to browse the records that you want to view or print. If you plan to print only one record, be sure that the record is selected in Browse mode before using the Print command.

I tell you about using the Find and Show All Records commands in the section titled "Finding Records" on page 133.

Sorting Records

As you've probably guessed, the order in which records appear in Preview mode or on paper when printed depends on the current sort order. Therefore, before you either Preview or print records, you may want to use the Sort command to put them in the desired order.

I tell you about using the Sort command in the section titled "Sorting Records" on page 153.

Using the Page Setup or Print Setup Dialog Box

The Page Setup (Mac OS) and Print Setup (Windows) dialog boxes enable you to set print options for your specific printer. In most cases, you'll set these options once, then use them again and again for all your layouts. But if you want to set special options for a layout, you must open the dialog box and set them before previewing or printing.

NOTE *The Page Setup (Mac OS) and Print Setup (Windows) dialog boxes vary depending on the printer. If this section does not adequately address the options that you see in the Page Setup or Print Setup dialog box on your computer, consult the manual that came with your printer for additional information.*

Setting Options in the Page Setup Dialog Box (Mac OS Only)

The Page Setup dialog box enables you to set a variety of options for your printer, including page attributes like paper size, orientation, and scaling.

Opening the Page Setup Dialog Box

To open the Page Setup dialog box, choose Page Setup from the File menu (see Figure 14-8, left). The Page Setup dialog box appears (see Figure 14-9).

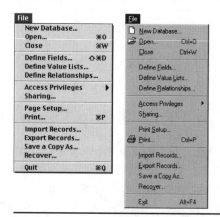

FIGURE 14-8. The File menu on Mac OS (left) and Windows (right).

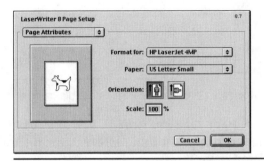

FIGURE 14-9. The Page Setup dialog box with the Apple LaserWriter 8 printer driver selected on Mac OS.

NOTE *The appearance of the Page Setup dialog box varies based on the currently selected printer driver. The options that appear, however, are similar for each printer. Figure 14-10 shows two more examples of Page Setup dialog boxes.*

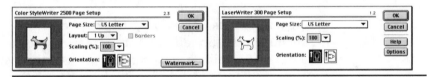

FIGURE 14-10. Two more Page Setup dialog box examples: the dialog box with the Color StyleWriter 2500 (left) and LaserWriter 300 (right) printer driver selected.

Setting Page Setup Options

You change options in the Page Setup dialog box by choosing menu options, clicking buttons, or entering values as follows:

CHANGING THE PAPER SIZE Choose a paper size option from the Paper menu (see Figure 14-11). Only the options supported by your printer will appear on this menu.

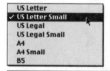

FIGURE 14-11. The Paper menu in the Page Setup dialog box on Mac OS.

CHANGING THE PAGE ORIENTATION   Click one of the Orientation buttons. The left button in Figure 14-9 is for portrait orientation; the right button is for landscape (sideways) orientation.

NOTE   *Envelope layouts are normally designed to print with landscape orientation.*

CHANGING THE SCALING   Enter a value in the Scale box. This affects the size of layout objects when printed and has nothing to do with the zoom controls at the bottom of the document window.

CHANGING POSTSCRIPT OPTIONS   Choose PostScript™ Options from the menu at the top-left side of the Page Setup dialog box. The contents of the dialog box change to display PostScript-related options (see Figure 14-12). Toggle check box settings as desired.

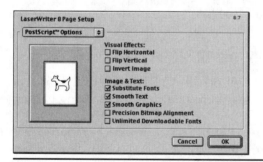

FIGURE 14-12. PostScript Options in the Page Setup dialog box on Mac OS.

NOTE   *PostScript options are available for PostScript-compatible printers only.*

Saving Page Setup Options

To save the settings in the Page Setup dialog box, click the OK button. The settings are saved and will remain in effect until they are changed.

TIP *Page Setup options can be restored to previous settings by scripts, which are also handy for recording all steps necessary to produce a frequently generated report. I tell you about scripting in Chapter 11.*

Setting Options in the Print Setup Dialog Box (Windows Only)

The Print Setup dialog box enables you to set a variety of options for your printer, including page attributes like paper size, orientation, and source.

Opening the Print Setup Dialog Box

To open the Print Setup dialog box, choose Print Setup from the File menu (see Figure 14-8, right). The Print Setup dialog box appears (see Figure 14-13). Remember, the options that appear may vary slightly from one printer to another.

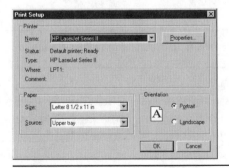

FIGURE 14-13. The Print Setup dialog box on Windows.

Setting Print Setup Options

You change options in the Print Setup dialog box by choosing menu options and selecting radio buttons as follows:

CHANGING THE PAPER SIZE Choose a paper size option from the Size menu (see Figure 14-14). Only the options supported by your printer will appear on this menu.

FIGURE 14-14. The Size menu in the Print Setup dialog box on Windows.

CHANGING THE PAPER SOURCE Choose a paper source option from the Source menu (see Figure 14-15). Only the options supported by your printer will appear on this menu.

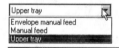

FIGURE 14-15. The Source menu in the Print Setup dialog box on Windows.

CHANGING THE PAGE ORIENTATION Select one of the Orientation options.

 NOTE *Envelope layouts are normally designed to print with landscape orientation.*

CHANGING PRINTER PROPERTIES Click the Properties button. The Printer Properties dialog box appears (see Figure 14-16). Make changes as desired and click OK to save them.

FIGURE 14-16. The Printer Properties dialog box on Windows.

 NOTE *You can learn more about printer properties in the documentation that came with your operating system or printer.*

Saving Print Setup Options

To save the settings in the Print Setup dialog box, click the OK button. The settings are saved and will remain in effect until they are changed.

TIP *Print Setup options can be restored to previous settings by scripts. I tell you about scripting in Chapter 11.*

Using Preview Mode

Before you print a layout, it's a good idea to preview it. That's what Preview mode is for. It enables you to view a layout with data as it would appear when printed on paper.

In this section, I tell you all about Preview mode, including why you should use it to view certain layouts that you don't even plan to print.

Why Use Preview Mode?

The way I see it, there are two good reasons to use Preview mode:

- If you have a layout that includes subsummary parts, you *must* switch to Preview mode (or print) to view the subsummary values. There's no choice if you want to view them on screen—subsummary values simply do not appear in Browse mode. I tell you more about subsummaries in the section titled "Using Summary Parts and Fields" on page 265.

- Preview mode can save time, paper, and toner (or ink). By previewing a report *before* you print it, you can make sure the report looks just the way you want it to. If it doesn't, you can quickly switch back to Layout mode to fix the problem, then switch back to Preview mode to check it again. If you skip the preview step and print a report that isn't quite right, you've wasted time, paper, and toner— three things that I don't like to waste.

Switching to Preview Mode

Switching to Preview mode is easy. Either choose Preview Mode from the View menu (see Figure 14-17) or press Command-U (Mac OS) or Control-U (Windows). The current layout is displayed in Preview mode (see Figure 14-18).

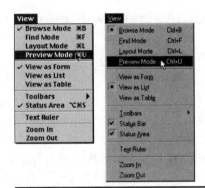

FIGURE 14-17. Choosing Preview Mode from the View menu on Mac OS (left) and Windows (right).

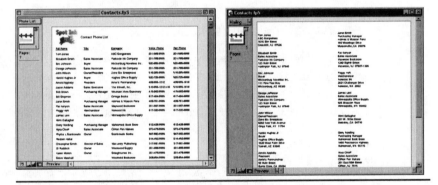

FIGURE 14-18. A columnar report layout on a Mac (left) and a mailing labels layout on Windows (right) in Preview mode.

TIP   *To see more of the page, use the zoom controls at the bottom of the status area to zoom out to a smaller percentage. Figure 14-18 shows two examples of layouts in Preview mode viewed at 75% magnification. I tell you more about the zoom controls in the section titled "Zoom Controls" on page 19.*

Viewing a Layout in Preview Mode

Preview mode displays a layout one page at a time. Here's some additional information for viewing a layout in layout mode.

About the Gray Area

The gray area around the edge of the page is the page margin. The width of the gray area varies based on the margin settings, which I discuss briefly in the section titled "Setting Margins" on page 534 and in more detail in "Margins" on page 227. Don't worry, you won't get a gray border around the edge of the layouts you print because that gray area doesn't print at all.

About the Status Area

In Preview mode, the status area displays the Layouts pop-up menu, the book, and the number of pages in the printed document. I tell you all about the status area in the sections titled "Status Area" on page 17 and "The Status Area in Preview Mode" on page 22.

 If the total number of pages in the document displays as a question mark, you can drag the bookmark to the bottom of the book to force FileMaker Pro to calculate the total number of pages. Be aware, however, that this may take time for lengthy reports.

Fixing Problems You Find in Preview Mode

If you discover a problem with a layout while viewing it in Preview mode, you can fix it before you print.

FIXING A PROBLEM WITH THE POSITION OR FORMAT OF A LAYOUT OBJECT Switch to Layout mode to modify the layout. I tell you all about working in Layout mode in Chapters 5, 6, and 7.

FIXING A PROBLEM WITH DATA   Switch to Browse mode to modify the contents of fields. I tell you about entering and editing data in Browse mode in Chapter 3.

FIXING A PROBLEM WITH THE FOUND SET   Switch to Find mode to find the records that you want to preview or print. I tell you about finding records in the first half of Chapter 4.

FIXING A PROBLEM WITH THE SORT ORDER   Choose Sort from the Records menu and use the Sort Records dialog box to sort the records as desired. This command is available from within Preview mode. I tell you about sorting records in the second half of Chapter 4.

 TIP   *When you are finished fixing a problem, don't forget to switch back to Preview to check your work.*

Printing

In many cases, the last step in building a database will be printing a report using one of its layouts. In this section, I tell you all about printing.

About the Print Dialog Box

You set up a print job in the Print dialog box, which differs in appearance for Mac OS and Windows. In this section, I provide some general information about using the Print dialog box.

Opening the Print Dialog Box

To open the Print dialog box, choose Print from the File menu (see Figure 14-8) or press Command-P (Mac OS) or Control-P (Windows). The Print dialog box appears (see Figure 14-19).

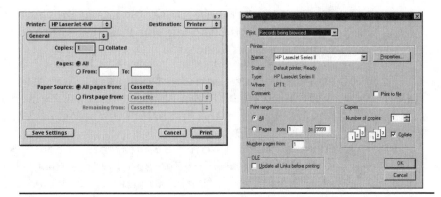

FIGURE 14-19. The General options in the Print dialog on Mac OS with the Apple LaserWriter 8 printer driver selected (left) and the Print dialog box on Windows (right).

NOTE *The appearance of the Print dialog box on Mac OS varies based on the printer driver. Some printer drivers display both general and FileMaker Pro options in the same windows. You can see examples of this in Figure 14-20.*

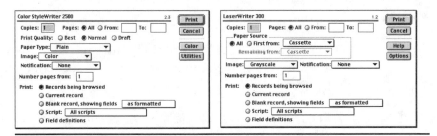

FIGURE 14-20. Two more Print dialog box examples on Mac OS: the dialog box with the Color StyleWriter 2500 (left) and LaserWriter 300 (right) printer driver selected.

Setting General Options

You can use the Print dialog boxes in Figure 14-19 to set general options—those options that are not specific to FileMaker Pro.

SPECIFYING THE NUMBER OF COPIES Enter a value in the Copies (Mac OS) or Number of copies (Windows) box.

PRINTING ALL PAGES Make sure the All option is selected.

PRINTING SPECIFIC PAGES Select the From (Mac OS) or Pages (Windows) option, then enter starting and ending page numbers in the From and To boxes.

SELECTING A PAPER SOURCE (MAC OS ONLY) Choose options from the Paper Source menu(s).

PRINTING TO A POSTSCRIPT FILE INSTEAD OF A PRINTER Choose File from the Destination menu (Mac OS) or turn on the Print to File check box (Windows). When you print, a Save As dialog box will appear so you can name and specify a disk location for the file.

TIP   *You may want to use the Print to file option to create an Adobe Acrobat PDF file of the document. You'll need the complete Adobe Acrobat package to do this, however. Consult the documentation that comes with that software for more information.*

Setting FileMaker Pro-Specific Options

FileMaker Pro-specific printing options are those available only when printing FileMaker Pro documents. Where these options appear depends on your operating system and, in the case of Mac OS, your printer driver:

- **Mac OS systems using the LaserWriter 8 printer driver** must select the FileMaker Pro option on the menu beneath the Printer menu in the upper-left corner of the dialog box. This displays the FileMaker Pro printing options (see Figure 14-21).

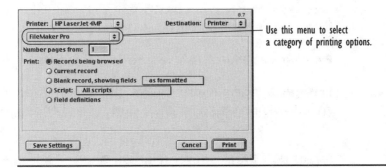

FIGURE 14-21. The FileMaker Pro options in the Print dialog box for the LaserWriter 8 printer driver.

- **Mac OS systems using a printer driver other than the LaserWriter 8 driver** can set FileMaker Pro printing options in the Print dialog box. Figure 14-20 shows two examples.

- **Windows systems** can set FileMaker Pro printing options in the Print dialog box (see Figure 14-19).

SPECIFYING THE START NUMBER FOR PAGE NUMBERING   Enter a value in the Number pages from box. This is the number that will be used as the page number on the first page of the report—if the page number symbol (##) has been included on the layout. I tell you more about including page numbers in layouts in the section titled "Pasting Static or Dynamic Informational Text" on page 239.

NOTE   *Don't confuse the page range option with the page numbering option. The page range option lets you specify which pages should be printed. The page numbering option lets you specify what number should appear as the page number on the first page of the report.*

There are other FileMaker Pro-specific printing options. I tell you about them next in the sections titled "Preparing to Print Records" on page 555 and "Preparing to Print Other Stuff" on page 555.

Mac OS systems using the LaserWriter 8 printer driver can access other printing options by choosing a category from the pop-up menu beneath the Printer pop-up menu in the Print dialog box (see Figure 14-21).

Preparing to Print Records

In most cases, when you print from FileMaker Pro, you'll print records.

PRINTING ONE RECORD Before opening the Print dialog box, browse the record that you want to print. Then open the Print dialog box. Select the Current record option (Mac OS; see Figures 13-20 or 13-21) or choose Current record from the Print menu (Windows; see Figure 14-22).

FIGURE 14-22. The Print menu on Windows.

PRINTING ALL THE RECORDS BEING BROWSED In the FileMaker Pro options of the Print dialog box, select the Records being browsed option (Mac OS; see Figures 13-20 or 13-21) or choose Records being browsed from the Print menu (Windows; see Figure 14-22).

Preparing to Print Other Stuff

Records aren't the only thing you can print. You can also print a blank record, script, or field definitions.

PRINTING A LAYOUT WITHOUT DATA Before opening the Print dialog box, switch to the layout that you want to print. Then open the Print dialog box. Select the Blank record showing fields option (Mac OS; see Figures 13-20 or 13-21) or choose Blank record showing fields from the Print menu (Windows; see Figure 14-22). Then choose an option from the corresponding menu (see Figure 14-23):

- **As formatted** prints the layout with fields formatted as they are in the layout. You might find this handy to document your layouts or review them on paper.

- **With boxes** prints the layout with boxes around the fields. This may be useful for printing a form that can be filled in the old fashioned way: with a pen or pencil.

- **With underlines** prints the layout with underlines where the fields are. This is also useful for printing a fill-in form.

FIGURE 14-23. The pop-up menu with options for printing a blank record on Mac OS (left) and Windows (right).

PRINTING SCRIPTS   In the Print dialog box, select the Script option (Mac OS; see Figure 14-20 or Figure 14-21) or choose Script from the Print menu (Windows; see Figure 14-22). Then choose an option from the corresponding menu (see Figure 14-24):

- **All scripts** prints all scripts in the database file.

- *Script name* prints just the corresponding script.

FIGURE 14-24. The menu with options for printing scripts on Mac OS (left) and Windows (right).

NOTE   *To print more than one script but not all the scripts, you must use the Print dialog box to select each script that you want to print, one at a time, clicking the Print button after each selection.*

PRINTING FIELD DEFINITIONS In the Print dialog box, select the Field Definitions option (Mac OS; see Figures 13-20 or 13-21) or choose Field definitions from the Print menu (Windows; see Figure 14-22).

NOTE   *Field definitions are printed in the order in which they are listed in the Define Fields dialog box. I tell you more about the Define Fields dialog box in the section titled "Using the Define Fields Dialog Box" on page 60.*

Printing

Once you've set options in the Print dialog box, you're ready to print. Make sure your printer is turned on and warmed up. Then click the Print (Mac OS) or OK (Windows) button. The job is sent to the printer.

WARNING   *The Print option you selected in the Print dialog box remains selected until you change it. For example, if you printed the current record, the Current record option remains set. Remember to check this option each time you print; otherwise you might be surprised by what comes out of your printer!*

TIP   *Print options are included with Page Setup options that can be restored to previous settings by scripts. I tell you about scripting in Chapter 12.*

Step-by-Step

Here's your chance to work with preview and printing options. In this section, I provide step-by-step instructions for preparing, previewing, and printing layouts in the Contacts.fp5 database file you've been working on at the end of each chapter. If you've been skipping around and don't have the completed files from Chapter

13, you can download them from the companion Web site for this book, http://www.gilesrd.com/fmprocomp/.

Printing the First Page of a Mailing Labels Layout

In this exercise, you'll find all contacts, sort by zip code, preview the Mailing Labels layout, and print the first page of mailing labels.

1. Open the file named Contacts.fp5 and, if necessary, switch to the Mailing Labels layout.

2. Choose Find All from the Select menu to find all records.

3. Choose Sort from the Sort menu. In the Sort dialog box that appears, set the Sort Order to Zip and click the Sort button.

4. Choose Page Setup (Mac OS) or Print Setup (Windows) from the File menu. Use the Page Setup (Mac OS) or Print Setup (Windows) dialog box that appears to make sure the paper size is set to letter and the orientation is set to portrait. Click OK.

5. Choose Preview from the Mode menu to switch to Preview mode. Use the book to view the first few pages of the document.

6. Choose Print from the File menu. Use the Print dialog box that appears to set the page range from 1 to 1 (thus printing just the first page). Click the Print button to print.

Previewing and Fixing a Phone List

In this exercise, you'll make the button on the Phone List layout in Contacts.fp5 a non-printing object, then find all Vendors, sort by last name, preview, and fix problems you find.

1. If necessary, open the Contacts.fp5 file.

2. Switch to the Phone List layout and switch to Layout mode.

3. Click once to select the $ button on the far left side of the body.

4. Choose Sliding/Printing from the Format menu. In the Set Sliding/Printing dialog box that appears, turn on the Do not print the selected objects check box. Click OK.

5. Switch to the Contact Entry Form layout.

6. Choose Find from the Mode menu. Select the Vendor radio button and then click the Find button.

7. Choose Sort from the Mode menu. In the Sort dialog box that appears, set the sort order to last name. Click Sort.

8. Switch back to the Phone List layout.

9. Choose Preview from the Mode menu. Examine all pages of the document. Do you see any problems with it? Here are some hints:

   - The Company field appears too narrow to hold all its data. In Layout mode, you can either make the field wider (at the cost of making other fields narrower) or reduce the font size so more information fits in the field.

   - The Company field contains data that has double-quotation marks. (Remember, this data was imported from a tab-separated text file.) In Browse mode, you can manually delete these unwanted characters or use the Replace command with the SUBSTITUTE function to strip them out.

   - The Voice Phone and/or Fax Phone fields are empty for some records. You can revise the Find request to add an additional request that omits records with the Voice Phone field empty.

- The layout could benefit from a print date in the footer. In Layout mode, you can insert the Date symbol (//) in the footer beside the page number symbol.

10. Fix the problems you found in the previous step. You can find the instructions you need throughout this book. Then check again.

Sharing Information

15

One of the strengths of FileMaker Pro—and a feature that makes it especially popular in the business world—is its built-in networking capabilities. Not only can FileMaker Pro database files be shared over a network, but they can be accessed by multiple Mac OS and Windows users at the same time. In addition, you can even share FileMaker Pro data with other applications using ODBC technology.

In this chapter, I explain how to prepare FileMaker Pro and database files for sharing over a network, as well as how to open, use, and close shared files. I also tell you how you can make your FileMaker Pro data accessible via ODBC for access with other applications. If you're in a networked environment, this chapter will help you and your co-workers be more productive using FileMaker Pro.

FileMaker Pro Network Sharing

FileMaker Pro includes built-in networking features that enable you to share FileMaker Pro database files with other FileMaker Pro users on a *local area network (LAN)* or *wide area network (WAN)*.

In this section, I explain how FileMaker Pro Network Sharing works, how you set it up, and how you can use it to share FileMaker Pro files.

How It Works

When you or another network user share a FileMaker Pro file, it becomes available in a special Hosts dialog box. The user who opened the file is the *host*. Other network users who want to open the file do so as *guests* by selecting the file in the Hosts dialog box and clicking Open.

 TIP   *You can prevent unauthorized access to your database file by setting up database access privileges. I tell you how to use FileMaker Pro's built-in security feature in Chapter 17. This chapter's discussions of access to shared files assumes that there are no restrictions set with access privileges.*

Guests to a shared file can access its data and layouts to perform a wide variety of tasks. When multiple users access the same file at the same time, there may be minor access limitations—for example, if one network user is updating a record, another network user cannot update the same record. I provide details about what you can and cannot do with a shared file in the section titled "Working with Shared Files" on page 567.

When a guest closes a shared file, it remains available to other guests. But when the host closes the shared file, all guests must close the file until someone else opens it as a host.

What You Need

To take advantage of FileMaker Pro's networking feature, your computer must have the following:

• Mac OS or Windows with appropriate network software installed and properly configured.

• Network connection.

• FileMaker Pro with the correct network options selected.

NOTE *Although FileMaker Pro Server software is not required to share database files with less than 10 users, it does offer additional features that may be useful in large network environments. For more information about FileMaker Pro Server, visit the FileMaker Pro Web site at http://www.filemaker.com/.*

Setting the Network Protocol

In order to share files, all computers on the network must be using the same network *protocol*. A protocol is a collection of instructions that the computer and software use to exchange data.

Network Protocol Options

FileMaker Pro supports two or three network protocol options, depending on your computer platform. Here are your choices and how they correspond to each other:

Mac OS	Windows
AppleTalk	n/a
n/a	IPX/SPX
TCP/IP	TCP/IP

The option you choose depends on two things:

- **What is the protocol in use by the network?** If the network utilizes one of these protocols, that will probably be the protocol you select.

- **What are the other FileMaker Pro users on the network using?** To share FileMaker Pro files with other network users, you must have the same protocol selected.

What? No "Real" Network?

If you don't have a "real" network—just a bunch of Mac OS and Windows computers strung together with LocalTalk or Ethernet cables—you should probably choose TCP/IP and set up a "fake" TCP/IP network. I tell you more about this in the section titled "Setting Up (or Faking) a TCP/IP Connection" on page 586.

When I worked on the FileMaker Pro version 4 edition of this book a few years ago, I didn't have a real network. All I had was a handful of Macs and a PC connected via LocalTalk. Unfortunately, TCP/IP wouldn't work properly with LocalTalk on my PC. I had to upgrade from a LocalTalk network to a Ethernet network—not the kind of thing I like to do in the middle of working on a book. When the dust settled, I found (to my relief) that the new configuration worked fine and I could share my FileMaker Pro files on all computers on the network.

Of course, if you just have a bunch of Macs, you can use the AppleTalk protocol and things will work just fine—either with LocalTalk or Ethernet—without dealing with TCP/IP configurations or upgrades.

Selecting the Network Protocol

You select the network protocol for FileMaker Pro on your computer in the Application Preferences dialog box.

Choose Application from the Preferences submenu under the Edit menu (see Figure 15-1). In the General tab of the Application Preferences dialog box that appears (see Figure 15-2), choose the appropriate protocol from the Network protocol menu (see Figure 15-3). When you're finished, click OK.

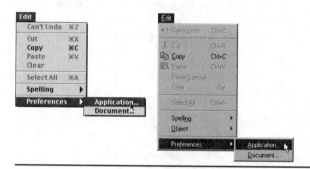

FIGURE 15-1. Choosing Application from the Preferences submenu under the Edit menu on Mac OS (left) and Windows (right).

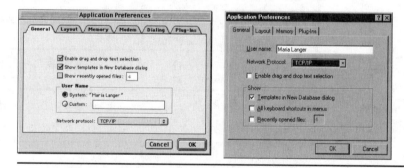

FIGURE 15-2. The General tab of the Application Preferences dialog box on Mac OS (left) and Windows (right).

FIGURE 15-3. The Network Protocol menu on Mac OS (left) and Windows (right).

WARNING *If you do not select the same network protocol as all the other FileMaker Pro users on the network, you will not be able to share FileMaker Pro files with other network users.*

If you changed the Network Protocol selection, you must restart FileMaker Pro for your changes to take effect. Choose Quit (Mac OS) or Exit (Windows) from the File menu (see Figure 15-4). Then open the FileMaker Pro application or one of its documents to continue working with FileMaker Pro.

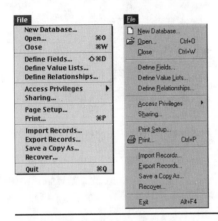

FIGURE 15-4. The File menu on Mac OS (left) and Windows (right).

NOTE *You set this option just once, no matter how many files you want to share on a network.*

Turning on FileMaker Network Sharing

To make a file accessible to others on the network, you must turn on FileMaker network sharing for the file. You do this with the File Sharing dialog box within FileMaker Pro.

NOTE *Don't confuse FileMaker network sharing with Mac OS or Windows file sharing. They're different. You can use FileMaker network sharing with Mac OS or Windows file sharing turned off.*

Choose Sharing from the File menu (see Figure 15-4). In the File Sharing dialog box that appears (see Figure 15-5), select one of the options in the FileMaker Network Sharing area:

- **Single User** disables file sharing for the file.

- **Multi-User** enables file sharing for the file.

- **Multi-User (Hidden)** enables file sharing for the file but does not display the file's name in the Hosts dialog box. This enables you to make the file available if it is needed for a relationship without actually displaying the file to network users.

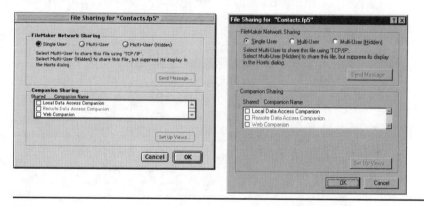

FIGURE 15-5. The File Sharing dialog box on Mac OS (left) and Windows (right).

Then click OK to save the file sharing setting with the file.

Working with Shared Files

Once a file is set up for sharing, multiple users can access it at the same time. In this section, I tell you how to open a FileMaker Pro file as a host and as a guest, how to work with files, and how to close them when you're finished.

Opening a Shared File

The way you open a shared file varies depending on whether you are the first person to open the file or you are opening the file after it has already been opened by another user. Here are the details.

OPENING A SHARED FILE AS THE HOST   If you are the first person to open a file, you will be opening it as the host. Choose Open from the File menu (see Figure 15-4) or press Command-O (Mac OS) or Control-O (Windows). Use the Open File dialog box that appears (see Figure 15-6) to locate and open the file. As the file opens, a message appears briefly, telling you that the file is being opened as multi-user to allow guest access over the network.

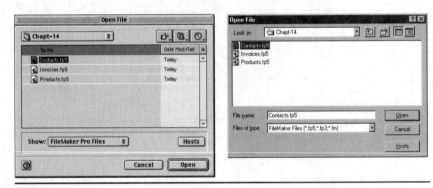

FIGURE 15-6. The Open File dialog box on Mac OS (left) and Windows (right).

OPENING A SHARED FILE AS A GUEST   If a file is already open and you want to access it, you must open it as a guest. Choose Open from the File menu (see Figure 15-4) or press Command-O (Mac OS) or Control-O (Windows) to display the Open File dialog box (see Figure 15-6). Click the Hosts button. The mouse pointer turns into an animated, double-headed arrow, indicating that FileMaker Pro is searching the network. After a moment, the Hosts dialog box appears (see Figure 15-7). It lists all the computers on the LAN that are hosting FileMaker Pro files and the names of the files they are hosting. To open a file as a guest, select the name of the file that you want to open and click the Open button. As the file opens, a message appears briefly, telling you that the file is being opened as a guest.

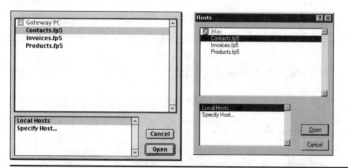

FIGURE 15-7. The Hosts dialog box on Mac OS (left) and Windows (right). There are slight differences in the appearance of this dialog box if your computer is on a network with zones or you have selected a protocol other than TCP/IP.

TIP *To display the Hosts dialog box without first displaying the Open File dialog box, hold down the Option key (Mac OS) or the Shift and Control keys (Windows) while choosing Open from the File menu (see Figure 15-4).*

More about the Hosts Dialog Box

Here are a few additional tips and instructions that you might find useful when working with the Hosts dialog box.

OPENING A SHARED FILE ON A NETWORK WITH ZONES Follow the instructions in the section titled "Opening a Shared File as a Guest" on page 568, but select the appropriate zone from the list at the bottom of the dialog box before selecting the file that you want to open.

OPENING A SHARED FILE ON A HOST COMPUTER THAT IS NOT LISTED IN THE HOSTS DIALOG BOX (TCP/IP ONLY) Click the Specify Host item in the list at the bottom of the Hosts dialog box (see Figure 15-7). In the Specify Host dialog box that appears (see Figure 15-8), enter the name or IP address of the host computer that you want to access. If desired, you can turn on the Permanently add entry to Hosts list check box to have FileMaker Pro automatically list the host each time you open the Hosts dialog box. Then click the Open (Mac OS) or OK (Windows) button. The host computer is added to the list at the bottom of the Hosts dialog box. Any files that computer is hosting appear in the list at the top of the dialog box. Select the name of a file and click Open to open it.

FIGURE 15-8. The Specify Host dialog box on Mac OS (left) and Windows (right).

 You can use the Specify Host dialog box to enter the IP address of a computer on the Internet that is hosting FileMaker Pro files, thus accessing files through the Internet. I tell you more about sharing files via the Internet in Chapter 16.

Using a Shared File

Once you've opened a shared file, you can use it just like any other FileMaker Pro file—well, almost. Here's a quick summary of the things you can—and can't—do with a shared file.

WHAT EVERYONE CAN DO The host and all guests can perform the following functions:

- Find, sort, and browse records.

- Switch from one layout or mode to another.

- Import or export data.

- Check the spelling of the records being browsed.

- Set Page Setup (Mac OS) or Print Setup (Windows) options and print.

- Perform a script listed on the Script menu or accessible by clicking a button.

- Change the contents of a global field. Only the host's changes are saved with the file.

WHAT ONLY ONE PERSON AT A TIME CAN DO The host and all guests can perform the following functions, but only one at a time. This means that if one person is performing one of these functions, no one else can perform the same function until it is complete.

- Edit a record, layout, or script. The record, layout, or script can be viewed by others while it is being edited, but no one else can edit it until the person who is editing it either completes the editing in Browse mode or switches to another layout or mode.

- Define or edit value lists.

- Define or change relationships.

- Open and use the ScriptMaker dialog box.

- Change passwords.

WHAT ONLY THE HOST CAN DO Only the host can perform the following functions. While they are being performed, all guests must close their connections to the file.

- Define fields or edit field definitions.

- Change the order of layouts.

- Change file sharing settings between single-user and multi-user.

- Use the Save a Copy As command.

- Define, edit, or delete groups and access privileges.

- Close a shared file.

- Set access privileges.

More about the File Sharing Dialog Box

If you are hosting a database file, you can use the File Sharing dialog box (see Figure 15-5) to monitor file sharing status and communicate with file guests.

MONITORING FILE SHARING STATUS To see how many users are connected to a file that you are hosting, activate that file, then choose Sharing from the File menu (see Figure 15-4). The FileMaker Network Sharing area of the File Sharing dialog box provides information about the number of guests connected to the file (see Figure 15-9).

FIGURE 15-9. The FileMaker Network Sharing area of the File Sharing dialog box with guests connected to a file on Mac OS (left) and Windows (right).

COMMUNICATING WITH GUESTS The host has the ability to communicate with guests by sending a message to all guests connected to the file. Activate the file that you want to send a message about, then choose Sharing from the File menu (see Figure 15-4) to open the File Sharing dialog box. Click the Message button in the FileMaker Network Sharing area (see Figure 15-9). Enter the text of the message that you want to send in the Send Message dialog box that appears (see Figure 15-10) and click the OK button to send it.

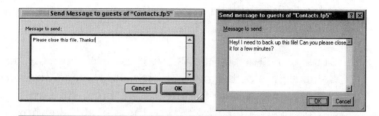

FIGURE 15-10. The Send Message dialog box on Mac OS (left) and Windows (right).

RECEIVING A MESSAGE FROM A HOST A message sent by a host is immediately sent over the network to all guests connected to the file. It appears in a dialog box on guests' screens (see Figure 15-11). To dismiss the message, click the Cancel button or the close button (Windows only). The message disappears automatically after 30 seconds.

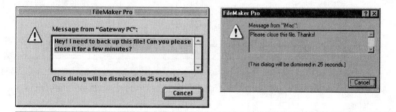

FIGURE 15-11. A message sent from a host to guests on Mac OS (left) and Windows (right).

Closing a Shared File

When you're finished using a shared file, you should close it. What happens when you close it varies, depending on whether you are a guest or the host.

CLOSING A SHARED FILE AS A GUEST When you have opened a database file as a guest, closing it isn't a big deal. It's just one less person connected to the file. Close the file the usual way: Choose Close from the File menu (see Figure 15-4), press Command-W (Mac OS) or Control-W (Windows), or click the file's close box

(Mac OS) or close button (Windows). The file closes. That's all there is to it.

CLOSING A SHARED FILE AS THE HOST When you have opened a database file as the host, closing the file has direct impact on any guests connected to the file. Close the file the usual way. If one or more guests are connected to the file, a dialog box like the one in Figure 15-12 appears, listing all the guests connected to the file. You have two choices. Click the cancel button to leave the file open. Click the Ask button to politely ask guests to close the file. When all guest names disappear from the dialog box in Figure 15-12, the file closes automatically on the host's computer.

FIGURE 15-12. The dialog box that appears on Mac OS (left) and Windows (right) when you attempt to close a file that has guests connected to it.

RECEIVING NOTIFICATION THAT A FILE IS BEING CLOSED When a file's host clicks the Ask button to ask guests to close a file, the Close File dialog box appears (see Figure 15-13) on the screens of all guests connected to the file. The guest has the option of clicking the Cancel button to finish up a few things before closing the file or clicking the Close Now button to close the file immediately. If the guest doesn't do either, the file will close automatically (if possible) within 30 seconds.

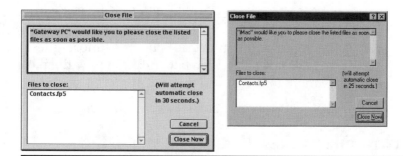

FIGURE 15-13. The Close File dialog box on Mac OS (left) and Windows (right).

Tips for Improving Performance

Network performance is a major concern of many network administrators and end users. The bigger and more complex the network, the slower performance can be. The same holds true for the number of users accessing a FileMaker Pro File.

Here are a few tips for getting the best performance from File-Maker Pro files shared on a network. Although you may not be able to apply all of them to your situation, you should be able to apply enough to make a difference.

- **Host the file on the computer on which the file resides.** This is probably the best (and easiest) thing you can do to increase performance. When the file is first opened on the same computer on which it is stored, less information needs to be transferred over the network.

- **If you have a dedicated host computer, optimize it.** In other words, if you have a computer whose sole job is to host FileMaker Pro database files, keep its configuration simple by minimizing the number of hardware devices attached to it and the number of software programs running on it. This helps keep the machine fast. A fast processor and a fast hard disk can also help. Keeping FileMaker Pro the foreground application also helps FileMaker Pro to run more quickly.

- **Consider investing in FileMaker Pro Server software.** This software optimizes FileMaker Pro network performance and can act as a host for more guests. Check the FileMaker Pro Web site, http://www.filemaker.com/, for more information.

Sharing Filemaker Pro Data via ODBC

Open Database Connectivity (*ODBC*) is an application programming interface (API) that enables various applications to share data. For example, you can set up a FileMaker Pro database file to share its data via ODBC and then access that data via another application, such as Microsoft Excel. ODBC can share information on the same computer or with another computer accessible via TCP/IP network.

Sharing data via ODBC is an advanced feature of FileMaker Pro and other applications. A complete discussion is beyond the scope of this book. In this section, however, I tell you about the two ODBC plug-ins that come with FileMaker Pro and explain how to use them to share your FileMaker Pro data with other applications.

ODBC Plug-Ins

FileMaker Pro's plug-in feature enables FileMaker, Inc. and third-party software developers to expand the capabilities of FileMaker Pro. FileMaker Pro comes with two plug-ins that add ODBC capabilities.

LOCAL DATA ACCESS COMPANION This plug-in enables sharing via ODBC on the same computer. For example, you share FileMaker Pro data on your computer and access it with Microsoft Excel on your computer.

REMOTE DATA ACCESS COMPANION This plug-in enables sharing via ODBC across a TCP/IP network. For example, you share File-Maker Pro data on your computer and someone on another computer accessible via TCP/IP accesses the data with Microsoft Excel.

Enabling the ODBC Plug-In

You enable plug-ins with the Plug-In tab of the Application Preferences dialog box. Choose Application from the Preferences submenu under the Edit menu (see Figure 15-1). In the Application Preferences dialog box that appears, click the Plug-Ins tab to display its options (see Figure 15-14). Turn on the check box beside the plug-in(s) you want to enable and click OK.

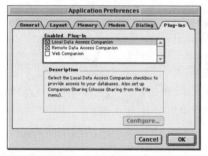 

FIGURE 15-14. The Plug-Ins tab of the Application Preferences dialog box on Mac OS (left) and Windows (right).

NOTE *You set this option just once, no matter how many files you want to share via ODBC.*

Turning on Companion Sharing

To make a file accessible via ODBC, you must turn on companion sharing for the file. You do this with the File Sharing dialog box within FileMaker Pro.

Choose Sharing from the File menu (see Figure 15-4). In the File Sharing dialog box that appears (see Figure 15-5), turn on the appropriate check boxes in the Companion Sharing area (see Figure 15-15). Then click OK to save your settings with the file.

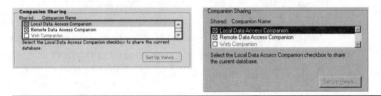

FIGURE 15-15. The Companion Sharing area of the File Sharing dialog box on Mac OS (left) and Windows (right).

The file can now be accessed by another application using ODBC.

Step-by-Step

Are you ready to experiment with sharing FileMaker Pro files? I'm making a big assumption here—that you have a network. After all, if you don't have a network, why would you bother reading this chapter?

In this section, I provide step-by-step instructions for setting up the Contacts.fp5 database file for file sharing, then connecting to it from another computer on the network. You can use the same file if you like—it's available on the Companion Web site to this book, http://www.gilesrd.com/fmprocomp/—or you can use any other FileMaker Pro file you have sitting around on your hard disk.

Setting Up a File for File Sharing

In this section, I provide instructions for checking your network protocol settings and turning on file sharing for a file.

1. Use the Application preferences dialog box to check to be sure that the Network Protocol option is correct for your network. If it is not correct, change it and restart FileMaker Pro.

2. Open Contacts.fp5 (or any other file that you want to share).

3. In the File Sharing dialog box, select the Multi-User button and click OK to save your change.

You are now hosting a file that is available to other users on the network.

Connecting to a Shared File

In this section, I provide instructions for opening a file as a guest.

1. Move to another computer on the network, preferably one whose owner doesn't mind you borrowing it for a few moments.

2. If necessary, start FileMaker Pro.

3. Use the Application preferences dialog box to check to be sure that the Network Protocol option is set the same as it is on your computer. If it is not, change it and restart File-Maker Pro.

4. Hold down the Option key (Mac OS) or Shift and Control keys (Windows) while choosing Open from the File menu to display the Hosts dialog box.

5. If necessary, select the network zone that your computer is a member of.

6. Locate your computer in the list of computers sharing files. Then select Contacts.fp5 (or the file you set up for sharing) and click the Open button.

You are now connected to the file as a guest.

Publishing Data on the Web

16

One of the great features of FileMaker Pro is its built-in Web publishing capabilities. With FileMaker Pro and an intranet or Internet connection, you can make your database files available to your entire company or to the world.

In this chapter, I tell you how to use FileMaker Pro's built-in Web publishing features to get your data on an intranet or the World Wide Web.

About Publishing Data on the Web

For the past few years, there's been an explosion of Web publishing. Individuals and organizations have learned that the Web's graphic user interface is a great way to share formatted information with graphics and hyperlinks. In this section, I provide an introduction to the Web and Web publishing and introduce you to the Web publishing tools built into FileMaker Pro.

Intranets and the Internet

Before you can start thinking about Web publishing, you must consider the network on which the Web is built. Technically speaking, you can use the Web's graphic user interface to publish data on two kinds of networks:

- An *intranet* is an internal network that uses TCP/IP to exchange information. Intranets are widely used in large organizations to share information internally.

- The *Internet* is a worldwide network of computers that exchange information via TCP/IP.

Both intranets and the Internet offer a variety of data communication options, including FTP, e-mail, and the World Wide Web. Therefore, the World Wide Web and Internet are not the same, as many people believe. The Web is merely a part of the Internet.

TIP   *Intranets are often connected to the Internet to enable computers on the intranet to access the Internet. Special software called a* firewall *can protect the intranet from unauthorized access by Internet users. A more complete discussion of this is beyond the scope of this book. But if you plan to publish FileMaker Pro database information from within an intranet, you may want to speak to the system administrator to see how you may be affected by a firewall or other security options.*

Web Publishing

To publish a document on the Web, you use *HyperText Markup Language* (*HTML*) to add formatting and other tags to the document's contents. You then save the document as a plain text file, normally with a .htm or .html extension. The file, which is stored on a network server computer, is made available to the intranet or Internet through the use of *Web server* software.

Web browser software like Netscape Navigator and Microsoft Internet Explorer can open the HTML documents, which are known as *Web pages*, interpret the HTML tags, and display the data as formatted text and graphics with hyperlinks. A *hyperlink*, which can be text or a graphic, displays another Web page or other document when clicked. This provides a level or interaction that enables viewers to navigate to the documents they want to see.

There are several ways to create HTML documents:

- **Manual coding** (the old fashioned way) requires that you type text and HTML tags to create properly coded documents. This is time consuming and not very much fun. It requires extensive knowledge of HTML. In addition, even the smallest typo or syntax error can cause undesirable results on the finished Web page.

- **Web authoring software**, such as Claris Home Page, Adobe PageMill and GoLive, Microsoft Front Page, and Macromedia Dreamweaver, offers a word processor-like interface for creating HTML documents. You enter and format text in a window, and the software enters all the HTML codes for you in the background. This is a quick and easy way to create Web pages, and requires little knowledge of HTML. It does, however, have some limitations in that the software seldom supports all the available HTML tags.

- **Server plug-ins and CGIs** work with the Web server software to get information from specific types of documents. Some of these programs can create Web pages on the fly based on user input and preprogrammed commands in HTML form documents. Blueworld Communications' Lasso, Pervasive Software's Tango, and Web Broadcasting's Web•FM are three examples of server plug-ins or CGIs that work with FileMaker Pro.

FileMaker Pro's Built-in Web Publishing Tools

FileMaker Pro has two built-in Web publishing tools. Here's a quick look at each of them.

Export to HTML Table

This Web publishing method lets you export information from a FileMaker Pro database to a text document coded with HTML table tags. The information can then be displayed on a Web page in table format.

There are pros and cons to using this method. On the pro side, it is the quickest and easiest way to get data into HTML format. It does not require a direct connection to an intranet or the Internet—simply upload the completed HTML document to the Web server and the information is made available via the Web server software.

On the con side, this method doesn't change automatically when the FileMaker Pro database changes. In addition, it doesn't allow any interaction between the viewer and the database.

NOTE *In my opinion, exporting to an HTML table is a great way to get static, seldom-changing information online. But if the information frequently changes or you need viewers to interact with it, this method simply won't cut it.*

I tell you more about exporting data to an HTML table in the section titled "Exporting Data as an HTML Table" on page 589.

Instant Web Publishing

Instant Web Publishing uses the FileMaker Pro Web Companion plug-in to turn FileMaker Pro into a database Web server. You specify layouts that contain the fields that you want to display online and those layout fields appear on a Web page in either a table, single-page form, or a search form.

The main benefit of this method is its simplicity—you can set it up in just minutes. And since viewers have real-time access to the database, they can work with its data to query, sort, and edit records.

This method does, however, require direct access to an intranet or the Internet. In addition, there's very little control over the design of the Web pages in which data appears.

NOTE   *What I like best about Instant Web Publishing is how easy it is to set up and use. While it isn't exactly "instant," it certainly is quicker than "cook and serve." (I've been eating a little too much chocolate pudding these days.)*

I tell you more about Instant Web Publishing in the section titled "Using Instant Web Publishing" on page 595.

NOTE   *FileMaker Pro version 5 also indirectly supports the Custom Web Publishing features that were available in FileMaker Pro version 4.x. To take full advantage of these features, however, you need the Developer version of FileMaker Pro 5. Because of this, a discussion of Custom Web Publishing is beyond the scope of this book.*

What You Need

What you need to get started with FileMaker Pro Web publishing depends on what method you use to put your data on the Web.

Export to HTML Table

Export to HTML Table requires a Web server to which you have either direct or modem access. Once you create the HTML table with database information, you place it in the appropriate location on the Web server. It can then be opened and viewed by anyone who can access the server with a Web browser.

Instant Web Publishing

Instant Web Publishing requires a computer running FileMaker Pro that is connected directly to the intranet or Internet via a TCP/IP connection. You place the FileMaker Pro files that you want to publish on the computer's hard disk and open them with FileMaker Pro. The viewer accesses the built-in Home page to get access to the databases that are available online.

A Web server or Web server software is *not* required for Instant Web Publishing. FileMaker Pro Web Companion enables File-Maker Pro to act as a server for FileMaker Pro database files.

NOTE *The standard version of FileMaker Pro limits the number of users who can connect to your database via Instant Web Publishing to only 10 IP addresses in a rolling 12-hour period. To publish your database to a wider audience, you need FileMaker Pro Unlimited, which, as the name suggests, has no connection limitations.*

Setting Up (or Faking) a TCP/IP Connection

While developing and testing your database Web publishing solutions, you might find it more convenient to use local computers rather than computers that are actually on the intranet or Internet. Then, when your solution is fully developed and tested, you can move it to a computer with a live connection to the network.

To do this, however, you must convince FileMaker Pro that it is indeed part of a TCP/IP network, even when it isn't. This is where you can prove that you're smarter than your computer by faking it out if you have to.

About IP Addresses

An IP address consists of four groups of digits separated by periods. An example is the one I usually use for testing: 192.0.1.2.

IF YOUR COMPUTER IS ALREADY PART OF A TCP/IP NETWORK You *must* use the IP address that has been assigned to your computer. In that case, you probably won't need to fake a connection— you're already set up for one, even if it doesn't include access to the Internet. You can skip the rest of this section.

IF YOUR COMPUTER IS NOT PART OF A TCP/IP NETWORK You can select a random IP address and assign it to your computer. File-Maker, Inc. recommends that you select an IP address that begins with a number between 192 and 223 because it's easier to set up a subnet mask (255.255.255.0) if you need one. The second and third set of digits in the IP address must be between 0 and 255. The last set of digits in the IP address should be between 2 and 254; the other digits are served for special use.

Setting Up TCP/IP on Mac OS

Use the MacTCP control panel or TCP/IP control panel (see Figure 16-1) to set up a configuration that identifies the computer with a fixed IP address—either the one assigned to your computer if you're part of a TCP/IP network or the one you picked at random if you're not part of a TCP/IP network. If a subnet is required (see Figure 16-1, right), enter either the one assigned to your computer if you're part of a TCP/IP network, or 255.255.255.0 if you chose a random IP address beginning with 192 or higher.

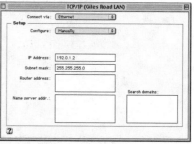

FIGURE 16-1. The TCP/IP control panel for AppleTalk (left) and Ethernet (right) connections on Mac OS after configuring it for a fake TCP/IP network connection.

TIP   *If you have a dial-up TCP/IP connection using PPP, don't change its configuration. Instead, create a new configuration for your fake LAN using the IP address you selected. This will make it easy to switch back to the dial-up configuration when you need to connect to your ISP.*

Setting Up TCP/IP on Windows

Use the Network control panel to set Properties for the TCP/IP protocol. (If this protocol is not listed in the Network control panel, you must add it; consult the manual that came with your operating system for details.)

The properties you must set (at a minimum) are as follows.

- **IP Address** (see Figure 16-2, left) should be either the one assigned to your computer if you're part of a TCP/IP network or the one you picked at random if you're not part of a TCP/IP network.

- **Subnet Mask** (see Figure 16-2, left) should be either the one assigned to your computer if you're part of a TCP/IP network or 255.255.255.0 if you chose a random IP address beginning with 192 or higher.

- **Gateway Address** (see Figure 16-2, right) is usually your IP address with the number 1 replacing the last set of digits.

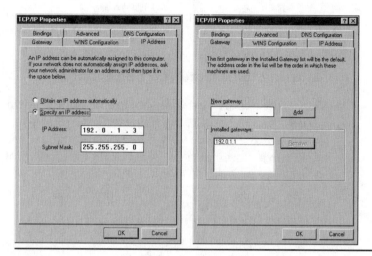

FIGURE 16-2. TCP/IP Properties on Windows after configuring it for a fake TCP/IP network connection.

Exporting Data as an HTML Table

When you export data as an HTML table, you create a specially formatted text file that contains both the data and the HTML tags that format it as a table. All this is done with the Export Records command, which I discuss in detail in the section titled "Exporting Records" on page 521. In this section, I provide specific details for using the HTML Table export format.

Preparing the Database

Before you export records to an HTML table, there are three things you need to consider:

- Which records will be exported?

- In what order should the records be exported?

- Do any fields require special formatting?

Here's how you can prepare your database for the answers to these questions.

Gathering the Records To Be Exported

When you export records—no matter which format you export to—only the records being browsed (the found set) are exported. This means that before you export, you must use the Find or Show All Records command to browse the records that you want to export.

I explain how to use the Find and Show All Records commands in the section titled "Finding Records" on page 133.

Sorting the Records To Be Exported

As you may have guessed, records are exported in the order in which they are being browsed. This means that, before you export, you should use the Sort command to put the records in the found set in the order in which you want them to appear in the HTML table.

I tell you how to use the Sort command in the section titled "Sorting Records" on page 153.

Formatting Fields

When you export records, you have the option of applying a number, date, or time field's formatting to the data it contains when exported. Additional characters such as currency symbols, decimal points, trailing decimal places, and other formatting components are then exported with the data.

To take advantage of this feature, you should switch to a layout that includes the formatting that you want the exported fields to use. If such a layout does not exist, either modify an existing layout to add the desired formatting or create a new one.

I tell you all about working with layouts in Chapters 5 through 8.

Exporting the Data

When you're ready to export, choose Export Records from the File menu (see Figure 16-3).

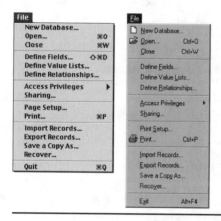

FIGURE 16-3. The File menu on Mac OS (left) and Windows (right).

Specifying a File Name, Location, and Type

The Export Records to File dialog box appears (see Figure 16-4).

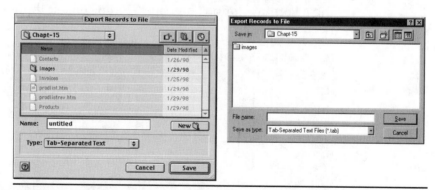

FIGURE 16-4. The Export Records to File dialog box on Mac OS (left) and Windows (right).

Use it to choose a location and enter a name for the HTML table. Do not include spaces in the filename, but do include the appropriate filename extension: .html or .htm. Then choose HTML Table from the Type (Mac OS) or Save as type (Windows) menu (see Figure 16-5). Click the Save button.

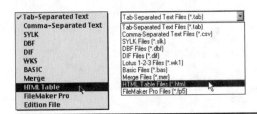

FIGURE 16-5. Choosing HTML Table from the Type menu on Mac OS (left) and the Save as type menu on Windows (right).

Setting Up the Export

The Specify Field Order for Export dialog box appears next (see Figure 16-6). Use this dialog box to select and set the order for the fields that you want to export. If you want number, date, and time fields to be formatted as they are in the current layout, be sure to select the option for Format output using current layout at the bottom left of the dialog box. I provide details for using this dialog box in "Specifying the Export Order" on page 524 and "Selecting a Format Option" on page 526, so consult those sections if you need assistance.

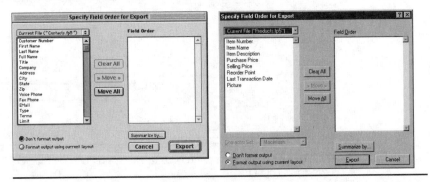

FIGURE 16-6. The Specify Field Order for Export dialog box on Mac OS (left) and Windows (right).

Exporting the Records

When you are finished setting options in this dialog box, it might look something like the illustrations in Figure 16-7.

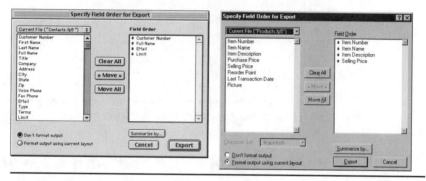

FIGURE 16-7. Two examples of field order and options set for records to be exported as HTML tables.

Click the Export button. A new file with the name you specified is created. The records are exported to it as an HTML table.

Viewing the HTML Table with a Web Browser

Once you've exported records to HTML Table format, you can look at the table with a Web browser (see Figure 16-8). Use one of these techniques:

- Drag the icon for the HTML table you created onto the icon for your favorite Web browser application. When you release the mouse button, the browser should launch and open the page.

- Start your favorite Web browser. Use its Open or Open File command to open the HTML table file you created.

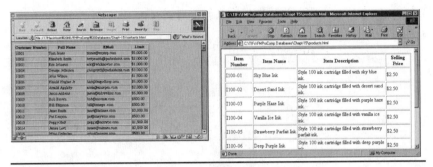

FIGURE 16-8. HTML tables viewed with Netscape Communicator on Mac OS (left) and Microsoft Internet Explorer on Windows (right).

Viewing the HTML Table with a Text Editor

The exported HTML table is nothing more than a text file with HTML tags. If you want to view or edit the HTML that FileMaker Pro composed for you, you can open the exported file with a text editor or word processor (see Figure 16-9).

FIGURE 16-9. Raw HTML viewed in SimpleText on Mac OS (left) and in WordPad on Windows (right).

TIP *If you want to make the HTML table more attractive—or at least add a title or heading to the page—you can open and edit it with a text editor like the ones in Figure 16-9 or with a Web authoring tool such as Claris Home Page.*

Using Instant Web Publishing

Instant Web Publishing adds an element of interactivity to a published database file. In this section, I explain how to set up Instant Web Publishing and use it to publish a database on the Web.

Enabling and Configuring Web Companion

The first step to using Instant Web Publishing is to enable and configure FileMaker Pro Web Companion.

TIP *You only have to perform this procedure once, no matter how many databases you publish on the Web.*

Enabling the Web Companion Plug-In

To enable the Web Companion plug-in, begin by choosing Application from the Preferences submenu under the Edit menu (see Figure 16-10).

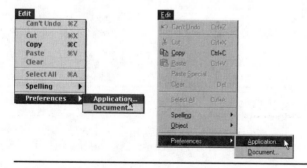

FIGURE 16-10. Choosing Application from the Preference submenu under the Edit menu on Mac OS (left) and Windows (right).

In the Application Preferences dialog box that appears, click the Plug-Ins tab to display Plug-Ins preferences. Turn on the check box to the left of Web Companion in the list (see Figure 16-11).

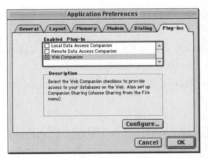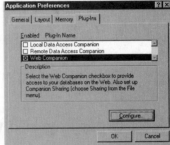

FIGURE 16-11. The Plug-Ins preferences of the Application Preferences dialog box on Mac OS (left) and Windows (right).

Configuring the Web Companion Plug-In

To configure Web Companion for Instant Web Publishing, click the Configure button. The Web Companion Configuration dialog box appears (see Figure 16-12).

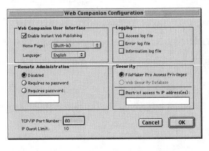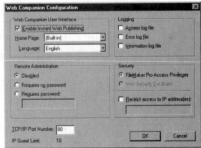

FIGURE 16-12. The Web Companion Configuration dialog box on Mac OS (left) and Windows (right).

There are several settings you must check and, if necessary, change:

• Turn on the Enable Instant Web Publishing check box.

• Choose (Built-in) from the Home Page menu. This enables FileMaker Pro to generate a Home page that lists all open FileMaker Pro documents being shared via Instant Web Publishing.

- If the computer's TCP/IP port number 80 is in use by another application—such as a Web server—you must change the value in the TCP/IP Port number box to 591. (This number has been registered with the Internet Assigned Numbers Authority for FileMaker Pro Web Companion.)

You can leave other options set the way they are in Figure 16-12. Click OK to save your settings and dismiss the Web Companion Configuration dialog box. Then click Done in the Application Preferences dialog box to save changes and dismiss it, too.

Preparing the Database for Publishing

Instant Web Publishing displays differently formatted pages or *views* of the database information:

- **Table View** displays multiple records at a time. It's a lot like a FileMaker Pro columnar report layout.

- **Form View** displays only one record at a time. It's like a FileMaker Pro single-page form layout.

- **Search Page** displays a form for entering search criteria. This is similar to displaying a FileMaker Pro single-page form layout in Find mode.

- **Sort Page** enables users to sort records based on a pre-defined sort order or sort fields.

These views or pages are created based on layouts and sort orders that you define before publishing the database on the Web. Their overall appearance is governed by a Web style you select and apply when setting up the views.

Creating the Layouts

To display a specific group of fields on a Web page, you must have a corresponding layout that includes just those fields.

Depending on the Web style you select (more on that in a moment), FileMaker Pro may display layouts as you designed them, including graphics, formatting, and field positioning. But the most important aspects of a layout that FileMaker Pro *always* uses when creating a Web page are the fields included on the layout and the formatting of number, date, or time fields (or calculation fields formatted as numbers, dates, or times).

Consider the Table View, Form View, and Search Page that File-Maker Pro will display for Instant Web Publishing. Now ask yourself these questions and act accordingly:

- Do you have one or more layouts that include the fields you want to display in each view or page? If so, are the number, date, and time fields formatted as desired? If the answer to these questions is yes, you don't have to do any additional work on your layouts. If the answer is no, you must create or modify layout(s) to meet your Web publishing needs.

- Do you want to include all database fields in any of these views or pages? If so, is default formatting acceptable for number, date, and time fields? If the answer to these questions is yes, you can use FileMaker Pro's default layout. Just keep in mind, however, that field repetitions and related fields do not appear if you use this option.

About Web Styles

FileMaker Pro version 5 enables you to apply *Web styles* to pages published with Instant WebPublishing. These styles determine two things:

- The overall appearance—primarily the color scheme—of the pages.

- Whether all layout objects will appear on the Web page as formatted and positioned in the actual layout.

What this means is that you can customize the appearance of the Web pages FileMaker Pro creates by choosing a particular Web style. Certain styles—Fern Green and Blue and Gold 2—are compatible with most Web browsers, but they do not display your database layouts as you created them. Although other styles do display your layouts as you created them, they are compatible only with Web browsers capable of displaying cacading style sheets, such as Microsoft Internet Explorer 4.0 or later.

You don't have to worry much about the compatibility issue. If a Web browser incapable of displaying cascading styles sheets accesses a database that uses a Web style that requires cascading style sheets, FileMaker Pro automatically displays the pages with the Fern Green style, which is compatible with most browsers.

Enabling Companion Sharing and Setting Up Views

When your layouts are complete, you're ready to set up Instant Web Publishing views. Choose Sharing from the File menu (see Figure 16-3) to display the File Sharing dialog box. To enable Companion Sharing, turn on the check box beside Web Companion in the Companion Sharing area (see Figure 16-13).

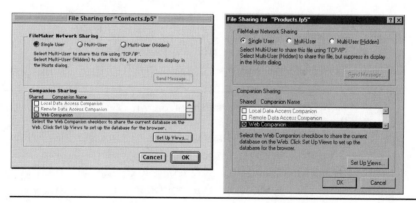

FIGURE 16-13. The File Sharing dialog box on Mac OS (left) and Windows (right).

Next, click the Set Up Views button. The Web Companion View Setup dialog box appears (see Figure 16-14). Use this dialog box to specify Web style options and layouts for each view.

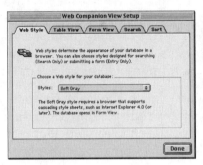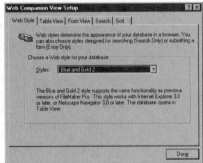

FIGURE 16-14. The Web Style tab of the Web Companion View Setup dialog box on Mac OS (left) and Windows (right).

SELECTING A WEB STYLE If necessary, click the Web Style tab in the Web Companion View Setup dialog box to display its options (see Figure 16-14). Choose one of the options from the Styles menu (see Figure 16-15). A description of the style appears beneath the menu.

FIGURE 16-15. The Styles menu on Mac OS (left) and Windows (right).

SETTING TABLE VIEW OPTIONS Click the Table View tab at the top of the Web Companion View Setup dialog box to display its options (see Figure 16-16). Use the Layout menu (see Figure 16-17) to choose a layout that contains the fields that you want to display in Table View. If you want to display all fields in the view, choose All Fields (no layout).

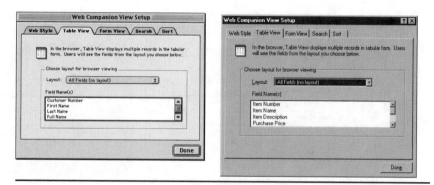

FIGURE 16-16. The Table View tab of the Web Companion View Setup dialog box on Mac OS (left) and Windows (right).

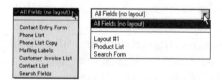

FIGURE 16-17. The Layout menu on Mac OS (left) and Windows (right). These two illustrations were taken from different files—that's why their options are different.

SETTING FORM VIEW OPTIONS Click the Form View tab at the top of the Web Companion View Setup dialog box to display its options (see Figure 16-18). Use the Layout menu (see Figure 16-17) to choose a layout that contains the fields that you want to display in Form View.

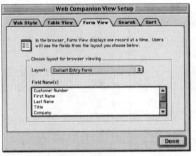
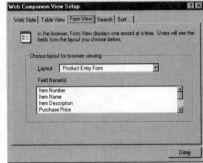

FIGURE 16-18. The Form View tab of the Web Companion View Setup dialog box on Mac OS (left) and Windows (right).

SETTING SEARCH PAGE OPTIONS   Click the Search tab at the top of the Web Companion View Setup dialog box to display its options (see Figure 16-19). Use the Layout menu (see Figure 16-17) to choose a layout that contains the fields that you want to display on the Search page. If you want to display all fields on the page, choose All Fields (no layout).

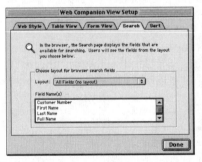
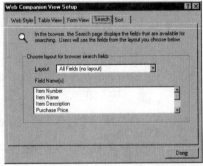

FIGURE 16-19. The Search tab of the Web Companion View Setup dialog box on Mac OS (left) and Windows (right).

SETTING SORT OPTIONS   Click the Sort tab to display Sort options (see Figure 16-20). Then select one of the three options.

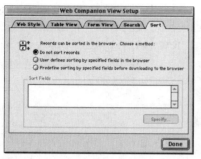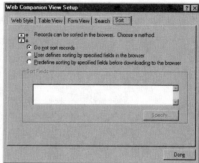

FIGURE 16-20. The Sort tab of the Web Companion View Setup dialog box on Mac OS (left) and Windows (right).

- **Do not sort records** displays the records in the order in which they were entered into the database.

- **User defines sorting by specified fields in the browser** enables you to select the fields by which the viewer can sort records. When you select this option, click the Specify button, then use the standard Specify Sort dialog box that appears to select the fields by which a viewer can sort. The fields appear in the list in the Web Companion View Setup dialog box (see Figure 16-21).

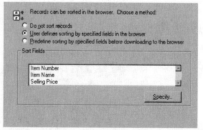

FIGURE 16-21. Examples of sort fields listed in the Web Companion View Setup dialog box on Mac OS (left) and Windows (right).

- **Predefine sorting by specified fields before downloading to the browser** enables you to set up a sort order in advance. When you select this option, click the Specify button, then use the standard Specify Sort dialog box that appears to specify a sort order. The sort order appears in the list in the Web Companion View Setup dialog box (see Figure 16-22). When the user views the database, the data is sorted automatically in the order you specify.

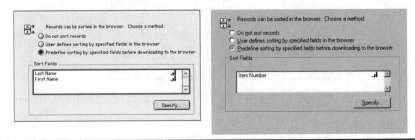

FIGURE 16-22. Examples of sort order displayed in the Web Companion View Setup dialog box on Mac OS (left) and Windows (right).

NOTE *If you need help using the Specify Sort Order dialog box, consult the section titled "Setting Sort Order" on page 153 where I discuss it in detail.*

SAVING STYLE, VIEW, AND SORT OPTIONS When you're finished setting options in the Web Companion View Setup dialog box, click the Done button. This saves your settings and dismisses the dialog box. Click OK in the File Sharing dialog box to dismiss it.

Viewing the Published Database on the Web

If you followed all the instructions up to this point, left the database file open, and have a live connection to the Internet, the database is now available on the Web. You can (and should) check it out for yourself.

Opening the Database with a Web Browser

Open your favorite Web browser and use it to open a URL consisting of the characters *http://* followed by the IP address of the computer that is being used as a FileMaker Pro Web server. For example, my two systems are set up as 207.138.23.228 and 207.138.23.229, so I'd view *http://207.138.23.228* or *http:// 207.138.23.229*. Figure 16-23 shows the Home page FileMaker Pro displays on each of these systems.

 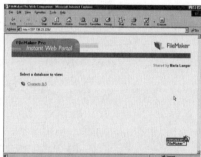

FIGURE 16-23. The Home page FileMaker Pro displays for Instant Web Publishing with Netscape Communicator on Mac OS (left) and Microsoft Internet Explorer on Windows (right).

WARNING   *If you had to change the TCP/IP port in the Web Companion Configuration dialog box (see Figure 16-12) as instructed in the section titled "Configuring the Web Companion Plug-In" on page 596, you must append the port number to the IP address like this:* http://192.0.1.2:591. *Otherwise, the application using port 80 will respond to the browser's request instead of FileMaker Pro.*

Exploring the Database

To access a database listed on the Home page, click its name, which is formatted as a link. This displays the database in Table View (see Figure 16-24, left) or Form View (see Figure 16-24, right), depending on the Web style and the browser used to access the database.

FIGURE 16-24. A Table View page with the Fern Green Web style on Mac OS (left) and a Form View page with the Soft Gray Web style on Windows (right).

Explore the rest of the database that you publish on the Web on your own. Be sure to try out all the buttons and links, experiment with the Search Page, and check to see if sorting works the way you expect. To make changes to what you see on your published pages, you must make changes to the corresponding FileMaker Pro layouts and configuration options as discussed throughout this section.

Security

Are you worried about security? If so, you're not alone. Fortunately, you don't have to worry much about security for the databases you publish on the Web. FileMaker Pro offers two ways to protect them from unauthorized access: FileMaker Pro Access Privileges and restricting access by IP address.

In this section, I tell you about both types of security, as well as security concerns of special interest to database Web publishers.

Setting Up Security

There are two methods of protecting the database files that you publish on the Web from unauthorized access.

FileMaker Pro Access Privileges

The access privileges feature, which is part of FileMaker Pro's built-in security, can also cover databases published on the Web.

Access privileges protect your databases two ways:

- **Passwords** enables you to control the tasks that a user can perform with a file. With password privileges, for example, you can prevent a user from creating a new record, editing a record, or deleting a record.

- **Groups** enables you to control the layouts and fields that a user can view and whether the user can modify specific layouts or fields. With group privileges, for example, you can prevent a user from seeing any combination of fields or allow the user to see a field but not edit it.

Access privileges are relatively easy to set up and use. In most cases, this security feature will meet your needs. And since this option is already enabled in the Web Companion Configuration dialog box (see Figure 16-12), all you need to do is set up access privilege security in a Web published database to protect it.

I cover access privileges in detail in Chapter 17; check that chapter for more information and step-by-step instructions.

Restricting Access by IP Address

You can increase security by restricting access to Web-published databases by IP address. This enables you to lock out anyone attempting to access the database from an unauthorized computer.

To set up this feature, begin by choosing Application from the Preferences submenu under the Edit menu (see Figure 16-10) to display the Application Preferences dialog box. Click the Plug-Ins tab to display its options (see Figure 16-11). Select Web Companion and click the Configure button to display the Web Companion Configuration dialog box (see Figure 16-12).

In the Security area, turn on the check box beside Restrict access to IP address(es). Then enter the IP addresses of the computers that are allowed to access the FileMaker Pro databases published by your computer. Be sure to include all periods (.) within the IP addresses and to separate each address with a comma. When you're finished, click OK to save your settings and dismiss the Web Companion Configuration dialog box. Then click OK again to dismiss the Application Preferences dialog box.

TIP   *You can include the * wildcard character in an IP address. For example, 192.0.* says to allow all computers with IP addresses that begin with 192.0.*

Opening a Secured Database File

What happens when you open a secured database file depends on the type of security set up for it.

OPENING A DATABASE SECURED WITH ACCESS PRIVILEGES   When you open a database file that is protected by access privileges, your Web browser displays a dialog box that you can use to enter your user name and password (see Figure 16-25). Enter the required information in the appropriate boxes and click OK to access the file.

FIGURE 16-25. The password dialog box displayed by Netscape Navigator on Mac OS (left) and Microsoft Internet Explorer on Windows (right). The appearance of the dialog box varies based on the browser application and the operating system.

NOTE *FileMaker Pro ignores anything in the Name or User Name field of the password dialog box.*

OPENING A DATABASE FILE PROTECTED WITH IP ADDRESS RESTRICTIONS When you open a database that is protected with IP address restrictions, nothing special happens—unless your IP address is locked out. In that case, a dialog box like the one in Figure 16-26 appears. Just click OK; you can't open the file.

FIGURE 16-26. The dialog box that appears when your IP address is restricted from opening a database file on Mac OS (left) and on Windows (right).

Additional Security Concerns

Here are a few additional things you should keep in mind concerning security over databases published on the Web.

Related Fields

If you use Instant Web Publishing and have selected a layout that includes related fields, there are two things you should be aware of:

- Related fields will be completely accessible to users no matter how security is set in FileMaker Pro access privileges for the database in which they reside.

- The database in which related fields reside will automatically be listed on the built-in Home page that FileMaker Pro displays (see Figure 16-23). You can prevent a file from

being listed on this page by including an underscore character at the end of the file name before any extensions, as in
Contacts_.fp3.

"No Password" Passwords

If a "no password" password exists for a file, the password dialog
box in Figure 16-25 will not appear. Instead, all users will have the
same limited access assigned to users who access the database
without a password. I tell you more about the "no password"
password in the section titled "Creating a "No Password" Password" on page 624 and "Opening a Secured Database without a
Password" on page 632.

The Export Records Access Privileges

Anyone who has the Export records access privilege turned on for
his or her password in a database can publish that database on the
Web. I tell you more about access privileges for passwords in the
section titled "Options in the Define Passwords Dialog Box" on
page 621.

Step-by-Step

Ready to publish a database on the Web? In this section, I provide
step-by-step instructions for publishing information in the file
named Products.fp5 that you have been working on at the end of
each chapter. If you've been skipping around and don't have the
completed files from Chapter 13, 14, or 15 (it doesn't matter
which), you can download them from the companion Web site to
this book, http://www.gilesrd.com/fmprocomp/.

Exporting to an HTML Table

In this exercise, you'll sort and export records to an HTML table. Then, if desired, you can view the completed table with a Web browser or open its HTML document with an HTML editor to customize it.

1. Open the file named Products.fp5.

2. Display all records and sort by Item number.

3. Export the records to an HTML Table named prodlist.htm. The following fields should be exported: Item Number, Item Name, Item Description, and Selling Price. Be sure to format output using the current layout before exporting.

4. Open your favorite Web browser and use it to open the prodlist.htm file you just created.

5. If desired, open prodlist.htm with your favorite HTML editing software and modify it to include a title and a description of what the page contains.

Instant Web Publishing

In this exercise, you'll use Instant Web Publishing to put a product catalog for Products.fp5 on the Web.

1. Check the MacTCP or TCP/IP control panel (Mac OS) or the TCP/IP Properties dialog box in the Network control panel (Windows) to make sure they are properly configured. If they are not, configure them as instructed in the section titled "Setting Up (or Faking) a TCP/IP Connection" on page 586. Make a note of the IP address assigned to the computer and close the control panel.

2. If necessary, open Products.fp5.

3. Use the Plug-Ins tab of the Application Preferences dialog box to enable the Web Companion plug-in.

4. Use the Web Companion Configuration dialog box to enable Instant Web Publishing, and choose the built-in home page. Save your settings.

5. Switch to Layout mode.

6. Create a new layout called Product List with the following fields: Item Number, Item Name, Selling Price. Format the Selling Price field to display the value in currency with two decimal places.

7. Create a new layout named Catalog Page with the following fields: Item Number, Item Name, Item Description, Selling Price, and Picture. (Note: You can omit the picture field if your copy of the database does not include pictures.) Format the Selling Price field to display the value in currency with two decimal places.

8. Create a new layout named Search Fields with the following fields: Item Number, Item Name, Item Description, Selling Price. (Note: If you omitted the Picture field from the previous layout, you can skip this step and use the Catalog Page layout when Search Fields layout is required in the following instructions.)

9. Open the File Sharing dialog box and enable Web Companion sharing.

10. Open the Web Companion View Setup dialog box.

11. In the Web Style tab, choose any Web style you like.

12. In the Table View tab, choose Product List from the Layout menu.

13. In the Form View tab, choose Catalog Page from the Layout menu.

14. In the Search tab, choose Search Fields from the Layout menu.

15. In the Sort tab, select the User defines sorting by specified fields in the browser option. Then use the Specify Sort dialog box to add the following fields to the sort order list: Item Number, Item Name, and Selling Price. Click OK to dismiss the Specify Sort Order dialog box.

16. Dismiss the Web Companion View Setup and File Sharing dialog boxes.

17. Open your favorite Web browser. Use it to view the IP address you noted earlier in these instructions. The built-in Home page should appear with Products.fp5 listed among the published files. Click its name to open it, then try all the views, buttons, and other features you included in the Instant Web Publishing solution.

Protecting and Maintaining Database Files

This part of the book provides a wealth of valuable information about protecting database files from unauthorized access and data loss and maintaining database files. Its two chapters are:

17

Securing Database Files

In Chapter 15, I explain how to share your database files with other members of a network. In Chapter 16, I explain how to publish database information on the World Wide Web. If you take advantage of either of these FileMaker Pro features, security is probably important to you. If it isn't, maybe it should be!

Fortunately, FileMaker Pro has flexible built-in security features. In this chapter, I tell you how to secure your database files against unauthorized access.

NOTE   *Don't confuse FileMaker Pro's access privileges with the access privileges of your network. They are completely separate.*

How Security Works

FileMaker Pro's built-in security feature, which is also known as *access privileges*, uses *passwords* and *groups* to offer two kinds of security. In this section, I tell you how access privileges work.

Passwords and Groups

Access privileges are determined by setting options for passwords and groups:

- **Passwords** enables you to assign privileges such as the ability to edit a record, design layouts, or even open the file. Passwords also enables you to control how FileMaker Pro menus appear. The *master password*—which is required to set up access privileges—allows full access to the file.

- **Groups** enables you to assign access to specific layouts and fields within the database file.

Passwords and groups work together. You associate passwords to groups to fully control access to data.

An Example

The best way to see how passwords and groups work together is to look at an example.

The Premise

Sal works in Sales. Alice works in Accounting. They both need access to a file full of customer information.

- Sal needs to be able to get the contact information for the customers. He needs to be able to create and print form letters that introduce new products. He doesn't need to see accounting-related information.

- Alice needs to be able to get the contact information and invoice history for a customer. She needs to be able to update a customer's credit limit. She doesn't need to modify any layouts or print any records.

The Solution

First, create three passwords:

- The individual responsible for creating and maintaining the database file must be assigned the master password. This gives him full access to the file.

- Create a password for Sal that enables him to browse, create, edit, and print records and design layouts.

- Create a password for Alice that enables her to browse and edit records.

Then create two groups:

- Create a group for the Sales Department.

- Create a group for the Accounting Department.

Next, associate passwords to groups:

- Associate the Sales group with Sal's password and the passwords for any other members of his department.

- Associate the Accounting group with Alice's password and the passwords for any other members of her department.

Finally, associate each group with the appropriate password(s):

- Allow the Sales group to view the layouts that show contact information and Sales Department form letters. Give this group access to all fields except those related to accounting information, such as credit limit and terms.

- Allow the Accounting group to view the layouts that show contact information and credit limit. Give this group access to all fields.

This is a very simple example. With large, complex organizations and database files, access privileges can also be very complex.

Setting Up Security

As the example hints, setting up security is a four-step process:

1. Create passwords for specific tasks or privileges.

2. Create groups of users.

3. Associate passwords to groups.

4. Set access privileges for groups.

Here are the details for these steps and the options they offer.

Passwords

Passwords determine which users can open a file and what tasks each user can perform. You create and modify passwords in the Define Passwords dialog box (see Figure 17-1).

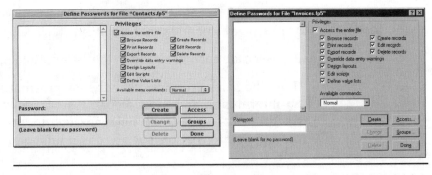

FIGURE 17-1. The Define Passwords dialog box on Mac OS (left) and Windows (right).

Options in the Define Passwords Dialog Box

The Define Passwords dialog box enables you to set two kinds of privileges for each password you create.

TASK PRIVILEGES   One type of privilege controls the specific tasks that a user can perform on a file. You set these privileges by turning check boxes on or off. Here's a complete list, with descriptions and chapter cross-references:

- **Access the entire file** enables the user to do anything with the file. When this check box is turned on, all the others are automatically turned on.

- **Browse records** enables the user to view, find and sort records. I tell you about browsing records throughout this book and about finding and sorting records in Chapter 4.

- **Print records** enables the user to print records. I cover printing in Chapter 14.

- **Export records** enables the user to export records or copy the found set. I discuss importing and exporting records in Chapter 13.

WARNING   *The Export records privilege also enables the user to access the File Sharing dialog box, thus giving him the ability to share a file on a LAN or publish it on the Web. I tell you about file sharing in Chapter 15 and Web publishing in Chapter 16.*

- **Override data entry warnings** enables the user to override validation options set in the Entry Options dialog box for a field. I tell you about validation options in Chapter 9.

- **Design layouts** enables the user to create or modify layouts. I discuss working with layouts in Chapters 5 through 8.

- **Edit scripts** enables the user to create or modify scripts with ScriptMaker. I tell you about scripting in Chapter 12.

- **Define value lists** enables the user to create or modify value lists. I cover value lists in Chapter 9.

- **Create records** enables the user to create new records and enter information into them. I tell you about creating records in Chapter 3.

- **Edit records** enables the user to edit the information in records. I also tell you about editing records in Chapter 3.

- **Delete records** enables the user to delete records. I cover deleting records in Chapter 3, too.

MENU PRIVILEGES The other type of privilege controls the menu commands that are available to the user. Use the Available menu commands menu (see Figure 17-2) to choose from among three options.

FIGURE 17-2. The Available menu commands menu in the Define Passwords dialog box on Mac OS (left) and Windows (right).

- **Normal** enables all menu commands that would normally appear in FileMaker Pro except those for task privileges that are turned off. For example, if the Create records privilege is turned off, the New Record command under the Mode menu will be gray.

- **Editing Only** enables only basic entry and editing commands, except those for task privileges that are turned off.

- **None** disables almost all menu commands.

TIP *If you choose the None option, you can include buttons on layouts to enable the user to perform tasks with the file. I tell you how to create buttons in the section titled "Including Buttons in Layouts" on page 481.*

Creating Passwords

Here are the details you need to open the Define Passwords dialog box, and to create, modify, and delete passwords.

OPENING THE DEFINE PASSWORDS DIALOG BOX   Choose Define Passwords from the Access Privileges submenu under the File menu (see Figure 17-3) or click the Passwords button in the Define Groups dialog box (see Figure 17-7). The Define Passwords dialog box appears (see Figure 17-1).

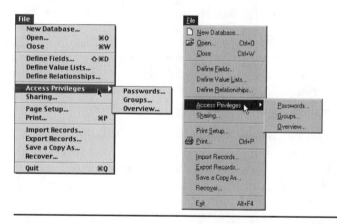

FIGURE 17-3. The Access Privileges submenu under the File menu on Mac OS (left) and Windows (right).

CREATING A MASTER PASSWORD   Enter the password that you would like to use as the master password in the Password box. Make sure the Access the entire file check box is turned on and that the Available menu commands menu is set to Normal. Then click the Create button. The password appears in the list on the left side of the dialog box (see Figure 17-4).

WARNING   *You must create a master password for your database file. FileMaker Pro will not allow you to set access privileges without it. You can have more than one master password if desired.*

CREATING A USER PASSWORD Enter the password that you would like to use as a user password in the Password box. Then set the check boxes and the Available menu commands menu in the privileges area as desired. When you're finished, click the Create button. The password appears in the list on the left side of the dialog box (see Figure 17-4).

CREATING A "NO PASSWORD" PASSWORD Follow the steps in the previous paragraph to create a new password, but leave the Password box empty. When you click the Create button, *(no password)* appears in the list on the left side of the dialog box (see Figure 17-4).

NOTE *With a "no password" password set up, users without a password can still open the file.*

WARNING *Do not use a "no password" password for a master password. Doing so defeats the whole security system by allowing anyone access to the whole file!*

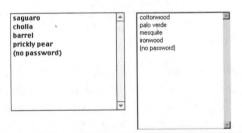

FIGURE 17-4. Passwords listed in the Define Passwords dialog box on Mac OS (left) and Windows (right).

CHANGING A PASSWORD OR ITS SETTINGS Click the password in the list on the left side of the window (see Figure 17-4) to select it. Then:

- To change the password itself, enter a new password in the Password box.

- To change the password's settings, make changes to privileges check boxes and the Available menu commands menu as desired.

When you're finished, click the Change button.

DELETING A PASSWORD   Click the password in the list on the left side of the window (see Figure 17-4) to select it. Then click the Delete button. A dialog box like the one in Figure 17-5 appears. Click the Delete button. The password is deleted.

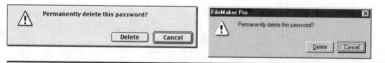

FIGURE 17-5. The dialog box that appears on Mac OS (left) and Windows (right) when you delete a password.

SAVING CHANGES IN THE DEFINE PASSWORDS DIALOG BOX   Click the Done button. The Confirm dialog box appears (see Figure 17-6). Enter a master password for the file—your entry is displayed as bullet characters (Mac OS) or asterisks (Windows). Click the OK button. Your changes are saved, and the two dialog boxes disappear.

FIGURE 17-6. The Confirm dialog box on Mac OS (left) and Windows (right).

TIP   *If you need to set up other security options, you can click the Access or Groups button in the Define Passwords dialog box to switch to the Access Privileges (see Figure 17-10) or Define Groups (see Figure 17-7) dialog box.*

Groups

Groups enable you to specify which layouts and fields are accessible to users. You create and modify group names in the Define Groups dialog box (see Figure 17-7).

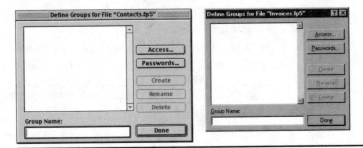

FIGURE 17-7. The Define Groups dialog box on Mac OS (left) and Windows (right).

 NOTE *The Define Groups dialog box is just for creating, renaming, and deleting groups. You assign privileges for groups in the Access Privileges dialog box.*

OPENING THE DEFINE GROUPS DIALOG BOX Choose Define Groups from the Access Privileges submenu under the File menu (see Figure 17-3) or click the Groups button in the Define Passwords dialog box (see Figure 17-1).

CREATING A GROUP Enter a name for the group in the Group Name box. Click the Create button. The group name appears in the list (see Figure 17-8).

FIGURE 17-8. Groups listed in the Define Groups dialog box on Mac OS (left) and Windows (right).

RENAMING A GROUP   Click the name of the group in the list (see Figure 17-8) to select it. Enter a new name for the group in the Group Name box and click the Rename button. The group name changes.

DELETING A GROUP   Click the name of the group in the list to select it (see Figure 17-8). Then click the Delete button. A dialog box like the one in Figure 17-9 appears. Click the Delete button. The group is deleted.

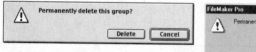 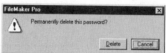

FIGURE 17-9. The dialog box that appears on Mac OS (left) and Windows (right) when you delete a group.

SAVING CHANGES IN THE DEFINE GROUPS DIALOG BOX   Click the Done button. Your changes are saved, and the dialog box disappears.

TIP   *If you need to set up other security options, you can click the Access or Passwords button in the Define Groups dialog box to switch to the Access Privileges (see Figure 17-10) or Define Passwords (see Figure 17-1) dialog box.*

Access Privileges

The Access Privileges dialog box is where you associate passwords with groups and specify which layouts and fields are visible to each group.

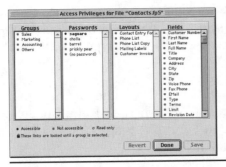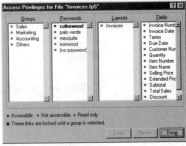

FIGURE 17-10. The Access Privileges dialog box on Mac OS (left) and Windows (right).

NOTE *I think the Access Privileges dialog box is one of the most confusing dialog boxes in FileMaker Pro. In fact, when I haven't used the dialog box for a while, I have to reach for this book to remind me how to use it. It's not difficult if you understand the logic behind it, but I forget the logic. It's a good thing that I write these things down.*

Options in the Access Privileges Dialog Box

The Access Privileges dialog box offers three possible privileges that you can change by clicking the marker to the left of an item.

- **Accessible**, which is indicated with a black bullet, means that the item can be viewed and modified.

- **Not accessible**, which is indicated with a gray bullet, means that the item can't even be seen.

- **Read only**, which is indicated with an empty circle (or white bullet), means that the item is visible but cannot be changed.

Setting Up Access Privileges

Here are the details for setting up access privileges.

OPENING THE ACCESS PRIVILEGES DIALOG BOX Choose Overview from the Access Privileges submenu under the File menu (see Figure 17-3) or click the Access button in the Define Passwords (see Figure 17-1) or Define Groups (see Figure 17-7) dialog box. The Access Privileges dialog box appears (see Figure 17-10).

ASSIGNING PASSWORDS TO A GROUP Click the name of the group in the Groups list to select it. Then click on the bullets to the left of the passwords in the Passwords list to change the access. (Do not click the passwords themselves.) Your options will be black (assigned to the group) or gray (not assigned to the group). When you click another group to assign passwords to it, a dialog box like the one in Figure 17-11 appears. Click Yes to save changes before changing the next group.

FIGURE 17-11. The dialog box that appears on Mac OS (left) and Windows (right) when you finish changing settings for one group and select another to change.

NOTE *You cannot change the setting for the master password, which appears in bold and is accessible for all groups.*

ASSIGNING LAYOUT AND FIELD ACCESS TO A GROUP Click the name of the group in the Groups list to select it. Then click on the bullets to the left of the layout names in the Layouts list or the field names in the Fields list to change the access, as discussed in "Options in the Access Privileges Dialog Box" on page 628. (Do not click the layout or field names themselves.) When you click another group to assign passwords to it, a dialog box like the one in Figure 17-11 appears. Click Yes to save changes before changing the next group.

SAVING ALL ACCESS PRIVILEGES SETTINGS AND CLOSING THE ACCESS PRIVILEGES DIALOG BOX If necessary, click the Save button at the bottom of the Access Privileges dialog box (see Figure 17-10). Then click the Done button. The dialog box disappears.

Two Examples

If you're confused, stop right here, take a deep breath, and clear your mind. Then look at the following two examples. They should help you understand.

In Figure 17-12, the passwords *cholla* and *prickly pear* are part of the *Sales* group. That group has access to all layouts except the Customer Invoice List layout. It has access to all fields except the Terms field, which is not accessible at all, and the Limit field, which can be seen but not changed.

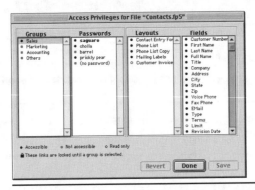

FIGURE 17-12. Example of Access Privileges set up for the Sales group on Mac OS.

In Figure 17-13, the password *no password* is part of the *Others* group. That group has access to the only available layout, but it has very limited access to fields.

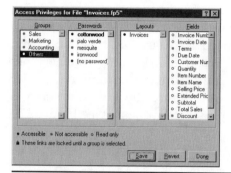

FIGURE 17-13. Example of Access Privileges set up for the Others group on Windows.

A Review of the Logic

If you understand the logic behind FileMaker Pro's access privileges, setting up security is a breeze. Here's the bottom line:

• Passwords, which can be assigned to one or more people, determine what a user can do with a file.

• Groups, to which multiple passwords can be assigned, determine what users can see in a file.

This means that it's possible to have two users in the same group who can see the same layouts and fields but can't work with the data the same way—one may be able to create and edit records while the other may only be able to browse records.

Accessing a Secured File

Once a file has been secured, access is controlled by the password that the user enters. In this section, I tell you how to open and work with a secured file.

Opening a Secured File

You open a secured database file the same way you open any other FileMaker Pro database file—use the Open command or double-click the file's icon in the Finder (Mac OS) or Windows Explorer (Windows). Before the file completely opens, a dialog box requesting a password appears (see Figure 17-14).

FIGURE 17-14. The Password dialog box on Mac OS (left) and Windows (right).

ENTERING A PASSWORD   Enter a valid password for the file in the Password box. Your entry is displayed as bullet characters (Mac OS) or asterisks (Windows). Then click OK to finish opening the file. If you enter a password that is not valid for the database file, a dialog box like the one in Figure 17-15 appears. Click OK to try again.

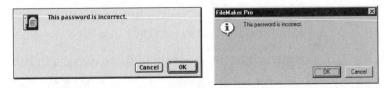

FIGURE 17-15. The dialog box that appears on Mac OS (left) and Windows (right) when you enter an invalid password.

NOTE   *FileMaker Pro passwords are not case-sensitive. That means you can enter characters in uppercase or lowercase, no matter how they appear in the Define Passwords dialog box.*

OPENING A SECURED DATABASE WITHOUT A PASSWORD   If a secured database file includes a "no password" password, the dialog box in which you enter a password will include a note telling you that you can leave the Password box blank to open the file with limited access. You can see this in Figure 17-14. If this is the case, you can open the file without entering a password. Just leave the Password box empty and click OK. If the database does not include a "no password" password, the dialog box in Figure 17-15 will appear if you attempt to open the file without a password.

Providing a Default Password for a File

If you have the master password for a file, you can set the file up so that it automatically opens using a default password. This is particularly useful when a file has few passwords and most users will open the file with the same password.

SETTING UP A DEFAULT PASSWORD   Open the file with the master password. Choose Document from the Preferences submenu under the Edit menu (see Figure 17-16). In the Document Preferences dialog box that appears, turn on the Try default password check box (see Figure 17-17), then enter the default password in the box beside it. Click the Done button to save your changes.

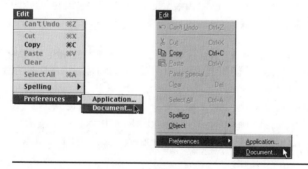

FIGURE 17-16. Choosing Document from the Preferences submenu under the Edit menu on Mac OS (left) and Windows (right).

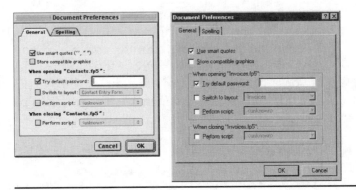

FIGURE 17-17. The Document Preferences dialog box on Mac OS (left) and Windows (right).

WARNING   *Do not enter the master password as the default password. Doing so enables anyone to open the file with the master password, thus giving them full access to the file.*

OPENING A SECURED FILE WITH THE DEFAULT PASSWORD   Open   the file the usual way. FileMaker Pro automatically tries the default password when it opens the file. If the password is valid, the file opens with the privileges assigned to that password.

OPENING A FILE WITH A PASSWORD OTHER THAN THE DEFAULT PASSWORD   Hold down the Option (Mac OS) or Shift (Windows) key while selecting the file in the Open File dialog box or while double-clicking the file's icon in the Finder (Mac OS) or Windows Explorer (Windows). The dialog box in Figure 17-14 appears, allowing you to enter the password of your choice.

Working with a Secured File

Once you've opened a secured file, access to layouts and fields is determined by the privileges for the group to which your password belongs. Here's how the access restrictions might affect you.

Using Commands

Options set in the Define Passwords dialog box affect the menu commands that are available for a password.

IF A COMMAND IS ACCESSIBLE   It appears in black on its menu and can be selected.

IF A COMMAND IS NOT ACCESSIBLE   It appears in gray on its menu and cannot be selected.

Viewing and Modifying Layouts

Options set in the Access Privileges dialog box affect the layouts that are accessible to a group. Since a password determines a user's group, it also determines the access privileges for a layout.

IF A LAYOUT IS ACCESSIBLE   It will appear and behave as normal. You will not be able to modify the layout, however, if the Design Layouts option is turned off for your password.

IF A LAYOUT IS NOT ACCESSIBLE   It will appear in gray, with the words *Access Denied* on it (see Figure 17-18).

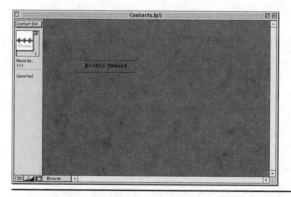

FIGURE 17-18. A layout that is not accessible to a password's group on Mac OS.

IF A LAYOUT HAS READ ONLY ACCESS It will appear as normal, but if you try to modify it, a dialog box like the one in Figure 17-19 appears—even if the Design Layouts option is turned on for your password.

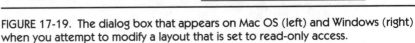

FIGURE 17-19. The dialog box that appears on Mac OS (left) and Windows (right) when you attempt to modify a layout that is set to read-only access.

Viewing and Modifying Field Contents

Options set in the Access Privileges dialog box affect the fields that are available for a group. Since a password determines a user's group, it also determines the access privileges for a field.

IF A FIELD IS ACCESSIBLE It will appear and behave as normal. You will not be able to modify its content, however, if the Edit Records option is turned off for your password.

IF A FIELD IS NOT ACCESSIBLE It will appear as a gray box (see Figure 17-20).

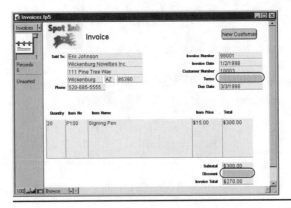

FIGURE 17-20. Fields that are not accessible to a password's group on Windows.

IF A FIELD HAS READ ONLY ACCESS It will appear as normal, but if you try to modify it, a dialog box like the one in Figure 17-21 appears—even if the Edit Records option is turned on for your password.

FIGURE 17-21. The dialog box that appears on Mac OS (left) and Windows (right). when you attempt to modify a field that is set to read only access.

Changing a Password

Passwords can be changed if necessary. How it is done depends on the password used to open the file.

CHANGING PASSWORDS WITH THE MASTER PASSWORD When you open the file with the master password, you have full access to the Define Passwords dialog box. You can change the master password or any other password in the file. I explain how in the section titled "Changing a Password or Its Settings" on page 624.

CHANGING A PASSWORD WITH A USER PASSWORD When you open the file with a password other than the master password, you can only change your own password. Choose Change Password from the File menu (see Figure 17-22). In the Change Password dialog box that appears (see Figure 17-23), enter your old password and your new password in the appropriate boxes. Then click OK. The password is changed.

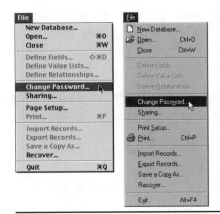

FIGURE 17-22. Choosing Change Password from the File menu on Mac OS (left) and Windows (right).

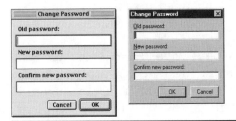

FIGURE 17-23. The Change Password dialog box on Mac OS (left) and Windows (right).

CHANGING A PASSWORD WITH THE "NO PASSWORD" PASSWORD
When you open the file with the "no password" password, you cannot change the password. The Change Password command under the File menu is gray.

Step-by-Step

Ready to try setting up access privileges for a file? In this section, I provide step-by-step instructions for protecting the Contacts.fp5 file that you've been working on at the end of each chapter from unauthorized access. If you've been skipping around in the book and don't have the completed exercise files from one of the last five chapters (it doesn't matter which), you can download them from the companion Web site for this book, http:// www.gilesrd.com/fmprocomp/.

Setting Up Access Privileges

Contacts.fp5 is widely used throughout Spot Ink, Inc. and will need access privileges that protect data from being seen by the wrong people or changed by the wrong people. I'll start by introducing a company's needs, then provide the procedure for setting up access privileges, one step at a time.

Some Background Information

The people who use Contacts.fp5 at Spot Ink, Inc. can be broken down into three categories:

- Sales, which uses the data to contact customers about new products and send out marketing materials.

- Marketing, which enters data for potential customers.

- Accounting, which uses the data to contact customers and vendors and keep track of invoices by customer. Accounting personnel also enter data for new vendors.

The Sales Manager, Steve, is responsible for creating form letters, reviewing the entries made by Marketing, and suggesting payment terms and credit limits. His entries into the Terms and Limit fields are checked and sometimes changed by the Credit Manager, Cathy, who is the only person in Accounting who is authorized to change these fields for either customers or vendors. Both Steve and Cathy know FileMaker Pro relatively well.

Of course, as the individual responsible for information management, you have complete control over the file.

Defining Passwords

The first step is to define the passwords that will be used to access the file.

1. If necessary, open Contacts.fp5.

2. Choose Define Passwords from the Access Privileges submenu under the File menu to display the Define Passwords dialog box.

3. Enter *master* in the Password box. Make sure the Access the entire file check box is turned on and click the Create button.

NOTE *I'm purposely keeping passwords obvious so the example is easier to understand; don't use* master *as the master password or user names as passwords in your files!*

---

4. Enter *steve* in the Password box. Make sure only the following check boxes are turned on: Browse records, Print records, Design Layouts, Create records, and Edit records. Choose Normal from the Available menu commands menu. Then click Create.

5. Enter *othersales* in the Password box. Make sure only the following check boxes are turned on: Browse records, Print records, Create records, and Edit records. Choose Editing Only from the Available menu commands menu. Then click Create.

6. Enter *allmarket* in the Password box. Make sure only the following check boxes are turned on: Browse records, Print records, Create records, Edit records, and Delete records. Choose Editing Only from the Available menu commands menu. Then click Create.

7. Enter *cathy* in the Password box. Make sure only the following check boxes are turned on: Browse records, Print

records, Override data entry warnings, Define Value Lists, Create records, Edit records, and Delete records. Choose Normal from the Available menu commands menu. Then click Create.

8. Enter *otheracct* in the Password box. Make sure only the following check boxes are turned on: Browse records, Print records, Create records, Edit records, and Delete records. Choose Editing Only from the Available menu commands menu. Then click Create.

9. Clear the contents of the Password box. Make sure only the Browse records check box is turned on. Choose Editing Only from the Available menu commands menu. Then click Create. *(no password)* should appear with the other passwords in the list.

10. Click the Done button. In the Confirm dialog box that appears, enter *master* and click OK.

Defining Groups

The next step is to define the groups for the file.

1. Choose Define Groups from the Access Privileges submenu under the File menu to display the Define Groups dialog box.

2. Enter *Sales* in the Group Name box and click Create.

3. Repeat the previous step to create groups named *Marketing, Accounting, Others,* and *Management.*

4. Click the Done button.

Associating Passwords with Groups

The next step is to associate passwords with groups.

1. Choose Overview from the Access Privileges submenu under the File menu to display the Access Privileges dialog box.

2. Select the *Sales* group. Click the bullets to the left of appropriate passwords so that only the *master, steve,* and *othersales* passwords have black bullets. (The others should be gray.) Click the Save button.

3. Select the *Marketing* group. Click the bullets to the left of appropriate passwords so that only the *master* and *allmarket* passwords have black bullets. Click the Save button.

4. Select the *Accounting* group. Click the bullets to the left of appropriate passwords so that only the *master, cathy,* and *otheracct* passwords have black bullets. Click the Save button.

5. Select the *Others* group. Click the bullets to the left of appropriate passwords so that only the *master* and *(no password)* passwords have black bullets. Click the Save button.

6. Select the *Management* group. Click the bullets to the left of appropriate passwords so that only the *master, steve,* and *cathy* passwords have black bullets. Click the Save button.

Assigning Privileges to Groups

The last step is to assign layout and field privileges to groups.

1. Select the *Sales* group. Click the bullets to the left of the appropriate layouts so that all layouts have black bullets except Customer Invoice List (the last one), which should be gray. Then click the bullets to the left of the appropriate fields so that all fields have black bullets except *Terms, Limit, Limit Average,* and *Customer Total,* which should be gray, and *Revision Date,* which should be white. Click the Save button.

2. Select the *Marketing* group. Click the bullets to the left of the appropriate layouts so that only the *Contact Entry Form* layout has a black bullet in front of it. The others should be gray. Then click the bullets to the left of the appropriate fields so that all fields have black bullets except *Terms, Limit, Limit Average, Customer Total,* and *Revision Date,* which should be gray. Click the Save button.

3. Select the *Accounting* group. Click the bullets to the left of the appropriate layouts so that only the *Contact Entry Form* and *Customer Invoice List* layouts have a black bullet in front of them. The others should be gray. Then click the bullets to the left of the appropriate fields so that all fields have white bullets. Click the Save button.

4. Select the *Others* group. Click the bullets to the left of the appropriate layouts so that only the *Contact Entry Form* and *Phone List* layouts have a black bullet in front of them. The others should be gray. Then click the bullets to the left of the appropriate fields so that all fields from *Customer Number* (the first field) through *Type* have white bullets and the rest of the fields have gray bullets. Click the Save button.

5. Select the *Management* group. Click the bullets to the left of the appropriate layouts so that all layouts have gray bullets. Then click the bullets to the left of the appropriate fields so that all fields have black bullets. Because both users who belong to this group also belong to another group, the two group privileges are added to each other to provide the access they need. Click the Save button.

6. Click the Done button.

Testing Access Privileges

Before releasing the revised database to the Spot Ink, Inc. users, you must check to make sure that privileges are set up the way they should be. The only way to do this is to open the database with each of the passwords, view all the layouts, and try all the fields.

As you try the passwords out, ask yourself two questions:

- Does the user have the access he or she needs to get the job done? The answer to this question should be yes.

- Does the user have additional access that he or she does not need that puts the data or organization at risk? The answer to this question should be no.

If you got the right answer to both questions for each user password, you've successfully set up access privileges.

Extra Credit

Since Contacts.fp5 includes related fields from Invoices.fp5, complete security should include the setting of access privileges in Invoices.fp5. Why not try that on your own?

18

Backing Up and Maintaining Database Files

Many FileMaker Pro database files are continuously accessed throughout their existence—sometimes for years. When in use in a large organization, the same database file may be accessed by dozens of users every day.

Can you say the same things about the letters or reports you create with a word processor or the worksheets you create with a spreadsheet program? Clearly, FileMaker Pro files are different. Because of that, they deserve special attention when it comes to backing up and maintaining them.

In this chapter, I tell you some things you can do to give your File-Maker Pro files the tender loving care they deserve. You'll find that, by following my suggestions, your files will live long, trouble-free lives.

Backing Up Database Files

One of the most important—yet most neglected—responsibilities of a computer user is backing up data. The consequences of data loss can be trivial or far-reaching. Lose a file that you threw together for a specific job three years ago, and it might not be a big deal. But lose a file that forms the basis of your company's sales system, and the company could lose millions of dollars and have to lay off hundreds of people while rebuilding the sales system from scratch.

In this section, I attempt to explain the importance of backing up your files—not just FileMaker Pro database files but *all* data files—and then provide some tips for doing it properly.

WARNING *Skipping this section could cause data loss. You wouldn't want that to happen, would you?*

A True Story

Once upon a time, not long ago, a computer book author was working hard on a project. She was very smart about backing up her work at the end of each day—after all, if a hard disk problem occurred, she didn't want to lose all the work she'd done on the project. Unfortunately, she didn't see the big picture and failed to back up the FileMaker Pro database file that listed all the contact information for the hundreds of people she'd met and worked with over the past seven years.

You can probably guess what happens next. I'll tell you just in case you can't.

On the morning of March 1, 1993, she turned on her computer and found that it wouldn't start. After hours of troubleshooting, she came to the conclusion (which was later verified by other experts) that her 4-month-old hard disk had died. Her manuscript was safe. But she lost all that contact information.

She learned a valuable lesson that day that she will never forget: *If it's important, back it up!*

Knowing Which Files to Back Up

If you're not sure whether a file is important enough to back up, ask yourself these questions:

- If the file was lost or damaged, would you have to recreate it? If yes, how long would it take? Can you spare the time to recreate something that you could have easily protected from loss? Wouldn't you rather protect it from loss?

- If the file was lost or damaged, would other people be affected? If yes, could it prevent people from doing their jobs? Could it cause loss of revenues or increased expenses?

- If the file was lost or damaged, could you get in trouble with your boss? If yes, would it be enough trouble to cost you your job? Do you like your job? Could you get another job quickly if you had to?

By considering the answers to these questions, you should be able to estimate the importance of a file and determine whether it's worth backing up.

Knowing How Often to Back Up

The frequency of backups is determined primarily by how often the data changes.

Another Example

When I write a book, I back up the project's files at the end of every working day. Do I back up all the work I've done since the beginning of the project every day? No. I just back up the files that have changed since the last backup. It takes a matter of minutes. I'm comfortable with the knowledge that there are two copies of everything I've done up to that point.

The rest of my document files don't get as much attention. Since most of them do not change daily, I don't back them up daily. Instead, I back them up weekly or, when I'm being lazy, less frequently. But at least once a month.

TIP *It's a lot more convenient to back up data files if those files are not mixed in with program and other files that do not need to be backed up regularly. I have a Documents folder on each of my computers and that's where all my folders full of project documents reside. Backing up a project is as easy as backing up a folder; backing up all documents is as easy as backing up the Documents folder. Applications don't need to be backed up—I can always reinstall them from original program disks.*

About FileMaker Pro Files

FileMaker Pro database files change every single time the file is opened—even if no records are changed. Does that mean you should back them up every night? If it's convenient, why not? But if it isn't convenient, you should at least back up after every real change in the database contents.

"On a Regular Basis"

That brings up the phrase "on a regular basis," which I use quite often throughout this chapter. A regular basis can be daily, weekly, monthly, or annually. The frequency should be determined by how often and how much the file changes. Once the frequency is established, the backup procedure should become part of your work schedule, part of your job.

Backup Strategies

There are a number of different approaches you can take to back up your data. The approach(s) you select should depend on the importance of the data and the resources you are willing to spend protecting it.

WARNING *You cannot back up a FileMaker Pro file while it is open. Even if the backup appears successful, the backup copy will probably be corrupted.*

Copying Files to Diskette

If a file can fit on a diskette, there's no reason why you shouldn't—at the very least—copy the file to diskette on a regular basis.

This is a bare minimum backup procedure. Why? Because diskettes are unreliable. As they age, their magnetic properties break down. As their magnetic properties break down, data is lost.

But even a backup on diskette is better than no backup at all.

Copying Files to another Hard Disk

Copying files to another hard disk is a better way of backing up data, especially if that hard disk is on another computer, such as a file server. Hard disks are more reliable, have greater capacity, and are a lot easier to back up to. When things are easier, we tend to do them more often, don't we?

NOTE *I've got a spare 9GB drive that I use as a second backup for all my computers.*

Copying Files to High-Capacity Removable Media

High-capacity removable media is a fancy way of saying Zip, Jaz, or any other cartridge-like device that holds a lot of data. It includes tape drives, too.

This kind of media offers the convenience of a hard disk with the control of a floppy diskette. Once you copy files to one of these babies, you can keep it anywhere. (That's important, as I discuss in the section titled "Storing Backups" on page 652.)

NOTE *I used to use SyQuest 44MB cartridges, and then Zip disks. Now I use Jaz disks for my nightly backups. I can fit all documents stored on my main production computer—including three book manuscripts—on one Jaz disk. Not bad.*

Backing Up or Archiving Files to CDR

CDR—CD-ROM recordable discs—offer an extremely reliable media for backing up data. (CDs are about as permanent a storage media as you can get.) With capacities exceeding 600MB, they can hold really big files or lots of small ones.

Depending on the CDR software, backing up to CDR can be as easy as dragging file icons or as time-consuming as creating defragmented disk images. The standard media can only be used once, but rewritable CDRs are on the rise and may soon replace standard CDRs.

NOTE *About two and a half years ago, I spent $1700 for a 2x speed CD-ROM recorder. Better ones are now available for less than $500. The CDR media, which used to cost me about $12 each, now costs $1.70. Although I don't use CDR for backing up data, I do use it for archiving—long-term storage of data I might need to use someday in the future. Every book I write is archived to CD when completed.*

Multiple Backups

For really important files, one backup probably isn't enough. That's when it's time to consider multiple backups. There are two ways to do this, both of which require multiple sets of backup media.

MULTIPLE BACKUP COPIES With multiple backup copies, you have more than one copy of the same file backed up. If the original file goes bad, you can choose any of the copies to replace it. If one of the copies is bad, you still have at least one other copy to replace it.

MULTIPLE BACKUP VERSIONS With multiple backup versions (or *incremental* backups), you have more than one version of a file backed up. For example, say that you have three backup disks, labeled A, B, and C. On Monday, you use Disk A. On Tuesday, Disk B. On Wednesday, Disk C. On Thursday, you overwrite the contents of Disk A with a fresh copy of the file. On Friday, you overwrite Disk B. And so forth. This gives you three backups with three different versions.

NOTE *The main benefit to having multiple versions is that if the file becomes corrupted on Tuesday and you discover it on Wednesday, you can still go back to the last good version of the file, which was backed up on Monday.*

Using Backup Software

There are lots of software products out there that can help you back up your data. These products either copy individual files or create single files containing all your documents in compressed format. Some can work either way.

These software products are great because you can program them to run regularly at a scheduled time and back up only the files that have changed since the last backup. You can also program them to keep multiple backup versions automatically.

The only drawback to using backup software is setting it up. It takes time. But the time you spend now can save hours that will accumulate over the next few months or years.

NOTE   *There's a dedicated Web server in my office that automatically backs itself up to an external hard disk and restarts every morning at 6:00 AM—even when I'm not around to watch it.*

Storing Backups

Another important part of backing up data is the location of the backup media. Ideally, they should be stored in another location. Why? So when the building in which your computer resides burns to the ground, your backups don't burn too. And no, it isn't just fire that you should worry about. It's floods, earthquakes, theft, and anything else that can separate you from your data.

Consider these backup storage locations:

ANOTHER BUILDING   If your company does not provide a backup location, bring the backups home with you. If you work out of your home, bring the backups to a neighbor's house. Or your mother, father, sister, brother, son, daughter—you get the idea. It makes a nice excuse to visit these people. Just don't leave them in the car if you live in a very hot, cold, or damp place. The elements can destroy backup media just as easily as computers can.

ANOTHER ROOM   So you think your data isn't important enough to be stored in another building. OK. Mine isn't either. But how about another room in the same building? Swap backup files with a co-worker—you keep his backups in your office and he keeps yours in his office. Don't pick the guy in the office next door; when the sprinklers go on in your office, they'll probably go on in his, too. If you work at home, pick another room on the other side of the house. I store my backups in the kitchen.

A FIREPROOF SAFE   You have a fireproof safe? But is it rated to protect its contents from high temperatures? A burned disk is worthless, but so is a melted one. If the safe is truly safe for data storage, use it!

THE FILE SERVER   If you back up to a file server, you probably don't have to worry about backup storage location. Why? Because the system administrator gets paid a lot of money to make sure that the file server is backed up. So he's making backups of your backups. If he's not, he's making a bad career decision.

 TIP   *When disaster strikes and you weren't backed up, it might be time to give the folks at DriveSavers a call. These folks can perform miracles with crashed, water-soaked, partially melted, or otherwise mangled hard disks. Get more info now — before you need them — at http://www.drivesavers.com/.*

Maintaining Database Files

Backing up data prevents you from losing files. But it isn't always enough to prevent you from losing data.

In this section, I tell you about some things that you can do to protect your files from being corrupted and how to fix them when they're damaged. I also provide some additional maintenance tasks you should consider if you're responsible for the care and feeding of a large database file.

File Corruption

FileMaker Pro files differ from files created with other applications in that FileMaker Pro can write to them at any time while they're open. Because of this, the file is never properly closed until you close it or quit or exit FileMaker Pro.

If a file is not closed properly—either because of a power outage, computer crash, or other minor calamity—it can be damaged or corrupted.

The Consistency Check

FileMaker Pro knows when a file has not been closed properly. It displays a message on screen when it opens one of these files, telling you that it is performing a consistency check (see Figure 18-1).

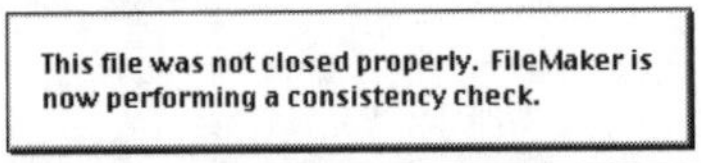

> This file was not closed properly. FileMaker is
> now performing a consistency check.

FIGURE 18-1. The message FileMaker Pro displays when it opens a file that wasn't closed properly.

In most cases, FileMaker Pro can automatically fix damaged files as it opens them. Sometimes, however, it can't. That's when it tells you to use the Recover command.

Recovering Damaged Files

The Recover command instructs FileMaker Pro to extract all the information it can from a damaged database file and rebuild that file from scratch.

To recover a damaged file, start by making sure that the damaged file is not open. Then choose Recover from the File menu (see Figure 18-2).

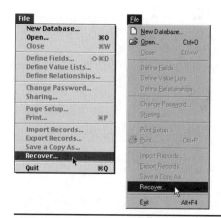

FIGURE 18-2. Choosing Recover from the File menu on Mac OS (left) and Windows (right).

The Open Damaged File dialog box appears (see Figure 18-3). Use it to locate and select the file that you want to recover. When you click the Open button, the Name Recovered File dialog box appears (see Figure 18-4). It suggests a name for the file, but you can name the file anything you like. Click the Save button to continue.

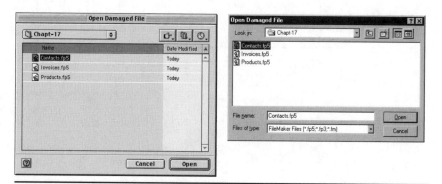

FIGURE 18-3. The Open Damaged File dialog box on Mac OS (left) and Windows (right).

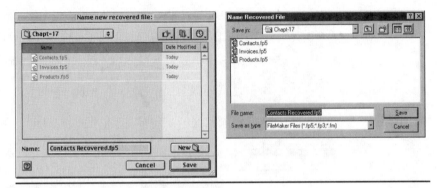

FIGURE 18-4. The Name Recovered File dialog box on Mac OS (left) and Windows (right).

Next FileMaker Pro displays the Recover dialog box (see Figure 18-5), which indicates the progress of the recover process. The amount of time that FileMaker Pro takes to completely recover a file varies based on the speed of your computer, the size of the file, and the severity of the file's problems. When it finishes, it displays a dialog box telling you what it did (see Figure 18-6).

FIGURE 18-5. The Recover dialog box on Mac OS (left) and Windows (right).

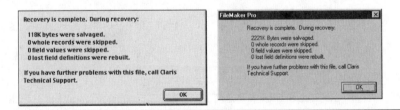

FIGURE 18-6. The dialog box that appears when the recovery process is complete on Mac OS (left) and Windows (right).

Click OK to dismiss the dialog box. Then open the recovered file and check it out.

NOTE   *My experience with the Recover command has been very positive. In the ten years I've been working with FileMaker Pro, I've only seen one instance where the Recover command could not recover a file. It just happened to be the biggest and most complex file I ever had to recover—good thing I had a recent backup!*

Other Maintenance Tasks

Here are a few other maintenance tasks you might consider to help keep your files fit and trim.

Cloning Files

When you clone a file, you create a copy of the file with no records in it. Everything else in the file is exactly the same.

Clones are good for two things:

- Clone a file to create a new database that is very similar to an existing one but with different records. One of my clients, for example, starts a new database file every year based on one I created for them three years ago. On January 2, they clone the previous year's file to start the new one.

- Clone a file, then import the original file's records into the clone. This forces FileMaker Pro to recreate a lot of the file structures that it maintains behind the scenes, like indexes. I tell you all about importing records in the section titled "Importing Records" on page 505.

TIP   *If you're having trouble with the Find command not finding the records that it should and the Recover command doesn't improve the situation, create a clone of the file and import the file's records into the clone. Chances are, the problem will go away.*

To create a clone, open the file that you want to clone, then choose Save a Copy As from the File menu (see Figure 18-7).

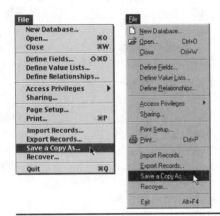

FIGURE 18-7. Choosing Save a Copy As from the File menu on Mac OS (left) and Windows (right).

In the Create Copy dialog box that appears (see Figure 18-8), choose clone (no records) from the Type (Mac OS) or Save a (Windows) menu (see Figure 18-9). Then use the dialog box to enter a name and choose a disk location for the clone and click the Save button. The new file is saved to disk.

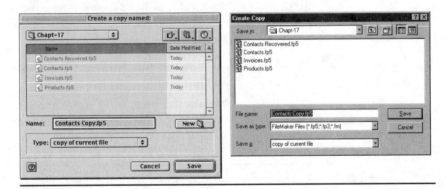

FIGURE 18-8. The Create Copy dialog box on Mac OS (left) and Windows (right).

FIGURE 18-9. The Type menu on Mac OS (left) and the Save a menu on Windows (right).

Compressing Files

As FileMaker Pro database files grow and evolve, they sometimes swell in size to be larger than they need to be. This often occurs when large numbers of records are deleted from a file—the file expands to make room for records, but doesn't collapse as much as possible when records are removed, leaving empty space in the file.

You can save a compressed copy of a file to make the file as small as it needs to be. This, in effect, squeezes out the empty space so the file is smaller.

NOTE *Don't confuse using FileMaker Pro to save a compressed copy of a file with using file compression software like StuffIt (Mac OS) or PKZip (Windows) to compress a file. They are completely different. When you save a compressed copy of a file within FileMaker Pro, the file is still usable as is; file compression software, however, squeezes the file so much that it must be uncompressed before it can be used.*

To save a compressed copy of a file, open the file that you want to shrink, then choose Save a Copy As from the File menu (see Figure 18-7). In the Create Copy dialog box that appears (see Figure 18-8), choose compressed copy (smaller) from the Type (Mac OS) or Save a (Windows) menu (see Figure 18-9). Then use the dialog box to enter a name and choose a disk location for the file and click the Save button. The new file is saved to disk.

NOTE *You must give the file a different name when saving it; you cannot overwrite an open FileMaker Pro file. When the new file has been saved, you can rename the old file and keep it as a backup, then give the new file its original name.*

Removing Duplicate Records

One final thing you should do periodically, especially with a large database file, is check it for duplicate records and remove the duplicates you find.

Here's an example. I know for a fact that my name and address exist multiple times in certain mailing lists. I get mail addressed to *Maria Langer, Maria L Langer, Maria K Langer* (my Microsoft alias), *M Langer, Maria Langes, Marie Lange*—you get the idea. The addresses are all the same or close—some abbreviate the word *West* and others abbreviate the word *Drive*. Some spell *Wickenburg* as *Wichenburg* or *Wickenberg*. It seems to me that the folks who maintain these lists can save a lot of money for their companies by weeding out the duplicates so I get just one piece of junk mail from them rather than a half dozen.

Here are some things you can do to find and help prevent duplicate entries:

- Use the Duplicates symbol (!) in a database field to locate two or more records with the same value in a field (see "Finding Records" on page 133 and "Using Symbols" on page 139). You may have to use the command in multiple fields, one at a time. You'll probably have to go through the found set manually to weed out the bad entries.

- Include a revision date field in the database that automatically enters the date a record was changed (see "Auto Enter Options" on page 343 and "Creation/Modification Information" on page 343). This will help you identify the more recent record so you know which one is probably outdated.

- Require that the people entering data use the Find command to search for an existing record before entering data for it. You can build a script that makes it easy to perform the required search without knowing much about File-Maker Pro (see Chapter 12).

These are just a few ideas. The more you work with FileMaker Pro, the more ideas you'll come up with to make your databases better.

Step-by-Step

There isn't very much in this chapter for you to try out. Most of it is pretty straightforward and easy to figure out. What do you say we skip the Step-by-Step section for this chapter? After all, you've done enough in the other chapters. Back up your files, and take the rest of the day off.

Time for me to saddle up and head out.

Appendices

This part of the book provides three appendices full of useful reference information:

Appendix A: Menu and Keyboard Shortcut Reference

Appendix B: Function Reference

Appendix C: ScriptMaker Reference

Menu and Keyboard Shortcut Reference

Here's a reference guide for FileMaker Pro's menus, submenus, and keyboard shortcuts, organized by menu.

NOTE *The Windows menus throughout this Appendix are illustrated with the All keyboard shortcuts in menus option enabled in the Application Preferences dialog box. I tell you about this option in the section titled "Show All Keyboard Shortcuts in Menus (Windows Only)" on page 35.*

TIP *Windows users can also take advantage of mouseless menus. Press the Alt key to activate the menu bar, then press the keyboard key corresponding to the underlined letter or number of the menu name or command that you want. For more information about this Windows feature, consult the manuals that came with your operating system.*

File Menu Commands

FIGURE A-1. The File menu on Mac OS (left) and Windows (right).

Command	Mac OS Shortcut	Windows Shortcut
Open	Command-O	Control-O
Close	Command-W	Control-W
Define Fields	Shift-Command-D	Control-Shift-D
Print	Command-P	Control -P
Quit	Command-Q	n/a
Exit	n/a	Alt-F4 or Control-Q

Access Privileges Submenu

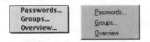

FIGURE A-2. The Access Privileges submenu under the File menu on Mac OS (left) and Windows (right).

NOTE *The Access Privileges submenu does not appear when the active FileMaker Pro file has been opened with a password other than the master password. Instead, the File menu displays the Change Password command.*

Edit Menu

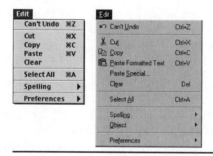

FIGURE A-3. The Edit menu in Browse mode on Mac OS (left) and Windows (right).

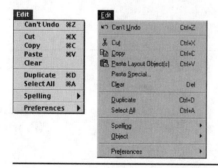

FIGURE A-4. The Edit menu in Layout mode on Mac OS (left) and Windows (right).

Command	Mac OS Shortcut	Windows Shortcut
In All Modes:		
Undo	Command-Z	Control-Z
Cut	Command-X	Control-X
Copy	Command-C	Control-C
Paste	Command-V	Control-V
Clear	n/a	Del
Select All	Command-A	Control-A
In Layout Mode Only:		
Duplicate	Command-D	Control-D

Spelling Submenu

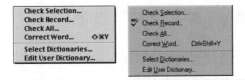

FIGURE A-5. The Spelling submenu under the Edit menu on Mac OS (left) and Windows (right).

Command	Mac OS Shortcut	Windows Shortcut
Correct Word	Shift-Command-Y	Control-Shift-Y

Object Submenu (Windows Only)

FIGURE A-6. The Object submenu under the Edit menu on Windows.

Preferences Submenu

FIGURE A-7. The Preferences submenu under the Edit menu on Mac OS (left) and Windows (right).

View Menu

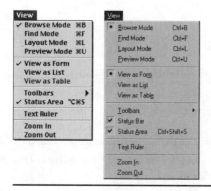

FIGURE A-8. The View menu in Browse mode on Mac OS (left) and Windows (right).

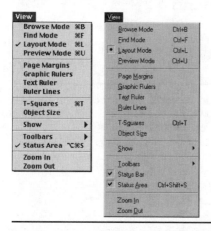

FIGURE A-9. The View menu in Layout mode on Mac OS (left) and Windows (right).

Command	Mac OS Shortcut	Windows Shortcut
In All Modes:		
Browse	Command-B	Control-B
Find	Command-F	Control-F
Layout	Command-L	Control-L
Preview	Command-U	Control-U
In Layout Mode Only		
T-Squares	Command-T	Control-T

Show Submenu

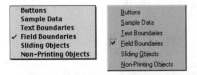

FIGURE A-10. The Show submenu under the View menu in Layout mode on Mac OS (left) and Windows (right).

Toolbars Submenu

FIGURE A-11. The Toolbars submenu under the View menu in Layout mode on Mac OS (left) and Windows (right). In all other modes, only the top two commands appear on this submenu.

Insert Menu

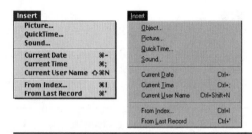

FIGURE A-12. The Insert menu in Browse mode on Mac OS (left) and Windows (right).

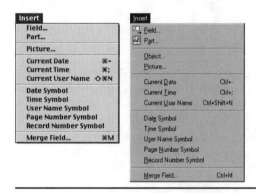

FIGURE A-13. The Insert menu in Layout mode on Mac OS (left) and Windows (right).

Command	Mac OS Shortcut	Windows Shortcut
In Browse, Layout, and Find Modes:		
Current Date	Command--	Control--
Current Time	Command-;	Control-;
Current User Name	Shift-Command-N	Control-Shift-N
In Browse and Find Modes Only:		
From Index	Command-I	Control-I
From Last Record	Command-'	Control-'
In Layout Mode Only:		
Merge Field	Command-M	Control-M

Format Menu

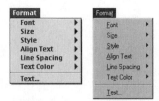

FIGURE A-14. The Format menu in Browse mode on Mac OS (left) and Windows (right).

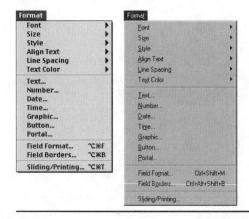

FIGURE A-15. The Format menu in Layout mode on Mac OS (left) and Windows (right).

Command	Mac OS Shortcut	Windows Shortcut
In Layout Mode Only:		
Field Format	Option-Command-F	Control-Shift-M
Field Borders	Option-Command-B	Control-Alt-Shift-B
Sliding/Printing	Option-Command-T	n/a

Font Submenu

FIGURE A-16. The Font submenu under the Format menu on Mac OS (left) and Windows (right). The font names listed on the Font submenu will vary depending on the fonts installed in your computer system.

Size Submenu

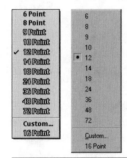

FIGURE A-17. The Size submenu under the Format menu on Mac OS (left) and Windows (right).

Style Submenu

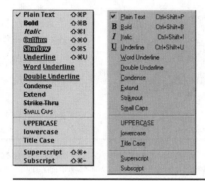

FIGURE A-18. The Style submenu under the Format menu on Mac OS (left) and Windows (right).

Command	Mac OS Shortcut	Windows Shortcut
Plain Text	Shift-Command-P	Control-Shift-P
Bold	Shift-Command-B	Control-Shift-B
Italic	Shift-Command-I	Control-Shift-I
Outline	Shift-Command-O	n/a
Shadow	Shift-Command-S	n/a
Underline	Shift-Command-U	Control-Shift-U
Superscript	Shift-Command-+	n/a
Subscript	Shift-Command--	n/a

Align Text Submenu

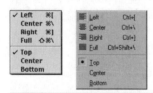

FIGURE A-19. The Align Text submenu under the Format menu in Layout mode on Mac OS (left) and Windows (right). In Browse mode, only the top four commands appear on this submenu.

Command	Mac OS Shortcut	Windows Shortcut
Left	Command-[	Control-Shift-L
Center	Command-\	Control-\
Right	Command-]	Control-Shift-R
Full	Shift-Command-\	Control-Shift-\

Line Spacing Submenu

FIGURE A-20. The Line Spacing submenu under the Format menu on Mac OS (left) and Windows (right).

Text Color Submenu

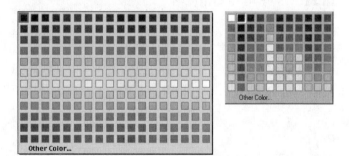

FIGURE A-21. The Text Color submenu under the Format menu on Mac OS with the Web palette selected (left) and on Windows with the System Subset palette selected (right).

Records Menu

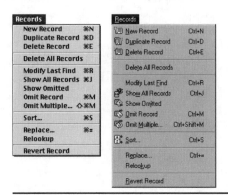

FIGURE A-22. The Records menu on Mac OS (left) and Windows (right). This menu only appears in Browse and Preview modes.

Command	Mac OS Shortcut	Windows Shortcut
In Browse Mode Only:		
New Record	Command-N	Control-N
Duplicate Record	Command-D	Control-D
Delete Record	Command-E	Control-E
Modify Last Find	Command-R	Control-R
Show All Records	Command-J	Control-J
Omit Record	Command-M	Control-M
Omit Multiple	Shift Command-M	Control-Shift-M
Replace	Command-=	Control-=
In Browse and Preview Modes Only:		
Sort	Command-S	Control-S

Requests Menu

FIGURE A-23. The Requests menu on Mac OS (left) and Windows (right). This menu appears only in Find mode.

Command	Mac OS Shortcut	Windows Shortcut
Add New Request	Command-N	Control-N
Duplicate Request	Command-D	Control-D
Delete Request	Command-E	Control-E
Show All Records	Command-J	Control-J
Perform Find	n/a	Enter

Layouts Menu

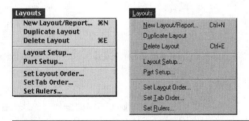

FIGURE A-24. The Layouts menu on Mac OS (left) and Windows (right). This menu appears only in Layout mode.

Command	Mac OS Shortcut	Windows Shortcut
New Layout/Report	Command-N	Control-N
Delete Layout	Command-E	Control-E

Arrange Menu

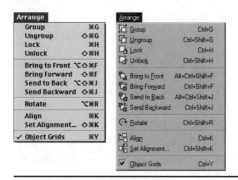

FIGURE A-25. The Arrange menu on Mac OS (left) and Windows (right). This menu appears only in Layout mode.

Command	Mac OS Shortcut	Windows Shortcut
Group	Command-G	Control-G
Ungroup	Shift-Command-G	Control-Shift-G
Lock	Command-H	Control-H
Unlock	Shift-Command-H	Control-Shift-H
Bring to Front	Shift-Option-Command-F	Alt-Control-Shift-F
Bring Forward	Shift-Command-F	Control-Shift-F
Send to Back	Shift-Option-Command-J	Alt-Control-Shift-J
Send Backwards	Shift-Command-J	Control-Shift-J
Rotate	Option-Command-R	Control-Shift-R
Align	Command-K	Control-K
Set Alignment	Shift-Command-K	Control-Shift-K
AutoGrid	Command-Y	Control-Y

Scripts Menu

FIGURE A-26. The Scripts menu on Mac OS (left) and Windows (right). The Scripts menu also displays the names of any scripts within the file that are set to appear on this menu.

Window Menu

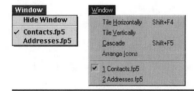

FIGURE A-27. The Window menu on Mac OS (left) and Windows (right).

Command	Mac OS Shortcut	Windows Shortcut
Tile	n/a	Shift-F4
Cascade	n/a	Shift-F5

Help Menu

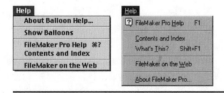

FIGURE A-28. The Help menu on Mac OS (left) and Windows (right).

Command	Mac OS Shortcut	Windows Shortcut
FileMaker Help	Command-?	F1
What's This?	n/a	Shift-F1

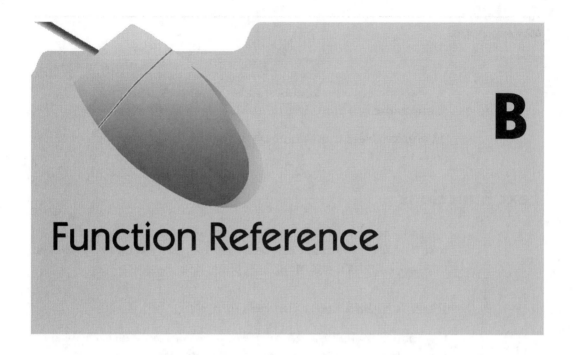

Function Reference

B

Here's a reference guide for all of FileMaker Pro's functions, which can be used in the Specify Calculation dialog box. I tell you about creating calculations and using functions in Chapter 10.

Function Syntax

In FileMaker Pro, most functions use the following syntax:

FunctionName (parameter1, parameter2, etc.)

where:

- *FunctionName* is the name of the function. It determines the type of calculation and the number and purpose of each of its parameters.

- Parentheses are used to enclose all parameters that work with a function.

- Parameters are values, fields, or expressions that work with the function.

- Commas are used to separate parameters.

Text Functions

Text functions return information about or perform operations on text. The *text* parameter can be a field name or literal text enclosed in double-quote characters.

Exact (*original text, comparison text*)

Compares *original text* to *comparison text* for an exact, case-sensitive match. Result is Boolean: 1 for a match or 0 for no match.

Example: Exact ("hello", "goodbye") = 0

Left (*text, number*)

Returns the *number* of characters in *text*, counting from the left. Result is text.

Example: Left ("FileMaker", 4) = File

LeftWords (*text, number of words*)

Returns the *number of words* in *text*, counting from the left. Result is text.

Example: LeftWords ("FileMaker Pro is great!", 2) = FileMaker Pro

Length (*text*)

Returns the number of characters in *text*. Result is a number.

Example: Length ("FileMaker Pro") = 13

Lower (*text*)

Converts *text* to lowercase. Result is text.

Example: Lower ("FileMaker Pro") = filemaker pro

Middle (*text, start, size*)

Returns *size* characters in *text,* from the *start* character. Result is text.

Example: Middle ("FileMaker Pro", 3 , 4) = leMa

MiddleWords (*text, starting word, number of words*)

Returns the middle *number of words* words in *text,* starting with the number of *starting word.* Result is text.

Example: MiddleWords ("FileMaker Pro is Great!", 2, 2) = Pro is

PatternCount (*text, search string*)

Returns the number of occurrences of *search string* in *text.* Result is a number.

Example: PatternCount ("FileMaker Pro", "le") = 1

Position (*text, search string, start, occurrence*)

Returns the position number of *occurrence* of *search string* in *text* from *start.* If *search string* does not occur after *start,* returns 0. Result is a number.

Example: Position ("FileMaker Pro", "le", 4, 3) = 0

Proper (*text*)

Converts the first letter in each word of *text* to uppercase and remainder of characters to lowercase. Result is text.

Example: Proper ("FileMaker Pro is great!") = Filemaker Pro Is Great!

Replace (*text, start, size, replacement text*)

Replaces the *size* characters in *text* with *replacement text*, from *start*. Result is text.

Example: Replace ("FileMaker Pro", 3, 4, "hello") = Fihelloker Pro

Right (*text, number*)

Returns the *number* of characters in *text*, counting from the right. Result is text.

Example: Right ("FileMaker Pro", 5) = r Pro

RightWords (*text, number of words*)

Returns the *number of words* in *text*, counting from the right. Result is text.

Example: RightWords ("FileMaker Pro is great!", 2) = is great!

Substitute (*text, search string, replace string*)

Replaces each occurrence of *search string* in *text* with *replace string*. Result is text.

Example: Substitute ("FileMaker Pro is great!", " ", "-") = FileMaker-Pro-is-great!

TextToDate (*text*)

Converts *text* entered in MM/DD/YYYY format to a date. Result is a date.

Example: TextToDate ("10/11/1998") = 10/11/98

TextToNum (*text*)

Converts *text* to a number. Result is a number.

Example: TextToNum ("43") = 43

TextToTime (*text*)

Converts *text* entered in HH:MM:SS format to a time. Result is a time.

Example: TextToTime ("4:15:29") = 4:15:29

TIP   *The TextToDate, TextToNum, and TextToTime functions enable you to calculate a date, number, or time entered as text.*

Trim (*text*)

Removes leading and trailing spaces from *text*. Result is text.

Example: Trim ("   FileMaker Pro   ") = FileMaker Pro

Upper (*text*)

Converts *text* to uppercase. Result is text.

Example: Upper ("FileMaker Pro") = FILEMAKER PRO

WordCount (*text*)

Returns the number of words in *text*. Result is a number.

Example: WordCount ("FileMaker Pro is great!") = 4

Number Functions

Number functions return information about or perform operations on single numbers. The *number* parameter can be a field name or a number.

Abs (*number*)

Returns the absolute value of *number*. Result is a number.

Example: Abs (–43.4) = 43.4

Exp (*number*)

Returns the value of e raised to the power of *number*. Result is a number.

Example: Exp (4) = 54.5981500331442

Int (*number*)

Returns the whole number portion of *number*. Result is a number.

Example: Int (–43.4) = –43

Mod (*number, divisor*)

Returns the remainder after *number* is divided by *divisor*. Result is a number.

Example: Mod (43.4, 4) = 3.4

NumToText (*number*)

Converts *number* to text. Result is text.

Example: NumToText (43.4) = 43.4

Random

Returns a random number between 0.0 and 1.0 for each record in the database. There is no parameter. Result is a number.

Example: Random = .30059519051601

Round (*number, precision*)

Returns *number* rounded to the number of decimal places in *precision*. When *precision* is negative, all decimal places are dropped and *number* is rounded to nearest 10 for –1, 100 for –2, 1000 for –3, etc. Result is a number.

Example: Round (43.4534, 2) = 43.45

Sign (*number*)

Returns -1 when *number* is negative, 0 when *number* is zero, and 1 when *number* is positive. Result is a number.

Example: Sign (–43.4) = -1

Sqrt (*number*)

Returns the square root of *number*. Result is a number.

Example: Sqrt (4) = 2

Truncate (*number, precision*)

Returns *number* truncated to the number of decimal places in *precision*. Result is a number.

Example: Truncate (43.4534, 3) = 43.453

Date Functions

Date functions return information about or perform operations on dates. The *date* parameter can be a field name or a date.

NOTE *In the examples in this section,* DateField *is the name of a field containing the date 6/30/1961.*

Date (*month, day, year*)

Returns the calendar date of *month, day, year*. The *year* parameter must be four digits. Result is a date in the format specified in your computer system.

Example (6, 30, 1961) = 6/30/61

DateToText (*date*)

Converts *date* to text. Result is text.

Example: DateToText (DateField) = 6/30/61

Day (*date*)

Returns the day number of *date*. Result is a number.

Example: Day (DateField) = 30

DayName (*date*)

Returns the weekday name of *date*. Result is text.

Example: DayName (DateField) = Friday

DayofWeek (*date*)

Returns the weekday number of *date*, from Sunday (1) to Saturday (7). Result is a number.

Example: DayofWeek (DateField) = 6

DayofYear (*date*)

Returns the number of days since January 1 of the year in *date*. Result is a number.

Example: Day of Year (DateField) = 181

Month (*date*)

Returns the month number of *date*. Result is a number.

Example: Month (DateField) = 6

MonthName (*date*)

Returns the month name of *date*. Result is text.

Example: MonthName (DateField) = June

Today

Returns the current date, as set in your computer system. There are no parameters. Result is a date.

Example: Today = 2/3/98

WeekofYear (*date*)

Returns the number of weeks since January 1 of the year in *date*. Fractions of weeks are counted as whole weeks. Result is a number.

Example: WeekofYear (DateField) = 26

WeekofYearFiscal (*date, starting day*)

Returns the number of weeks since the first week of the year in *date*, using *starting day* (1 through 7, where 1 is Sunday) as the first day of the week. The first week of the year is the first week that contains at least four days of that year. Result is a number.

Example: WeekofYearFiscal (DateField, 2) = 26

Year (*date*)

Returns the year number of *date*. Result is a number.

Example: Year (DateField) = 1961

Time Functions

Time functions return information about or perform operations on times. The *time* parameter can be the name of a time field or a time.

 In the examples in this section, TimeField is the name of a field containing the time 6:15 PM.

Hour (*time*)

Returns the hour number of *time*. Result is a number.

Example: Hour (TimeField) = 18

Minute (*time*)

Returns the minute number of *time*. Result is a number.

Example: Minute (TimeField) = 15

Seconds (*time*)

Returns the seconds number of *time*. Result is a number.

Example: Seconds (TimeField) = 0

Time (*hours, minutes, seconds*)

Returns the time of *hours, minutes, seconds* in the current time field format. Result is a time.

Example: Time (18, 15, 0) = 6:15 PM

TimeToText (*time*)

Converts *time* to text. Result is text.

Example: TimeToText (TimeField) = 6:15 PM

Aggregate Functions

Aggregate functions perform calculations on nonblank values in one or more repeating fields or related fields. The *field* parameter can be the name of one or more fields. (If more than one field, separate field names with commas.) The result of all of these functions is a number.

NOTE *In the examples in this section,* RepeatingField *is the name of a repeating field containing the values 10, 20, and 30.*

Average (*field*)

Returns the average of nonblank values in *field*.

Example: Average (RepeatingField) = 20

Count (*field*)

Returns the number of nonblank values in *field*.

Example: Count (RepeatingField) = 3

Max (*field*)

Returns the maximum value of nonblank values in *field*.

Example: Max (RepeatingField) = 30

Min (*field*)

Returns the minimum value of nonblank values in *field*.

Example: Min (RepeatingField) = 10

StDev (*field*)

Returns the standard deviation of the sample represented by nonblank values in *field*.

Example: StDev (RepeatingField) = 10

StDevP (*field*)

Returns the standard deviation of a population represented by nonblank values in *field*.

Example: StDevP (RepeatingField) = 8.16496580927726

Sum (*field*)

Returns the sum of nonblank values in *field*.

Example: Sum (RepeatingField) = 60

Summary Functions

Summary functions perform calculations on summary fields. The *summary field* parameter must be a summary field; the break field parameter must be the field by which you want to summarize information.

GetSummary (*summary field, break field*)

Returns the value of *summary field* for the current range of records when records are sorted by *break field*.

Repeating Functions

Repeating functions return information about or perform operations on repeating fields. The *repeating field* parameter must be a field name.

NOTE   *In the examples in this section,* RepeatingField *is the name of a repeating field containing the values 10, 20, and 30.*

Extend (*nonrepeating field*)

Allows the value of a nonrepeating field to be used in a calculation that requires repeating fields.

GetRepetition (*repeating field, number*)

Returns the contents of the repetition *number* of *repeating field*.

Example: GetRepetition (RepeatingField, 2) = 20

Last (*repeating field*)

Returns the last nonblank value in *repeating field*.

Example: Last (RepeatingField) = 30

Financial Functions

Financial functions perform financial calculations on numbers. Each parameter can be a constant number or a number field name. The result of each of these functions is a number.

NOTE   *In the examples in this section,* RepeatingField *is the name of a repeating field containing the values 100, 200, and 300.*

FV (*payment, interest rate, periods*)

Returns the future value of an investment based on *interest rate* and *payment* for *periods*.

Example: FV (500, .07, 5) = 2875.369505

NPV (*payment, interest rate*)

Returns the net present value of a series of unequal *payments* (in a repeating field) made at regular intervals using a fixed *interest rate* per interval.

Example: NPV (RepeatingField, .07) = 513.035052647132

PMT (*principal, interest rate, term*)

Returns the periodic payment needed to pay *principal* with a fixed *interest rate* over *term*.

Example: PMT (5000, .07, 5) = 1219.45347220687

PV (*payment, interest rate, periods*)

Returns the present value of equal *payments* made at regular *periods* with a fixed *interest rate* per period.

Example: PV (500, .07, 5) = 2050.0987179738

Trigonometric Functions

Trigonometric functions perform trigonometric calculations on a single number. The *number* parameter can be a constant number or a number field name. The result of each of these functions is a number.

Atan (*number*)

Returns the arc tangent of *number*.

Example: Atan (45) = 1.54857776146818

Cos (*number*)

Returns the cosine of *number*.

Example: Cos (45) = .52532198881772

Degrees (*number*)

Converts *number* from radians to degrees.

Example: Degrees (45) = 2578.31007808936

Ln (*number*)

Returns the base-*e* logarithm of *number*.

Example: Ln (45) = 3.80666248977032

Log (*number*)

Returns the common logarithm of a positive *number*.

Example: Log (45) = 1.65321251342397

Pi

Returns the value of pi. There are no parameters for this function.

Example: Pi = 3.141592653589

Radians (*number*)

Converts *number* from degrees to radians.

Example: Radians (45) = .78539816339725

Sin (*number*)

Returns the sine of *number*.

Example: Sin (45) = .85090352453411

Tan (*number*)

Returns the tangent of *number*.

Example: Tan (45) = 1.61977519054387

Logical Functions

Logical functions perform a test, then return a value based on the result of the test. The parameters of logical functions can include values, expressions, and field names.

Case (*test1, result1* [, *test2, result2, default result*]...)

When *test1* is true, returns *result1*; when *test2* is true, returns *result2*, etc. When no test is true, returns nothing or *default result*.

Example: Case (5<3, "hello", 3<8, "goodbye", "get lost") = goodbye

Choose (*test, result0* [, *result1, result2,*]...)

Evaluates *test* to produce an index number used to choose a result. When the index number is 0, returns *result0*; when the index number is 1, returns *result1*, etc. When there is no corresponding result, returns nothing.

Example: Choose (1+1, "hello", "goodbye", "get lost") = get lost

If (*test, result one, result two*)

When *test* is true, returns *result one*. When *test* is false, returns *result two*.

Example: If (5<3, "hello", "goodbye") = "goodbye"

IsEmpty (**field**)

Returns 1 when *field* is empty. Returns 0 when *field* is not empty.

IsValid (*field*)

Returns 0 when *field* is missing from the file or contains an invalid value. Returns 1 when *field* is present in the file and contains a valid value.

Status Functions

Status functions return information about the state of the database file or your computer. Status functions have predefined parameters; they are not based on constant values, fields, or expressions.

Status (CurrentAppVersion)

Returns the version of the FileMaker Pro application in use. Result is a number.

Status (CurrentDate)

Returns the current date. Result is a date.

Status (CurrentError)

Returns a number for the current error value. Result is a number.

 TIP   *The Status (CurrentError) function is often used in scripts to trap or identify errors.*

Status (CurrentFieldName)

Returns the name of the current field. Result is text.

Status (CurrentFileName)

Returns the name of the current file. Result is text.

Status (CurrentFileSize)

Returns the size in bytes of the current file. Result is a number.

Status (CurrentFoundCount)

Returns the number of records in the current found set. Result is a number.

Status (CurrentGroups)

Returns the group or groups of which the current user is a member, based on his or her password. Result is text.

Status (CurrentHostName)

Returns the host name that FileMaker Pro registers on the network. Result is text.

Status (CurrentLanguage)

Returns the current language set on the system. Result is text.

Status (CurrentLayoutCount)

Returns the number of layouts in the database. Result is a number.

Status (CurrentLayoutName)

Returns the name of the current layout. Result is text.

Status (CurrentLayoutNumber)

Returns the number of the current layout. Result is a number.

Status (CurrentMessageChoice)

Returns a number corresponding to the button clicked in a message displayed with the Show Message script step: 1 is for OK, 2 is for Cancel, and 3 is for the third button. Result is a number.

Status (CurrentMode)

Returns the number for the current FileMaker Pro mode: 0 for Browse, 1 for Find, or 2 for Preview. Result is a number.

Status (CurrentModifierKeys)

Returns a number corresponding to a keyboard modifier key currently being pressed. Result is a number.

Status (CurrentMultiUserStatus)

Returns 0 for a single user file, 1 for a multiuser file opened as a host, and 2 for a multiuser file opened as a guest. Result is a number.

Status (CurrentNetworkChoice)

Returns the name of the currently selected network protocol. Result is text.

Status (CurrentPageNumber)

Returns the page number currently printing or being previewed. If no page is being previewed or printed, returns 0. Result is a number.

Status (CurrentPlatform)

Returns a number for the computer platform currently in use: 1 for Mac OS and 2 for Windows. Result is a number.

Status (CurrentPortalRow)

Returns the number of the current row in a selected portal. When no portal is selected, returns 0. Result is a number.

Status (CurrentPrinterName)

Returns the name of the current printer. Result is text.

Status (CurrentRecordCount)

Returns the number of records in the current file. Result is a number.

Status (CurrentRecordID)

Returns the unique internal ID number for the current record. Result is a number.

Status (CurrentRecordNumber)

Returns the number of the current record in the found set. Result is a number.

Status (CurrentRepetitionNumber)

Returns the current repetition number of the current repeating field. When the field is nonrepeating, returns 1. Result is a number.

Status (CurrentRequestCount)

Returns the current number of defined find requests. Result is a number.

Status (CurrentScreenDepth)

Returns the number of bits needed to represent the color of a pixel on the computer screen. Result is a number.

Status (CurrentScreenHeight)

Returns the number of pixels displayed vertically on the computer screen. Result is a number.

Status (CurrentScreenWidth)

Returns the number of pixels displayed horizontally on the computer screen. Result is a number.

Status (CurrentScriptName)

Returns the name of the script currently running or paused. Result is text.

Status (CurrentSortStatus)

Returns a number representing the current sort status: 0 for unsorted and 1 for sorted. Result is a number.

Status (CurrentSystemVersion)

Returns the system version currently in use. Result is a number.

Status (CurrentTime)

Returns the current time. Result is a time.

Status (CurrentUserCount)

Returns the number of users accessing the file. Web users are not counted. Result is a number.

Status (CurrentUserName)

Returns the name of the current user as specified in General Application Preferences. Result is text.

Design Functions

Design functions return information about the structure of any database file that is currently open on your computer. The parameters of design functions are normally the names of databases, layouts, or fields.

DatabaseNames

Returns the names of the currently opened databases. This function has no parameters.

FieldBounds (*database name, layout name, field name*)

Returns the location and size of *field name* in *layout name* of *database name*.

FieldNames (*database name, layout name*)

Returns the number of fields in *layout name* of *database name*. To get the names of all fields in a database, enter a pair of double-quotes for *layout name*.

FieldRepetitions (*database name, layout name, field name*)

Returns the number of field repetitions in *field name* within *layout name* of *database name*.

FieldStyle (*database name, layout name, field name*)

Returns formatting information about *field name* in *layout name* of *database name*.

FieldType (*database name, field name*)

Returns the type of *field name* in *database name*.

LayoutNames (*database name*)

Returns the names of the layouts in *database name*.

RelationInfo (*database name, relationship name*)

Returns the name of the related file for *relationship name* in *database name*.

RelationNames (*database name*)

Returns the names of all relationships defined in *database name*.

ScriptNames (*database name*)

Returns the names of all scripts defined in *database name*.

ValueListItems (*database name, value list name*)

Returns the values defined for *value list name* in *database name*.

ValueListNames (*database name*)

Returns the names of all value lists in *database name*.

ScriptMaker Reference

Here's a reference guide for all of FileMaker Pro's script steps. I tell you about scripting in Chapter 12.

Control Steps

Control steps give you control over the flow of the script's execution of steps.

Perform Script

Performs a script either within the database or within another database (an external script). Options:

- Perform sub-scripts check box
- Specify menu (to select a script)

Pause/Resume Script

Pauses a script or resumes a paused script. Options:

- Specify button (to set duration of pause)

Exit Script

Exits the current script. If the current script is a subscript of another script, returns to the main script.

Halt Script

Stops performing all scripts.

If

Performs steps if the result of a calculation is true (not zero). Options:

- Specify button (to specify a calculation)

Else

Performs another set of steps if the result of a calculation is false (zero). Else is used within the If/End If construction.

End If

Marks the end of an If statement. Added to script automatically when the If step is added.

Loop

Repeatedly performs a series of script steps.

Exit Loop If

Stops execution of looped script steps if the result of a calculation is true (not zero). Options:

• Specify button (to specify calculation)

End Loop

Marks the end of a loop. Added to script automatically when the Loop step is added.

Allow User Abort

Allows or prevents users from stopping a script. Options:

• On and Off options

Set Error Capture

Allows or prevents an error message from displaying. Used to change the way FileMaker Pro handles error messages when a script is running. Options:

• On and Off options

Navigation Steps

Navigation steps let you navigate through your database file.

Go to Layout

Switches to the specified layout. Options:

• Refresh window check box

• Specify menu (to select layout)

Go to Record/Request/Page

Switches to a record in Browse mode, find request in Find mode, or page in Preview mode. Options:

* Specify menu (to select record, request, or page)

Go to Related Record

Moves to the current related record in the related file. Options:

* Show only related records check box
* Specify menu (to select relationship)

Go to Portal Row

Moves to a portal row or a specific field in a portal row. Options:

* Select entire contents check box
* Specify menu (to select the portal row)

Go to Field

Moves to a field in the current layout. Options:

* Select/perform check box
* Specify field check box and button

Go to Next Field

Moves to the next field on the current layout. The next field is determined by the tab order.

Go to Previous Field

Moves to the previous field on the current layout. The previous field is determined by the tab order.

Enter Browse Mode

Switches to Browse mode. Options:

- Pause check box

Enter Find Mode

Switches to Find mode. Options:

- Restore find requests check box
- Pause check box

Enter Preview mode

Switches to Preview mode. Options:

- Pause check box

Sort/Find/Print Steps

Sort/Find/Print steps let you sort or unsort, find, show all, omit, and print records.

Sort

Sorts records in the found set. Options:

- Restore sort order check box
- Perform without dialog check box

Unsort

Restores records to the order in which they were entered into the database.

Show All Records

Shows all records in the file.

Show Omitted

Shows the records that are not in the found set.

Omit Record

Removes the current record from the found set.

Omit Multiple

Removes a number of records, starting with the current record, from the found set. Options:

- Perform without dialog check box
- Specify record check box and button

Perform Find

Finds records that match the find request(s). Options:

- Restore find request check box

Modify Last Find

Displays the last find request for modification.

Page Setup (Mac OS) or Print Setup (Windows)

Sets the Page Setup (Mac OS) or Print Setup (Windows) options. Options:

- Restore setup options check box
- Perform without dialog check box

Print

Prints information from the current file. Options:

- Perform without dialog check box

Editing Steps

Editing steps let you edit database contents.

Undo

Undoes the last action.

Cut

Moves the contents of a field to the clipboard. Options:

- Select entire contents check box
- Specify field check box and button

Copy

Copies the contents of a field to the clipboard. Options:

- Select entire contents check box
- Specify field check box and button

Paste

Pastes the contents of the clipboard into a field. Options:

- Select entire contents check box
- Paste without style check box
- Specify field check box and button
- Link if available check box

Clear

Removes the contents of a field. Options:

- Select entire contents check box
- Specify field check box and button

Select All

Selects the entire contents of a field.

Field Steps

Field steps let you change or otherwise work with the contents of fields.

Set Field

Replaces the contents of a field with the results of a calculation. The field does not have to be on the current layout. Options:

- Specify field check box and button
- Specify button (to specify calculation)

Insert Text

Inserts a text string into a field. Options:

- Select entire contents check box

- Specify field check box and button

- Specify button (to enter the text string)

Insert Calculated Result

Inserts the result of a calculation into another field on the current layout. Options:

- Select entire contents check box

- Specify field check box and button

- Specify button (to specify the calculation)

Insert from Index

Inserts a value from the index into a field. Options:

- Select entire contents check box

- Specify field check box and button

Insert from Last Record

Inserts the value from the last active record into the same field of the current record or find request. Options:

- Select entire contents check box

- Specify field check box and button

Insert Current Date

Inserts the current date into a field. Options:

- Select entire contents check box

- Specify field check box and button

Insert Current Time

Inserts the current time into a field. Options:

- Select entire contents check box

- Specify field check box and button

Insert Current User Name

Inserts the current user name, as set in the General Application Preferences, into a field. Options:

- Select entire contents check box

- Specify field check box and button

Insert Picture

Inserts a picture from a file into a container field. Options:

- Specify file check box and button

Insert Movie (Mac OS) or Insert QuickTime (Windows)

Inserts a movie file into a container field. Options:

- Specify file check box and button

Insert Object (Windows Only)

Inserts an embedded or linked object into a container field. Options:

- Specify check box with Object button

Update Link (Windows Only)

Updates an OLE link in a container field. Options:

- Specify check box with Field button

Records Steps

Records steps let you work with records and find requests.

New Record/Request

Creates a new record in Browse mode or find request in Find mode.

Duplicate Record/Request

Duplicates the current record or find request.

Delete Record/Request

Deletes the current record or find request. Options:

- Perform without dialog check box

Delete Portal Row

Deletes the current portal row. Options:

- Perform without dialog check box

Revert Record/Request

Returns the current record or find request to the way it was before you changed it. Options:

• Perform without dialog check box

Exit Record/Request

Exits the current record or find request to update the field and make no field active.

Copy Record

Copies the data in the current record to the clipboard.

Copy All Records

Copies the data in the current found set that is visible in the current layout to the clipboard.

Delete All Records

Deletes all records in the found set. Options:

• Perform without dialog check box

Replace

Replaces the contents of a field in all records of the found set. Options:

• Perform without dialog check box
• Specify field check box and option
• Specify button (to set replace options)

Relookup

Updates a lookup value for records in the found set. Options:

- Perform without dialog check box
- Specify field check box and option

Import Records

Imports records into the database. Options:

- Restore import order check box
- Perform without dialog check box
- Specify file check box and button

Export Records

Exports records in the found set to another file. Options:

- Restore export order check box
- Perform without dialog check box
- Specify file check box and button

Windows Steps

Windows steps let you work with document windows.

Freeze Window

Stops updating the window, thus hiding actions from users.

Refresh Window

Redraws the screen or resumes updating after the Freeze Window step. Options:

- Bring to front check box

Scroll Window

Scrolls the active window. Options:

- Specify menu (to select scroll option: Home (top), End, Up, Down, or To Selection)

Toggle Window

Hides or changes the size of the active window. Options:

- Specify menu (to select window view option: Zoom, Unzoom, Maximize, or Hide)

Toggle Status Area

Shows, hides, or locks the status area. Options:

- Lock check box

- Specify menu (to select status area display option: Show, Hide, or Toggle)

Toggle Text Ruler

Shows or hides the text ruler. Options:

- Refresh window check box

- Specify menu (to set ruler display option: Show, Hide, or Toggle)

Set Zoom Level

Reduces, enlarges, or locks the contents of a window. Options:

- Lock check box

- Specify menu (to select zoom percentage)

View As

Displays the records individually or in a list. Options:

- Specify menu (to select view as display option: View as Form, View as List, View as Table, or Cycle)

Files Steps

Files steps let you work with database files.

New

Creates a new file.

Open

Opens an existing file. Options:

- Open hidden check box

- Specify File check box and button

Close

Closes a file. Options:

- Specify File check box and button

Change Password

Modifies an existing password.

Set Multi-User

Turns network access on or off for the current file. Options:

- Specify menu (for setting option: On, On (Hidden), or Off)

Set Use System Formats

Specifies whether the date, time, and number formats of the system should be used. Options:

- On and Off options

Save a Copy as

Saves a copy of the current file. Options:

- Specify file check box and button

Recover

Opens a damaged file. Options:

- Perform without dialog check box
- Specify file check box and button

Spelling Steps

Spelling steps let you include spelling check commands in your scripts.

Check Selection

Checks the spelling of text in a field. Options:

- Select entire contents check box
- Specify field check box and button

Check Record

Checks the spelling of text in the current record.

Check Found Set

Checks the spelling of text in the found set.

Correct Word

Displays the spelling dialog box so you can correct a misspelled word. The Spell check as you type option must be turned on in the Spelling Document Preferences dialog box.

Spelling Options

Displays the Spelling Options dialog box.

Select Dictionaries

Displays the Select Dictionaries dialog box.

Edit User Dictionary

Displays the Edit User Dictionary dialog box.

Open Menu Item Steps

Open Menu Item steps let you include commands to open certain dialog boxes, such as the Preferences, Define Fields, and Help dialog boxes.

Open Application Preferences

Displays the Application Preferences dialog box.

Open Document Preferences

Displays the Document Preferences dialog box.

Open Define Fields

Displays the Define Fields dialog box.

Open Define Relationships

Displays the Define Relationships dialog box.

Open Define Value Lists

Displays the Define Value Lists dialog box.

Open Help

Displays the FileMaker Pro Help Contents window.

Open ScriptMaker

Displays the Define Scripts dialog box. FileMaker Pro stops performing a script after this step.

Open Sharing

Display the File Sharing dialog box.

Miscellaneous Steps

Miscellaneous steps let you perform a variety of other tasks that don't fit in any other category.

Show Message

Displays an alert message. Options:

* Specify button (to specify message and response buttons)

Beep

Plays the system alert sound.

Speak (Mac OS only)

Produces speech from text. Options:

* Specify button (to specify text and speech options)

Dial Phone

Dials a phone number. Options:

* Perform without dialog check box

* Specify button (to specify the phone number)

Open URL

Opens a URL. Options:

- Perform without dialog check box

- Specify button (to specify the URL)

Send Mail

Sends an e-mail message. This command only works with MAPI-compliant e-mail applications. Options:

- Perform without dialog check box

- Specify button (to specify the To, Cc, Subject, and Message fields)

Send Apple Event (Mac OS only)

Sends an Apple Event to another application. Options:

- Specify button (to specify the Apple Event options)

Perform AppleScript (Mac OS only)

Performs AppleScript commands. Options:

- Specify button (to specify AppleScript commands)

Send DDE Execute (Windows only)

Sends a Dynamic Data Exchange (DDE) command to another application. Options:

- Specify button (to set the Service Name, Topic, and Commands)

Send Message (Windows only)

Starts an application or opens or prints a document in another application. Options:

• Specify button (to set the message options)

Comment

Adds descriptive notes to a script. Options:

• Specify button (to specify the comments)

Flush Cache to Disk

Saves the FileMaker Pro internal cache to disk.

Quit Application (Mac OS) or Exit Application (Windows)

Quits (Mac OS) or exits (Windows) FileMaker Pro.

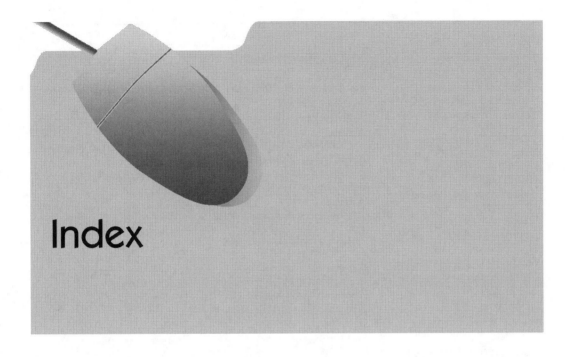

Index

Symbols/Numbers

:: (paired colons)
    as dynamic text symbol, 187
    as relational field indicator,
        428, 444, 445
... (ellipsis) search symbol,
    141–142
* (asterisk)
    as mathematical operator,
        387
    as wildcard character in IP
        address, 608
@ (at sign)
    as dynamic text symbol, 188
    as search symbol, 142–143
? (question mark)
    as dynamic text symbol, 187
    as search symbol, 142
/ / dynamic text symbol, 187
/ / search symbol, 142
/ mathematical operator, 387
- (minus sign) mathematical
    operator, 387

<< >> merge symbols, 171–
    172, 188, 236
<> comparison operator, 388
<= comparison operator, 388
= comparison operator, 387–
    389
> comparison operator, 388
>= comparison operator, 388
dynamic text symbol, 187,
    554
| | dynamic text symbol, 187
+ mathematical operator, 387
^ mathematical operator, 387
! search symbol, 142, 660
< search symbol, 139
<= search symbol, 140
= search symbol, 141
== search symbol, 143
> search symbol, 140
>= search symbol, 140–141
& text operator, 385
¶ text operator, 386

"" (double quotes) text
    operator, 385–386, 389
() mathematical operator, 386–
    387, 389
≥ comparison operator, 388
≥ search symbol, 140–141
≤ comparison operator, 388
≤ search symbol, 140
12-hour clock, 310
24-hour clock, 310
216-color palette, 37
256-color palette, 37
8-dot-3 file-naming
    convention, 53
88-color palette, 37

A

Abs (absolute value) function,
    686
Access privileges
    assigning to groups, 627–631
    how they work, 617–618